SECOND EDITION

Invention Analysis
AND Claiming A PATENT
LAWYER'S
GUIDE

Ronald D. Slusky

AMERICAN BAR ASSOCIATION
**General Practice,
Solo & Small Firm
Division**

Cover design by Mary Anne Kulchawik/ABA Publishing

The materials contained herein represent the opinions and views of the authors and/or the editors, and should not be construed to be the views or opinions of the law firms or companies with whom such persons are in partnership with, associated with, or employed by, nor of the American Bar Association or the General Practice, Solo & Small Firm Division, unless adopted pursuant to the bylaws of the Association.

Nothing contained in this book is to be considered as the rendering of legal advice, either generally or in connection with any specific issue or case. Readers are responsible for obtaining advice from their own lawyers or other professionals. This book and any forms and agreements herein are intended for educational and informational purposes only.

© 2007, 2012 American Bar Association. All rights reserved.

No part of this publication may be reproduced, stored in a retrieval system, or transmitted in any form or by any means, electronic, mechanical, photocopying, recording, or otherwise, without the prior written permission of the publisher. For permission, contact the ABA Copyrights and Contracts Department at copyright@americanbar.org or via fax at 312-988-6030, or complete the online form at http://www.americanbar.org/utility/reprint.html.

Printed in the United States of America.

19 18 17   8 7 6

Library of Congress Cataloging-in-Publication Data

Slusky, Ronald D.
 Invention analysis and claiming : a patent lawyer's guide / my Ronald
D. Slusky. — 2nd ed.
    p. cm.
 Includes bibliographical references and index.
 ISBN 978-1-61438-561-5 (print : alk. paper)
1. Patent laws and legislation—United States. 2. Patent
lawyers—United States—Handbooks, manuals, etc. I. Title.
 KF3131.S58 2012
 346.7304'86—dc23

                                                                2012018185

Discounts are available for books ordered in bulk. Special consideration is given to state bars, CLE programs, and other bar-related organizations. Inquire at Book Publishing, ABA Publishing, American Bar Association, 321 North Clark Street, Chicago, Illinois 60654-7598.

www.ShopABA.org

For my family
—
Stephen M. Gurey (1947–2007)

CONTENTS

DETAILED CONTENTS

PART II
DRAFTING INDIVIDUAL CLAIMS

PART III
THE CLAIM SUITE AND THE ANTICIPATED
ENFORCEMENT SCENARIO

ACKNOWLEDGMENTS

An author's acknowledgments typically express his appreciation to those who made it possible for him to pull his book together—mentors, colleagues, and friends who read and critiqued the chapters as they were written; editors; and others involved in producing the published work. I, too, have such people to acknowledge. But first, thanks to those who were deserving of acknowledgment long before this book was even a gleam in its author's eye.

I owe my biggest debt of gratitude to my employer of 31 years, Bell Laboratories. It was Bell Labs—originally a division of AT&T and now of Lucent Technologies—that accepted me into its patent training program in 1970 and launched my career as a patent lawyer. The Bell Labs legal organization afforded me the opportunity to learn the patent craft in an environment that emphasized excellence in all aspects.

Don Snedeker was my first mentor. Don showed me how to write a structured patent application—one that uses consistent terminology to tell the invention story in a logical sequence and leave no doubt as to what the inventive concept is. And Don's clear, direct writing style served as a model that I still struggle to emulate.

My across-the-hall neighbor in those early Bell Labs years was Roy Lipton—an attorney's son who became an attorney's attorney. I can see him still, chair canted back on two legs against my office wall, one hand hooked under the seat, the other, outstretched, holding a yellow legal-size sheet containing a freshly typed claim proffered for comment by a neophyte yearning to be just like him. Roy's greatest gift to me was his jurisprudentially focused approach to patent prosecution. "Jurisprudentially speaking" has become a favorite expression of mine that a former colleague has said that he misses hearing me say. I know the feeling. Hardly a day goes by that I don't think back wistfully to the innumerable "jurisprudentially speaking" discussions I had with Roy.

My later career was nurtured by AT&T's Patent Counsel, John McDonnell. The idea of defining the invention in a single sentence—the problem-solution statement that informs so much of this book—was something I learned from John. And it was he who entrusted me with many high-visibility projects and later promoted me to a managerial position at Bell Labs.

I am also indebted to attorneys I have been privileged to mentor over my career. Their questions often forced me to put into words the concepts I had internalized during my early training. I owe them a lot for having been the willing guinea pigs for many of the techniques presented in this book.

I am indebted to the following mentors, colleagues, and others who reviewed the drafts, shared unstintingly of their time and their ideas, and encouraged me in so many ways: Bob Ardis, Henry Brendzel, Jeff Brosemer, Ken Brown, Sam Dworetsky, Jim Falk, Mike Fogarty, Barry Freedman, Marc Goldring, Steve Gurey, Dave Hurewitz, Kasey Keegan, Irena Lager, Ben Lee, Roy Lipton, John McDonnell, Scott McLellan, Mike Morra, Gene Nelson, Harry Newman, Anthony Olivetto, Fred Padden, Frank Politano, Peter Priest, Greg Ranieri, Tom Restaino, Eugene Rosenthal, Bruce Schneider, Richard Sharkansky, David Tannenbaum, Chuck Warren, and Jeff Weinick. Special thanks are due to Ben Lee, Jeff Weinick, and most of all to Peter Priest for many hours of helpful discussions and to Frank Politano for his special words of encouragement and detailed reading of the entire manuscript.

My search for interesting patents from the past was greatly aided by the privately published work by Thomas J. Perkowski, *Claims to Fame and Fortune: A Survey of Pioneer Inventions in America*.

Ann Taylor helped me edit the manuscript throughout its years of gestation, with an attention to detail that I can only marvel at.

I was carried along to the finish line by the enthusiasm of my book proposal editor, Ashley Shelby, and by the team at ABA Publishing: Rick Paszkiet, Sandra Johnson, and Kelly Keane.

Special thanks to Barbara Appelbaum. Her comments were invaluable in helping a writer with a patent-centric view of the world appreciate how things that patent attorneys take for granted might be confusing and need to be painstakingly explained.

ABOUT THE AUTHOR

Ronald D. Slusky is a patent attorney in private practice in New York City. He previously was in-house counsel at Bell Laboratories—originally a unit of AT&T and later Lucent Technologies—where he was privileged to mentor dozens of patent attorneys over a career spanning 31 years.

The author holds B.S. and M.S. degrees in electrical engineering from Columbia University and a J.D., cum laude, from Seton Hall University.

INTRODUCTION

Almost every patent matter—whether involving procuring a patent, licensing the patent, or enforcing it in court—brings up the same fundamental question:

What Is the Invention?

The question is simple, but deceptively so, because the answer is sometimes maddeningly elusive. Yet the skill with which the answer is pursued is crucial to maximizing a patent's economic value. A skillfully discerned answer to *What Is the Invention?* results in patent claims that secure protection far beyond the inventor's specific prototype, or "embodiment," to ideally encompass all alternative designs that incorporate the essence of what was invented. By the same token, an incomplete or wrong answer may create loopholes in the patent that allow competitors to incorporate the essence of the inventor's teachings in their own products without infringing the patent.

The difficulty in answering *What Is the Invention?* arises in part because from the patent perspective an invention is not a physical thing but a concept. Even the inventor may not appreciate what that concept is. Scientists and engineers are typically focused on getting some product designed and built, or a material formulated and tested, and getting the thing to market. Abstract notions like "inventive concept" are largely irrelevant to someone charged with working out the bugs, finishing the project on time, and meeting a budget. The task of identifying the inventive concept—answering *What Is the Invention?*—falls mostly to the patent attorney.

This book shows how to capture the inventive concept in the form of a problem-solution statement. This is a sentence of the form:

The problem(s) of _____ is(are) solved by _____.

Here, for example, is a problem-solution statement defining the seminal invention patented by rocket pioneer Robert Goddard.[1] The inventive

---

1. United States Patent No. 1,103,503 (issued Jul. 14, 1914).

concept is Goddard's recognition that a rocket could be made to travel further for a given amount of fuel by storing the fuel in a casing separate from the combustion chamber and feeding the fuel into the combustion chamber as needed.

> The *problem of* enabling a rocket to carry a large amount of combustible material while keeping the weight of the rocket as low as possible is solved by successively feeding portions of the material to the rocket's combustion chamber from a separate casing containing the supply of combustible material.

The book then shows how the problem-solution statement can be used as the basis for drafting the patent application's broadest claims. Indeed, an overarching theme of the book is the critical importance of first analyzing an invention from the problem-solution perspective and only then drafting the patent application's claims based on the results of the analysis. For example, the above problem-solution statement for Goddard's invention is readily transformed into the following claim:

> A rocket apparatus having, in combination, a combustion chamber, a casing containing a supply of combustible material, and means for successively feeding portions of said material to said combustion chamber.

Indeed, virtually every topic in this book—from identifying the invention and its fallback features; to drafting claims of varying scope that define the invention and its features; to preparing the specification; to amending the claims during prosecution—is directly or indirectly informed by the problem-solution paradigm.

Summary of the Book

This book is presented in four parts.

Part I—Identifying the Invention

We see in Part I how to identify the inventive concept and how to develop a problem-solution statement as broad as the prior art will allow. Also presented is the use of the problem-solution paradigm to identify the invention's fallback features—features of the inventor's embodiment(s) that can serve as the basis for patentability if prior art that comes to light after the patent application is filed reveals that the invention is narrower than originally thought. The fallback features inform the patent application's intermediate- and narrow-scope claims developed pursuant to what the book calls the Planned Retreat.

Part II—Drafting Individual Claims

Having identified the invention and its fallback features, we are ready to draft claims that define them. Part II presents two basic techniques for drafting claims to the broad invention, both based on the problem-solution statement. The first of these is problem-solution-based claiming. Here a claim is derived directly from the problem-solution statement, with very little being added or taken away. The second technique is inventive-departure-based claiming. This approach also relies heavily on the problem-solution thought process, but is more open-ended. The claim drafter is set free to bring creativity to bear, allowing a wide range of claim structures and ways of expressing the broad invention. Part II also presents various types of intermediate- and narrow-scope claims, including claims in dependent and independent form. These include claims directed to the fallback features, claim differentiation claims, independent embodiment claims, and maximized royalty base claims. Such claims implement the Planned Retreat, and they serve other functions as well. Definition claims, which function to define terminology used in their parent claims, are also presented. We then look at how best to arrange dependent claims within a given claim family. Finally, we present a law-focused discussion of functional language in claims, generally, and means-plus-function claiming in particular.

Part III—The Claim Suite and the Anticipated Enforcement Scenario

It is not enough to be able to draft claims in isolation. The patent application's overall claim suite needs to be assembled with the anticipated enforcement scenario in mind. Even in the hands of a skilled attorney, the patenting process is fraught with uncertainties. Prior art that lies undiscovered until after the patent issues may render some or all of the patent's claims invalid. Changes in the direction of technology may render some or all of the claims irrelevant to the marketplace.

Part III shows how to assemble an overall claim suite in a way that anticipates and addresses those uncertainties. We see, for example, that the claim suite should include claims defining the invention in all of its commercially significant settings. A video encoding invention, for instance, should be claimed in both the encoder setting and the decoder setting. Most, if not all, of the claims should capture the activities of individual (as opposed to co-acting) direct infringers. The invention should be claimed in all the appropriate statutory classes, which often means both as a method and as an apparatus. The claim suite should also have as much diversity as possible. This means that the invention is defined using, for example, different claim formats and varying terminology or with the claim elements presented in a different order. Diversity in the claim suite addresses the possibility that any one claim may contain an unappreciated infringement loophole, or may be declared invalid based on prior art or indefiniteness, while another claim may not.

Part IV—Preparing and Prosecuting the Patent Application

The problem-solution paradigm informs not only the preparation of claims but the drafting of the specification and prosecuting of the application in the Patent and Trademark Office. We see in Part IV how the problem-solution statement can serve as the backbone of an effective, story-telling patent specification. It describes how the problem-solution paradigm can be used to amend claims in the most effective way. Part IV also discusses how practitioners can make best use of their most important information resource—the inventor.

Invention Examples

Patent attorneys like to make up technology to illustrate patent law principles. The author recalls, for example, Professor Irving Kayton using the "discovery" that ketchup applied to a bald head can promote hair growth to illustrate the point that one can patent a new use for an old substance.

In that spirit, the author has taken the liberty of making up a few things here and there. The inventions are real—among them the chair, paper clip, microwave oven turntable, traffic signal, and backspace key. Some of the examples, however, make possibly incorrect assumptions about what the prior art was when those inventions were made. That lack of historical accuracy is hopefully compensated for by the pedagogical value of the examples.

Terminology Conventions

The book uses the following terminological and typographic conventions:

Attorney	The word "attorney" is used herein to refer to both patent attorneys and patent agents.
Competitors	Others who may practice an invention are referred to as the patent owner's "competitors" even though

	the patent owner may not have any intention or ability to practice the invention himself and, if so, does not have competitors.
Inventor	An invention is often made by two or more "joint" inventors. For simplicity, this book always uses the singular form.
Embodiment	Although the inventor often devises multiple embodiments, the book often uses the singular form.
His/Her	Feminine pronouns are used when referring to the inventor and masculine pronouns for patent attorneys and other dramatis personae.
Specification	For readability, initial capital letters are used when Sections referring to the main sections of the patent specification, e.g., Background, Summary of the Invention ("Summary"), and Detailed Description.
Claim numbers	Claim numbers in patents are sequential integers, but for ease of reference, claims are denoted 1.1, 1.2, . . . in Chapter One, 2.1, 2.2, . . . in Chapter Two and so forth.

Reading and Using This Book

This book can be read and used as a reference work. The various sections are fairly self-contained, and liberal cross-referencing enables the reader interested in a particular topic to come on board with any terminology or concepts that might have been introduced earlier.

The book was also designed with another use in mind. Much effort was invested in producing a work that both the new and experienced practitioner could—and would want to—pick up and read from start to finish. The topics build on one another in a logical sequence and with as much of a narrative arc as was possible to provide in a book of this type. The book endeavors not to be simply a compilation of information, but to mentor the reader in an overall approach to analyzing inventions, to discovering the inventive concept and its features, and to then define them in a comprehensive and sophisticated set of claims.

Beyond the claims, the principles presented in this book enable the patent practitioner to prepare a pedagogically satisfying patent specification. Armed with a fully thought-out answer to the question *What Is the Invention?*, the practitioner finds that the narrative flow takes on a certain single-mindedness as the writing proceeds and a convincing invention story emerges. It is easier to get everything down in the right sequence and at the right level of detail. It becomes clear what is to be put in and what is to be left out. Less editing and rearranging will be required. The claims will almost write themselves. The overall task becomes pleasurable and satisfying, giving the attorney impetus to work in a concentrated, productive fashion.

Most importantly, the principles presented in this book enable the practitioner to produce a superior product.

For the inventor, that superior product is a patent specification that tells a convincing invention story and effectively showcases the inventor's contribution to the art. For the patent owner, it is a claim suite that broadly and precisely answers the question *What Is the Invention?* and thereby maximizes the economic value of the issued patent.

And for the patent attorney, it is a legal task whose completion produces those feelings of well-being and satisfaction that come from a job well done.

Introduction to the Second Edition

The patent law has evolved significantly since the first edition of this book appeared in 2007. Congress passed the America Invents Act in 2011; the U.S. Supreme Court rendered its opinions in *Mayo v. Prometheus* in 2012[2] and *Bilski v. Kappos*[3] in 2010 (clarifying the boundaries of statutory subject matter) and *KSR v. Teleflex*[4] in 2007 (interpreting 35 U.S.C. 103); and the Federal Circuit issued a significant number of decisions on a wide range of topics.

However, the principles of invention analysis that inform the major portions of the book are timeless and thus little affected by changes in the patent law. *What Is the Invention?* is, first and foremost, a *technological* question. Even those court rulings that affected claiming practices[5] were of relatively minor consequence in the overall context of the book.

Why then a second edition?

Functional Language in Claims—Means-Plus-Function and Otherwise

Sometime after the first edition went to press, the author realized that an important topic had not been covered—functional language in claims.

2. *Mayo Collaborative Servs. v. Prometheus Labs., Inc.*, 132 S. Ct. 1289, 565 U.S. ___ (2012).
3. *Bilski v. Kappos*, 130 S. Ct. 3218, 561 U.S. ___ (2010).
4. *KSR v. Teleflex*, 550 U.S. 398 (2007).
5. *In re Nuijten*, 500 F.3d 1346, 84 USPQ2d 1495 (Fed. Cir. 2007) (propagated signal claims are nonstatutory); *Abbott Labs. v. Sandoz Inc.*, 566 F.3d 1282, 90 USPQ2d 1769 (Fed. Cir. 2009) (en banc in part) (product-by-process claims only infringed if the alleged infringing product was made by the recited process).

This oversight has now been corrected by way of a new chapter—Chapter Twelve—directed to this topic.

It was also only after the first edition was published that the author was finally disabused of his wishful notion that, "any day now," the Supreme Court or the U.S. Congress would straighten out the means-plus-function mess that has beset our jurisprudence. The liberal use of means-plus-function examples in the first edition erroneously implied that all was hunky-dory in that corner of our practice. The author's belated attention to this topic can only be chalked up to a complacency born of some 35-plus years of uneventful means-plus-function claiming and a *Who-Moved-My-Cheese?*[6] mentality. In any event, the book's means-plus-function claims have now been re-cast and/or supplemented by non-means-plus-function versions. And a new chapter directed to means-plus-function claiming has been added. That chapter—Chapter Thirteen—addresses the history and current status of means-plus-function claiming and offers some practical guidance for defining claim elements functionally while avoiding what the Federal Circuit refers to as "means-plus-function treatment."

Chapter Review Questions and Exercises

In preparing the first edition, the author envisioned the book's principal audience as practitioners already admitted to USPTO practice.

There were two surprises on this front.

Given the book's hands-on nature, the author had not expected that that book would find much, if any, use in law schools. It turns out, however, that about a dozen law schools offering claim drafting courses or advanced patent seminars have incorporated the book into their curricula. This second edition has thus been supplemented at the end of each chapter with a Chapter Review section that those teaching from this book—as well as those studying on their own—may find helpful. The chapter review items include: questions readily answered based on material in the chapter (Confirm Your Understanding); questions that call for analysis, synthesis or that solicit reader opinion (Questions for Further Thought); and hands-on invention analysis and claim drafting exercisees (Sharpen Your Skills). An answer guide is available to law professors at no charge. Contact the author at 212.246.4546 or rdslusky@gmail.com.

The other surprise on the readership front was the extent to which the book was sought out by inventors planning to use the book in the course of preparing and filing their own patent applications. This

---

6. Spencer Johnson's book *Who Moved My Cheese?* (Putnam, 2002) is a parable about attitudes toward change.

book can certainly help inventors become better-educated consumers of patent attorney/agent services. However, doing it yourself is a big mistake. Not even a whole shelf-full of books can substitute for the mentoring and experience required to learn how to prepare an adequate specification, properly analyze the invention, and draft appropriate claims. (The author is reminded of the supposedly humorous book cover from his junior-high-school days: *Brain Surgery Self-Taught* by Lance Boyle, M.D.). Write a patent application and its claims yourself, if you are so inclined, but then take it to a patent professional.

Revisions to the Text

One of the book's prescriptions is *Consult with Colleagues*.[7] This is a complex practice and it is easy to miss something or go off in a bad direction. As a colleague of the author once observed, "If this was easy everybody would be doing it." Indeed, the author had the privilege of consulting with many colleagues since the book's introduction, particularly while presenting the book's material in public and in-house seminars. In addition to questioning the author's over-fondness for means-plus-function claiming, some of the more experienced seminar participants offered insights that resulted in changes throughout the book. Among those were a re-vamping of the claims for the microwave oven turntable example that appears in several places and the Planned Retreat for the invention of the chair appearing in Chapter Six.

   Other revisions reflect changes in the law relating to propagated signals and product-by-process claims.[8] Case law citations have been updated to reference the most recent cases on point, and Appendix D has been revised in light of statutory changes embodied in the America Invents Act of 2011.

   This edition also features an expanded the index.

Statutory References—America Invents Act

The America Invents Act (AIA), enacted in 2011, amended a number of sections of Title 35 including §§ 102, 103, and 112 cited throughout this book. Those amendments will become effective up to a year after this second edition has issued. However, the AIA's new sub-sectioning scheme has been incorporated into the text in order to make the book as useful as possible for the long term. Thus, for example, the various provisions of § 112 currently denoted by paragraph number are referenced herein by their AIA designations—§ 112(a)–(f).

---

7. p. 45.
8. *See* note 5.

PART I

Identifying the Invention

Introduction to Part I:

Identifying the Invention

PART I—*Identifying the Invention*—takes as its central premise that an invention is not a thing, but a concept. We have to know what the inventive concept is to be able to reliably draft claims capturing the invention at its full breadth.

CHAPTER ONE introduces the notion of inventive concept, taking as its example the ballpoint pen, patented in 1888. Also introduced is the idea that the most effective route to the inventive concept is a process that moves forward from the problem the invention solves to identify the inventive solution, not backward from the inventor's specific embodiment(s).

CHAPTER TWO expands upon this concept. It uses the paper clip to illustrate how things can go quite wrong if the analysis of an invention is embodiment-based rather than problem-solution-based.

CHAPTER THREE focuses on the centerpiece of problem-solution invention analysis—the problem-solution statement. A problem-solution statement is a definition of the invention setting forth the problem the inventor sought to solve and the inventor's solution to that problem in terms that are as broad as the prior art will allow. The problem-solution statement provides a foundation for the patent application's broadest claims, as presented in Part II of the book.

CHAPTER FOUR offers ways of analyzing the invention to ensure that the problem-solution statement is not unduly narrow, while CHAPTER FIVE presents the opposite side of the coin. It discusses how we can determine when a problem-solution statement is too broad and how it can be narrowed without being made too narrow. The techniques discussed in these two chapters can also be used when drafting claims.

CHAPTER SIX introduces the concept of the Planned Retreat. The metaphor of the Planned Retreat is a strategy for identifying and prioritizing the invention's fallback features. These are aspects of the inventor's embodiment(s) that can serve as a basis for patentability if what we thought was the broad invention turns out to be in the prior art.

CHAPTER ONE

Inventions Are Concepts

For most people, an invention is something tangible. One thinks of mechanical devices like the zipper or manufactured substances like tetracycline. Even a process invention like pasteurization evokes the physical reality of the milk being heated.

For patent lawyers, however, an invention is not something physical, but a concept. Indeed, in his 1933 book *Double Patenting*, patent law author Emerson Stringham goes so far as to state that an invention is an abstraction:

> The difficulty which American courts . . . have had . . . goes back to the primitive thought that an "invention" upon which the patent gives protection is something tangible. The physical embodiment or disclosure, which, in itself is something tangible is confused with the definition or claim to the inventive novelty, and this definition or claim or monopoly, also sometimes called "invention" in one of that word's meanings is not something tangible, but is an abstraction. *Definitions are always abstractions.* This primitive confusion of "invention" in the sense of physical embodiment with "invention" in the sense of definition of the patentable amount of novelty, survives to the present day, not only in the courts, but among some of the examiners in the Patent Office [emphasis added].[1]

There is no possibility of clear thinking, says Stringham, until it is understood that an invention as protected by a patent is an abstraction.

Patent practitioners refer to that abstraction as the "inventive concept."

The patent attorney's primary mission is to discover the inventive concept underlying the inventor's embodiment, and then to capture the inventive concept in the patent claims. To fail in that mission is to open the door for a competitor to take advantage of the inventor's contribution to the art while avoiding liability under the patent.

---

1. Emerson Stringham, *Double Patenting* (Washington, D.C.: Pacot Publications, 1933).

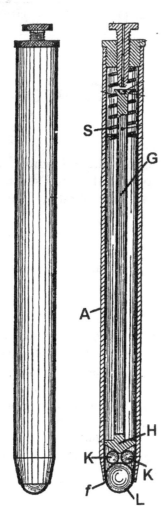

**FIGURE 1–1 John
Loud's ballpoint pen.**

This chapter uses John Loud's invention of the ballpoint pen, patented in 1888,[2] to illustrate the idea of inventive concept. Loud's embodiment is shown in Figure 1–1.[3] The ball L is held against the contracted mouth f of tube A by spring S, which pushes against rod G, bearing H, and anti-friction balls K. The spring yields when the ball is pressed against paper, thereby regulating the flow of ink onto the ball and from there onto the paper as the pen is moved.

Claim 1.1 defines Loud's pen:

---

2. U.S. Patent No. 392,046 (issued Oct. 30, 1888).

3. Loud's embodiment was not practical. A Hungarian journalist named Laszlo Biro is credited with having invented the modern ballpoint pen in 1938.

1.1 A pen comprising
a tube having a contracted mouth and adapted to hold ink,
a spheroidal marking point projecting from the mouth, and
an ink flow regulator[4] that resiliently holds the marking point
against the mouth.

This claim seems pared down to the absolute minimum. Desirably, the claim even reads on the pen empty of ink since the claim calls for a tube adapted to hold ink, but it does not recite the ink as an element of the claimed combination. As such, the claim reads on pens in their manufactured form and could be asserted against manufacturers who might have sold the pen without ink, like fountain pens of the day.

Yet claim 1.1 would be of little value if Loud's patent were still in force. Modern ballpoint pens do not have anything like Loud's "ink flow regulator that resiliently holds the marking point against the mouth." Instead, the ink is kept from leaking out by virtue of a tight fit between the ball and its socket and by using ink that has just the right level of viscosity.

Granted, it would have required a visionary of considerable insight to have anticipated the advent of the technology required to manufacture today's modern ballpoint pens. However, it does not require a visionary to recognize that advances do occur. Indeed, the patent attorney's task is to draft claims that preserve a patent's value *despite* such advances if improved devices embody the inventor's original work.

Loud's attorney, William Dowss, was in fact up to the task. Claim 1.1 and its "ink flow regulator" is not Dowss's claim, but was written for this example by the author. If the Loud patent were still in force, Dowss's claims would command a royalty for every ballpoint pen on the market because Dowss successfully isolated—in a 10-word claim—the concept that underlies every ballpoint pen:

1.2 A pen having a spheroidal marking-point, substantially as described.

That's it! A pen having a spheroidal marking-point. A pen cannot be a ballpoint pen without one. Another claim in the Loud patent is similarly terse.

1.3 A pen having a marking sphere capable of revolving in all directions, substantially as and for the purposes described.

_____

4. A means-plus-function version of this element might be "means for resiliently holding the marking point against the mouth." The means-plus-function construct is used only sparingly throughout the book, for reasons made apparent in Chapter Thirteen.

There are myriad different ballpoint pens on the market. Yet each implements the concept that Loud was the first to embody in a pen and that Dowss was skilled enough to claim. Loud's embodiment did not have a replaceable cartridge, a plastic barrel, or a retractable tip. The technology needed to create the tiny balls and tight-fitting sockets used in modern fine-line ballpoint pens probably did not exist in 1888. Today's metals, plastics, and ink compositions were not available. Nonetheless, every ballpoint pen produced since Loud's original embodies a concept that transcends these embodiment details—the concept of a pen "having a spheroidal marking-point."

It is easy enough now to recognize the shortcomings of claim 1.1. But how would one know that it is not the broadest definition of the invention? It is the rare invention that can be claimed in as few words as claims 1.2 and 1.3, and therefore a claim even as short as claim 1.1 would seem to be quite broad. How did patent attorney Dowss have the insight to foresee in 1888 that future pens would not need claim 1.1's spring-loaded "ink flow regulator"?

Dowss may not have had that insight. But Dowss's claims clearly evince his understanding that implementational details—like an "ink flow regulator" or a tube with a contracted mouth—were irrelevant to the essence of Loud's invention.

How did Dowss come to that understanding? And how can the practicing patent attorney today know when the inventive concept has truly been found and properly claimed?

The answer to that question is an approach to invention analysis that lies at the heart of this book.

Begin from the Problem

The path to the inventive concept begins with the problem that the inventor solved. The inventive concept is the inventor's solution to that problem, when broadly articulated at a conceptual level. Given any detail in the inventor's embodiment—a physical element, a method step, a particular functionality, or a specific relationship among these—one can ask whether that detail is essential to solving the problem at least to some extent. If not, that detail is not intrinsic to the inventive concept.

The problem Loud addressed was that existing (fountain and quill) pens could not write on rough surfaces, such as wood or leather. Central to his solution is the ball itself. Problem solved. Claim 1.1's "ink flow regulator" tells how such a pen could be constructed, not about how the problem of writing on rough surfaces can be solved. If the ink could somehow regulate itself, we would still have a pen of the type Loud envisioned. Never mind that Loud probably never considered whether such an ink could exist. It is possible to formulate a statement of something new—a pen with a spheroidal marking-point—without having to describe how such a pen might be constructed.

Perhaps somewhat more subtle is the question of the contracted mouth of the pen barrel, which one might think is absolutely required. How else could the ball be held in place?

It doesn't matter.

Imagine a tiny genie whose job is to hold the ball in place. Loud's spheroidal marking-point pen would still be a novel writing implement, even with that genie hanging on for dear life as the pen wiggles across the paper. Distinguishing Loud's pen from those that came before does not require saying that the pen has a contracted mouth or an ink flow regulator. Advantageous or not, these are only implementational details not going to the essence of solving the problem of writing on rough surfaces.

Dreaming up what the book calls "far-fetched embodiments," like our genie, is a powerful invention analysis tool.[5]

It is sometimes thought there is no harm in including an implementational detail in an invention definition if the detail is absolutely needed to implement the invention. This is a dangerous view to take. We can never be certain that any particular detail always *will* be needed. Technology marches on. New ways of doing things are invented every day.

Moreover, whether something seems required to *implement* an inventive concept is irrelevant to the task of *claiming* it. No argument in this regard comes from the Patent Office of 1888. The Patent Office issued Loud's patent with claims 1.2 and 1.3 just as presented above. Indeed, upon eliminating the "substantially as described" construct not used in modern practice, and assuming that ballpoint pens had not yet been invented, those same claims would be patentable today.

―――――――――――

Inventive concepts underlie every kind of invention, not just mechanical devices like ballpoint pens. Appendix A presents a number of them, including such pioneering inventions as Birdseye's method for packaging frozen food, Camras's technique for magnetic recording, and L'Esperance's laser vision surgery.

It is no surprise that such breakthrough inventions can be articulated broadly and claimed tersely. But week in and week out the Patent and Trademark Office issues patents with similarly broad claims that are directed to more modest advances. Appendix A provides examples of these as well.

――――――――

5. *See* p. 39.

CHAPTER REVIEW—Inventions Are Concepts

Confirm Your Understanding

1. Why is it important for a patent's claims to capture the invention's underlying concept?
2. What is the harm in including a claim limitation that any practical embodiment is going to have to have anyway?

Questions for Further Thought

3. How is it possible to reconcile the idea of claiming the inventive concept with the principle that abstract ideas are not the proper subject of a patent claim? See, generally, *Diamond v. Diehr*, 450 U.S. 175, 209 USPQ 1 (1981); *State Street Bank & Trust Co. v. Signature Financial Group, Inc.*, 149 F.3d 1368, 47 USPQ2d 1596 (Fed. Cir. 1998).
4. None of Loud's ballpoint pen claims (p. 6) encompass the felt-tip pen. Assuming that a claim could be drafted that would cover both ballpoint and felt-tip pens, while not reading on the prior art fountain pens and quills, do you think Loud should have been entitled to such a claim?
5. Do you agree with the author's contention that claims 1.2 and 1.3 would be patentable today, assuming no ballpoint pen prior art existed? Why or why not?
6. How would you respond if an examiner were to reject claims 1.2 and 1.3 based on
   a. 35 U.S.C. 101 as not being directed to an inventive "manufacture" but only a concept?
   b. 35 U.S.C. 112(b) as being "vague and indefinite"?

Sharpen Your Skills

7. Identify the problem solved and inventive concept(s) underlying the inventions listed below, based on the prior art indicated.

Invention	Prior Art	Problem Solved	Inventive Concept
Ballpoint pen	Quills; fountain pens	Pen can't write on rough surfaces	Pen with a spheroidal marking-point
Bubble wrap	Shredded paper; packing peanuts	?	?
Pocket door	Hinged door	?	?
Computer spreadsheet	Pencil and paper; word processing	?	?

CHAPTER TWO

Begin from the Problem
(Not the Embodiment)

The problem-solution approach illustrated in Chapter One for the ball-point pen is summarized by the prescription *Begin from the Problem (Not the Embodiment)*. That prescription should be followed in the analysis of every invention.

This chapter uses the invention of the paper clip to illustrate in greater detail what can go wrong if the analysis begins from the embodiment rather than the problem and how beginning from the problem can improve the odds of capturing others' products that implement the inventor's teachings.

What Is the Problem?

Build a better mousetrap, it is said, and the world will beat a path to your door.

It rarely happens.

Consider the mousetrap itself. Only a few kinds of mousetraps are found on store shelves, even though hundreds of mousetrap designs have been patented over the years, and even though each is "better" in *some* way, even the best idea is unlikely to achieve commercial success unless midwifed into the marketplace through attractive pricing, concerted marketing, and effective advertising. Contrary to the expectations of many first-time patentees, obtaining a patent is rarely the end of a process; it is usually only a beginning.

Yet the invitation to build a better mousetrap embodies the important idea that a good invention solves a problem that its predecessors solved less well or not at all. Not merely different from the prior art, a good invention corrects for some deficiency in it. For example, some people find the standard spring-loaded mousetrap hard to set. Others recoil from its violent nature and don't like having to look at the dead mouse, preferring to trap the mouse alive and release it outdoors. The few "better" mousetraps that have enjoyed marketplace acceptance have done so by addressing one or more such problems.

Answering the quintessential patent question posed in this book's Introduction—*What Is the Invention?*—therefore, requires answering the question *What Is the Problem?* Until the problem is fully appreciated, the solution cannot be fully appreciated either.

Not all practitioners begin from the problem. Many attorneys are taught to begin by focusing on the solution—the specific embodiment that the inventor designed. Typically a claim to the embodiment is drafted. The claim is then progressively broadened through a process of "pruning and distilling." Terms that are narrow are made general. For example, "screw" becomes "fastener." Separately recited physical elements or method steps are coalesced into more all-encompassing elements or steps. For example, the dual steps of "pointing [to an icon]" and "clicking" are distilled into the single step of "selecting." Other limitations are removed altogether. Pruning and distilling continue until any further broadening would cause the claim to read on the prior art. That which remains is supposedly the broadest possible claim to the invention. Similar approaches prune and distill a sketch of the embodiment or a list of components or steps, and a claim is directed to what is left.

A claim developed in any of these ways will certainly be broader—and therefore encompass more embodiments—than what was started with. However, the inventive concept may involve functions or relationships not present in the original claim, and it is unlikely that these will somehow find their way into the finished claim. Significant infringement loopholes can result. Even if such inventive-concept-defining functions or relationships are present in the original claim, they may unwittingly be excised during the claim-broadening process if their significance is not appreciated. Like the inhabitants of Flatland,[1] the attorney beginning an invention analysis from the embodiment may become trapped in a limited analytical framework and may be unable to discern a larger world beyond.

Object Lesson—The Konaclip Paper Clip

Let us look in detail at an example of how an embodiment-oriented, invention-analysis-by-claim-drafting approach described above can miss the broad invention. We will then see how the broad invention is readily uncovered by following the prescription to *Begin from the Problem (Not the Embodiment)*.

---

1. As recounted by Edwin A. Abbot in *Flatland: A Romance of Many Dimensions* (New York: Signet Classics, 1984), the inhabitants of Flatland—points, lines, and polygons—know nothing of the third dimension and are baffled by certain phenomena that occur when Flatland is visited by various three-dimensional objects.

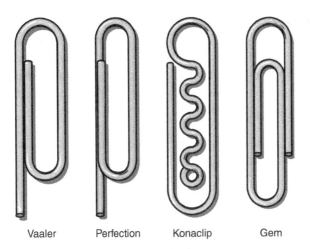

Vaaler   Perfection   Konaclip   Gem

FIGURE 2–1 The evolution of the paper clip.

The example is an early form of paper clip, marketed as the Konaclip, shown in Figure 2–1. Among the advantages touted for the Konaclip was the ability to hold a stack of paper securely while being easy to put on and take off without damaging the paper. This was a combination of properties that had eluded the prior art, exemplified by the Vaaler and Perfection clips also shown in Figure 2–1. The Vaaler clip did provide secure fastening; a corner of the paper stack was woven around and through the clip's overlapping arm portion. However, this was tedious and permanently creased the paper. The Perfection clip was easy to put on and take off. And it was gentle on the paper. But its paper-holding power was quite poor.

Not that the Konaclip worked all that well either; papers in the middle of the stack still tended to fall out. But the Konaclip did work better than the Perfection clip in that regard and, like the Perfection, did not damage the paper.

Also shown in Figure 2–1 is the now ubiquitous Gem. Although the historical record is not clear, it is assumed for this example that the Gem was invented after the Konaclip.[2]

Our ill-fated invention-analysis-by-claim-drafting approach begins by drafting a claim to the Konaclip embodiment. Claim 2.1 is such a claim. Note how claim 2.1 recites the Konaclip's inwardly deflected leg extending down the middle of the clip. This is the Konaclip's most distinctive physical feature and clearly distinguishes the Konaclip from the prior art Vaaler and Perfection clips.

---

2. A fascinating account of the development of the paper clip is presented in Henry Petroski, *The Evolution of Useful Things* (New York: Alfred A. Knopf, 1992).

> 2.1 A clip constructed of a single length of spring-steel wire bent to form an elongated frame having a pair of opposing rounded end portions, an end portion of the wire deflected inwardly within and near one end of the frame and within the plane thereof, and extended longitudinally along and within substantially the full length of the middle of the clip, the end portion having a serpentine shape and terminating in an eye.

Claim 2.1 is narrower than it has to be. Limitations that have nothing to do with the Konaclip's central leg—the terms "single," "spring-steel," and "pair of opposing rounded end portions"—can be pruned out of this claim without causing it to read on the prior art, but while still having a claim that "hangs together." This is shown by marked-up claim 2.2. Indeed, those limitations also apply to the Vaaler and/or Perfection clips and, as a result, limit the claimed subject matter without helping to distinguish the invention from the prior art anyway.

> 2.2 A clip constructed of a ~~single~~ length of ~~spring-steel~~ wire bent to form an elongated frame ~~having a pair of opposing rounded end portions~~, an end portion of the wire deflected inwardly within and near one end of the frame ~~and within the plane thereof~~, and extended longitudinally along and within substantially the full length of the middle of the clip, the end portion having a serpentine shape and terminating in an eye.

Still remaining in this claim are various features of the central leg—its serpentine shape, its length, its position within the plane of the overall frame, and the little eye at the end. None of these are necessary to distinguish the Konaclip from the prior art either, since the prior art clips have no central leg whatsoever. Striking those features from the claim makes it even broader while still not causing the claim to read on the prior art, as shown by marked-up claim 2.3.

> 2.3 A clip constructed of a length of wire bent to form an elongated frame, an end portion of the wire deflected inwardly within and near one end of the frame ~~and within the plane thereof~~, and extended longitudinally along and within ~~substantially the full length of~~ the middle of the clip, ~~the end portion having a serpentine shape and terminating in an eye~~.

Ultimately, then, it is the recitation of the central leg that is extended "longitudinally along and within the middle of the clip" that distinguishes the Konaclip from both the Vaaler and Perfection clips. Claim 2.4 is the final version.

2.4 A clip constructed of a length of wire bent to form an elongated frame, an end portion of the wire deflected inwardly within and near one end of the frame, and extended longitudinally along and within the middle of the clip.

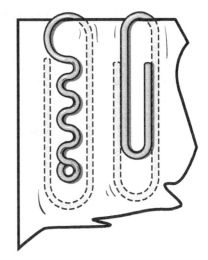

This claim is obviously much broader than the claim we started with. Indeed, claim 2.4 would encompass many Konaclip-like paper clips that differ from the particular embodiment shown in Figure 2–1.

Claim 2.4 does not encompass the later-invented Gem; the Gem does not have the Konaclip's central leg. Yet the Konaclip embodies a concept that carried over into the Gem. The Konaclip patent[3] did not have a claim directed to

FIGURE 2–2 The Konaclip and the Gem share a common concept that solves the paper-holding problem.

that concept, but it *could* have, and would have entitled the Konaclip patent owner to a royalty for every Gem sold.

Therein lies the moral of this tale.

The Konaclip's underlying concept readily reveals itself upon application of the rule *Begin from the Problem (Not the Embodiment)*. Recall that the problem the Konaclip was intended to solve was that prior art paper clips were not able to fasten a stack of papers securely without damaging them. What is really going on in the Konaclip in an attempt to solve that problem? A little thought reveals the answer. Part of the clip on one side of the paper urges the paper against a pair of opposing rails of the frame on the other side of the paper. This provides a great deal of frame surface area against which the paper is urged, and to some extent tucks the paper down into the space between the rails. Figure 2–2 shows how both the Konaclip and the Gem incorporate this concept.

Claim 2.5 is a claim drafted with that solution in mind. This claim reads not only on the Konaclip but also on the not-yet-invented Gem!

2.5 A clip constructed of a length of wire bent to form an elongated frame having a pair of opposing rails, an end portion of the wire being disposed inwardly within the frame and in the plane thereof, the end portion being so arranged as to cause a stack of paper inserted between

---

3. U.S. Patent No. 648,841 (issued May 1, 1900).

the end portion and the opposing rails to be urged substantially equally against both of the opposing rails.

There is little chance that any embodiment-based analysis of the Konaclip could ever result in claim 2.5. Without first considering what problem the Konaclip was intended to solve and how, broadly and functionally, the problem *was* solved, it is unlikely that words directed to the broad solution would ever find their way into the starting-point claim. Nor is it likely that such words would emerge as the result of any subsequent editing of the claim. The embodiment-based analysis of the Konaclip was doomed from the start. Claim 2.1 does contain a glimmer of the claim 2.5 language in its recitation that the end portion of the wire is "within the plane" of the frame. However, that language was pruned out of the claim during the broadening process.

Had the Konaclip patent included a claim like claim 2.5, the Konaclip inventor could have collected significant royalties from Gem manufacturers, notwithstanding the commercial failure of his own product. Unfortunately, the Konaclip patent focused solely on the Konaclip's geometry—its central leg—and not its underlying concept. Thus the potentially valuable Konaclip patent proved to be as worthless as the Konaclip itself.

Scenarios like this are common. All too often, a patent application's broadest claim arrived at through an embodiment-based analysis falls short of the mark, even when the conceptual underpinnings of the invention were right there, waiting to be discovered. The inventive concept often lies just as close to the surface as in this example, and a problem-solution-based analysis will readily uncover it.

Not that all inventions yield up their inventive essence as straightforwardly as the Konaclip. The subtleties of the concept underlying some inventions can make for a puzzle of Gordian knot proportions. All the more reason to begin from the problem, not the embodiment, if we are to have any chance of consistently capturing the inventive concept.

Pruning and distilling are invaluable tools for improving a claim. But what's needed in the early going is not a claim-drafting tool, but an invention-analysis tool. Sometimes we can get to where we need to be even when starting out from the embodiment. A perceptive attorney poring over a claim—particularly if helped along by an engaged inventor—may see an initial embodiment-oriented characterization of the invention transformed into an inventive-concept-capturing claim bearing little resemblance to the original. But there is little guarantee of that.

Drafting a broad claim that captures all of the inventor's embodiments is relatively simple. It is much harder to draft a claim that will capture others' future products before they have even been designed. Difficult or not, it is a task that must be tackled. We otherwise leave open the possibility that an inventor's original embodiment will be overtaken in the marketplace by "new and improved" implementations not covered by any claim in the issued patent. The Konaclip example makes that quite evident, as well as illustrating how beginning from the problem, not the embodiment, can help avoid that result.

The next chapter introduces a methodology that, indeed, begins from the problem to identify the broad invention and to define it in a problem-solution statement. That definition of the invention can serve as the basis for the patent application's broadest claims and, as we will see, the overarching theme of the entire patent application.

CHAPTER REVIEW—Begin from the Problem (Not the Embodiment)

Confirm Your Understanding

1. Explain why "pruning and distilling" a claim does not necessarily result in the broadest definition of the invention.

Questions for Further Thought

2. Why should the patent system allow someone like the Konaclip inventor to claim an invention so broadly as to capture something the inventor didn't actually think of, e.g., the Gem paperclip?
3. When might it be desirable to have claim(s) directed to the embodiment(s), i.e., claims that are narrower than made necessary by the prior art?

Sharpen Your Skills

4. Prune and distill the claims below to broaden them without the claims reading on the stated prior art. Are you happy with the breadth of the claims that result?

Problem	People may carry dangerous items into a restricted area, e.g., airport boarding area, school, etc.
Prior Art	"Pat down" people by hand
Inventor's Embodiment	Walk-through metal detector

Claim	Apparatus for detecting the presence of metal carried by a human being, comprising
	    an archway through which a person can pass,
	    an electromagnetic field generator disposed within the archway for generating an electromagnetic field that is changed when a metal object is passed through the archway,
	    a detector configured to detect changes in the magnetic field, and
	    an alarm operative in response to detection of the detected changes.

Problem	Foreign-language films cannot be understood by viewers who speak only English
Prior Art	Bilingual movie companion translates aurally in real time
Inventor's Embodiment	Add subtitles to film
Claim	A reel of a motion picture in which the dialog is in a language other than English, the motion picture film having printed thereon written translations of the dialog into English.

CHAPTER THREE

The Problem-Solution Statement

The centerpiece of problem-solution invention analysis is the problem-solution statement.

The problem-solution statement is a one-sentence statement of the invention. It states as broadly as possible, but without reading on the prior art, (a) the problem the invention solves, and (b) the inventor's solution to that problem. The problem-solution statement can serve as a foundation for the patent application's broadest claims. It is a benchmark against which the entire suite of claims in the patent application can be measured. And it can serve as the backbone of an effective story-telling patent specification.

The problem-solution statement is of the following form:

> *The problem(s) of* _____ *is(are) solved by* _____.

Here, for example, are problem-solution statements for the ballpoint pen and Konaclip inventions discussed in the previous chapters:

> *The problem of* a pen being able to write on rough surfaces *is solved by* the pen having a spheroidal marking-point.

> *The problem of* securely fastening sheets of paper without damaging the paper and while being able to unfasten the sheets easily *is solved by* a wire clip bent into an elongated frame having a pair of opposing rails and at least one inner portion within a single plane and arranged such that a stack of paper inserted between the inner portion and the opposing rails is urged substantially equally against both of the opposing rails by the inner portion.

Appendix A presents more examples in a variety of technologies.

Some inventions can be broadly characterized in more than one way. We saw this in the case of Loud's ballpoint pen.[1] If differing ways of characterizing the invention surface as the analysis proceeds, we should

---

1. *See* p. 7.

consider creating separate problem-solution statements for each. Such alternative characterizations of the invention provide a basis for alternative ways of claiming it.

Start Early

A first draft of the problem-solution statement should be formulated as soon as we have enough information about the problem and the general outlines of the solution to do so. Starting early counteracts the tendency for unessential implementational details to taint our notion of what the broad invention is. It protects us from becoming blindsided by the details and going too narrow right at the outset. Waiting until all the details have been laid out, and then trying to synthesize the invention out of all that, opens the door to an analysis that is embodiment-based rather than problem-solution-based. It is difficult to be misled by what we don't know.

Our introduction to the invention may be a technical paper or other written description supplied by the inventor. In that case, we should have the problem-solution paradigm in mind as soon as we begin to read. As the inventor's exposition unfolds, we mentally separate what seems to be the problem from what seems to be the solution, as well as separating what seem to be implementational details from what seems to be at the heart of the inventive concept. The task is often made easy by an inventor who has had prior exposure to the patenting process and has been inculcated with the problem-solution approach to describing an invention. The inventor's write-up may then quite clearly lay out the problem-solution story, as well as prior attempts to solve the problem and the shortcomings of those approaches. In any event, we should formulate a first version of the problem-solution statement as soon as the information gathered from the inventor's write-up makes it possible to do so—if not on paper in the first instance, then at least in our minds.

Or our introduction to the invention may occur in a face-to-face or telephone conversation with the inventor. Here, again, the problem and solution should be the early focus. The inventor should be set on a problem-solution course, being asked what problem she set out to solve and what she knows about prior art attempts to solve it.

The inventor can then be asked to explain how she solved the problem. A useful way of setting the stage for this is to bring the inventor back in time to the moment of inventive realization and to prompt her to articulate her solution in terms that put a heavy emphasis on function with as few implementational details as possible.

"Marla, given the problem that we just talked about, what would you say—in one sentence if you can—is fundamentally at the heart of

how you solved that problem? If you can bring yourself back to that moment when you thought you had seen your way clear to a solution, what do you think you realized there at that outset? Taking a sort of top-down approach to what you invented, what do you think is the broadest, most general way you can articulate your solution?"

It would be nice if the inventor could thereupon bring forth a broad, elegantly articulated solution, like Athena springing fully formed from the head of Zeus. Occasionally it does happen that way. More typically, however, the inventor picks up her pencil and begins explaining her solution in the context of the embodiment. This is not surprising. Inventors are used to thinking about their work in the tangible realm rather than the conceptual. Nonetheless, given the attorney's exhortation to describe the solution broadly and functionally, the inventor will present it in at least *some* level of generality, which is fine for a start. Techniques for ensuring that the problem-solution statement is as broad as it can be are presented in the next chapter.

The attorney should therefore stay alert for what could be the broad solution and take an initial stab at the problem-solution statement as soon as it appears possible to do so. That initial view of the invention can then be presented to the inventor for discussion.

If the attorney is not familiar with the technology at hand, his initial take on the problem-solution statement can be wildly overbroad. It is nonetheless desirable to start early and aim high even though it may well mean having to fall back to a more limited view of the invention once the full extent of the prior art becomes clear. The alternative of holding back and aiming lower in the first instance may result in an invention definition that is unduly narrow. Having been apprised by the inventor that the proposed problem-solution statement is too broad, the attorney can simply prompt the inventor to pick up the thread of her story, staying alert for an opportunity to formulate a problem-solution statement that is better focused on her contribution to the art.

Think Big

A companion idea to the prescription *Start Early* is *Think Big.*

Having been exposed to the broad functionality of the embodiment early on in his discussion with the inventor, the attorney who thinks big says to himself, "imagine the value of this patent if only we could capture the naked notion of *that*," meaning the broad functionality of the embodiment stripped of its implementational trappings. The earlier in the process we start thinking in these terms, the better.

 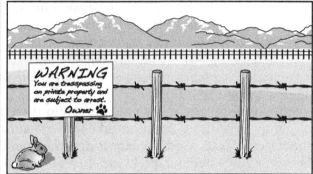

FIGURE 3–1 An attorney "thinking big" is unsatisfied with a limited, albeit easily obtained, parcel of intellectual property if a more expansive parcel can be staked out with additional effort.

Imagine the first alarm clock. An embodiment-based analysis of this device would have focused on its various components—an analog clock face, a bell, a hand to indicate the desired alarm time, and so forth. However, an attorney who was thinking big at that time would have been asking himself, "Is it possible that we could get (i.e., claim) the naked notion of alarming at a selectable time? Think of royalties! Think of the market share!" And then, "What's the prior art? Can it stop us? How can we get around it?" How much easier to capture the alarm clocks of the future—electrical clocks, electronic watches, personal digital assistants, and so on—if the patent is not limited to any particular configuration of the timekeeping device or any particular alarming mechanism.

Or consider the computer mouse. An attorney thinking big would want his client to own the naked notion of random-access control of a display screen cursor. Such a claim would encompass such postmouse innovations as the trackball, joystick, touch pad, or even cursor control with voice commands.

To *Think Big* means not being satisfied to pursue a limited parcel of intellectual property, even though it may be relatively easy to acquire. It means having a persistent, relentless mind-set of trying to secure as expansive a parcel of intellectual property as possible, even though it may be more difficult to do so.

Of course, the problem-solution statement cannot be so broad as to encompass prior art. It would be great to own the naked notion of sending moving pictures over the airwaves, but that idea is already almost a century old. So at some point our grandiose ideas of how broadly the invention can be defined may have to give way to reality.

Better, however, to aim high and have to fall back somewhat than to aim low and achieve a lesser goal, only to realize too late in the game—when others enter the marketplace with a variant of the inventor's embodiment not captured by the patent's claims—that more could have been achieved.

Don't Be Misled by the Inventor's Embodiment Focus

The broad invention is often some new functionality. How the embodiment implements that functionality is of secondary importance. The inventor may not appreciate the distinction, however, and may lead the attorney to assume that the new functionality is already known in the art. The opportunity to define the inventor's contribution at its full breadth may then become lost.

The attorney can usually forestall such a result by keeping his ears open and, again, starting early and thinking big.

Consider, for example, the drip-style coffeemaker shown in Figure 3–2. When the carafe is not in place, a valve in the coffee basket prevents liquid from dripping out of the coffee basket onto the burner or countertop. Sliding the carafe into place pushes up on a pin, which opens the valve and allows coffee to flow. If the carafe is removed, the valve is again closed.

At the time the inventor devised this pin-and-valve design, the broad concept of shutting off the flow of liquid if the carafe is not in place may have been in the prior art. But it may not have been. In that case, the inventor would be entitled to a claim encompassing all ways of confirming the presence of the carafe—a photocell, a microswitch, a weight sensor, and so on.

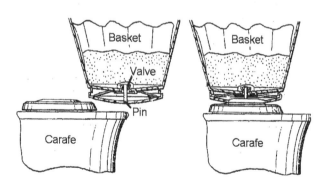

FIGURE 3–2 Coffeemaker with anti-drip feature.

Unfortunately, the inventor may describe the problem she set out to solve not as the problem of dripping coffee but the problem of how to shut off the flow. In so doing, she will have relegated her broad invention to the prior art. The attorney is less likely to be misled by such overly narrow thinking by beginning to formulate the problem-solution statement early on. He will then have the opportunity to explore with the inventor whether the invention can, indeed, be as broad as the naked notion of shutting off the flow if the carafe is not there.

First Be a Skeptic; Then Be an Advocate

The previous section describes a situation where the inventor doesn't appreciate the full breadth of the invention. The opposite is also possible. That is, the inventor's view of the breadth of her invention may be overly optimistic. This phenomenon is particularly common with the nonprofessional, armchair inventor who brings to her attorney *only* the very broad idea because the inventor does not have the engineering skills to design a working embodiment.

A truism of the patent business is that if a problem is one of long standing and could have been solved years ago, it probably was! Thus an attorney presented with an invention that solves an old problem and that was readily solvable with old technology should bring a healthy dose of skepticism to the invention-analysis process.

Consider, for example, a pager or a cell phone that automatically switches from audible ringing to its vibrate mode when an onboard microphone senses that the ambient noise level is so high—on a busy street, for example—that the audible ringing might not be heard. It's a cute idea. But the problem of not hearing an audio alert in a noisy environment is as old as the pager itself. And microphones tiny enough for sensing the ambient noise level have also been around for a long time. The problem could, therefore, have been solved years ago, and our intuition ought to suggest that this is not a new idea. In fact, it is not.[2]

How about a windshield wiper system that detects the level of precipitation and adjusts the speed of the wipers accordingly? Also an old idea.[3]

This does not mean the inventor should be sent packing based on mere suspicions about the prior art. What it does mean is that a prior art search should definitely be undertaken to either validate or disprove our suspicions.

---

2. U.S. Patent No. 5,646,589 (issued July 8, 1997).
3. U.S. Patent No. 5,949,150 (issued Sept. 7, 1999).

The role of the attorney as skeptic also extends to the question of obviousness under 35 U.S.C. 103. The attorney's experience may tell him that the invention as broadly presented by the inventor would likely be deemed obvious based on the prior art. The inventor needs to be challenged in such a case to articulate (with the attorney's help, as discussed below) why an invention so broadly defined would not have been so obvious after all.

The point of such skepticism is not to talk the inventor out of seeking a patent, at least not in the first instance. Indeed, the attorney's role is to be the inventor's advocate and help her secure whatever intellectual property protection she is entitled to. The point of such skepticism, rather, is to open a dialog that hopefully will bring to the fore possible arguments *against* the obviousness rejection that the attorney believes is likely to come if the present broad view of the invention is maintained.

Thus, once having laid out for the inventor the examiner's likely obviousness rejection, the attorney needs to switch roles and become an advocate *for* the invention. For example, the inventor should be encouraged to identify any incorrect assumptions underpinning the attorney's skepticism, such as the attorney's interpretation of what a particular prior art reference actually says. And the attorney should explore with the inventor whether any of the indicia of nonobviousness established by case law might apply. Among such indicia are

- the modification or combination of prior art references yielding unexpected results;
- the state of the art being such as to "teach away" from making the modification or combination of prior art references;
- the existence of so-called secondary considerations, such as long-felt need.[4]

Surprises often await the attorney on these fronts. The attorney is often surprised to hear from the inventor some cogent technological and/or legally sound reasons that the attorney's initial take on the obviousness question is not as open-and-shut as it first appeared.

Once it appears that all the relevant prior art is in hand and that at least some reasonable argument can be mounted against any anticipated case of obviousness, the attorney will be in a favorable position to advocate for the patentability of the invention if the expected obviousness rejection is actually made. However, the attorney's advocative

---

4. An enumeration of some of the indicia of nonobviousness is provided in *Manual of Patent Examining Procedure*, § 2145, ¶ X (8th ed., rev. July 2010).

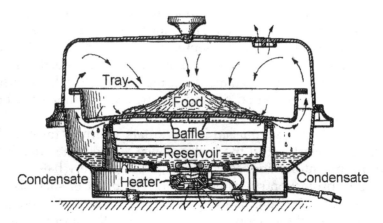

FIGURE 3–3 A food steamer that solves three problems with three separate solutions.

role should be engaged long before that. We will see in Part IV that an artfully crafted patent specification can serve as a powerful vehicle for advocating the patentability of the invention.

Keep Separate Inventions Separate

The broad invention may reside in the fact that two or more solutions have been brought together to achieve some unexpected result(s). However, a device or process may incorporate two or more solutions to respective problems, each being a separate invention (assuming that the requirements of novelty[5] and nonobviousness[6] are met). For example, the food steamer shown in Figure 3–3 solves at least three problems, each solved by a respective feature of the steamer, and each giving rise to its own problem-solution statement:

1. *The problem of* foul odors that occur if the steamer is allowed to boil dry *is solved by* preventing the condensate from draining back to the boiling-water reservoir.
2. *The problem of* the food getting soggy if allowed to remain in contact with the condensed steam *is solved by* a specially designed food tray that causes the condensate to drain away from the food.

---

5. 35 U.S.C. 102.
6. 35 U.S.C. 103.

3. *The problem of* long waiting times for initial steam formation to occur *is solved by* a baffle that promotes local heating of water in the boiling-water reservoir.

Identifying the separate inventions embodied in a particular device, method, or system, and pursuing them in separate patents, may be crucial to securing patents that competitors cannot easily design around. If the patent defines and claims the invention as a combination of multiple solutions to multiple problems, a competitor's product implementing less than all of those solutions escapes scot-free. It is therefore dangerous to lump all the solutions together and call *that* the invention without thinking through the possible problems that may arise when it comes time to license or enforce the patent. In general, a problem-solution statement should be formulated for each independently novel/nonobvious idea.

Define the Invention; Try It On for Size

The overall process of formulating a problem-solution statement is summarized by the prescription *Define the Invention; Try It On for Size*.

"Define the Invention" means formulating a problem-solution statement at some level of breadth. "Try It On for Size" means comparing that problem-solution statement to the prior art to determine whether it is too broad, too narrow, or "just right." The problem-solution statement may contain limitations—either in the problem or in the solution—not necessary to distinguish the invention from the prior art. In that case, the problem-solution statement needs to be made broader. Or the problem-solution statement may read on the prior art. In *that* case, the problem-solution statement needs to be made narrower.

The process is iterative. Once having redefined the invention, the new problem-solution statement must itself be tried on for size. A problem-solution statement that was too broad may now be too narrow, and vice versa. In fact, successive versions of the problem-solution statement may cross the line between "too broad" and "too narrow" any number of times until arriving at one that seems "just right." (See Figure 3–4.) This is analogous to adjusting a camera's focus or its zoom back and forth in smaller and smaller steps until the image is perfectly defined. This dynamic is evident in the author's "real-time" analysis of the backspace key presented in Appendix B.

Effective invention identification means getting a good handle on the prior art as soon as possible. We otherwise run the risk of investing time and effort in a problem-solution statement that is too broad. This can mean additional time and expense to reconfigure the patent application and its claims, assuming the undue breadth comes to light before the

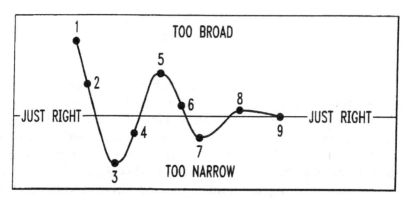

FIGURE 3–4 Formulating successive definitions of the invention and trying each one on for size is like adjusting a camera's focus or zoom back and forth in progressively smaller steps.

patent application is filed. And if anticipatory prior art comes to light later, during prosecution, we may be faced with an application that does not effectively advocate or adequately disclose the "real" invention.

It may be feasible for the attorney and inventor, while the two of them are together, to conduct an online prior art search at the United States Patent and Trademark Office (USPTO) website or at a commercial search site. Even if a prior art search was already undertaken, or the inventor is confident that she is already aware of all the relevant prior art, questions of further prior art that may be "out there" may arise after the problem-solution statement has been worked on and broadened. An updated search may then be appropriate.

The attorney and inventor will have done a lot at their first (and perhaps only) meeting even if they accomplish nothing more than to produce a finely honed problem-solution statement and identify the invention's important fallback features.[7] Getting the inventive concept locked down early paves the way for an efficiently written and sharply focused patent application.

Many practitioners like to sketch out at least one set of claims at the first meeting. This is fine as long as it is done after a problem-solution-based analysis has been undertaken. Drafting claims should not be the primary vehicle for discovering the invention. The structural formalisms of claim drafting, while perhaps familiar and facilitating, can all too easily mislead us into thinking we have discovered the inventive forest when we have actually only identified some of its trees. Drafting a claim

---

7. *See* Chapter Six.

without having analyzed the invention is like drawing a map without having first surveyed the terrain. The Konaclip example presented in Chapter Two should have convinced the reader of the importance of analyzing first, and claim drafting second.

A fundamental patent-drafting skill is the ability to evaluate an invention definition—be it in the form of a problem-solution statement or a claim—and to decide whether it is too broad, too narrow, or "just right." The reader will be helped in developing that skill by the material in the upcoming two chapters.

CHAPTER REVIEW—The Problem-Solution Statement

Confirm Your Understanding

1. Since a problem-solution statement is not a claim, what difference does it make if the problem-solution statement reads on the prior art?
2. Why bother with a problem-solution statement? Why not proceed directly to claiming the invention and be done with it?
3. What are the benefits of starting early to hypothesize what the broad invention is, as opposed to waiting until the inventor has explained everything about the embodiment(s) and *then* beginning the analysis?
4. What does the author mean when referring to the "naked notion" of an invention?
5. The patent attorney's job is to advocate for the nonobviousness of the invention. Why, then, is it appropriate for the attorney to be a skeptic on the question of nonobviousness in the initial discussions with the inventor? Why not just wait to see what the examiner says?
6. What is the danger in combining multiple solutions to multiple problems in the patent application's broadest claims?
7. Why is it important to get a good handle on the prior art as soon as possible?
8. What are the two main ways in which the breadth of a problem-solution statement needs to be "tried on for size"? Why are they both important?
9. What are the dangers in postponing consideration of what the real invention is until the first Patent Office action is received?

Questions for Further Thought

10. In what way(s) do inventors think differently about inventions from the way patent attorneys do? What are the implications of those differences for the analysis of an invention?
11. Thinking Big (p. 21) often results in a characterization of the invention that is far broader than the inventor had ever contemplated. Does/ should this make the patent attorney a coinventor?
12. Patent attorneys who Think Big often come up with embodiments of the inventive concept that the inventor-client never dreamed of. How should the patent specification be prepared, and the invention claimed, in order to best protect the client's interests in such a case?
13. An old device that inherently solves a previously unappreciated problem is not a patentable invention. See, for example, *Abbott Labs. v. Baxter Pharm. Prods. Inc.*, 80 USPQ2d 1860 (Fed. Cir. 2006). Why, then, do we bother to define the invention in terms of both a problem and a solution? That is, if the solution portion of the problem-solution statement reads on the prior art, why aren't we "dead in the water" no matter what the problem portion says?

14. Does being able to broadly characterize an invention in more than one way, as in the case of Loud's ballpoint pen (p. 6), mean that there is more than one invention?

15. In the coffeemaker example (p. 23), the author asserts that the inventor who was first to teach the desirability of shutting off the flow of coffee in the absence of the carafe would have been entitled to a claim that encompasses all ways of doing that, even though the inventor's only embodiment was the pin-and-valve approach. Do you agree?

16. How does the author's assertion square with the provision of 35 U.S.C. 112(f) stating that a means-plus-function recitation—e.g., "means for shutting off the flow of liquid if the carafe is not in place"—shall be construed to cover

> the corresponding structure, material, or acts described in the specification *and equivalents thereof* [emphasis added].

That is, is a mechanical pin-and-valve shutoff the "equivalent" of, say, a photocell?

17. The author refers to the domain of exclusivity granted by a patent as a *"parcel* of intellectual property." In what way(s) is this real property analogy an apt one? Can you think of another legal construct to which a patent claim might be analogized?

18. The book explains the dangers of lumping together two or more inventive solutions in one claim. What options might be pursued if the client does not, at least initially, want to pay for multiple patent applications to cover the various inventive solutions?

Sharpen Your Skills

19. Following the prescription to *First Be a Skeptic; Then Be an Advocate,* try to think of way(s) to advocate for the patentability of the following ideas, given the prior art shown and any other prior art that you think would be "problematic."

a. Repeated Subway Ads	**Embodiment**	**Prior Art**

	All ads on at least one side of the interior of a subway car advertise the same organization, e.g., the U.S. Army.	In the prior art, the ads are for different products/ organizations.

b. Upside-Down Ketchup Label

Embodiment

Prior Art

Upside-down ketchup label allows the bottle to be stood upside down so that ketchup will always be near the mouth of the bottle but the label will be right-side up.

---

c. Art Restorer's Adhesive

Embodiment

Prior Art

Material called B-72 is discovered to be a great adhesive for repairing valuable museum objects. It is most useful to restorers as an adhesive when dispensed from a tube, because in a tube it will stay fresh for a long period of time.

B-72 was known in the prior art, but only came in solid pellets that were mixed with a solvent by the user to form a liquid that was used only as a varnish, not as an adhesive. B-72 will quickly dry out when kept in a jar due to air exposure.

---

d. Word Processor Highlighting

Embodiment

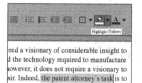

Prior Art

A "highlighting function" in a word processor allows the writer to highlight selected words.

CHAPTER FOUR

The Problem-Solution Statement— Reaching for Breadth

The prescriptions *Start Early* and *Think Big* presented in the previous chapter give us a good start in making the problem-solution statement, and ultimately the claims, as broad as they can be. This chapter presents a number of other prescriptions and ideas that can be brought to bear in that quest. These techniques can be applied in the very earliest stages of our thinking, even before the first draft of the problem-solution statement has been committed to paper. They can also be used later on, when the problem-solution statement is being tried on for size in the search for infringement loopholes.

The problem-solution statement will serve as the basis for some of the patent application's broadest claims.[1] However, the ideas in this chapter can also be used when drafting claims directly.

Envision the "Opposing Team"

True or false? In characterizing an invention, one should try to capture the inventor's contribution to the art.

The answer would certainly seem to be "true," but it is not the complete answer. The value of a patent is not determined by how cleverly or well its claims define the product or method that the inventor designed. A patent is valuable when its claims read on what somebody *else* will market or, at least, *would* market but for the existence of the patent. If it is expected that competitors will slavishly "knock off" a copy of the inventor's marketed product, there is no real issue—almost any claim will do. But that rarely happens. More often a competitor implementing the essence of the inventor's teachings does so in a way that departs significantly from the inventor's design.

Thus when we are drafting the problem-solution statement—which will serve as the basis for the patent application's broadest claims—the appropriate mind-set is not one of defining what our inventor has done.

---

1. *See* Chapter Seven.

FIGURE 4–1 The Opposing Team scrutinizes every word as the prosecuting patent attorney writes it, waiting for him to create an infringement loophole.

Rather, our mind-set needs to be one of defining what some competitor may do that *takes advantage of* what our inventor has done—particularly a competitor who is intent on doing so while avoiding the claims of our inventor's patent.

A powerful way of putting ourselves in that mind-set is to conjure up the image of a potential infringer and his patent attorney. The book refers to them as the "Opposing Team." These adversaries will be poring over the claims after the patent issues, looking either for limitations that their product does not meet or for some way to redesign the product to that end.

At the very same time, then, that we are formulating a problem-solution statement or a claim, we should imagine ourselves to *be* the Opposing Team. As each word, phrase, and structural element appears on the screen or on our yellow pad, we should try to think of a way around it, just like the real-life Opposing Team will do. Indeed, the author often has a sense of the Opposing Team standing over his shoulder as he writes, watching for something to appear that will make it possible to design around the issued patent or argue that their product does not infringe.

This constant awareness of the Opposing Team enables us to serve as our own worst critic or perhaps, one might say, our own *best* critic. It helps us become aware of unduly limiting aspects of a problem-solution statement (or a claim) in real time so that problems can be fixed as they arise.

Adopting the Opposing Team's mind-set can also help us identify potential arguments that the problem-solution statement is too broad or ambiguous, rendering any claims that may be based on it unpatentable (pending claim) or invalid (issued claim).

The inventor should also be made aware of the Opposing Team—if not by name, at least in concept. When first drafting or later editing the problem-solution statement or a claim, we can emphasize to the inventor that the goal is to define the inventive concept in a way that precludes a motivated competitor from "ripping off" the invention. The inventor can be encouraged to help think about how the invention might be appropriated by a competitor without coming within the ambit of the current problem-solution statement. Inventors are often captivated by the puzzle-like aspect of this challenge and find loopholes that the attorney might never have considered.

One of the author's colleagues puts it this way:

> *"Once I believe that I understand the invention's kernel, I challenge the inventor by asking questions like: "You say that the invention requires x+y+z at a minimum. If you were to find someone building x+y, but not using z, would you feel upset that this someone can do it without paying you a royalty?" This, in my experience, very quickly causes the inventor to think about how this "someone" will try to get away with using the invention without using some of what the inventor thought was necessary in the presented embodiment, and focus on the kernel of the invention."*
>
> *—HTB*

Another of the author's colleagues compares the Opposing Team to a computer hacker. Although his description speaks in terms of analyzing a claim, the idea applies equally well to the problem-solution statement.

> *"I approach claim analysis much as a hacker approaches systems analysis. Although people usually look at a system from the standpoint of what it does right, a hacker looks at the edges to see what it does wrong. Thus, my mind-set when drafting claims is that of a person skilled in the art who reads the specification and then tries to extract commercial value from its teachings while skirting the boundaries of whatever has been claimed. I ask myself what would I do/build/argue to get around any claim, regardless of how well drafted, if I were a commercial competitor (or his shrewd lawyer). In this sense my claim drafting tends to have a pessimistic, or at least a very defensive, bent.*
>
> *I tend to work in a constant feedback loop on every claim limitation that suggests itself to me, trying to understand how each limitation poses a "vulnerability"—an infringement loophole—within the context of the setting at hand."*
>
> *—BSL*

In short, the patent attorney endeavoring to further his client's interests is aided in that task by taking on the mind-set of a competitor's attorney endeavoring to further *his* client's interests.

Mine the Embodiments

We have seen the dangers of beginning from the embodiment when analyzing an invention. A properly focused study of the embodiments can, however, help uncover the breadth of the invention in the context of a problem-solution analysis. The prescriptions presented in this section help us to do so.

Investigate What's Really Going On

One way of gaining insight into the breadth of the invention is to ask, *What's Really Going On?* or—more completely—*What's Really Going On to Solve the Problem?* The word "really" emphasizes a search for the fundamental problem and the fundamental solution. What is going on *really*?

The answer to *What's Really Going On?* can usually be expressed in functional terms, so we should think more functionally than structurally, in verbs rather than nouns, in method steps rather than structural elements.

The exhortation to discover *What's Really Going On?* invites us to exercise our technological curiosity; to dig down and discover what the invention is accomplishing at its essence; to understand what is going on at the 50,000-foot level; to see the invention in terms of fundamental causes and ultimate effects, without all the stuff in between.

Answering *What's Really Going On?* means, then, figuring out what solves the problem in at least a rudimentary way—not what solves the problem in the most elegant, efficient, or commercially attractive way. It means discovering which aspects of the embodiment(s) are essential to solving the problem *at all*. Competitors rarely implement an invention exactly as the inventor did. Indeed, competitors may sacrifice a measure of elegance, efficiency, or even commercial attractiveness in their products if it means being able to get into the market or avoid paying a patent royalty. Or they may devise their *own* elegant, efficient, or commercially attractive implementations. The more limitations in a problem-solution statement (and ultimately a claim that is based on it), the easier it is for a potential infringer to render himself a *non*infringer.

If the inventor has devised two or more embodiments, we should try to identify what is common among them. If they are different embodiments of what is truly the same invention, *What's Really Going On?* will be the same in each of them. If the inventor has devised only one embodiment, we can encourage her to think of others—even some "far-fetched" ones, as described below[2]—and then identify what is common among all of them.

The prescription to investigate *What's Really Going On?* can be used not only when planning out the first draft of a problem-solution statement but also to weed out undue limitations in a problem-solution statement or claim already under way. Given an aspect of the embodiment(s)—a physical element, a method step, a functionality, or a relationship among

---

2. *See* p. 39.

these—we should ask whether it is essential to the solution or, on the other hand, only an aspect of how the inventor happened to *embody* the solution. Any element or detail not contributing to the core of the solution is probably not part of what's really going on and not an indispensable part of the broad invention. Such an element or detail may create an infringement loophole, enabling others to take advantage of the inventor's teachings without coming within the ambit of her patent.

The inventor sometimes insists that the invention cannot be implemented without some particular implementational detail. Or she may insist that the invention is applicable only to a narrow technological environment. If the inventor is correct, defining the invention to include that detail or environment would not be damaging. Indeed, there would be a potential benefit. The more limited the invention definition (as ultimately embodied in the patent claims), the more difficult it is for the patent examiner to find prior art that anticipates it. This can reduce legal costs and lead to a quicker issuance of the patent.

However, one can rarely guarantee that the inventor's view is correct. An inventor is often too wound up in her embodiment(s) to appreciate how her basic ideas may be implemented by others. She often fails to appreciate how her particular embodiments may be but trees in a larger inventive forest. It is often easy enough, however, for the attorney to help the inventor appreciate what's really necessary for the invention by conjuring up a few commercially plausible alternative embodiments that do not include one or more details that the inventor insisted were so indispensable.

Separate What from How

Certain aspects of the inventor's embodiment(s) may allow the problem to be solved more completely or more advantageously than if the invention were implemented some other way. But the invention is not about preferred ways of solving the problem. It is about solving the problem, period. To *Separate What from How* means to figure out *what* solves the problem, as contrasted with *how* the embodiments just happen to implement the solution.

The process to *Separate What from How* focuses not on what the broad invention *is,* but what it is *not.* The question is: Would the invention as currently defined solve the problem to at least some extent even in the absence of a particular element, step, or interrelationship in the embodiment? If so, that aspect of the embodiment is most likely a *how* and not a *what,* relating not to the broad invention but to the implementation. We saw in our ballpoint pen example[3] that its embodiment's "ink flow

---

3. *See* pp. 6–8.

regulator" and contracted barrel mouth were not essential to solving the problem of writing with ink on a rough surface and, as such, were not necessary to define what the invention was.

This is not to say that the implementational details—the *hows*— are totally unimportant. Some of the embodiment's *hows* will serve as the basis for important fallback feature claims.[4] The *hows* of the embodiment(s) are also needed to satisfy the requirements of "enablement" and "best mode."[5] Our focus at the moment, however, is distilling the invention down to its bare essence.

The process to *Separate What from How* helps address one of the patent practitioner's more insidious demons—the almost irresistible mental hold that certain embodiment details can exert over us. Even the most experienced attorney can be seduced into thinking that some aspect of the embodiment(s) is necessary to the invention, when it is not. By working to *Separate What from How*, we steer our thought processes away from the embodiment and the lure of its implementational details toward a broader view of the invention.

A caveat: Used in isolation, the endeavor to *Separate What from How* may broaden out the embodiment but completely miss the invention, as we saw in the case of the Konaclip.[6] This technique should not be used, then, when formulating a problem-solution statement or a claim in the first instance. It should be used only after a problem-solution-based anal-

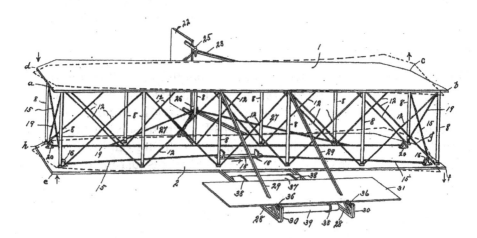

FIGURE 4–2 The Wright brothers' "aeroplane," patented in 1906.

---

4. *See* Chapter Six.
5. 35 U.S.C. 112(a).
6. *See* pp. 12–16.

ysis is already under way or when we are intentionally setting out to draft a claim of less than fully broad scope.[7]

Our view of the *what* vs. *how* status of an embodiment detail may change once the problem-solution statement is compared to the prior art. For example, a feature of the Wright brothers' 1906 flying machine was a wing-warping mechanism, as shown by the dashed lines in Figure 4–2. Wing warping provided lateral control during flight, allowing the pilot to keep the wings level. Providing lateral control would certainly seem to be an implementational detail—a *how* not essential to a definition of a machine capable of heavier-than-air flight. One might therefore think to characterize the Wrights' invention as comprising nothing more or less than a lift-producing wing and a source of motive energy, as in the following problem-solution statement:

> The problem of achieving heavier-than-air flight is solved by the combination of (a) a wing structure that provides lift when moved relative to the atmosphere and (b) a source of motive power to provide said relative motion.

This problem-solution statement is too broad, however. At least one flying machine having a lift-producing wing and a source of motive power was built prior to the Wrights by one Clement Ader some 13 years before Kitty Hawk. Ader's craft was impractical; it had no lateral control mechanism and, as a result, was incapable of sustained flight beyond perhaps 150 feet.[8] Even so, the above problem-solution statement characterizes not only the Wrights' 1906 flying machine, but Ader's as well. It also reads on flying dinosaurs and most species of birds.

We see, therefore, that changing the wing configuration to achieve lateral control was not an aspect of *how* the Wright brothers implemented their invention. It *was* the invention and, indeed, is recited in even the broadest claims of their 1906 patent.[9]

Dream Up Alternatives, Including Some Far-Fetched Ones

A powerful tool for finding loopholes in an invention definition is to dream up some alternatives to the inventor's embodiment(s), including

---

7. *See* Chapter Nine.

8. Tom D. Crouch, *A Dream of Wings: Americans and the Airplane, 1875–1905* (Washington, D.C.: Smithsonian Institution Press, 1989).

9. U.S. Patent No. 821,393 (issued May 22, 1906). Claim 1 of the Wrights' patent recites "In a flying-machine, a normally flat aeroplane [wing] having lateral marginal portions capable of movement to different positions above or blow [*sic*] the normal plane of the body of the aeroplane, . . ."

some alternatives that are far-fetched. These are embodiments that, while outlandish or "wacky," would nonetheless solve the problem to at least some extent. The more far-fetched the better. The point is not to claim, or even to disclose, these embodiments in the patent application. The point is that even a far-fetched embodiment can solve the problem without involving some of the implementational details required by practical embodiments. Dreaming up far-fetched embodiments is thus another way of isolating the essence of the invention from its implementational details and thereby identifying limitations in the problem-solution statement, or in a claim, that aren't needed after all.

For example, the push-button telephone introduced in the 1960s replaced the electrical pulses generated by a rotary dial with tones generated by electronic oscillators. Oscillators were the only way known at the time to generate tones electronically, and a physical switch (e.g., push-button) was the only way known for a user to indicate the digit she wanted to dial. Here is a possible problem-solution statement for this invention:

> The problem of slow dialing of rotary telephone instruments is solved by using oscillators to generate tones in response to user operation of push-buttons.

A far-fetched embodiment of a push-button telephone, however, might use trained miniature parrots to whistle the tones in response to verbal commands. Such an embodiment would not use oscillators or push-buttons. Yet it implements the same concept that underlies the "real" embodiment: signaling into the telephone network from the telephone customer's premises using tones rather than pulses. Thinking about whistling parrots and voice commands should lead us to a problem-solution statement that does not invoke oscillators or push-buttons:

> The problem of slow dialing of rotary telephone instruments is solved by a telephone dialer that generates for each of a plurality of unique dialing indications a respective unique signal comprising at least one tone.

This second problem-solution statement covers not only the original oscillator-plus-push-button embodiment but also the parrots-plus-spoken-command embodiment. The latter embodiment is not of practical interest, of course. Importantly, however, conjuring up that far-fetched embodiment led us to a problem-solution statement encompassing realistic embodiments that were probably unimagined, if not unimaginable, when the push-button telephone was conceived of. For example, there are now ways of generating tones without oscillators and ways of dialing a telephone number without the use of push-buttons, for example, by voice command or point-and-click dialing from a computer screen. Thus a patent claim based on the second problem-solution statement would potentially have had longer staying power, and would have covered more real-life, realistic embodiments, than a patent based on the first one. In this particular case, the patent would have expired long before non-oscillator-based tone generation came to market in any widespread way. In general, however, one never knows how quickly today's implementational imperative will become the old way of doing things. Dreaming up far-fetched embodiments helps us deal with that eventuality.

It may be unreasonable to expect an inventor or her attorney to divine the technological advances of the future, but it is not unreasonable to expect them to anticipate that advances of some kind will inevitably occur. Dreaming up various embodiments of the invention, including some far-fetched ones, helps us identify those aspects of the current problem-solution statement that are inherent in the underlying inventive concept from those that are merely illustrative details.

Broaden Out the Problem

When a problem-solution statement is too narrow, the offending language is usually in the solution portion. However, it is also possible for the problem to be stated too narrowly, which, just as in the case of the too-narrow solution, can lead to an unduly narrow claim.

One way the problem gets stated too narrowly is by being framed in view of the inventor's own work. As we saw in our discussion of the coffeemaker of Figure 3–2, this can result in at least some of the inventor's contribution being relegated to prior art status. This in turn can result in a too-narrow problem-solution statement and, ultimately, a too-narrow claim.

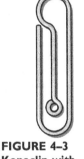

FIGURE 4–3
Konaclip with
straight central leg.

As another example, suppose the inventor of the Konaclip[10] had made a big point of the fact that the Konaclip would not hold paper very securely if its central leg were straight, as shown in Figure 4–3, rather than serpentine, as seen in Figure 2–1. From this perspective one might conclude that the straightness of the central leg is the problem, and the serpentine shape is the solution. That might be a correct

---

10. *See* pp. 12–16.

analysis if the straight-legged Konaclip had been in the prior art. But since *no* Konaclip-like paper clip previously existed, the analysis is too narrowly focused, leading to an invention definition that includes the serpentine central leg. The problem that the Konaclip inventor set out to solve was not the ineffectiveness of a Konaclip straight leg as compared to the serpentine leg. He *invented* the Konaclip, after all. Rather, the problem that the Konaclip inventor set out to solve was the more general problem of secure and convenient holding of a stack of paper without damaging it. That, then, is the appropriate problem statement for the Konaclip.

Another way the problem gets too narrowly stated is when the environment or context for the invention has not been fully explored and ultimately gets characterized too narrowly.

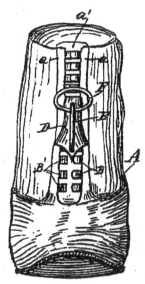

FIGURE 4–4 The problem that Judson's "clasp locker" (later, the "zipper") was originally intended to solve was the inconvenience of shoe buttons.

For example, what problem did the zipper solve? Knowing all the ways in which zippers have come to be used—clothing, zippered ring binders, backpacks—it would be apparent to us today that the generic problem solved by the zipper is how to quickly and easily join and later separate the margins of two pieces of flexible material. But, the original use envisioned for the zipper was very specific. Its inventor, Whitcomb Judson, developed his invention as a replacement for shoe buttons, which were tiny and required the use of a buttonhook—a tedious and time-consuming process. Judson's "clasp locker," shown in Figure 4–4, promised to be a boon to shoe-wearers the world over. As a result, the inventor might well have become so fixated on shoes as to overlook the possibility that the problem solved could go far beyond the problem of shoe closure. Judson and his patent attorney might therefore have developed a problem-solution statement such as the following (where the shoe-related terminology is underscored) and called it a day:

The problem(s) attendant to fastening a <u>shoe</u> using <u>shoe</u> buttons *are solved by* (a) a row of clasps made with interlocking parts disposed on opposing <u>flaps of the shoe</u>, which when in position, can only engage each other when at an angle to the line of strain, and (b) a movable guide having two guideways which are separated at one end and converge into a single guideway at the other end.

Happily, they were smarter than that. Although Judson and his patent attorney James Williamson could have been blinded by a shoe-centric view of the invention, at least one of them understood that the problem solved was not limited to shoe closure. As related in Judson's 1893 patent,[11]

> [t]he invention was especially designed, for use as a shoe-fastener; but is capable of general application wherever clasps consisting of interlocking parts may be applied, as for example, to mail-bags, belts, and the closing of seams uniting flexible bodies.

Indeed, most of the claims of the patent embody this realization, as evidenced by their preambles.

> 4.1 A device for engaging and disengaging a series of two-part clasps upon a shoe *or other article*, consisting of ...
>
> 4.2 A hand device for locking or unlocking a series of two-part clasps or similar interlocking parts, which engage or disengage by an angular movement, the said device consisting of ...

A great many other pioneering inventions proved to have much wider applicability than the specific application originally envisioned by their inventors. These include the atmospheric steam engine (originally developed to pump water out of coal mines); bar coding (railroad freight cars); and the vacuum tube amplifier (radio broadcasting). It is not important for our discussion here whether the patents for those inventions claimed them broadly beyond the inventors' originally envisioned application, or whether technology or the marketplace would have been ready for other applications before their patents might have expired. We never know how soon the world may find uses for an invention beyond those originally contemplated by the inventor. Thus in trying the problem-solution statement on for size, it is important to think beyond the initial problem environment to see if the problem statement is narrower than it needs to be.

---

11. U.S. Patent No. 504,038 (issued Aug. 29, 1893). Judson's embodiment didn't work well. An improved version, much more akin to the zippers we know today, was invented by Gideon Sundback, for which he was granted U.S. Patent No. 1,219,281 (issued March 13, 1917).

Many of the tools and paradigms helpful in broadening the solution part of the problem-solution statement can also be helpful in broadening the problem. For example;

- Ask *What Problem Is Really Being Solved?* The answer for the zipper, for example, is the problem of being able to join flexible bodies, not just shoe flaps.
- Dream up alternative, possibly even far-fetched, environments as a way of seeing the problem in a more generic context.
- See if the problem can be stated more generally by pruning and distilling it down from its current formulation.

Prune and Distill

Pruning and distilling are among the more mechanical techniques available to broaden a problem-solution statement or a claim. They might even be thought of as a kind of word processing.

Pruning means completely eliminating limitations not needed to distinguish the invention from the prior art. Each element, each function, each adjective needs to be examined to see if it is really necessary.

Distilling is a related technique. Rather than totally pruning away a limitation, it may be possible to make it more general. Or it may be possible to combine two or more recited functions or elements into a single, more generic or overarching function or element. For example, we might replace "bolt" with the more general term "fastener" or combine the individual steps of "point" and "click" with the single step "select."

Not only should whole elements come under scrutiny, but individual words as well. Adjectives should get particular attention. Sometimes a judicious adjective or two may be the most effective way of distinguishing the invention from the prior art. However, adjectives mostly narrow an invention definition without enhancing its differentiation from the prior art. Adjectives are usually just surplusage that we can safely prune away and thereby broaden the problem-solution statement. Examples we will encounter later in the book include *automobile* floor mat and *extendible and retractable* structure.[12]

Pruning and distilling were presented in a negative light when introduced in Chapter Two.[13] In that context, however, the starting point was a claim intentionally directed to the embodiment. Language going to the heart of the invention is not guaranteed to be present at the outset. Even if such language were present at the outset, we have no principled way

---

12. *See* pp. 106–107.
13. *See* p. 12.

of preventing it from being inadvertently lost during the pruning/distilling process.

The reason it is safe to prune and distill at *this* point is that the words being worked over do not constitute a description of the embodiment, but a definition of the invention in problem-solution terms.

Consult with Colleagues

There are as many approaches to analyzing inventions as there are attorneys plying this trade. The analysis of virtually any invention can therefore invariably be enhanced by discussing it with a colleague. It is rare that another patent attorney will not have some probing question or insight that can shed further light on the problem and/or the solution.

This section presents some invention identification ideas that a number of practicing patent attorneys have shared with the author. Not surprisingly, the author's and the other attorneys' approaches coalesce into a few thematic strains. We are, after all, all focused on the same goal— determining *What Is the Invention?*

First "See" the Invention

One colleague refers to his starting-point process as "seeing" the invention. The paradigm is a powerful one. The notion of seeing the invention implies a mind's-eye grasp of an answer to the question, *What's Really Going On?*[14]

> *"Before beginning the claim-drafting process, one must first 'see' the invention, and not just an embodiment of the invention, although sometimes it is not easy to distinguish between the two. Nonetheless I believe that the key to understanding the invention is to gain a fundamental understanding of the concept(s) behind the embodiment(s). By understanding the principle behind the result, the claim drafter should be able to draw a broader claim than otherwise.*
>
> *I usually get there by continuing to ask questions of the inventor, each time stripping away verbally the extra stuff so that I can change the example that had been presented and still have the inventor say, 'Yes, that is what I mean.' Or, 'Yes, that will work also!'*
>
> *I was trained to always write a problem-solution and a claim. Now I boil the invention down by simply writing a claim that reflects my thought process. But I think that in the back of my mind I have*

---

14. *See* p. 36.

*worked through the problem and solution while forming the claim in
my mind."*

—DHT

Use the European ("Jepson") Claim Format as an Invention-Analysis Model

Another attorney recommends thinking about the invention in terms
of the European, or Jepson-type, claim format at the invention-analysis
stage, whether or not one ultimately wants to have claims of that type
in the patent application. Readers may well already be familiar with this
format, in which the so-called inventive departure is set off from the rest
of the claim by a transitional phrase such as "the improvement comprising" or "characterized in that."

Here, for example, is a European-style claim directed to the idea of
chair legs ("elongated support members"):

> 1. Apparatus comprising
> a seat, and
> a seat support supporting the seat above an underlying surface,
> CHARACTERIZED IN THAT the seat support includes one or
> more elongated support members.

Such point-of-novelty claiming might not be where you want to end
up. However,

> *"it may be a place that you want to start your thinking process from. It
> helps one conceptualize what was done before, and what was added or
> changed by the inventor to solve the problem or yield the improvement.
> If the improvement is simply stated (just one element), you have a good
> start on a broad claim. Then, you look at the preamble—the words lead-
> ing up to 'the improvement comprising'—and see if the same improve-
> ment works in other environments."*

—BHF

This approach serves as the basis of a claim-drafting technique called
"inventive-departure-based claiming," presented in Chapter Eight.

Envision the Marketplace

Another attorney focuses on the ultimate marketing of the invention,
thereby engaging the inventor on his own terms.

"I ask the inventor to envision the marketplace. What would he tout about his invention if he had to actually sell it? Is it, for example, faster than the known alternatives? Lighter? Less expensive? More efficacious? Once he has told me, I ask him to point to what exactly it is in his system or process that makes those advantages possible. We then proceed to sketch out the invention on a piece of paper and refine the picture to a point where it contains only the minimum necessary prior art structure to support the thing that he pointed to. A particular benefit of this approach is that it enables the inventor to supply what the attorney needs within an analytical framework that is natural and routine to the inventor rather than my having to turn the inventor into a junior patent attorney in the first instance."

—GCR

Imagine You Have Only 60 Seconds to Describe the Invention

A colleague suggests that distilling the invention down to its essence can often be achieved by asking the question, "What would you say if you had to say it in 60 seconds?"

"When I supervised attorneys in a corporate setting, I recommended as follows: "Envision yourself having to explain the invention to a manager who holds the patent-filing purse strings. The manager is in a hurry to attend a meeting. Imagine that you have only 60 seconds to describe the invention's novelty while accompanying him to the meeting room door. What would you say in one or two sentences?"

I also strongly urged that any such one- or two-sentence description of the invention should focus on the inventive solution and its benefit. Knowing what the benefit is helps you identify those few things that are necessary to provide that benefit and thus those few things that should be contained in the broadest claim."

—HTB

In a similar vein, another attorney observes that unless one can give a short-and-sweet answer to *What Is the Invention?* more analysis is required.

"One needs to be able to answer the question 'What is the Invention?' without a lot of arm-waving and a half-hour diatribe. Otherwise, you have not grasped the essence of the invention. Once I can answer 'What is the Invention?' I can then draw a boundary around

those elements or functions—mechanical, electrical, or whatever—that allow the invention to overcome the problems unsolved by the prior art. I then try to distill the encircled elements into a single function by aggregating a number of more specific functions into a broader generic one."

—DRP

Cross-Examine the Inventor

In yet another approach, a colleague writes the patent application's Background and Summary early on in the process—preferably in collaborative engagement with the inventor. This gives him an opportunity to explore the problem and solution in narrative form. The inventor is cross-examined as the words evolve. (This is a favored approach of the author as well and is described later in the book.[15])

> *"Whenever possible, I write the patent application with the inventor sitting next to me, and I analyze the invention using a method that I call 'cross-examine the inventor.' As I initially write the background and summary based on what he tells me he thinks is the invention, I keep asking him if each thing I have written is essential. I try to think of cases where a particular thing might not be necessary, as if I were attacking the summary in court, and urge the inventor to do the same. When I'm done, I put it into claim form. Then I explain to the inventor what the claim is about, what the elements are, and that they all must be present for infringement. Then I go over each one again and see if any particular element seems optional. Then I go back to the summary if there are any changes. Of course, as I write the detailed description and begin to really understand what is going on and the inventor opens up more and explains more, thereby peeling back some of the layers he has unintentionally (or maybe even intentionally) hidden from me, I further refine the summary and claims in an iterative manner."*
>
> —EJR

Discovering the breadth of the invention is only half the story. We must also be able to evaluate a problem-solution statement or a claim to determine if it is so broad as to read on prior art and to fix it if it *is* too broad. That aspect of the practice is addressed next.

---

15. *See* pp. 330–332.

CHAPTER REVIEW—The Problem-Solution Statement— Reaching for Breadth

Confirm Your Understanding

1. What does the author mean by the "Opposing Team?" Why is it important to focus on the Opposing Team when analyzing an invention?

2. What is the danger in including a particular implementational detail in a problem-solution statement (or claim) based on the inventor's assurance that, as a practical matter, the invention cannot be implemented without that detail?

3. How does dreaming up "far-fetched embodiments" help identify the inventive concept?

4. Since the inventive method or apparatus is defined in the "solution" portion of the problem-solution statement, why should the process of reaching for breadth involve looking to possibly broaden the "problem" portion?

5. Some practitioners are taught to discover the broad invention by listing the individual elements of the inventor's embodiment and then separating those that aren't necessary to distinguish the invention from the prior art (the "hows") from those that are (the "whats"). What is the danger in using this technique as one's primary approach to identifying the inventive concept?

Questions for Further Thought

6. How is analysis of the invention helped along by thinking, as the author suggests (p. 36), "more functionally than structurally, in verbs rather than nouns, in method steps rather than structural elements?"

7. In what way is the search for breadth enhanced when the patent attorney has a strong technical background?

8. Is it realistic to be concerned about dinosaurs and birds being prior art to the Wrights' flying machine (p. 38)?

Sharpen Your Skills

9. Experienced attorneys have many ways of thinking about the process of reaching for breadth (p. 33). Ask some experienced colleagues in your workplace how *they* do it.

10. Reach for breadth in drafting a problem-solution statement for the fol-
    lowing inventions:

Invention	Prior art
Public restroom paper towel dispenser that uses an electric eye to dispense a fixed amount of paper from a continuous roll.	Dispenser responsive to user pulling down on one side of a looped cloth towel to expose a fixed amount of unused towel.
Car radio antenna or defroster wires embedded in car window.	Wire-reinforced glass in armored car.

CHAPTER FIVE

The Problem-Solution Statement—
Reining in Overbreadth

Just as a problem-solution statement can be too narrow, it can also be too broad. A pending claim based on an overly broad problem-solution statement will be rejected as unpatentable. An overly broad issued claim will be declared invalid.

Thus evaluating a problem-solution statement—trying it on for size—means not only determining whether it is too narrow but also whether it is too broad. Techniques for assuring ourselves that the problem-solution statement is as broad as it can be were presented in Chapter Four. This chapter presents ways of evaluating a problem-solution statement or a claim to make sure it is not *too* broad.

Read the Problem-Solution Statement as Broadly as Possible

A crucial skill for patent attorneys is the ability to appreciate what the words in a patent claim could be interpreted to mean—as compared with what we *intend* them to mean. The methodology described in these pages has us formulating a problem-solution statement rather than claims in the first instance. However, at least some of the patent application's claims will be based on the problem-solution statement, as we will see in upcoming chapters. Thus it is appropriate to evaluate the language of the problem-solution statement with possible overbreadth in mind.

An attorney trying on the problem-solution statement for size must not view his words through the lens of his own disclosure. The words of the problem-solution statement must be compared to the prior art as an examiner will do with the claims to see if there is some way—*any* way—that the words of the problem-solution statement can be made to read on prior art, whether relevant to the inventive contribution or not.

For example, an attorney writing a problem-solution statement for the first "horseless carriage" and following the prescription to *Think Big*[1] might have thought the invention to be the idea of mounting an engine on a wheeled vehicle and using its energy to rotate the wheels:

> *The problem of* moving people or things without the need of
> human or animal power *is solved by* mounting an engine on a wheeled
> vehicle and using energy generated by the engine to rotate the
> wheels.

However, the railroad locomotive, which long preceded the automobile, also meets this definition. So does the paddle-wheel steamboat. It would be of no matter that the attorney intended the term "wheeled vehicle" to mean something narrower. This problem-solution statement needs to be narrowed.

Indeed, cases are legion in which a patent applicant insisted that his claim language meant something specific, but the patent examiner, and ultimately the court, decided that it meant something broader. The patent applicants in one such case[2] argued that the claim limitation that A and B are "integrally formed" with one another meant that A and B must be fused into one piece, such as by being cast as a molded article or welded together. See Figure 5–1.

They needed that argument accepted to avoid prior art in which A and B were separate pieces that were bolted together. The Federal Circuit held, however, that the term "integrally formed" could, indeed, encompass such prior art two-piece structures and affirmed the examiner's finding of unpatentability. To similar effect was a case that broadly interpreted the terms "window" and "data" used in defining a computer interface.[3]

The message of such cases is that the meaning that will be ascribed to claim language is not necessarily as narrow as the patent applicant intended or—faced with new prior art—as narrow as the patent applicant may later want to argue. Rather, the meaning that will be ascribed to claim language can be virtually anything that is lexically reasonable. Indeed, examiners are duty-bound to give the words in a claim their plain meaning and to read the claims on prior art as broadly as the claim terms reasonably allow, even if that prior art has little or nothing to do with the

---

1. *See* p. 21.
2. *In re Morris*, 127 F.3d 1048, 44 USPQ2d 1023 (Fed. Cir. 1997).
3. *Apple Computer Inc. v. Articulate Systems Inc.*, 234 F.3d 14, 57 USPQ2d 1057 (Fed. Cir. 2000).

Applicant

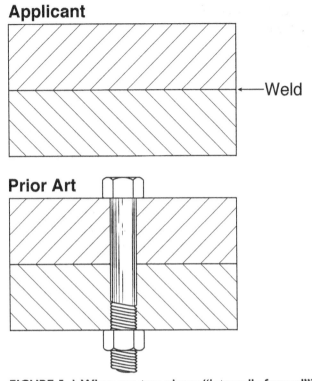

←—Weld

Prior Art

FIGURE 5–1 When are two pieces "integrally formed"?

subject matter invented and does not disclose the inventive concept.[4] This protects the public against patent owners who might attempt to enforce their claims against prior art subject matter once the patent is issued.

Absent an explicit definition in the specification, claim terminology means anything and everything that it reasonably *could* mean, not just what the applicant intends or argues it to mean.

The language of a problem-solution statement or a claim thus needs to be evaluated, and possibly narrowed, with the above ideas in mind.

Narrowing the Right Way

It is easy enough to narrow an overly broad invention definition in *some* way. Just find some aspect of the inventor's embodiment(s) not shown

---

4. *See, e.g., In re Suitco Surface, Inc.*, 603 F.3d 1255, 1259, 94 USPQ2d 1640 (Fed. Cir. 2010); *In re Morris, supra. Cf. In re Donaldson Co.*, 16 F.3d 1189, 29 USPQ2d 1845 (Fed. Cir. 1994) (en banc) (specification sets a limit on how broadly the Patent and Trademark Office may construe means-plus-function language under the rubric of reasonable interpretation).

in, nor obvious in view of, the prior art and add it to the problem-solution statement or claim being drafted.

That approach, however, is a recipe for disaster, as it may well result in a view of the invention that is much too narrow. As discussed in the following sections, we must continue to search for a broad and functional characterization of the solution to the problem that the invention solves. Moreover, we need to consider whether it is not the *solution* that is stated too broadly, but the *problem*—that is, the solution's *context*.

Continue to Focus on Breadth and Functionality

In deciding how best to narrow an overly broad problem-solution state-ment or claim, we need to stay focused on the principles presented above. For example, we need to ascertain what's really going on to solve the problem that is *not* going on in the prior art that makes the problem-solution statement too broad. It is all too easy—especially if we are men-tally fatigued after having pounded away at the invention for a while—to fall back on just any old embodiment detail as a way of fixing the problem-solution statement. That urge must be resisted, however, lest we arrive at a view of the invention that is unduly narrow.

Let us revisit Chapter Two's Konaclip example.[5] An initial problem-solution statement for the Konaclip might have been directed to a clip that slides onto both sides of the paper and uses spring action to hold the paper in place.

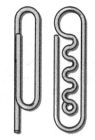

The *problem of* holding a stack of paper together securely without damaging the paper while being convenient to take on and off *is solved by* a bent-wire clip that includes at least two sections slidable onto respective sides of the stack of paper, each section being urged into the plane of the paper by spring action.

FIGURE 5–2 The Perfection and the Konaclip.

This statement of the Konaclip invention is too broad, however. It describes not only the Konaclip but also the prior art Perfection clip,[6] which also slides onto both sides of the paper and uses spring action to hold the paper in place. Figure 5–2 illustrates both clips.

Upon comparing the Konaclip and the Perfection, it would be tempt-ing to narrow this problem-solution statement by adding words directed

---

5. *See* pp. 12–16.
6. *See* p. 13.

to the Konaclip's central leg. Indeed, that unique feature of the Kona-clip clearly differentiates it from all the paper clips that came before it. Such a definition of the Konaclip, however, would not capture the Gem, which—in our example, at least—came later and, as we know, became the marketplace winner. Indeed, our previous analysis concluded that what is really going on in the Konaclip is its notion of equal pressure against opposing rails. Like the central leg, the equal-pressure aspect of the Konaclip distinguishes it from the Perfection. Unlike the central leg, however, the equal-pressure aspect of the Konaclip carried over into the Gem and, like the Gem, addressed the problem of holding a stack of paper securely, conveniently, and without damage. As we know, the Konaclip quickly dropped out of the marketplace; while its underlying concept, as embodied in the Gem, has survived to this very day.

Consider Narrowing the Problem Rather than the Solution

Inherent in the problem-solution statement formula

> *The problem(s) of _____ is(are) solved by _____.*

is the idea that an invention comprises not only a solution but the problem that is solved. As such, the problem-solution statement incorporates an environment or context for the invention. If a problem-solution statement is too broad, then, the best way to narrow it may not be to narrow the statement of the solution, but the statement of the problem. Even if the solution portion of the problem-solution statement reads on the prior art, the problem-solution statement as a whole may not be overly broad if (a) the solution appears in the prior art in a different environment or context, and (b) it would not have been obvious to use the stated solution in that environment or context.

For example, sometime after the microwave oven was invented, it was recognized that the food is heated more uniformly if it is moved around within the oven.[7] The uneven heating is caused by standing waves within the oven that create regions where the energy is more intense than average and regions where the energy is less intense than average. Moving the food around within the oven equalizes the energy received by the various parts of the food.

An attorney answering the question *What's Really Going On?* and "thinking big" would recognize that the turntable is only an implementational feature, and that the broad invention is simply to move the food around. The following problem-solution statement might result:

---

7. U.S. Patent No. 2,632,838 (issued March 24, 1953).

> *The problem of* nonuniform heating of food *is solved by* moving the
> food while the food is being heated.

This problem-solution statement is too broad, however. For example, it
reads on the prior art rotisserie oven. It even reads on a cooking spoon
stirring the contents of a saucepan on a stove.

The above problem-solution statement could be narrowed into the
realm of patentability by narrowing the solution to recite the turntable
(assuming that no food-cooking prior art shows a turntable). But our
problem-solution analysis has already told us that what's really going
on to solve the problem is not the use of a turntable but the fact that
the food is being moved around, however that might be accomplished.
This is confirmed by the fact that we can dream up a far-fetched embodiment that also solves the problem,[8] such as recruiting a band of little
microwave-impervious people to march the food around inside the oven.

The fix lies in amending the *problem*. The problem-solution statement
can be narrowed to avoid the rotisserie and cooking spoon prior art by
putting the invention into the microwave oven context.

> *The problem of* nonuniform heating of food <u>in a microwave oven</u>
> *is solved by* moving the food <u>within the oven</u> while the food is being
> heated.

The prior art's teaching of "moving the food" in more conventional
food preparation contexts would not have rendered it obvious to perform that step in a microwave oven, given that microwaves permeate the
oven enclosure and it wouldn't have been thought in the first instance
that there would be a nonuniform heating problem.

Upon reviewing this second problem-solution statement, however,
we find that it is still too broad. Early microwave food-heating apparatuses moved the food across the end of a waveguide out of which the
microwaves emanated, thereby anticipating the "moving the food" limitation.[9] (Figure 5–3.)

The way to fix the problem-solution statement is again to focus on
the problem and the context in which it arises. The prior art waveguide-
based microwave heating apparatus did not suffer from the standing
wave phenomenon, and therefore the nonuniform heating problem did
not arise. Standing waves occur when the microwaves are confined
within a so-called microwave cavity. The enclosed main chamber of the

---

8. *See* p. 39.
9. U.S. Patent No. 2,495,429 (issued Jan. 24, 1950).

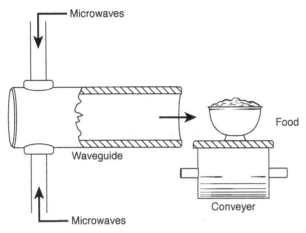

FIGURE 5–3 Early microwave oven.

modern microwave oven is such a cavity. Putting the invention into that context by including the word "cavity" in the *problem* portion of the problem-solution statement distinguishes the invention from the prior art without resorting to a "turntable" limitation in the *solution* portion:

> *The problem of* nonuniform heating of food in a microwave ~~oven~~ cavity *is solved by* moving the food within the cavity while the food is being heated.

Although this chapter is about reigning in overbreadth, we cannot leave our problem-solution statement—even though it has now been narrowed into the patentable realm—without considering whether it is too narrow. Maybe we are at a place like point 7 in Figure 3–4—sufficiently narrowed from where we started so that we are no longer reading on prior art but not as broad as we might be.

Two things come to mind.

The problem portion of the above problem-solution statement is a little too narrow in regard to its recitation of "food." The microwave oven doesn't care what is being heated and the turntable is going to turn no matter what is on it. This tells us that we should be able to say something broader than "food"—let's use "matter"—and still define a patentable invention.

Indeed, anything that might get put into the oven has the potential to be unevenly heated absent the invention. In addition, some alternative, and perhaps far-fetched, embodiments that solve the problem come to mind.[10] It is conceivable that instead of moving the matter to be heated, the standing wave pattern could be the thing that is moved—envision the movement of waves coming ashore. Or the standing waves could be somehow eliminated altogether. (We are presuming that until the time of this invention, the standing-wave phenomenon as the cause of nonuniform heating had not been recognized. Otherwise, merely stating the invention to be eliminating the standing waves would be an unduly functional characterization of the invention. See Chapter Twelve on this point.)

These additional considerations lead us to the following alternative problem-solution statement that encompasses all three scenarios: (a) moving the matter within the cavity, (b) moving the standing waves within the cavity, or (c) precluding standing waves altogether.

> *The problem of* nonuniform heating of matter heated with microwave energy in a microwave cavity *is solved by* at least one of (a) moving the matter within the cavity, (b) causing the microwave energy to be in the form of moving standing waves, or (c) causing the microwave energy to be in a form other than standing waves.

This can alternatively be stated as

> *The problem of* nonuniform heating of matter with microwave energy in a microwave cavity *is solved by* heating the matter other than with standing microwaves that are stationary relative to the matter.

Rethinking the Horseless Carriage

Returning now to our horseless carriage and the above overbroad problem-solution statement, we should ask ourselves what problem the horseless carriage solves as compared to the prior art "wheeled vehicles" such as the locomotive and the paddle-wheel steamboat. At least one answer is that the locomotive and steamboat are limited in that they can't go just anywhere, whereas a horseless carriage can travel over open ground and, certainly, along any sufficiently wide path or road. We might think to amend the above problem-solution statement thusly:

> *The problem of* moving people or things <u>over roads or open ground</u> without the need of human or animal power *is solved by* mounting an engine on a wheeled vehicle <u>capable of moving over the roads or</u>

---

10. *See* p. 39.

<u>open ground</u> and using energy generated by the engine to rotate the wheels.

This problem-solution statement, however, arguably says nothing more than that the inventor has solved a known problem. People already had vehicles capable of moving over roads or open ground (e.g., horse-drawn carriages and wagons), but these required animal power to pull them and, arguably, it was presumably a known notion prior to the invention of the automobile that it would be desirable to replace animal power with a mechanical energy source as was already in use in locomotives and ships. As discussed in Chapter Twelve, this renders the above problem-solution statement "unduly functional" and therefore too broad. But how to make the vehicle go where you want it to go? That problem is solved by having wheels that can be steered from within the vehicle, and that solution was no doubt one of the inventions that made the horseless carriage possible. Assuming that the steerable toy wagon came later, then, a not-unduly-broad problem-solution statement for the horseless carriage could be the following:

> *The problem of* moving people or things <u>in any desired direction</u> without the need of human or animal power *is solved by* mounting an engine on a wheeled vehicle having wheels <u>capable of being steered from on or within the vehicle</u> and using energy generated by the engine to rotate the wheels.

The principles presented thus far enable us to define the invention as broadly as we believe we are allowed to based on the prior art. That is, the prior art we are *aware* of. Other prior art can appear at any time after the patent application is filed, potentially invalidating any claim based on what may prove to be an overly broad problem-solution statement. Anticipating *that* possibility is the subject of the next chapter.

CHAPTER REVIEW—The Problem-Solution Statement— Reining in Overbreadth

Confirm Your Understanding

1. The book urges the reader to evaluate a problem-solution statement or claim as an examiner will in assessing whether the problem-solution statement is too broad. Isn't this working against ourselves? Why not just go with the broad definition we initially come up with and "tweak up" the claims after the first Patent Office action?

2. A possible approach to narrowing an overly broad problem-solution statement is to look for a feature of the inventor's embodiment(s) not shown in the prior art and add that to the problem-solution statement. Why does the author characterize this as a "recipe for disaster" (p. 54)?

3. Since the inventive structure is defined in the "solution" portion of the problem-solution statement, why should the process of reining in over-breadth involve looking to possibly narrow the "problem" portion?

Question for Further Thought

4. It is said that a patent applicant can be her own lexicographer. How does this square with the author's assertion (p. 52) that "the meaning that will be ascribed to claim language [used to define an invention] is not necessarily as narrow as the patent applicant intended . . . [and] . . . can be virtually anything that is lexically reasonable?"

Sharpen Your Skills

5. Each of the following problem-solution statements is too broad. State why, based on prior art you are aware of, and redraft the problem-solution statement into the patentable realm.

   a. **Sunscreen:** *The problem of* people getting sunburned *is solved by* covering the skin with a material that blocks sun rays.

   b. **Public restroom paper towel dispenser that uses an electric eye to dispense a fixed amount of paper from a continuous roll:** *The problem of* wastage of hand-drying material in a public restroom *is solved by* an apparatus that dispenses a discrete amount of hand-drying material at a time.

   c. **Cellular telephone:** *The problem of* the lack of portability of a voice communication instrument *is solved by* the voice communication instrument being arranged to communicate with another voice communication instrument using electromagnetic energy.

   d. **Tear-back tab on disposable coffee cup lid:** *The problem of* being able to get ready access to the liquid in a disposable beverage container while minimizing spillage when the container is being carried *is solved by* a lid for the container having a perforated tab.

CHAPTER SIX

Fallback Features
and the Planned Retreat

Prior art that comes to light after a patent application has been filed may render its broadest claims unpatentable or invalid. This chapter presents an invention analysis strategy—called the Planned Retreat—to take account of that possibility. At the heart of the strategy is the use of the problem-solution paradigm to identify the invention's "fallback features," which ultimately translate into intermediate- and narrow-scope claims for the patent application.

The Need for a Fallback (Retreat) Strategy

A patent application must include at least one claim.[1] Limiting ourselves to that one claim is not a good idea, however. We can never be sure that all the relevant prior art has been found and that the problem-solution statement—and any claim on which it is based—is not overly broad. There's a lot of prior art out there, including over 7 million patents issued in the United States and tens of millions more issued in countries around the world, not to mention all the journal articles and technical books ever written.

A patent application therefore needs claims of varying scope. This means not only claims that define the invention at what we believe to be its broadest, but also other claims, either in independent or dependent form, that stake out more modest parcels of intellectual property by qualifying the broad invention definition.

We hope that the patent application's broadest claims will survive patent examination, as well as any subsequent attack on patentability mounted by the Opposing Team. If the broadest claims do survive, the presence of narrower claims in the issued patent is of little moment; a patent is infringed even if only one of its claims is infringed. On the other hand, we never know what prior art may surface after the application is filed that will force a retreat from the invention boundaries

---

1. 35 U.S.C. 112(b).

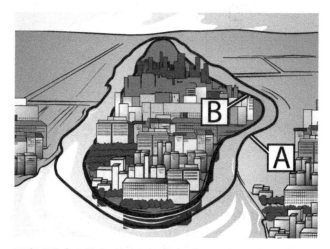

FIGURE 6–1 If the parcel of intellectual property initially staked out is too broad (**A**), a well-thought-out Planned Retreat enables us to give up as little valuable intellectual property as possible while establishing a defensible position for what's left (**B**).

initially staked out. Nor can we predict the necessary extent of such a retreat. Without a range of broad, intermediate-scope, and narrow claims in the issued patent to fall back on, the patent owner might be left with no enforceable patent rights whatsoever.

These are among the important reasons that a patent application should be filed with a suite of intermediate- and narrow-scope claims at the outset. Indeed, depending on (a) whether the patent is pending or issued, and (b) what was or was not disclosed in the patent application, it may be expensive or even impossible to secure the claims that best define the invention in view of newly discovered prior art.

The Planned Retreat

The Planned Retreat is a strategy for formulating an array of successively restricted fallback positions, each defined by a respective claim, to which we can retreat if newly identified prior art forces us to do so. Which fallback position we retreat to depends, of course, on what the prior art does or doesn't show.

The underlying philosophy of the Planned Retreat is that there is no point in surrendering an acre if, with a little thought and planning, a patentability issue can be resolved by giving up a square foot or two. That philosophy is implemented by selecting our successive stages of possible retreat—that is, each successively narrower claim—so as to fulfill two criteria. Those criteria are that each successively narrower claim should (a) give up as little valuable intellectual property as possible, and (b) establish a defensible position for what's left.

To "give up as little valuable intellectual property as possible" means preserving coverage for those features of the embodiment(s) that we think are more likely than others to appear in competitors' marketplace offerings. Such a feature for the broad idea of the double-hung window, for example, would be a mechanism that counterbalances the weight of the lower sash by pulling up on it, such as sash weights or

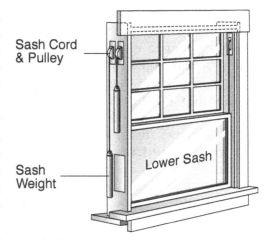

FIGURE 6–2 A sash weight or other mechanism to counteract the weight of a double-hung window's lower sash would be a valuable position of retreat in view of prior art disclosing only the window.

springs. We could envision that such a mechanism would be an indispensable feature of any commercially viable double-hung window, being more convenient than using a stick to prop up the sash or, perhaps, a tight friction fit. See Figure 6–2.

To "establish a defensible position for what's left" means that the narrower invention definition we may have to retreat *to* should have some additional likelihood of being patentable over the position we are retreating *from*. It does little good to establish a position of retreat—no matter how likely it is that the market will demand it—if the invention is no more patentable with that feature than without it.

Suppose, for example, that the broad invention is a new type of pen that turns out to be disclosed in a prior art patent that says nothing about the color of the ink. A position of retreat limiting the invention to pens of that type in which the ink is black would meet the Planned Retreat's first criterion of giving up as little valuable intellectual property as possible, given that black is probably the most popular ink-pen color. But "black ink" is not a defensible position of retreat. Even though the prior art patent says nothing about ink color, it is obvious that the ink in *any* pen can be black. If the broad pen claim falls, the narrower pen-plus-black-ink claim will fall right along with it.

The work stuff of the Planned Retreat is the invention's "fallback features"—also referred to by such terms as "inventive features," "backup positions," and "subsidiary inventions."

A fallback feature is a facet of the inventor's embodiment(s) that can serve as a basis for patentability if what we thought was the broad invention turns out to be in the prior art. Given a combination of elements comprising the broad invention, a fallback feature is a detail particularizing one or more of those elements; an additional element; or a particular relationship among the elements. For example, a fallback feature for the double-hung window is the provision of some mechanism for pulling up on the sash, as discussed above. A fallback feature of Loud's ballpoint pen was an antifriction bearing for the pen's spheroidal marking-point.[2]

An invention's Planned Retreat is formulated by identifying and prioritizing the fallback features in a way that achieves the above-stated goals of giving up as little valuable intellectual property as possible at each stage of retreat while establishing a defensible position for what's left. We will see later in this chapter how the problem-solution paradigm is enlisted in this effort. And we will see in Chapter Nine how the results of the analysis translate into intermediate- and narrow-scope claims for the patent application.

Let us take as our example the invention of the chair. The inventor's embodiment is shown in Figure 6–3, and the assumed prior art is shown in Figure 6–4. Based on this prior art, let us conclude that the broad invention is a seating device having one or more elongated support members. The inventor calls them "legs." The chair leg solves such seating-device problems as the undue weight and lack of portability that burdened the prior art seating devices, as reflected in the invention's problem-solution statement.

> *The problem of* providing a seating device that is lightweight and portable *is solved by* the seating device having one or more elongated support members.

FIGURE 6–3
The first chair.   **FIGURE 6–4 Prior art to the chair.**

---

2. *See* p. 6.

What, then, should our fallback positions be? What feature(s) of this embodiment of the chair give up as little valuable intellectual property as possible if retreat becomes necessary, while providing a defensible position for what's left?

If the marketplace moves fast enough, we may have the luxury of 20-20 hindsight. Claims directed to features that consumers have shown they value in a chair can be added to the patent application if it is still pending in the Patent Office and if those features were actually disclosed in the patent application.

Usually, however, we do not have the luxury of such hindsight. And there are typically too many things one can say about an embodiment to take a scattershot approach and claim them all, let alone claim them in various combinations.

The following, for example, is only a partial list of what we might say about our inventor's chair embodiment:

- Legs are perpendicular to seat.
- Legs are exactly four in number.
- Legs are made of wood.
- Legs are of equal length.
- Legs are cylindrical.
- Legs have rounded bottoms.
- Legs have a 3-square-inch cross section.
- Legs are at corners of a rectangular seat.
- Legs are permanently attached to seat (e.g., with tree resin used as an adhesive).

Note that all of these features involve the chair legs and not, for example, the seat back. Recall the admonition *Keep Separate Inventions Separate*.[3] The seat back is a separate invention, addressing the problem of sitter comfort rather than the problems of weight and portability solved by the use of elongated seat supports. A seating device could be outfitted with a seat back even in the absence of elongated supports, and vice versa. Indeed, based on the prior art shown in Figure 6–4, the chair back is a novel idea that could be the subject of its own patent application.

Looking then at the leg-related features listed above, it is not difficult *in hindsight* to pick out the features that give up relatively little compared to others and would well serve the goals of the Planned Retreat.

---

3. *See* p. 26.

For example, a definition that limits the claimed invention to a seating device having exactly four legs still encompasses a great deal of valuable intellectual property. Moreover, based on the prior art shown in Figure 6–4, four legs is a defensible position of retreat. For similar reasons, the idea of permanently attaching the legs to the seat is another very good fallback position.

Features such as the legs being perpendicular to the seat or being at the seat periphery also surrender relatively little, given that those proved to be desirable marketplace features. But the additional patentability afforded by these features is questionable given the prior art "bench" shown in Figure 6–4.

Other features' limitations give up a great deal and, as such, would be easy for competitors to circumvent while still having a marketable product. The leg's 3-square-inch cross section is one of these. Moreover, its defensibility as a position of retreat is questionable. If chair legs turn out to be known in the prior art, their cross section would no doubt be deemed a matter of design choice and, as such, obvious.

But, again, this is all in hindsight. We need to be able to determine *prospectively* which features of an invention will constitute the best fallback positions.

Identifying the Fallback Features Using the Problem-Solution Paradigm

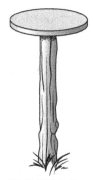

FIGURE 6–5
Assumed chair prior art.

The problem-solution paradigm again serves us in good stead.

Recall that the reason for identifying the fallback features is that what we thought was the broad invention may actually turn out to be in the prior art. All we need do, then, is assume the existence of rudimentary prior art that solves the same problem as the invention and solves it in the same way. We then carry out a problem-solution analysis with *that* as the assumed prior art.

In our chair case, then, we assume for purposes of analysis that the prior art already knew of a rudimentary seating device having one or more legs—perhaps the one-legged stool shown in Figure 6–5. We then ask what problems relative to legs are solved by the embodiment and we identify as our fallback features those solutions that appear to be the most defensible from a patentability standpoint. Here are the steps laid out more formally:

1. Assume the broad invention to be in the prior art.
2. Identify the significant subsidiary problem(s) the embodiment(s) solve.[4]
3. Characterize in broad terms the inventor's solution to each subsidiary problem.[5]
4. Identify as fallback features those solutions that best meet the Planned Retreat's dual criteria.
5. Apply steps 1 through 4 to each identified fallback feature to identify *its* fallback features, and do this iteratively until each significant subsidiary problem and its corresponding solution(s) have been explored.

We will see in the next section how four legs and permanent leg-seat attachment emerge as the clear winners based on such an analysis.

Planned Retreat for the Chair

Applying the problem-solution paradigm to our chair, as with reference to Figure 6–6, let's see what our chair inventor had to say about the problems that arose as she refined her prototype:

Stool A

> *"Once I came up with the idea of elongated support members—which I call 'legs'—in order to make my seating device lightweight and portable, my major concerns were stability and low cost.*
>
> *I never thought about having only one leg like you [patent attorney] are suggesting might be in the prior art. In fact I assumed at the beginning that there would always be three legs because it's the minimum number required for stability. It's sort of the obvious choice if you're going to have more than one.*
>
> *I decided to call my three-legged device a 'stool.'*
>
> *As I began to build, I realized that for maximum stability the bottoms of the legs should be far apart and should be noncollinear. And I also realized that the legs can support the most weight when they are perpendicular to the seat. The stool that I built on those principles I called 'Stool A.' Unfortunately, Stool A tended to tip over.*

Stool B

Stool C

FIGURE 6–6 Chair inventor's early embodiments

---

4. *See* Chapter Three.
5. *See* Chapter Four.

I then realized that I could make my stool more stable if I splayed out the legs, resulting in what I called Stool B.

However, people tended to trip over Stool B, so I had to reduce the splay angle in combination with attaching the legs somewhat away from the periphery. I called this my Stool C. Although Stool C was a little less stable than Stool B, Stool B proved to be unacceptable because of the tripping.

Note, also, that with either of my splayed configurations, the legs had to be made thicker than the perpendicular legs in order to hold up the same amount of weight. I also needed horizontal connecting pieces to keep the legs from breaking away from the seat. All this additional material added to the cost and weight of the stool, which is why I really liked the perpendicular legs in the first place, as in my Stool A. Again, however, Stool A was quite unstable.

So it looked like the best choice was either (1) Stool A if one's paramount concern would be to minimize weight or (2) Stool C if one's paramount concern would be stability.

But then I hit upon the idea of using four legs.

I found out, in fact, that there are a lot of advantages to having four legs, particularly if they are perpendicular to the seat and located at the corners of a quadrilateral seat. I called this four-legged configuration a 'chair.'

A four-legged device with perpendicular legs is much harder to tip over than a three-legged device with perpendicular legs. It's even more resistant to tipping when the legs are attached at the corners of the seat.

Three legs have the advantage that the device won't wobble at all because three points define a plane. But with careful cutting to make the legs as equal in length as possible, wobbling is not a major concern.

And although my chair requires material for four legs, instead of only three, each leg can be a little bit skinnier than in Stool A and still support the same load, so that the weight increase of having four legs isn't all that great and my chair certainly requires less material than the splayed-leg Stools B and C while exhibiting at least a comparable level of stability.

I was then thinking that if four legs are better than three, then maybe five legs are better than four. But that turned out not to be so. Five legs made the device more resistant to tipping over than with four legs, but the improvement was minimal. And five legs added to the wobbling problem, increased the chair's weight, and made it more expensive to build. So four legs is the ideal number.

Structural integrity was yet another issue, I found. As long as the chair was left in one spot, it was sufficient to have a friction fit of the legs into recesses in the seat bottom. But when the chair was moved, the legs tended fall out. I fixed this problem by permanently attaching the legs to the seat. This also made the chair more portable since it could be carried as a single unit."

Based on the foregoing, the following is a possible Planned Retreat for the chair:

I	Seat with one or more elongated supports ("legs")(indep. claim)
2	Legs are at least three in number
3	Legs are noncollinear
4	Legs are perpendicular to seat
4a	~~Legs are noncollinear~~
5	Legs at corners of a cornered seat
6	Legs are exactly four in number
6a	~~Legs at corners of a quadrilateral seat~~
7	Legs are splayed
8	Legs to not extend beyond seat edge
8a	~~Horizontal connectors~~
9	Horizontal connectors
10	Legs are perpendicular to seat
11	Legs are permanently attached to seat

And here is an explanation of how we might arrive at this particular Planned Retreat based on the two Planned Retreat criteria: commercial value and defensibility, beginning with the fallback positions that retreat directly from the broad inventive concept and then moving to the remaining, indirect, fallback positions.

Direct Fallback Position 2: Three or More Legs

Commercial Value (Planned Retreat Criterion I): This fallback position doesn't give up too much since having at least three legs solves the problem of stability in a major way. The marketplace is thus likely to demand this feature—and thus competitors' seating devices are likely to incorporate it—whether or not a seating device has any of the other features.

Defensibility (Planned Retreat Criterion II): Having three or more legs is arguably not obvious and thus appears to be a defensible position of retreat. Even if the prior art knew of a seating device with one or two elongated supports, the person of ordinary skill would arguably think that no more than two supports would ever be needed. Note that two supports is the maximum number known in the prior art.

On the other hand, if the prior art knows a seating device having exactly one elongated support, it is probably obvious, based on the bench prior art, to provide two elongated supports. Therefore a seating device having at least two elongated supports is not a very defensible position of retreat from a seating device having at least one elongated support. Thus our number-of-legs fallback position 2 is limited to three legs or more.

Direct Fallback Position 7: Legs That Are Splayed

Commercial Value: This feature ameliorates the stability problem and so should have some traction in the marketplace, whether or not a seating device with splayed legs has any of the other features. Fallback position 7 thus retreats directly from the broad inventive concept. Per our inventor's experiments, splaying the legs will probably entail additional cost and weight, but these issues may not be of particular concern to at least some buyers.

Defensibility: Fallback position 7 would appear to be a defensible position of retreat since we know of no prior art in which anything is splayed.

Direct Fallback Position 9: Horizontal Connectors

Commercial Value: This feature helps with structural stability and so should have some traction in the marketplace. Although the connectors are particularly advantageous in the context of the splayed legs, they obviously could be used when the legs are not splayed. Fallback position 9 thus retreats directly from the broad inventive concept. The connectors will probably entail additional cost and weight, but these issues may not be of particular concern to at least some buyers.

Defensibility: Fallback position 9 would appear to be a defensible position of retreat since we know of no prior art having such connectors.

Note that the subject matter of fallback position 9 also appears in fallback position 8a, which is discussed below.

Direct Fallback Position 10: Legs Are Perpendicular to the Seat

Commercial Value: This feature ameliorates the weight problem because it enables the legs to be less thick than if splayed legs are used, and the marketplace is thus likely to want perpendicular legs in at least many commercial seating devices, whether or not they have any of the other features. Thus fallback position 10 retreats directly from the broad inventive concept.

Defensibility: Fallback position 10 may not be a particularly defensible position of retreat. If it turns out that prior art knows of a seating device with a single elongated support, it is likely to be perpendicular to the seat, per Figure 6–5, rendering fallback position 10 anticipated. So if we are pressed on the fallback position count front, this is another fallback position we might consider omitting.

Note that the subject matter of fallback position 10 is also presented as fallback position 4 discussed below.

Direct Fallback Position 11: Legs Are Attached to the Seat

<u>Commercial Value</u>: This feature addresses the portability problem, and the marketplace is thus likely to want it in at least many commercial seating devices, whether or not they have any of the other features. Thus we have fallback position 11 retreating directly from the broad inventive concept.

<u>Defensibility</u>: This appears to be a defensible position of retreat since we are aware of no prior art seat support of any kind that is attached to the seat.

<u>Separate invention</u>: While the commercial value and defensibility of fallback position 11 seem good, we should recognize that attaching a seat support to the seat is advantageous for portability, independent of whether the seat support comprises "one or more elongated supports." So the idea of attaching a seat's support structure to the seat itself should be explored as a separate invention to be patented.

Indirect Fallback Position 3: Legs Are at Least Three in Number and Are Noncollinear

<u>Commercial Value</u>: Since our inventor expects that the vast majority of commercially offered seating devices will have three or four legs, and that most of them will have legs that are spread out around the periphery of the seat—and are thus "noncollinear"—we expect that most of the commercial offerings will incorporate both features.

<u>Defensibility</u>: First we should ask why the awkward locution *"noncollinear."* Why not say that that the legs are located at the seat periphery?

If it turns out that prior art knows of a device with a single elongated support, it could be argued with some force that it would have been obvious to modify the two supports of the prior art bench to be "elongated," thereby arriving at a structure with elongated support members at the periphery. And if the subject matter of fallback position 2—namely the idea of having at least three legs—were also known or obvious, then it would undoubtedly be obvious to provide a third elongated leg on the prior art bench somewhere between the ends, e.g., in the center. Given the log's narrowness, it could well be argued that any such third leg was also at the "periphery," since the word "periphery" could be construed to mean not only the ends of the log but also its sides.

Thus, a fallback position reciting three elongated legs at the periphery of the seat would be a weak position of retreat. Saying that the legs are "noncollinear," however, provides a defensible position of retreat since a third leg on the prior art bench would be collinear, not *noncollinear*. The fact that our inventor's supports are noncollinear is, in fact, what provides stability.

Indirect Fallback Position 4: Legs Are at Least Three in Number and Are Perpendicular to the Seat

Commercial Value: What we said about fallback position 3 has an analogy in fallback position 4. That is, since our inventor expects that the vast majority of commercially offered seating devices will have three or four legs, and that many of them—particularly those with four legs—will also have their legs perpendicular to the seat, we expect that some fair number of commercial offerings will incorporate both features.

Defensibility: Fallback position 4's combination of the "perpendicular leg" feature with the at least three legs feature of fallback position 2 is arguably more defensible than fallback position 2 standing by itself or fallback position 10 reciting the "perpendicular leg" feature in combination with the "at least one elongated support" of the broad inventive concept.

On the one hand, we have two prior art devices that can each be characterized as having at least one perpendicular support—the two-support "bench" and the one-elongated-support prior art seating device of Figure 6–5 that we hypothesize might be out there. We are thus faced with an argument that since the prior art knows of at least two devices having different numbers of perpendicular supports, the *number* of supports is a mere matter of design choice, rendering obvious the subject matter of fallback position 4.

The counterargument is that support perpendicularity in those two pieces of prior art is nothing more than a hindsight characterization that one would arrive at only given the benefit of the present inventor's teachings. Unless the prior art seating devices are explicitly characterized by the prior art as having perpendicular supports, it can be argued that, without more, the prior art doesn't teach a general principle to be used when the number of legs is scaled up.

Indirect Fallback Position 4a: Legs Are at Least Three in Number, Are Perpendicular to the Seat, and Are Noncollinear

Commercial Value: Even though fallback position 4a incorporates several different features, the inventor expects that quite a few commercial offerings will incorporate all of these features.

Defensibility: Fallback position 4a is shown crossed out because defensibility considerations make it expendable. If we are allowed a claim based on fallback position 3—which also encompasses the noncollinearity feature—fallback position 4a does not add any coverage since anything that is covered by fallback position 4a is also covered by fallback position 3 and then some.

On the other hand, if we are not able to overcome a novelty or nonobviousness rejection as to fallback position 3, then fallback position 4a would hardly provide a defensible position of retreat from fallback position 4 because if both the perpendicularity feature and the noncollinearity feature are known or deemed individually obvious for a three-legged device, it's hard to conjure up an argument as to why it wouldn't be obvious to have both features. Under this scenario, fallback position 4a is unnecessary.

Indirect Fallback Position 5: Legs at Corners of a Cornered Seat

Commercial Value: The inventor has told us that her chair is particularly resistant to tipping when there are four legs, each attached to a corner of a quadrilateral seat. We thus expect that some fair number of commercial offerings will incorporate this feature.

But this feature is positioned as a retreat from fallback position 2 because we recognize that this feature is not unique to four-legged seating devices. The inventor did not devise a chair with any other than four corners. However, we recognize that a three-legged seating device could be constructed with a triangular seat, and having the legs at the corners of such a seat would, in fact, enhance stability.

Defensibility: This is a defensible position of retreat. The prior art that we know of does not disclose cornered seats, let alone attaching a leg to each of its corners.

Indirect Fallback Position 6: Exactly Four Legs

Commercial Value: Four legs is the ideal number according to the inventor, as it solves the stability problem while requiring less material than a comparably stable three-legged device. Thus the marketplace is even more likely to demand four legs than three legs and, again, independent of any of the other features.

And even though specific in its requirement of "exactly" four legs, this fallback position would be expected to capture a great deal of the marketplace due to its superiority from so many perspectives, as the inventor discovered.

Defensibility: Having exactly four legs appears to be a more defensible position of retreat than three legs, per fallback position 2. Even if the art did suggest in a general way the notion of having more than two elongated supports, the obvious choice, per our inventor, is three legs, not four. And four legs provides unexpected results in that it has proven to be the exact best number of legs to provide good stability at the lowest cost and weight. Note that five legs are not as good as four because the fifth leg adds significantly to the weight while not improving stability all that much.

Indirect Fallback Position 6a: Four Legs at the Corners of a Quadrilateral Seat

Commercial Value: The inventor has told us that her chair is particularly resistant to tipping when there are four legs, each attached to a corner of a quadrilateral seat. We thus expect that some fair number of commercial offerings will incorporate this feature.

Defensibility: Fallback position 6a is shown crossed out because defensibility considerations make it expendable. The argument parallels what we said about claim 4a. If we are allowed a claim based on fallback position 5 (directed to the broader notion of legs at the corners of a cornered seat) fallback position 6a does not add any coverage since anything that is covered by fallback position 6a is also covered by fallback position 5 and then some.

On the other hand, if we are not able to overcome a rejection of fallback position 5, then fallback position 6a would hardly provide a defensible position of retreat from fallback position 4 because if it is known or obvious to put the legs at the corners of a cornered seat having, say, three corners, it's hard to conjure up an argument as to why it wouldn't be obvious to do it for four corners.

Indirect Fallback Position 8: Splayed Legs Not to Extend Beyond Seat Edge

Commercial Value: If you're going to have splayed legs, it would be good for people not to trip over them, so commercially offered seating devices with splayed legs are likely to have this feature.

Defensibility: The leg of the hypothesized one-legged seating device of Figure 6–5 does not extend beyond the seat edge. But how could it be otherwise? Thus we can argue in defense of this fallback position that the fact that we can characterize the Figure 6–5 seating device as having a leg that does not extend beyond the seat edge is a hindsight observation rather than a generalized principle known to those in the art.

Indirect Fallback Position 8a: Horizontal Connectors

Commercial Value: The commercial value considerations noted above relative to fallback position 9 apply here.

Defensibility: Fallback position 8a is probably a fallback position not to bother with. If fallback position 9 is not patentable because connectors for elongated supports are known for unsplayed legs, it doesn't seem that fallback position 8a, reciting connectors on splayed legs, is going to be any more patentable than fallback position 9.

Our Planned Retreat for the chair is shown below in claim form, with the various fallback features in italics and the claims shown indented to illustrate their position in the overall retreat plan. The claim numbers correspond to the fallback position designations used above; for example, fallback position 2 appears in claim 6.2.

6.1 Apparatus comprising
a seat, and
a seat support that supports the seat above an underlying surface, the seat support including *one or more elongated support members*.

6.2 The apparatus of claim 6.1 wherein the seat support includes *at least three support members*.

6.3 The apparatus of claim 6.2 wherein the one or more elongated support members are *noncollinear*.

6.4 The apparatus of claim 6.2 wherein the one or more elongated support members are substantially *perpendicular* to the seat.

6.5 The apparatus of claim 6.2 wherein the seat has a plurality of corners and each of the elongated support members *supports the seat substantially at a respective corner*.

6.6 The apparatus of claim 6.2 wherein the seat support includes *exactly four elongated support members*.

6.7 The apparatus of claim 6.1 wherein the one or more elongated support members are *splayed*.

6.8 The apparatus of claim 6.7 wherein the splayed support members *do not extend beyond the perimeter of the seat*.

6.9 The apparatus of claim 6.1 further comprising at least one *connector* connecting at least one pair of the elongated support members.

6.10 The apparatus of claim 6.1 wherein the one or more elongated support members are substantially *perpendicular* to the seat.

6.11 The apparatus of claim 6.1 wherein the one or more elongated support members are *permanently attached* to the seat.

Chapter Eleven presents a set of guidelines for arranging dependent claims in various combinations pursuant to the Planned Retreat strategy, as exemplified by the claim family above.

———————

This chapter ends Part I of the book, "Identifying the Invention." We've identified the inventive concept in problem-solution form and have mapped out a Planned Retreat. We are now ready—indeed, primed—to draft the claims.

CHAPTER REVIEW—Fallback Features and the Planned Retreat

Confirm Your Understanding

1. Why do we develop a Planned Retreat when deciding how we will claim an invention?
2. Why spend the time to develop a Planned Retreat when preparing the patent application when we can always amend the claims during prosecution after the full extent of the prior art becomes clear?
3. What is meant by (a) "claim scope" and (b) "fallback feature"?
4. What are the two components of an effective Planned Retreat? Why are both important?
5. How is the problem-solution paradigm used to develop a Planned Retreat?
6. Why subject the inventor of the chair in Figure 6–3 to the costs of a second patent to claim the concept of the seat back when the seat back could be recited in a claim dependent from the broad ("elongated support member") chair claim?
7. Give two reasons that an initially identified potential fallback feature may ultimately be deemed not worthy of being included in the Planned Retreat scheme for a particular invention.
8. What criteria should be used in determining where a particular fallback feature should be positioned within an overall Planned Retreat scheme? Why might certain features show up in more than one claim?

Questions for Further Thought

9. Why does the problem-solution paradigm work as well when identifying an invention's fallback features as it does for identifying the broad invention?
10. Why is the inventor's input important to the development of an effective Planned Retreat?
11. Assuming we've identified a significant number of embodiment features, why bother to do any further Planned Retreat analysis given that we can include each of them in its own dependent claim?
12. Which is more worthwhile, if one had to choose: (a) a highly novel fallback feature with low likelihood of use by others, or (b) a close-to-obvious fallback feature with a high likelihood of use by others? (N.B. This is an opinion question with no "right answer," involving consideration of a lot of issues and many unknowable contingencies. Thinking about this question, however, can help develop the reader's Planned Retreat analysis skills.)

13. Rather than trying to second-guess which fallback features will prove to be the ones that consumers will want and including them in the claims when the patent application is first filed, why not just keep the prosecution alive by filing a string of continuations until the "winning" features emerge in the marketplace and then direct claims to those particular features?

Sharpen Your Skills

14. Keeping in mind the dual criteria of the Planned Retreat (p. 62), outline a Planned Retreat, as illustrated on p. 62, for each of the inventions below. Use the problem-solution paradigm (p. 66) to identify the fallback features.

Inventive Concept	Embodiment
Traffic signal having automatically synchronized indicia for first and second roadways.	
Telephone that communicates with the telephone network over a wireless channel.	
Money drawer that has compartments for different denominations of coins and bills.	

PART II

Drafting Individual Claims

Introduction to Part II:
Drafting Individual Claims

Drafting patent claims can be a challenging task, particularly for the novice. The specter of that blank sheet of paper or empty computer screen can be daunting.

However, if a problem-solution statement has already been developed following the principles presented in Part I, the hard part will have already been done. Problem-solution statement in hand, the patent attorney can begin claim drafting not with an empty screen, but with a substantial kernel of inventive essence. The time invested in getting the problem-solution statement just right will now bear fruit. Far from being an isolated activity, drafting the claims becomes through this approach the capstone of a comprehensive invention-analysis process.

PART II—*Drafting Individual Claims*—shows how it is done.

CHAPTERS SEVEN and EIGHT present two techniques for drafting the patent application's broadest claims. Both techniques take advantage of the hard work that went into developing the problem-solution statement. These two techniques complement each other, helping us to achieve a healthy measure of diversity in the claim suite—the subject of Chapter Sixteen. The claim-drafting technique described in Chapter Seven is problem-solution-based claiming. This technique develops a claim directly from the problem-solution statement itself, with very little being added or taken away. Little thought needs to be given to the invention itself. All the thinking and analysis that went into developing the problem-solution statement gets directly applied to the claim. Chapter Eight's technique is inventive-departure-based claiming. This approach also relies heavily on the problem-solution thought process. It is more open-ended, however. The claim drafter is set free to bring creativity to bear, resulting in a virtually limitless variety of claim structures and ways of expressing the broad invention.

Claims of intermediate and narrow scope are the subject of CHAPTER NINE. These are claims that qualify or limit the broadly claimed invention by reciting additional elements, particularizing already-recited elements, or particularizing relationships among the recited elements. One can never be sure that all the relevant prior art is in hand. Claims of intermediate and narrow scope implement the Planned Retreat, providing somewhere to fall back to if the broadest claims turn out not to be patentable after all.

CHAPTER TEN discusses definition claims. These are claims typically in dependent form that define terminology in their parent claims. In so doing, definition claims address two potential parent claim deficiencies. One potential deficiency is that the parent claim may read on prior art that does not disclose the inventive concept. The other is that the parent claim may be indefinite because either the parent claim itself or a claim that it depends from contains indefinite terminology.

The whys and wherefores of chaining dependent claims are explained in CHAPTER ELEVEN.

CHAPTER TWELVE addresses the topic of functional language in claims—recitations that state what a claim element *does* (its "function") as compared with what it *is* structurally. Understanding the extent to which functional language is effective to distinguish an invention from the prior art is critically important, given how much of modern-day innovation resides not in the physical structure of things but, rather, in functionalities implemented by software.

A particular form of functional language is the means-plus-function element—the subject of CHAPTER THIRTEEN. Traditionally a staple of U.S. claiming practice, means-plus-function claiming has fallen into a state of virtual nonuse in the wake of a succession of Federal Circuit opinions that have severely limited its reach and that have imposed new requirements on the disclosure needed to support a means-plus-function recitation. The chapter offers guidelines for how to define claim elements functionally without invoking "means-plus-function treatment."

CHAPTER SEVEN

Problem-Solution-Based Independent Claims

The author has often thought of publishing a gag gift book entitled "Patent Claim Forms." All of its pages would be blank. The joke is one that only a patent lawyer can fully appreciate. Every invention is different, and there is no such thing as fill-in-the-blanks claiming. This start-from-scratch aspect of claim drafting is what makes it so challenging.

The claim-drafting technique described in this chapter—problem-solution-based claim drafting—is an effective way of meeting the challenge. It arrives at a claim by transforming the problem-solution statement into claim form, with very little being added or taken away. That such a technique exists should come as no surprise. Stringham reminds us that an invention is not a thing, but a definition.[1] A definition is made up of words. Thus no matter what *format* we may use to define an invention—a claim or a problem-solution statement—the *words* that inform that definition ought to be pretty much the same in either case.

The Five Steps

Problem-solution-based claim drafting transforms the problem-solution statement into claim form in five steps:

1. Choose one or more claim settings (as discussed below).
2. Choose one or more statutory claim types for each setting (as discussed below).
3. Remove the problem-related language and the boilerplate *"The problem of . . . is solved by,"* but retain language defining the environment or context in which the problem arises.
4. Stitch the remaining language into one or more claims, adding as few words as possible.

---

1. *See* p. 5.

5. Compare the resulting claim(s) to the problem-solution statement to verify the accuracy of the transformation(s).

These five steps will readily produce claim(s) as broad as the problem-solution statement itself. If more than one problem-solution statement was created when the invention was being analyzed, corresponding claims can be created by applying these steps to each problem-solution statement separately.

The reader may be somewhat skeptical. It is not uncommon to spend an hour or more drafting and redrafting a claim when writing it from scratch. How can five cookbook-like steps supplant all of that? How can all the critical thinking that traditionally goes into drafting a patent claim really be so readily bypassed?

Actually, none of that critical thinking *is* bypassed. We have already brought our best thinking to bear in identifying the problem and the solution and refining them into a sharply focused invention definition. In patent work, as in life generally, there is no free lunch. But by this point we've already *paid* for lunch.

This chapter illustrates the problem-solution-based claim-drafting process with two examples, after which a set of questions and answers explains the underlying theory of the problem-solution-based claim-drafting technique.

Examples of the Technique

The following are two examples of problem-solution-based claim drafting.

Uniform Microwave Oven Heating

The first example returns to the microwave oven improvement discussed earlier[2] based, first, on our broadest problem-solution statement:

> *The problem of* nonuniform heating of matter with microwave energy in a microwave cavity *is solved by* heating the matter other than with standing microwaves that are stationary relative to the matter.

We will choose as our setting the oven itself. (Another setting might be the turntable if there was something about the turntable used in the embodiment that could distinguish it from turntables generally.) And we have chosen to create both a method claim and an apparatus claim that uses the means-plus-function construct.

---

2. *See* p. 55–58.

1. Setting(s)	Oven
2. Statutory claim type(s)	Method and apparatus (with means-plus-function element)
3. Remove problem-related language and boilerplate	~~The problem of nonuniform~~ heating of matter with microwave energy in a microwave cavity ~~is solved by~~ heating the matter other than with standing microwaves that are stationary relative to the matter
4. Stitch	7.1 A method comprising heating matter in a microwave cavity with microwaves that are other than standing waves that are stationary relative to the matter
	7.2 Apparatus comprising
	a microwave cavity, and
	means for heating matter in the microwave cavity with microwave energy, said heating means heating the matter other than with standing microwaves that are stationary relative to the matter
5. Compare	The reader should verify the accuracy of the transformations

And here is the technique applied to our previously developed problem-solution statement that focuses on the preferred embodiment wherein the matter being heated is "food" and wherein the problem is overcome by moving the food:

> *The problem of* nonuniform heating of food in a microwave cavity *is solved by* moving the food within the cavity while the food is being heated.

Here we have chosen to draft our apparatus claim in non-means-plus-function form. As discussed below, this will involve adding a structural recitation of a "food support."

1. Setting(s)	Oven
2. Statutory claim type(s)	Method and apparatus (without means-plus-function elements)
3. Remove problem-related language and boilerplate	~~The problem of nonuniform~~ heating of food in a microwave cavity ~~is solved by~~ moving the food within the cavity while the food is being heated
4. Stitch	7.3 A method comprising moving food within a microwave cavity while the food is being heated within the cavity
	7.4 Apparatus for heating food comprising
	a microwave cavity, and
	a food support configured to move the food within the cavity while the food is being heated
5. Compare	The reader should verify the accuracy of the transformation

Traffic Signal

**FIGURE 7–1 Early
traffic signal.**

The traffic signal is our second example.

Early traffic signals were manual affairs in which "stop" and "go" placards were held up by a human operator. A major problem was that operator fatigue resulted in erratic timing of the presentation of the "stop" and "go" placards for the different directions of travel, confusing both drivers and pedestrians. The solution was an invention common to all modern traffic signals—namely the fact that the "stop" and "go" indicia change in automatic synchronism—an invention implemented in even the simple hand-cranked traffic signal shown in Figure 7–1.

Here is the problem-solution statement for this invention:

The problem of achieving safe and orderly traffic flow at a roadway intersection *is solved by* a traffic signal in which the display of "stop" and "go" indicia for traffic on a first roadway of the intersection is automatically changed in predetermined coordination with changes in the display of "stop" and "go" indicia for traffic on a second roadway of the intersection.

And below are the steps of the problem-solution-based claiming methodology applied to this problem-solution statement used, in this case, to produce two apparatus claims in two settings[3]—(a) the novel traffic signal, and (b) a roadway intersection that includes the novel traffic signal.

1. Setting(s)	(1) traffic signal, (2) roadway intersection having the traffic signal
2. Statutory claim type	Apparatus claims for both settings, one using means-plus-function recitations and the other not
3. Remove problem-related language and boilerplate	~~The problem of achieving safe and orderly traffic flow~~ at a roadway intersection ~~is solved by~~ a traffic signal in which the display of "stop" and "go" indicia for traffic on a first roadway of the intersection is automatically changed in predetermined coordination with changes in the display of "stop" and "go" indicia for traffic on a second roadway of the intersection

---

3. *See* pp. 88–89.

4. Stitch (two apparatus claims)	7.5 A traffic signal comprising
	"stop" and "go" indicia for traffic at a roadway intersection, and
	means for causing the display of the "stop" and "go" indicia for traffic on a first roadway of the intersection to be automatically changed in predetermined coordination with changes in the display of the "stop" and "go" indicia for traffic on a second roadway of the intersection
	7.6 In combination,
	a roadway intersection, and
	a traffic signal configured to display "stop" and "go" indicia for traffic on a first roadway of the intersection; to display "stop" and "go" indicia for traffic on a second roadway of the intersection; and to automatically change the "stop" and "go" indicia for traffic on the first roadway in predetermined coordination with changes in the display of the "stop" and "go" indicia for traffic on the second roadway
5. Compare to problem-solution statement	The reader should verify the accuracy of the transformation(s)

Stitching Options

There are a number of areas where the claim drafter has some options when carrying out stitching step 4.

Preamble

The claim evolving out of the stitching process may lend itself to a short, formulaic preamble and/or to a longer preamble incorporating substantive limitations. The choice typically comes down to which approach seems to work better for the problem-solution statement at hand and whether we are drafting an apparatus claim or a method claim. Often, both types of preamble work equally well.

Rearrangement and Repetition

We are allowed to rearrange the language of the original problem-solution statement. Indeed, some rearrangement is usually necessary. This is fine as long as the relationships among the elements of the problem-solution statement are preserved. Repeating a few words or phrases may also be necessary to make the claim hang together.

Statutory Claim Type

The problem-solution statement can be transformed into one or more of the statutory claim types: (a) method claims for "processes"; (b) apparatus claims for "machines" and "manufactures [manufactured items]"; and (c) composition claims for chemical compounds and other compositions of matter.[4] We saw, for example, how the problem-solution statement for our microwave oven invention was transformed into both method claims 7.1 and 7.3 and apparatus claims 7.2 and 7.4. If it proves difficult to convert the problem-solution statement into a claim of a particular statutory type, the problem-solution statement can be reworked with the desired statutory claim type in mind.

The advantages of defining an invention using any particular statutory claim type are discussed in Chapter Fifteen.

Structural Elements vs. Means-Plus-Function

Apparatus claims may recite one or more of their elements that have functional language either as means-plus-function elements,[5] as in claims 7.2 and 7.5 or as non-means-plus-function elements, as in claims 7.4 and 7.6. The problem-solution statement ideally expresses the invention in functional terms. It is therefore usually straightforward to transform a problem-solution statement into both a method claim and into an apparatus claim that defines the physical elements in functional terms, either using means-plus-function limitations or not.

There are many issues surrounding the use of means-plus-function claiming, as discussed in Chapter Thirteen. For present purposes, it will simply be noted that in order to avoid using the word "means" or other words that the Federal Circuit says are equivalent, such as "element," "mechanism," and "device," we may have to add a structural limitation not actually present in the problem-solution statement. In the case of claim 7.4, it is the limitation "food support."

Invention Setting

An invention setting is an environment or context in which the inventive concept is manifest. For example, one setting for our traffic signal invention is the traffic signal itself. Another setting is the roadway intersection where the signal is installed. Claims 7.5 and 7.6 claim the invention in those two settings. Claims 7.1 through 7.4 both claim the microwave

---

4. 35 U.S.C. 101.

5. "An element in a claim for a combination may be expressed as a means or step for performing a specified function." 35 U.S.C. 112(f).

oven invention in the same setting—the oven itself. However, another setting could be the oven's turntable if defined with sufficient particularity as to not read on other kinds of turntables.

Invention settings are treated in detail in Chapter Fourteen and so will not be discussed further here except to note that a problem-solution statement usually casts the invention in a particular one of its settings. The straightforward transformation of the problem-solution statement into claim form will usually result in a claim in that same setting. If some other setting for the claim is desired, it may be possible to change or add a few words to an already formulated problem-solution statement to get it into the desired setting. However, if changing more than a word or two proves necessary, it is better to draft a new problem-solution statement with the desired setting in mind. Too much ad hoc fussing with the original problem-solution statement increases the risk of the finished claim having undue limitations or reading on the prior art.

Questions and Answers

The following questions and answers explain the underlying theory of the problem-solution-based claiming methodology.

Why is the problem-related language removed?

Words in a claim that define only the problem to be solved do not enhance the claim's patentability and, accordingly, are surplus. A claim reading on prior art is unpatentable whether or not the prior art solves the problem or recognizes its existence.[6] The claimed combination of elements or steps must distinguish the invention on its own merits without regard for the problem it solves.

Problem-defining language can actually be damaging. Every word in a claim "can and will be used against you in a court of law." The Opposing Team may assert that their product or process solves a different problem from the one stated in the claim. And they will then argue that if the inventor did not intend the invention to be limited to solving any particular problem, she would not have included it in the claim. Meritorious or not, there is no point in opening the door to this kind of attack.

---

6. *In re Dillon*, 892 F.2d 1554, 13 USPQ2d 1337 (Fed. Cir. 1989) (en banc).

Why is the language defining the environment or context retained?

Language in the problem-solution statement defining the context or the environment is necessary to define the invention. If it were not necessary, we would have eliminated it when vetting the problem-solution statement.

In the microwave oven invention, for example, we saw earlier that distinguishing the invention over the prior art required defining the invention in the context of a microwave oven *cavity.* Indeed, that context-defining term was not removed during step 1 of the methodology.

Why is the stitching step made so constraining?

We worked hard to formulate a problem-solution statement that defines the invention in words that are "just right." This is not the time to get overly creative. It is all too easy for the effort expended in bringing the problem-solution statement hard up against the prior art to become compromised if we stray too far from its original language. Adding or changing words could narrow the invention definition in unappreciated ways. There will be plenty of opportunity for claim-drafting creativity with other claim-drafting strategies, such as inventive-departure-based claiming presented in Chapter Eight.

Why is step 5—comparing the claim to the problem-solution statement— necessary, given that the claim was produced so directly from the problem-solution statement?

We want to assure ourselves that the transformation to the claim form was carried out accurately and that nothing untoward has happened. Here are things to check:

- Are there any elements (apparatus elements or method steps) in the claim not having an explicit presence in the problem-solution statement?
- Did a single functional recitation become bifurcated into two or more claim elements?
- Were any modifiers (adjectives or adverbs)—which quite often have an unduly limiting effect on a claim—inadvertently introduced?
- Are there relationships between or among claim elements that do not exist in the problem-solution statement?

These kinds of discrepancies between the problem-solution state-ment and the claim can be loopholes for the Opposing Team to exploit in their quest to appropriate the essence of the inventor's contribution while avoiding infringement. If the steps of the methodology have been followed carefully, loopholes should be few and far between.

The "Too-Short" Claim

The terseness of claims that typically result from problem-solution-based claiming may give the reader pause. Problem-solution-based claims are typically quite short, containing a minimum number of apparatus ele-ments or method steps. This is the natural consequence of our efforts to minimize the number of words and limitations in the problem-solution statement.

A short claim is better than a long one. However, we sometimes hear that examiners don't "like" claims that are too short. They "like" to see lots of structure, and lots of claim elements. In short, lots of *limitations*. As a result, many practitioners do not claim the invention as broadly as they could, anticipating that unless the claim looks "long enough," the examiner will object to the claim based on its being, for example, func-tional or indefinite.

This does a disservice to the invention. We have already assured our-selves that the words of the problem-solution statement define subject matter that is "statutory," "novel," and "nonobvious."[7] Therefore, a claim based on that problem-solution statement should equally pass muster, no matter how few words or individual claim elements the claim contains. The fact that claim language may be highly functional, for example, or sets forth the invention in relatively few words, is not a proper basis for the claim to be rejected.[8]

Even in the absence of anticipatory prior art, examiners sometimes reject claims that they regard as too short or too functional based on the definiteness requirement of 35 U.S.C. 112(a)—the requirement that a pat-ent should have claims "particularly pointing out and distinctly claiming the subject matter which the applicant regards as his invention."

Such rejections are improper.

---

7. 35 U.S.C. 101–103.

8. *In re Swinehart*, 439 F.2d 210, 169 USPQ 226 (CCPA 1971); *K-2 Corporation v. Salomon SA*, 191, F.3d 1356, 1366–68, 52 USPQ2d 1001 (Fed. Cir 1999); *Wright Medical Technology, Inc. v. Osteonics Corp.*, 122 F.6d 1440, 1443–44, 43 USPQ2d 1837, 1840 (Fed. Cir. 1997).

A claim is indefinite only when the boundaries of the claimed subject matter cannot be understood from the claim language.[9] And there is nothing indefinite about a claim that defines an invention functionally rather than structurally, as in this example from an issued patent:[10]

> 7.7 A two-stroke engine having a pressurized air rail for producing an atomized fuel spray for injection into individual combustion chambers, in which oil for lubrication is atomized by metering said oil into a stream of compressed air taken from the rail or from a reservoir connected thereto and the resulting oil/air mist is injected into the crankcase directly upon points requiring lubrication.

Vigorously pursuing the rights of our clients means presenting the claims that our professional judgment says the clients are entitled to. We need to claim the invention *proactively*—the way *we* think it needs to be defined—not *reactively*—the way the examiner wants it to be.

That being said, there are certain practicalities. The patent owner may not have the financial resources, or the desire, for a protected battle in the USPTO. The beautiful, terse claims that we struggled over may have to be jettisoned in favor of claims that at least look longer in the interest of moving the case forward to an allowance. For those reasons, one may not want to even include such a claim in the application in the first instance.

A claim developed using the problem-solution-based approach can, however, serve as a touchstone against which other, less terse independent claims can be assessed. We can examine each recitation in those other claims and ask ourselves what, if anything, of significance is being given up by having included this or that recitation in the longer claim that does not appear in the shorter claim. Professional judgment then can be exercised to determine which direction to go in.

Appendix A presents the problem-solution statements for a number of inventions, along with the claims that result by applying the claim-drafting technique presented in this chapter. The reader is encouraged to try out the technique and compare the reader's claim to the version given in the appendix.

A further, more open-ended claim-drafting technique, inventive-departure-based claiming, is presented next.

---

9. *See, e.g., Power-One, Inc. v. Artesyn Technologies, Inc.*, 599 F. 3d 1343, 94 USPQ2d 1241 (Fed. Cir. 2010); *In re Borkowski*, 422 F.2d 904, 164 USPQ 642 (CCPA 1970).

10. U.S. Patent 5,375,573 (issued Dec. 27, 1994).

CHAPTER REVIEW—Problem-Solution-Based Independent Claims

Confirm Your Understanding

1. What are the three steps of problem-solution-based claim drafting?
2. In drafting a claim based on the problem-solution statement, why is
   a. the problem-related language removed?
   b. the language defining the environment or context retained?
   c. the stitching step made so constraining?
3. How is it possible for the cookbook-like procedure offered in this chapter to bypass the critical thinking that is traditionally required to draft a valid broad claim?

Questions for Further Thought

4. What is the benefit of converting a narrative definition of the invention (i.e., a problem-solution statement) into claim form as compared to just "diving in" and drafting the claim directly?
5. An unwritten rule in the USPTO is to find some way to reject a claim if it is "too short." How is it in the client's interest, then, to spend the time to draft very compact claims—such as those typically resulting from the methodology presented in this chapter—and/or to prolong the prosecution in order to fight for their allowance? Or is it, in fact, in the client's interest to do so?

Sharpen Your Skills

6. Convert the following problem-solution statements into claim form using the technique described in this chapter. Try to draft at least two claims in each case, using various stitching options and/or by claiming the invention in different settings (p. 215).

   a. Computer auto-dialing

   > *The problem (inconvenience) of* having to manually dial a telephone number after having looked it up in a computer *is solved by* a telephone-enabled computer that automatically dials the telephone number in response to an indication from a user [e.g., a mouse point-and-click] that a call to that number is desired.

   b. Spreadsheet program

   > *The problem of* having to manually update values in a paper-based spreadsheet *is solved by* a computer program that stores

mathematical relationships between dependent and independent variables as defined by a user and, upon a user inputting a new value for at least one of the independent variables, updates and displays the values of at least one of the dependent variables whose value was affected by the change in the independent-variable value.

c. Electric-eye-operated restroom apparatus (paper towel dispenser, water faucet, toilet flusher, etc.)

The problems of resource wastage and/or the spreading of germs in a public restroom *are solved by* operable restroom apparatuses that operate automatically in response to at least one of (a) the presence of a person in the restroom, or (b) the movement of a person in the restroom.

CHAPTER EIGHT

Inventive-Departure-Based Independent Claims

A patent should have at least one claim defining the invention as broadly as the prior art will allow. Otherwise competitors may find a way to appropriate the essence of the inventor's contribution to the art while avoiding all of the claims that *are* in the patent.

The ideal broad claim is perfectly congruent with the boundaries of the invention, encompassing all present and future implementations of the inventive concept while not reading on any prior art (Figure 8–1(A)). The previous chapter showed how a problem-solution statement, carefully crafted following the techniques presented in Part I, can take us a long way toward a claim that is as close to that ideal as our powers of human analysis and written expression can make it.

Our powers of analysis are hardly perfect, however. We may think we have distilled the inventive concept down to its most basic form, free of implementational details, but we may not have. The possible limiting effect of particular terminology in the problem-solution statement may have escaped our consideration. Or a potential licensee, putative infringer, judge, or jury may not interpret the claim language in the way that we or the patent examiner understood it. Our broadest claims, then, may be interpreted more narrowly than we had intended, possibly leaving some embodiments outside the boundaries defined by the claim (Figure 8–1(B)).

It is for these reasons that a patent application preferably includes a number of claims that each undertake to capture the invention at its full breadth. It will be harder for a competitor to design around two, three, or more claims defining the broad invention than to design around only one such claim. Recall, for example, John Loud's ballpoint pen patent[1] in which one claim recited "a spheroidal marking-point" and another recited "a marking sphere capable of revolving in all directions."

Moreover, having several broad claims in the application may save the day if one of them turns out to read on "invention-irrelevant" prior

---

1. *See* p. 7.

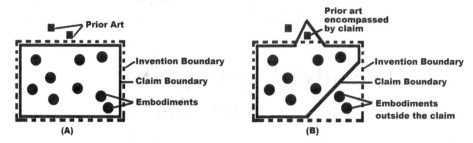

FIGURE 8–1(A) The theoretically perfect claim encompasses all possible embodiments of the invention (x) but no prior art (n). **FIGURE 8–1(B)** But what seems to be the broadest allowable claim may turn out to be too broad in one aspect and/or too narrow in another.

art, meaning prior art that does not teach the inventive concept but nonetheless anticipates the claim language (Figure 8–1(B)). In many Patent Office actions, this is the only type of prior art cited. We saw earlier, for example, how a claim that seemed to nicely define the concept of a heavier-than-air flying machine also managed to read on birds and flying dinosaurs.[2] Although a particular claim may be unintentionally overbroad in this way, another may not, thereby preserving coverage for the broad invention.

The problem-solution-based claim-drafting technique presented in the previous chapter is limited in the variety of claims that it can generate. This is a significant limitation. The above considerations require that the broad invention be expressed in a number of different ways, using various formats and different recitations of elements.

Some practitioners develop independent claims using an embodiment-oriented, invention-analysis-by-claim-drafting approach. A claim directed to the embodiment is drafted. The claim is then pruned and distilled, eliminating features that are clearly optional and consolidating multiple elements or functions into broader, overarching recitations.

Claims drafted in this way may capture the *embodiment(s)* at their broadest, but may miss the real invention—a point that has been emphasized throughout the book. The paper-clip discussion in Chapter Two[3] is as good an example as any of how an analysis that begins from the embodiment may fail to yield a claim capturing the inventive concept, no matter how much pruning and distilling is done.

2. *See* p. 39.
3. *See* pp. 12–16.

Embodiment-based claiming does have its place. Independent claims focusing on the embodiment(s) are an important component of the Planned Retreat. More about that in Chapter Nine. Moreover, sketching out a claim or two based on the embodiment(s) is a relatively painless way to get the claim-drafting juices flowing, a point discussed below under the heading "Separate What from How." Embodiment-based approaches leave a lot to be desired, however, when undertaking to claim the invention at its broadest.

How, then, to proceed?

There is no avoiding the need to identify the inventive concept at the outset. However, a fully thought through problem-solution statement is not necessarily required: a less-than-fully-formed idea of invention is sufficient to begin the process. The full breadth of the invention can be discovered as the claim takes shape. The key is to keep the goal of claiming the invention *conceptually* uppermost in our minds. This allows the claim-in-progress to be distilled down to the inventive essence. The claim itself, rather than the problem-solution statement, is what is iterated into a final, razor-sharp definition of the invention.

Central to this approach is the notion of "inventive departure," also referred to as the "inventive step," "inventive advance," "point of novelty," or simply "the improvement."

The inventive departure is a physical element, step, functionality, or a combination of these that defines how the invention departs from the prior art. In the earlier example of uniform microwave food heating,[4] the inventive departure at its broadest is "heating the matter other than with standing microwaves that are stationary relative to the matter," and for the preferred embodiment it is "move the food." In our chair example,[5] the inventive departure is "the seat support is elongated."

The inventive departure is akin to the solution portion of a problem-solution statement. But, the inventive departure does not have to involve a complete statement of the solution. Nor does it speak to the invention's environment or context. This is consistent with the notion of "departure." The inventive departure states the improvement without saying what is being improved—how the invention departs from the prior art without saying what is being departed *from*.

The inventive departures for other inventions already encountered in the book are shown below. Note that the inventive departure is not necessarily a complete thought. It is more like the germ of an idea—a germ out of which a full-blown claim can grow.

---

4. *See* p. 55.
5. *See* p. 64.

Invention	Inventive Departure
Ballpoint pen (p. 6)	Spheroidal marking-point
Konaclip/Gem paperclip (p. 13)	Equal pressure against opposing rails
Alarm clock (p. 22)	Alert at a selectable time
Nondripping coffeemaker (p. 23)	Coffee flow is shut off if carafe is not present
Aircraft lateral control (p. 39)	Controllable wing configuration
Traffic signal (p. 86)	Indicia are changed in coordination

The drafting of an inventive-departure-based claim starts from the inventive departure itself. The claim is built out from there, with just enough words being added to satisfy two requirements. One requirement is antecedent support for the inventive-departure-defining language. The other is defining an environment or context in which the inventive departure is novel and nonobvious.

An inventive-departure-based claim must be fussed over as carefully as a problem-solution statement. For example, the words that define the environment or context of the invention—what the inventive departure departs *from*—need to be worked over with as much care as when drafting a fully vetted problem-solution statement. The claim-drafting process, however, can begin without as much concern about exact wording in the early stages. Much of the necessary thinking and analysis can be done as the claim takes shape. Similar to problem-solution-based claim drafting, however, the inventive-departure-based approach requires ongoing focus on the invention at an abstract and functional level, lest we fall into the trap of simply cataloging piece-parts of the embodiment(s) and winding up with a claim that misses the inventive concept.

Inventive-departure-based claim drafting has five steps:

1. Choose one or more claim settings (as discussed below).
2. Choose one or more statutory claim types for each setting (as discussed below).
3. Identify the inventive departure.
4. Draft the claim based on the inventive departure.
5. Compare the finished claim to the problem-solution statement.

Steps 1 and 2: Setting(s) and Statutory Claim Types

These are the same as steps 1 and 2 of the problem-solution-based claim-drafting technique presented in Chapter Seven.

Step 3: Identify the Inventive Departure

There are many ways to identify the inventive departure.

The most formal way is to develop a complete problem-solution statement. The solution portion of the problem-solution statement is, or contains, the inventive departure. Different versions of the inventive departure will arise from different versions of the problem-solution statement.

Even if the claim drafter is intent on just digging in without writing and burnishing a full problem-solution statement, the same analytical techniques that go into developing a problem-solution statement can be used to identify the inventive departure, at least preliminarily, as discussed immediately below. The claim-drafting process itself can then be used to finish the job.

Consider the Problem and the Solution

We have seen throughout the book how the broad invention can be teased out of the embodiment(s) by asking what problem was intended to be solved and how, broadly speaking, it *was* solved. Aspects of the embodiment(s) that might have initially seemed central to the invention may no longer seem so when the invention is analyzed from the standpoint of being the solution to some problem. Thus, even without developing a formal problem-solution statement, it is still fruitful to take a problem-solution approach when attempting to identify the inventive departure.

For example, we saw earlier that the ballpoint pen addressed the problem that the previously existing (fountain and quill) pens could not write on a rough surface.[6] That problem was solved by the pen having a "spheroidal marking-point" or, alternatively stated, a "marking sphere capable of revolving in all directions." "Spheroidal marking-point" is one way to characterize the ballpoint pen's inventive departure. "Marking sphere capable of revolving in all directions" is another.

Figure Out "What's Really Going On"

Another way of identifying the inventive departure is to ask *What's Really Going On?* and then answering that question in functional terms. Any detail not helping to answer *What's Really Going On?* should be suspected as being not essential to the inventive departure.

Think in terms of verbs rather than nouns, in method steps rather than structural elements. In the book's example of uniform heating of food in a microwave oven,[7] the inventive departure is the verb phrase "moving the food or 'matter' . . . ," rather than the noun "turntable."

---

6. *See* p. 8.
7. *See* p. 55.

Identify what is common among the various embodiments. Thinking about alternative embodiments, including some "far-fetched" ones,[8] can help in this process.

Giving free rein to our technological curiosity is another way to get to the bottom of what's really going on—taking the thing apart in the mind's eye to understand what is going on at the 50,000-foot level.

Separate What from How

A broad invention is not about preferred ways of solving the problem, but about solving the problem, period. To *Separate What from How* means to figure out *what* solves the problem, as compared to *how* the embodiments just happen to implement the solution.

The inventive departure is the *what* of this paradigm.

The task to *Separate What from How* focuses not on what the invention *is*, but what it is *not*. An aspect of the embodiment is not intrinsic to the broad invention if the problem is at least partially solved without that aspect. It is the ball of the ballpoint pen that solves the problem of how to write on a rough surface. All the other parts of the embodiment relate to *how* the inventive concept is implemented, and do not inform the inventive departure.

The pitfalls of an embodiment-based approach to analyzing an invention are emphasized throughout the book. See, for example, the Konaclip discussion at pp. 12–16. However, the exercise of drafting an embodiment-based claim *can* facilitate separating "what" from "how" and thereby help us identify the inventive departure. Writing down potential claim limitations and seeing how they interplay can sharpen our understanding of the inventive departure at its essence. Once having identified the inventive departure in this way, however, we should use it as the starting point for drafting a new claim using the techniques described in this chapter.

One of the author's colleagues finds that this kind of claim-drafting exercise helps him gain a broad perspective on the invention:

> "I begin by crafting a one-sentence statement of the invention. One must be patient and spend whatever time this takes. Then I write a claim of medium to medium-narrow scope and then roughly sketch (outline) broader claims up to the broadest claim. I don't reach for the broadest claim in the beginning because it is the crown jewel and I want to have considered all the angles first. One can often gain a

---

8. *See* p. 40.

broader perspective on the invention by working the medium scope claims first."

—JPM

Step 4: Draft the Claim Based on the Inventive Departure

Before beginning to draft the claim, we should decide on a statutory claim type for the claim—method, apparatus, or composition of matter. We should also decide on a setting in which the claim will define the invention. An invention setting is an environment or context in which the inventive concept is manifest. We saw, for example, in the previous chapter that two settings for a novel traffic signal could be (a) the traffic signal itself, and (b) a roadway intersection where the novel traffic signal is installed.[9] Statutory claim types and invention settings are discussed in detail in Chapters Fourteen and Fifteen.

Once having decided on an invention setting and statutory claim type, and having identified the inventive departure, we are ready to draft the claim. It is assumed in what follows that the reader is familiar with claim-drafting mechanics—the need for proper antecedent basis for claim recitations, the fact that a claim element should be affirmatively recited only once in a given claim, and similar claim-drafting standards.[10]

Begin with the End in Mind

In his book *The 7 Habits of Highly Effective People*,[11] personal effectiveness author Stephen Covey urges readers to "begin with the end in mind." Being effective in life, Covey says, requires first deciding what one's goals are. That goal is Covey's "end in mind." Once a goal is clearly in mind, action can be taken to achieve it.

Beginning with the end in mind is also a powerful claim-drafting paradigm. The "end in mind" is the inventive departure. The claim drafting begins by writing down the inventive departure—typically as a method step or an apparatus element. The process proceeds backward from there. The claim is completed by adding only so much additional language as necessary to do two things:

1. Provide *antecedent support* for the language used to express the inventive departure.

---

9. *See* p. 86.
10. For claim drafting guidance, *see, e.g.*, Robert C. Faber, *Faber on Mechanics of Patent Claim Drafting* (New York: Practicing Law Institute).
11. Stephen R. Covey, *The 7 Habits of Highly Effective People* (New York: Fireside, 1989), p. 95.

2. If necessary, put the inventive departure into a *particular context* in which the claimed subject matter is novel and nonobvious.

Working backward from the inventive departure helps ensure that only essential limitations make their way into the claim. It also helps for us to take on the mind-set of the Opposing Team, as one of the author's colleagues observed when describing his approach to inventive-departure claiming:

> *"I focus on the departure or difference from the prior art that the invention contains and build a claim around that. Drafting the claim is then a matter of writing something down that recites the difference and then thinking of ways to avoid the language of the claim, yet still practice the invention. This forces you to think of generic terms that keep that from happening. Of course, removing limitations that are not needed in order to provide a context for the inventive distinction is part of that process."*
>
> —HLN

We return to the book's microwave oven example[12] for an illustration of the technique. Recall that the inventive departure is the idea of heating the matter other than with standing microwaves that are stationary relative to the matter—an inventive departure formulation that encompasses three embodiments: (a) moving the matter within the cavity, (b) moving the standing waves within the cavity, or (c) precluding standing waves altogether.

Let us draft an apparatus claim, beginning by writing a generic preamble and a "payoff limitation" that states that inventive departure as a means-plus-function element. The whole middle of the claim is blank at this point:

8.1 Apparatus comprising . . .
.
.
.

. . . means for heating the matter other than with standing microwaves that are stationary relative to the matter.

---

12. p. 55.

Applying criterion (1) above, we see that antecedent support is required for "the matter." That support can be put in the claim preamble.

> 8.2 Apparatus for heating matter, the apparatus comprising ...
>
> .
>
> .
>
> .
>
> ...means for heating the matter other than with standing microwaves that are stationary relative to the matter.

Applying criterion (2) above, we recognize that claim 8.2 reads on the operation of a rotisserie oven, not to mention stirring the contents of a saucepan heating on a stove. In our (commendable) striving for breadth, we forgot all about the microwave oven context for the food-moving. This leads us to claim 8.3:

> 8.3 Apparatus for heating matter, the apparatus comprising ...
>
> .
>
> .
>
> .
>
> ...means for heating the matter with microwave energy, the heating means heating the matter other than with standing microwaves that are stationary relative to the matter.

So far so good, but single-means claims are not permitted,[13] so let's add something that we are undoubtedly going to need in any practical embodiment—a support for the matter to be heated:

> 8.4 Apparatus for heating matter, the apparatus comprising
> a support for the matter, and
> means for heating the matter with microwave energy, the heating means heating the matter other than with standing microwaves that are stationary relative to the matter.

Recall,[14] though, that the prior art knew to heat food by conveying it across the open end of a microwave waveguide. Claim 8.4 reads on that prior art, which is overcome by putting the invention into the context of a "microwave cavity." And since the "support" is within or might be a

---

13. 35 U.S.C. 112(f) permits means-plus-function recitations in a claim "to a *combination* [emphasis added]."

14. *See* p. 56.

part of the cavity, we don't need it to be our second element and we can eliminate it:

> **8.5** Apparatus for heating matter, the apparatus comprising
> a microwave cavity,
> a support for the matter within the cavity, and
> means for heating the matter with microwave energy, the heating means heating the matter other than with standing microwaves that are stationary relative to the matter.

Now we're good, except that we may want to avoid our claim being given what the Federal Circuit calls "means-plus-function treatment."[15] To this end—as discussed in detail in Chapter Thirteen—we want to avoid using the word "means" and its generic stand-ins, "element," "mechanism," "device," and the like. We also want the claim recitation in question to be as structural as possible.

On the other hand, we want to maintain the breadth that we secured by building up our claim from a broad functional inventive departure. So "turntable" or "displacement device" are nicely structural but using them to avoid "means-plus-function treatment" will unduly narrow the claim since the broad invention, we have decided, includes the three possibilities of (a) moving the matter within the cavity, (b) moving the standing waves within the cavity, or (c) precluding standing waves altogether.

It turns out that a useful claim-drafting construct is to introduce a phantom element for carrying out the desired broad functionality and to imbue the phantom element with structural character by building into it one or more structural elements that we need anyway. This preserves the breadth of the inventive departure without the phantom element engendering any narrowness of its own. The phantom element is, in effect, a custom label that we've created to encompass two or more structural elements that we are content to have in the claim anyway.

In the case at hand, we can create a phantom element called "a heating subsystem" that includes a source of microwave energy and a support for the matter:

> **8.6** Apparatus comprising
> a microwave cavity, and
> a heating subsystem comprising (a) a source of microwave energy for the cavity and (b) a support for the matter,

---

15. *See, e.g., Welker Bearing Company v. PHD, Inc.,* 550 F.3d 1090, 89 USPQ2d 1289 (Fed. Cir. 2008).

> the heating subsystem being configured to heat the matter other than with standing microwaves that are stationary relative to the matter.

Even though "subsystem" standing by itself might be deemed a generic term like "means" or "element," the fact that it is defined using structural recitations should save it from "means-plus-function treatment."[16]

The balance of this chapter presents further ideas for drafting inventive-departure-based claims with "the end in mind" to help implement the technique when the inventions are more complex.

Pack Only What You Need

The process of working backward from the inventive departure is summarized by the prescription *Pack Only What You Need.*

Claim drafting can be compared to packing clothes for a winter vacation. Whether you pack your heavy outerwear or your shorts and swimsuit depends on where you're going—to the Rockies for skiing or to the Caribbean for golf and the beach. You certainly wouldn't pack for both destinations but would take only what you need.

In the claim-drafting context, the "destination" is the inventive departure. You can't know whether you should "pack" a particular limitation into a claim until you know what inventive departure you are heading for.

Should a microwave oven claim recite a "power-level selector"? Not if the inventive departure is the idea of "moving the food within the oven cavity during the heating." The food is heated uniformly with or without a power-level control.

Should a claim directed to a chair invention include a "back support?" Not if the invention is the use of elongated support members. The problem of chair portability solved by elongated support members is solved equally well whether or not the chair has a back.

Determining whether a limitation is necessary to define an invention is often not so clear when reviewing a claim already written. Working backward from the inventive departure and packing only what you need avoids having to ferret out unnecessary limitations after they have inveigled their way into the fabric of the claim.

The prescription *Pack Only What You Need* applies not only to the body of a claim but also to its preamble. In fact, the preamble is frequently where undue limitations show up.

Unnecessary limitations typically fall into one of four categories:

---

16. *See* pp. 193–194.

1. Descriptive labels and modifiers
2. Unnecessary elements
3. Advantages of the invention
4. Intended use of the invention

Let us consider each of these types of limitations in turn in the preamble context, recognizing that such limitations can *also* be unduly narrowing when appearing in the *body* of the claim.

Descriptive Labels and Modifiers

Descriptive labels and modifiers in a preamble rarely buy any patentability but yet may be given limiting effect when it comes time to enforce the claim.

For example, consider claim 8.7:

> **8.7 An *automobile* floor mat comprising**
> a semirigid monolayer having a gradually sloping edge portion extending outward from a central section, the edge portion terminating in a lip disposed at an elevation above the central portion, the lip having a plurality of indentations disposed at regular intervals around its periphery.

The descriptive label "automobile" buys no patentability in claim 8.7, because a preamble claim term is not given any patentable weight "where a patentee defines a structurally complete invention in the claim body and uses the preamble only to state a purpose or intended use for the invention."[17] That is certainly the case here. There is nothing in the body of the claim that intrinsically limits the defined structure to being an *automobile* floor mat. Thus if the examiner finds a prior art mat described by the body of the claim, he will reject the claim whether or not the prior art mat was designed for use in an automobile (or, for that matter, intended to be placed on a floor).

Although the descriptive label "automobile" will be of no help in securing *allowance* of this claim, it will come back to bite us when we go to *enforce* the claim. The patent owner could be out of luck if the Opposing Team uses the claimed semirigid monolayer to construct mats intended for use in trucks or locomotive cabs and that are not capable of being used in automobiles due to, for example, the mats' size or shape.

Claim 8.8 presents another example of descriptive preamble labels or modifiers that can get us in trouble. The claim is directed to a telescoping

---

17. *Rowe v. Dror*, 112 F.3d 473, 42 USPQ2d 1550 (Fed. Cir. 1997).

radio/TV antenna, which the claim calls "an extendible and retractable structure."

> **8.8** An *extendible and retractable* structure comprising
> a plurality of structural sections, mounted to be slidable in the direction of their length relative to each other, each structural section including [details omitted] . . .

The uniqueness of this antenna is the particular conformation of the sliding structural sections as recited in the details omitted from the claim above. The recited geometry of those sections and their arrangement in the finished antenna is what renders the structure "extendible and retractable." The terms "extendible" and "retractable" in the preamble are, therefore, redundant and do not enhance the claim's patentability. Yet, a competitor's antenna having sections exactly like the inventor's may be designed to permanently lock the sections in place when the antenna is initially extended. Such an antenna might be intended for delivery to a remote site—like a mountaintop or Mars—extended in place, and left for good. Because the sections are permanently locked in place once extended, the antenna is arguably nonretractable and, as a result, noninfringing.

Undue limitations like these can be avoided by not packing a limitation into the preamble until the structure of the evolving claim makes it clear that it is needed. A good practice is to start with the simplest preamble possible, such as "A method comprising. . . ." As the claim begins to take shape, it may turn out that the preamble is, in fact, the best place for certain limitations. That's fine. Preamble limitations will be given limiting effect, thereby supporting a claim's patentability, if they tie into the rest of the claim recitations.

Unnecessary Elements

Working a claim bottom-up from the inventive departure rather than top-down from the preamble can help keep not only unnecessary labels and modifiers out of the preamble, but entire elements as well.

For example, claim 8.9 is directed to a method for operating an engine in which the inventive departure involves using a fuel containing certain additives to keep the engine parts clean.

> **8.9** A method for operating an engine *having a fuel pump,* the method comprising:
> operating the engine using a fuel containing [certain recited additives] under conditions sufficient to clean performance-inhibiting deposits from *the fuel pump or other fuel system elements.*

Although the inventor was primarily concerned about fuel pump deposits, the claim drafter, thinking broadly, structured the claim to recite that the deposits were cleaned from the "fuel pump *or* other fuel system elements." This is all to the good. Unfortunately, the preamble explicitly limits the claimed method to an environment that includes a fuel pump. An accused infringer whose engine does not have a fuel pump will argue that this claim does not apply to him.

This claim bears the telltale evidence of a preamble that was drafted before the rest of the claim. The preamble probably includes the phrase "having a fuel pump" because the claim drafter was focused on the embodiment. If the body of the claim had been written *before* the preamble, it would probably have been drafted to call for deposits being cleaned from "fuel system elements" or even from "a fuel pump or other fuel system elements." There would then have been no impetus to pack a "fuel pump" limitation into the preamble, because the claim would have been complete without it.

Advantages or Intended Use of the Invention

Finally, in the following examples, the preamble language explains an advantage or intended use for the invention. As such, the preamble potentially limits the applicability of the claim to potential infringers without the claim gaining patentability in return:

Preamble	Infringement-Avoidance Scenario
A high-speed rotor of a type *applicable for use with a flywheel*, the rotor comprising [no flywheel mentioned in the rest of the claim] . . .	The alleged infringer discovers a non-flywheel-based application for the novel rotor.
An optical system in which at least two out-of-phase light beams of different frequencies are combined *with improved output efficiency* . . .	The alleged infringer selects an operating parameter for the optical system to achieve increased processing speed without the improved output efficiency that the claim calls for.
An on chip debug system for a programmable *very large scale integration (VLSI)* processor. . .	The level of integration regarded in the industry as being "very large scale" constantly changes as advances in technology enable components to be made increasingly smaller. The alleged infringer, whose processor uses a state-of-the-art level of integration, argues that VLSI should be interpreted to mean what it meant at the time the patent application was filed.

Define, Don't Explain

Patent attorneys love to explain things. This is great when we are writing the specification. But it can get in the way when drafting claims. It is hard to resist the urge to liven up a claim's dull litany of elements by explaining that the claimed subject matter is an *automobile* floor mat, or an optical system with *improved output efficiency*, or a rotor *applicable for use with a flywheel.*

That urge to explain must be resisted nonetheless.

A claim's function is to define the boundaries of the patent owner's intellectual property, not to explain or help readers to understand something. An explanatory-type limitation, such as an advantage or intended use, may seem harmless enough, but we need to take it as an article of faith that every extra word in a claim is a potential loophole for infringers to exploit.

Limitations should be suspected of explaining rather than defining if they set forth any of the following:

- The advantage of the invention, or what it is "good for."
- How the recited combination can integrate with the external environment.
- Motivations (e.g., for doing a particular step or including a particular element).
- How to carry out a recited function where the recitation of the function itself imbues the claim with patentability.
- How inputs get generated.
- The source of something that the claimed method or apparatus works on.

We should consider deleting any limitation that meets one of these criteria. If the claim distinguishes over the prior art without the limitation, it isn't necessary to the invention and the claim is well rid of it.

We have seen examples of limitations meeting some of the above criteria in the previous discussion of claim preambles. The following are further examples of claims with explanatory language, but in these examples they are in the body of the claim. The lined-out material in the examples is merely explanatory and thus can be deleted. Underscoring in some of the examples designates language inserted to complete the claim once the lined-out language has been removed.

In claim 8.10, the "enabling" step serves only to provide a motivation for providing the novel message content of the "inserting" step. It is only the latter that imparts novelty to the claim, which is equally patentable without the "enabling" step.

8.10   A method for use by a transmitting terminal, the method comprising

~~enabling a receiving terminal to determine if messages transmitted by the transmitting terminal are being missed, the enabling including~~

inserting into each message that originates from the transmitting terminal (a) an identification of the transmitting terminal and (b) a sequence character that is advanced for every N messages transmitted by the transmitting terminal.

In claim 8.11 the fact that the recited apparatus may include a timer as a way of measuring the time interval in question merely explains how to carry out the function of the "means for redirecting." The claim is equally patentable without reciting the timer.

8.11 Apparatus for processing a message, comprising

a timer, and

means for redirecting the message from a primary location to a secondary location if a predetermined interval timed by the timer expires before the message has been acted upon at the primary location,

...

Claim 8.12 illustrates the power of the phrase "as a function of" as a way of enabling the claim drafter to eliminate claim elements that merely explain how to carry out a function that is novel in and of itself. The inventive departure in this claim is forming a data symbol decision based on a certain sum. That sum is generated in the penultimate step in the original claim.

8.12 A method for forming a decision as to the value of a data symbol carried in a data signal, the method comprising

receiving the data signal,

generating samples of the data signal

generating a plurality of coefficients,

multiplying the coefficients with respective ones of the samples,

generating a sum of the resulting products, and

forming the data symbol decision based on the sum <u>as a function of the sum of the products of a plurality of coefficients with respective samples of the data signal.</u>

In the revised claim, the phrase "as a function of" enables the final, "forming" step to treat the sum produced by the five preceding steps of the original claim as a computational *fait accompli*. Six steps in the original claim are thereby collapsed into one.

The advantage of claim 8.12 in its revised form is huge. We would be hard-pressed to prove that each of the individual steps of the original claim is carried out in our competitor's embodiment. The advantages would be even greater in the case of an apparatus version of claim 8.12, since it may be difficult to prove that the competitor's product has six individual components that carry out the recited "receiving," "generating," and "multiplying." Moreover, the competitor's product might not even carry out one or more of the generating steps, or the multiplying step. Rather, the competitor's product might use a lookup table in which precomputed results for the various computations and/or precomputed coefficients are stored.

Claim 8.13 illustrates the use of the phrase "in such a way that" to similar effect. The inventive departure, as set forth in the last paragraph of the claim, is the idea of adjusting a sampling phase in a data equalizer in such a way that two coefficients used in the equalizer are kept substantially equal to one another:

> 8.13 A method comprising
> forming a decision as to data symbols carried by a data signal in response to the sum of the products of an ordered plurality of coefficients with respective samples of the signal,
>> periodically updating the values of the coefficients, and
>> adjusting the phase with which the samples are formed *in such a way that* an adjacent pair of the coefficients are maintained substantially equal to each other.

Note that this claim doesn't explain how the sampling phase is adjusted to keep the two coefficients equal to one another; adjusting the sampling phase to achieve the equality was the inventive departure in and of itself. Note, too, that claim 8.13 avoids reciting any motivation for the method in that it doesn't explain why one would *want* to keep the coefficients equal to one another. That is the role of the specification. Defining the invention requires us only to recite that the sampling phase is adjusted in such a way as to achieve the recited equality, in whatever way that might be accomplished.

In the end, however, there is perhaps no better exemplar of a claim that follows the prescription *Define, Don't Explain* than the ballpoint pen claim drafted by patent attorney William Dowss:[18]

---

18. *See* p. 7.

8.14 A pen having a spheroidal marking-point, substantially as described.

A working ballpoint pen needs to have some way to hold the marking-point in place, and the pen needs some way for the marking-point to be inked. But claim 8.14 doesn't explain any of that. Nor did it need to. Dowss's claim serves as a powerful reminder of how precisely an invention can be claimed by hewing to the principle that the function of a claim is not to *explain* the embodiment(s), but to *define* the invention.

Use Functional Recitations to Minimize the Number of Claim Elements

Infringement loopholes become increasingly likely as the number of individual claim elements increases. Given a dozen individual claim elements, a determined competitor will undoubtedly be able to find a way to implement all of their functions with only 11 elements, or with only 10 or with 9, thereby implementing the inventor's teachings but avoiding literal infringement.

Pruning and distilling the claim goes a long way toward closing up any such loopholes in both method and apparatus claims. However, another way of eliminating potential loopholes in apparatus claims is to recite a specific limitation in functional terms without calling for a specific structure by which to do it. For example, the following claim incorporates the *function* of a hinge without reciting the hinge itself:

8.15 Apparatus comprising
a door frame,
a door mounted on the door frame in such a way that it can swing into and out of the plane of the door frame,
...

These considerations apply not only to independent claims like claim 8.15, but dependent claims as well.

For example, claim 8.16 recites a signal converter configured to generate a revised version of an input signal. Its dependent claim 8.17 calls for an explicit structural element, reciting that the signal converter includes a separate encoder configured to encode the input signal. By contrast, dependent claim 8.18 presents that encoding functionally, reciting that the signal converter encodes the input signal without calling for a separate element to do so.

8.16. Apparatus comprising
an input port adapted to receive an input signal,

a signal converter configured to generate a revised version of the input signal, . . .

8.17. The apparatus of claim 8.16 wherein the signal converter includes an encoder configured to encode the input signal to generate the revised version.

8.18. The apparatus of claim 8.16 wherein the signal converter is configured to encode the input signal to generate the revised version.

Scrutinize Every Modifier

Beware the insidious modifier, particularly adjectives. Most of them are unnecessary in a broad claim, serving to explain rather than define. Each modifier in a claim should be scrutinized to see if the claim will support patentability without it. If so, the modifier is probably expendable.

Examples from earlier in this chapter include *automobile* floor mat,[19] *extendible and retractable* structure,[20] and *very-large-scale* integration.[21] Here are some other examples:

Claim Language	Infringement-Avoidance Scenario
Decoding a *transmitted* video signal by . . .	Opposing Team carries out all the steps of the claim except that the video signal was not "transmitted" from anywhere but read out of a storage device.
High-resolution filter	Opposing Team asserts that their filter does not meet the limitation "high-resolution," because there are filters that have even higher resolution than theirs.
Rapidly removable label	Opposing Team asserts that their label isn't any more rapidly removable than is typical and therefore not "rapidly" removable.

The patent owner may have a comeback for such Opposing Team challenges. But the real question is: *What are these limitations doing here?* If a particular modifier is needed in order to define the invention in view of the prior art, that is one thing. But if not helping define the invention, the modifier is only serving to explain something about the embodiment(s), and the claim could just as easily have been allowed without it.

Another potential problem for certain modifiers is their potential for being declared indefinite. The terms "high-resolution" and "rapidly"

---

19. *See* p. 106.
20. *See* p. 107.
21. *See* p. 108.

certainly fit this category. Claim indefiniteness is discussed in further detail in Chapter Ten.

Be Sure the Claim Says What You Mean

Claims sometimes don't say what we mean them to say.

The following are typical examples of claim language gone awry, based on claim language reported in cases or personally encountered by the author.

The ways in which misstatements can arise are, of course, innumerable. These examples, then, are simply illustrative of the need to be sensitive to what our words really mean.

"Heating said block of material to 500°F"

Consider a process in which, according to the specification, a block of material should be put in a 500°F oven. A claim drafter not paying close attention to what his words mean might recite this step as "heating said block of material to 500°F."

This recitation is inaccurate. What it says is that the block of material is heated until the material itself reaches 500°F, not that the material is put in a 500°F environment. A competitor following the teachings of the specification by putting the material in a 500°F oven for some period of time but removing it before the material itself reaches 500°F does not infringe the claim. Moreover, the claim is invalid as not pointing out "that which the applicant regards as the invention."[22]

The correct recitation would be "putting said block of material in a 500°F environment."

"First and second transistors having first and second emitters"

This recitation is ambiguous. A transistor can have one, two, or more emitters, raising the question in this case as to whether (a) the first transistor has the first emitter and the second transistor has the second emitter, or (b) the first transistor has first and second emitters and the second transistor also has its own separate first and second emitters. The recitation should be made clear by reciting whichever of these meanings is intended:

- a first transistor having a first emitter and a second transistor having a second emitter

---

22. 35 U.S.C. 112(b).

OR

• first and second transistors *each* having first and second emitters

"Wherein"

Claim drafters develop a lexicon of pet words and phrases. We have gotten so used to them that they are skimmed over when a claim is reviewed because they fit a pattern or "sound right" even when they don't belong or don't mean what we intended.

The word "wherein" is one of the most widely misused words in patent claims. It means "in which," and, accordingly, is perfectly fine in constructions such as:

> The apparatus of claim 1 *wherein* the top surface of the armrest is other than horizontal.

> The method of claim 1 further comprising tumbling the gem in an abrasive medium *wherein* silicon carbide is one of the medium's abrasive components.

These claims make perfect sense if the word "wherein" is replaced by its synonym "in which."

By contrast, "wherein" is improperly used in the following recitation, as is made clear by replacing "wherein" with "in which":

> . . . a wheel that perforates the card stock, *wherein* the card stock is held in place during the perforating ...

What does the "wherein" refer to here? In *what* is the card stock held in place? The wheel? The card stock? Neither of these constructions makes any sense. This recitation would be better cast as

> . . . a wheel that perforates the card stock, the card stock being held in place during the perforating . . .

The author has often thought of marketing a novelty item for patent lawyers: a sweatshirt bearing the slogan "Words Matter." The above examples—and others presented in Chapter Twelve—illustrate that they indeed do.

Assume That Input Signals and Data/Parameter Values Are Already in Hand—Don't Generate Them in the Claim

Both apparatus and methods often operate on input signals or may use data values, parameters, measurements, counts of things, and so forth.

When claiming the broad invention, however, it is usually desirable to treat input signals, data/parameter values, and the like as already existing—handed to us by a genie, perhaps—rather than explicitly generating them within the claim. For example, we saw in claim 8.12 how *six* claim steps could be coalesced into *one* claim step by treating the sum that is used to form the data symbol decision as an already existing or available quantity rather than by generating that sum in the claim.

As another example, suppose the invention is the idea of adjusting the output rate of a manufacturing process once the number of widgets produced within the previous hour reaches a certain limit. The invention *could* be defined in two steps—a counting step and an adjusting step:

> 8.19 A method for use in a machine that manufactures widgets, the method comprising
>   counting the number of widgets manufactured in an hour's time, and
>   adjusting the output rate of the machine when the count reaches a predefined limit.

Note, however, that it is irrelevant to the inventive concept *how* the number of widgets manufactured in an hour is determined. Indeed, instead of counting the widgets, the Opposing Team might use the cumulative weight of an hour's output to determine how many widgets were produced and, in so doing, avoid a literal infringement of claim 8.19.

By assuming that the widget count is already in hand and available to the adjusting step, the entire counting step can be eliminated:

> 8.20 A method for use in a machine that manufactures widgets, the method comprising
>   adjusting the output rate of the machine when the number of widgets manufactured within an hour's time reaches a predefined limit.

In a similar vein, we can assume that an originally analog, but now digital, signal operated on within a claim has been handed to us in digital form when the inventive process set forth in the claim begins to operate on the signal. A claim explicitly reciting an analog-to-digital converter or conversion step may well prove to be an unfortunate limitation, as in the following scenario reported to the author:

> "A claim I once litigated called for an analog-to-digital converter to convert analog signals received by a cellular telephone base station into digital form for further processing. The problem was that by the time the patent was in litigation—10 years after it had been filed—no

one was connecting analog lines to base stations anymore; most (or all) telephone lines connected to base stations delivered signals to the base station already in digital form. It was irrelevant to the 'real' invention whether the digital signals were received digitally or converted locally in the base station and so A/D conversion added nothing to the validity of the claim. It just pulled in an extra element that created real problems for us in making out the case for infringement."

—MJF

The reader will recognize how inclusion of the A-to-D converter in the claim of the above story violated any number of the prescriptions set forth in the book, including the prescription *Define, Don't Explain.*[23]

Save Dependent Claim Limitations for the Dependent Claims

Supervising attorneys sometimes encounter a limitation in a trainee's claim that serves no purpose in the claim. When asked why the limitation is there, the trainee may explain, "I need it to support the dependent claim." Claims 8.21 and 8.22 exemplify this. Claim 8.21 is the parent claim on which claim 8.22 is dependent. The parent claim is burdened by a fuel pump limitation that is meaningful only in the dependent claim.

This is a claim-drafting error. A parent claim should not be burdened with limitations needed only to support a dependent claim recitation. Whatever antecedent support is needed for a dependent claim should be put into *that* claim, not its parent. This is a further illustration of the prescription *Pack Only What You Need.*

The fix is incorporated into claims 8.23 and 8.24. Parent claim 8.23 has become unburdened of the fuel pump limitation, which is now totally contained within the dependent claim 8.24.

"Burdened" Parent	"Unburdened" Parent
8.21 An engine comprising a fuel system *including a fuel pump,* and a fuel injector configured to inject first and second types of fuel into the fuel system in such a way that . . .	8.23 An engine comprising a fuel system and a fuel injector configured to inject first and second types of fuel into the fuel system in such a way that . . .
8.22 The invention of claim 8.21 wherein *the fuel pump* includes a diaphragm and wherein at least one of the types of fuel is sprayed onto the diaphragm.	8.24 The invention of claim 8.23 *wherein the fuel system includes a fuel pump,* wherein the fuel pump includes a diaphragm, and wherein at least one of the types of fuel is sprayed onto the diaphragm.

---

23. *See* p. 109.

If it proves awkward to introduce the necessary antecedent support into a dependent claim, the claim can always be written in independent form and the limitation introduced there.

Write the Claim Out of Your Head, Not Off the Drawing

Many practitioners refer to the patent application drawings when drafting claims. This is useful when intermediate- or narrow-scope claims are being drafted[24] since such claims intentionally incorporate embodiment details.

However, the drawings may interfere with the required conceptual thinking that is so desirable when we are drafting broad claims. As Stringham reminds us,[25] an invention is an abstraction, not something tangible. Yet, it is all too easy for the drawings to draw our attention away from the abstract, exposing us to the siren song of the embodiment and its tangible details—details that can unduly narrow a claim.

It is much harder to be attracted to embodiment details when they are not staring up at us from the drawing. Thus the broadest claims should be written directly out of the claim drafter's head. The mind's eye should be able to so clearly see those few functionalities and interrelationships that define the broad invention as to render reference to the drawing unnecessary.

If we find ourselves unable to write the claim without looking at the drawings, it may be time to stop and reengage the invention conceptually. Only when a crystal-clear answer to the question *What Is the Invention?* is in hand should we return to the claim drafting per se. Indeed, the author finds that once the inventive concept is fixed in his mind, the drawings and their details can become an out-and-out distraction from the enjoyable activity of engaging the invention and drafting claims in the purely conceptual realm.

Strive for Simplicity

Simplicity is a key to clarity. Convoluted interrelationships or claim language that is difficult to read through can signal that the invention has not been captured at its essence. Often buried in such a claim are ambiguities or unduly limiting recitations that aren't necessary to the invention.

The architectural philosophy of *form follows function* applies here. A claim whose *form* is clean and simple is more likely to serve the *function* of defining the invention cleanly and simply (read "broadly"). The

---

24. *See* Chapter Nine.
25. *See* p. 5.

hallmark of a well-written claim is one that the inventor can understand without a lot of attorney explanation.

Once it becomes apparent that a claim-in-progress is evolving into an awkward mess, it is best to stop and rethink the approach. Often the culprit is that the limitations are introduced in a less-than-optimal order. Indeed, limitations that had seemed so necessary may simply fall away once the claim elements are rearranged.

Another clue that there is some underlying flaw or untoward assumption about the claim structure is when we find ourselves churning the claim—working and reworking, flip-flopping between certain ways of expressing or arranging the limitations, and being never satisfied with the result. We may have been assuming that a particular element needs to be introduced in the claim before other(s), but that may not be so. Other possibilities are that too much or too little has been placed in the preamble, or that the claim is not being tightly enough focused on the selected invention setting.

There is little point in fighting a recalcitrant claim. Efforts to wrestle it into submission may well prove to be futile in any event. Better to look for that underlying assumption and start over. It can be hard to force ourselves to put on the brakes and abandon a claim when a lot of time has already been invested. It is therefore a good idea to stay alert to the possibility that things are beginning to deteriorate and to regroup sooner rather than later.

Step 5: Use the Problem-Solution Statement as a Benchmark

The problem-solution statement is a benchmark against which all claims can be measured.

Presuming that we intended to write a claim that captures the invention at its broadest, we should assure ourselves that all of the claim's steps, elements, and so forth should really be there. Anything in a claim that does not appear in the problem-solution statement is suspect and should be critically evaluated.

This chapter and the previous chapter provide two approaches to drafting claims that define the invention as broadly as we believe the prior art allows us to. We also need to develop intermediate- and narrow-scope claims to implement a Planned Retreat for the invention because other prior art may lurk in the patent's future. Claims of less than fully broad scope serve other functions, as well. All of that is addressed next.

CHAPTER REVIEW— Inventive-Departure-Based Independent Claims

Confirm Your Understanding

1. What is meant by the statement that "the ideal broad claim is perfectly congruent with the boundaries of the invention"?
2. What are the dangers in defining the broad invention in only one way?
3. What is meant by "inventive departure"?
4. What are the three steps of inventive-departure-based claiming?
5. What are the benefits of writing a claim "backward," i.e., beginning from the inventive departure and then "filling in" the rest of claim afterward?
6. List some ways to identify the inventive departure.
7. An inventive-departure-based claim is fleshed out by adding only so much additional language to the inventive departure as is needed to do two things. What are they?
8. What is meant by "pack only what you need" when drafting a claim?
9. Why is it necessary to closely scrutinize descriptive labels and modifiers when reviewing a claim?
10. What is the danger in a claim reciting (a) advantages or (b) intended uses of the invention?
11. What is the benefit of such claim-drafting constructs as "as a function of" and "in such a way that"?
12. Why is it desirable to minimize the number of structural elements or method steps in a claim?
13. What is the danger in using the following claim limitations?
    a. "generating a video signal" in a claim directed to a video-processing chip
    b. "measuring the temperature inside the oven" in a claim directed to an industrial fabrication method
    c. "summing A and B" in a claim that goes on to do a calculation based on the sum A+B
14. What is the benefit of drafting claims without referring to the drawings as one does so?

Questions for Further Thought

15. What advantages (if any) and disadvantages (if any) do you see in the practice of routinely giving a name of the claimed invention in the preamble, e.g., "An automobile floor mat comprising. . . ."?
16. What are dangers in including claim recitations that state
    a. the advantage of the invention or what it is "good for";
    b. how the recited combination can integrate with the external environment;

    c. motivations (e.g., for doing a particular step or including a particular element);

    d. how to carry out a recited function where the recitation of the function itself imbues the claim with patentability;

    e. how inputs get generated;

    f. the source of something that the claimed method or apparatus works on.

17. Examiners sometimes reject claims containing recitations such as "doing X in such a way that Y happens" (p. 111) on the grounds that a proper claim cannot merely recite a desired object but, rather, must recite the structure or affirmative steps that achieve the object. In what situations might such a rejection be proper? Improper?

18. What is the danger in including a recitation in a parent claim solely for the purpose of providing antecedent support for terminology in a dependent claim?

Sharpen Your Skills

19. Although modifiers (e.g., "foldable," "variable," "concurrently") are often surplusage in a claim, such a modifier may sometimes be the hook for patentability, i.e., it may be the inventive departure. For example, in the first digital watches, the colon between the hours and minutes indications was static and users had no confirmation that their watch was actually running, leading someone to invent the blinking colon, which could have been defined as follows:

> A numeric time display having a blinking indicator between the hours indication and the minutes indication

Sketch out a claim or problem-solution statement for at least three everyday devices or methods that can be distinguished from some assumed prior art using a single modifier.

20. Draft an inventive-departure-based claim for the following inventions using the methodology presented in this chapter. Be particularly mindful of assessing the breadth of the invention when assembling the words that define the inventive departure, including the possibility that the underlying concept might have applicability beyond the specific context of the embodiment, as in the case of the zipper (p. 42).

a. Conference Call Tones

Embodiment

Enter call Leave call

A two-pitch sequence when someone enters or leaves a conference call goes low-to-high when someone joints the call and high-to-low when someone leaves.

Prior Art

Enter call Leave call

The same pitch is used for entering or leaving the call.

---

b. Bicycle Lock

Embodiment

U-style lock

Prior Art

Padlock and chain

---

c. Bubble Pack

Embodiment

Prior Art

Crumpled paper

Packaging "peanuts"

CHAPTER NINE

Intermediate- and Narrow-Scope
Claims

A patent application should be filed not only with claims defining the invention at its broadest, but with claims of intermediate and narrow scope as well. A claim of intermediate scope includes perhaps one, two, or three limitations not required to define the broad invention. A claim of narrow scope includes even more.

Intermediate- and narrow-scope claims serve a number of functions. Most importantly, they implement a Planned Retreat for the invention so that if prior art makes it necessary to retreat from the application's broadest claims, those that remain will have given up as little valuable intellectual property as possible while providing a defensible position for what's left.[1] They can also trigger application of the doctrine of claim differentiation[2] and expand the royalty base.[3] That and other functions of intermediate- and narrow-scope claims are discussed in this chapter.

Fallback Feature Claims

Fallback feature claims are the Planned Retreat's front line of defense and are a mainstay of patent-claiming practice. A fallback feature claim is typically in dependent form and narrows the subject matter of the claim from which it depends—its "parent"—by reciting a feature of the invention that may be relied on for patentability if prior art renders the parent claim unpatentable.

Drafting a set of fallback feature claims is usually straightforward once the fallback features have been identified. Identifying the fallback features themselves is the heart of the matter. Chapter Six presents a problem-solution-based process for doing so. Per that process, the broad invention is regarded as being in the prior art for analysis purposes. A

---

1. *See* pp. 62–63.
2. *See* p. 124.
3. *See* p. 133.

problem-solution analysis is then carried out based on that assumed prior art. The reader may wish to refer back to that discussion at this point.[4]

A fallback feature claim can add its subject matter to its parent claim in various ways, depending on the nature of the feature itself. A fallback feature claim can further limit the subject matter of its parent by (a) adding one or more additional elements to the elements contained in the parent claim, (b) particularizing an already recited element in the parent claim, or (c) particularizing the relationship between already recited elements. Those three alternatives are illustrated by dependent claims 9.2 through 9.4 of the following claim family defining the pencil:

> 9.1 A writing implement comprising
> a rod made of a material that is transferred to a writing surface when the rod is moved across a writing surface, and
> an encasement for the rod.
>
> 9.2 The invention of claim 9.1 further comprising
> an eraser affixed to an end of the writing implement, the eraser being adapted to remove the transferred material from the writing surface when the eraser is rubbed thereon. (Adds an element)
>
> 9.3 The invention of claim 9.1 wherein the rod is made of graphite and the encasement is made of wood. (Particularizes elements)
>
> 9.4 The invention of claim 9.1 wherein the encasement is in the form of a cylinder and the rod is disposed along the central axis of the cylinder. (Particularizes a relationship)

Guidelines for assembling the fallback feature claims (and definition claims[5]) into claim families are presented in Chapter Eleven.

Claim Differentiation Claims

The doctrine of claim differentiation is sometimes advanced as a reason to include claims of intermediate and narrow scope in a patent application. This rule of claim interpretation provides that when an independent claim is limited by recitations in a dependent claim, the first claim must be regarded as being broader.[6] Otherwise the second claim would be superfluous, something that is "presumptively unreasonable."[7] A depen-

---

4. *See* pp. 66–67.

5. *See* Chapter Ten.

6. *See, e.g. In re Tanaka,* 640 F. 3d 1246, 98 USPQ2d 1331 (Fed. Cir. 2011); *Dow Chemical Co. v. United States,* 226 F.3d 1334, 56 USPQ2d 1014 (Fed. Cir. 2000).

7. *Beachcombers, International, Inc. v. WildeWood Creative Products, Inc.,* 31 F.3d 1154, 1161, 31 USPQ2d 1653, 1659 (Fed. Cir. 1994).

dent claim included in a claim family with this doctrine in mind is here referred to as a claim differentiation claim.

Consider, for example, claim 9.6, reciting that the elongated support member (chair leg) of claim 9.5 is cylindrical.

> 9.5. Apparatus comprising
> a seat, and
> a seat support that supports the seat above an underlying surface,
> the seat support including one or more elongated support members.
>
> 9.6 The apparatus of claim 9.5 wherein the one or more elongated support members are cylindrical.

The fact that claim 9.5 has a dependent claim stating that the chair legs are cylindrical supports an argument that claim 9.5 should not be interpreted as being limited to legs that are cylindrical, even if every chair leg disclosed in the specification is cylindrical.

The doctrine of claim differentiation is usually invoked in litigation when the patent owner needs a claim term to be interpreted expansively to make it read on the accused product or process. Anticipating the day when their claims may be litigated, attorneys sometimes include claim differentiation claims in their applications as a way of bolstering the case for a broad interpretation of the claims from which they depend. Such a claim might not otherwise be included in the claim suite if the limitation in question did not constitute a meaningful fallback feature.

There is no harm in having claims of this type in the claim suite. They may not carry the day, however. The doctrine of claim differentiation is only a guide to claim construction, not a rigid rule.[8] Certainly the Opposing Team will argue against the application of the doctrine or at least against the particular interpretation being argued by the patent owner.

A more reliable way of ensuring that claim language is interpreted broadly is to point out explicitly in the specification that certain illustrative details of the embodiments are no more than that—illustrative details—and that there are, or at least may be, alternatives. Even better is to present examples of such alternatives. In the chair example, the specification would explicitly make the point that the chair legs need not be cylindrical:

> Although the elongated support members of the sitting devices disclosed herein are cylindrical, that is, have circular cross sections,

---

8. *ICU Medical, Inc. v. Alaris Medical Systems, Inc.*, 558 F. 3d 1368, 90 USPQ2d 1072 (Fed. Cir. 2009).

other cross sections are possible, including cross sections that are squares or ovals or are nonregular in shape, as well as cross sections that vary in shape along the length of the member.

Independent Embodiment Claims

An independent embodiment claim is a claim in independent form that includes one or more details of the disclosed embodiment(s)—details not included in claims intending to define the invention at its full breadth. As such, an independent embodiment claim necessarily stakes out a more modest parcel of intellectual property than the application's broadest independent claims.

It might seem that there is no need for such claims. After all, we can always include embodiment details in one or more *dependent* claims. However, as we will see, independent embodiment claims can close up potential infringement loopholes, and overcome other problems, that are actually created by claims being in dependent form.

The Question of Breadth

An independent claim reciting specific embodiment details can actually be broader than a dependent claim reciting those same details. The reason is that the details in a dependent claim may render certain limitations in its parent claim(s) redundant. A dependent claim is always burdened

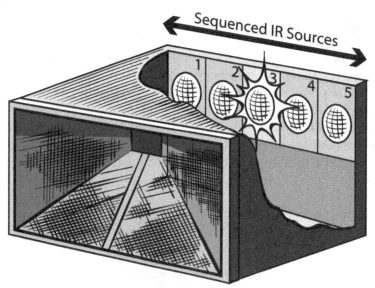

FIGURE 9–1 Snake trap with sequenced infrared sources simulating the movement of prey.

with all of its parent's limitations—redundant or not—and we should take it as a matter of faith that any redundant words in a claim have the potential to narrow it, even if the redundant words seem "harmless enough." Any extra word in a claim can and will be used against you in a court of law.

Functional claim language in the parent claim is often redundant in this way. Such language may serve as the very basis for patentability in the parent claim. It may not, however, be needed in order to distinguish the invention from the prior art once a dependent claim adds specific structural elements that carry out the recited function.

Claim 9.7 is an example of a claim with functional language that may become redundant once certain embodiment details are introduced in a dependent claim. This claim broadly defines an animal trap that lures the animal with an infrared or other electromagnetic energy source that simulates the movement of prey within the trap enclosure. The trap could be used to capture snakes, for example, many of which are able to detect the infrared (heat) energy given off by their prey. See Figure 9–1.

> 9.7 An animal trap comprising:
> an enclosure adapted to trap an animal that enters the enclosure, and
> an energy source that generates electromagnetic energy detectable by the animal, the energy being generated in a way that simulates the movement of prey for the animal within the enclosure.

The assumed prior art includes (a) a trap with a mechanically manipulated lure shaped like a mouse or other prey; and (b) an insect trap having a stationary, visible light source that blinks on and off. Claim 9.7 distinguishes over both because a mechanical lure does not generate electromagnetic energy and a blinking light does not simulate the movement of prey.

Claim 9.7 does not limit the invention to the use of infrared energy, nor to any particular pattern that simulates the movement of prey. Those various embodiment details, rather, are pushed down into dependent claims 9.8 through 9.10.

> 9.8 The apparatus of claim 9.7 wherein the energy of the energy source is substantially all infrared energy.
> 9.9 The apparatus of claim 9.7 wherein the energy source comprises a plurality of individual energy sources that are activated and deactivated in such a way that at least one source is activated while at least one other source is deactivated.
> 9.10 The apparatus of claim 9.9 wherein the individual energy sources are arranged in a line and are activated in sequence along the line.

Now consider independent embodiment claim 9.11. The hook for patentability in this claim is its recitation that the lure comprises a plurality of individual energy sources that go on and off but not all at the same time. This language was lifted directly out of dependent claim 9.9 but, unlike the latter, independent embodiment claim 9.11 is not burdened by claim 9.7's movement-of-prey limitation.

> 9.11 An animal trap comprising:
> an enclosure adapted to trap an animal that enters the enclosure, and
> a plurality of electromagnetic energy sources that are activated and deactivated in such a way that at least one source is activated while at least one other source is deactivated.

Claim 9.11 could prove to be quite valuable. The inventor may have *thought* that her trap worked as well as it did because the infrared pattern was simulating the movement of prey. But a competitor may discover that at least some heat-detecting animals are attracted to apparent changes in the position of the infrared source, whether or not those changes mimic the movement of any real-world creature. The competitor may thus produce a product where the on-and-off pattern is random, arguably avoiding the movement-of-prey limitation called for in claims 9.7 through 9.10. The competitor's random-pattern trap *would*, however, infringe independent embodiment claim 9.11 since that claim says nothing about the movement of prey.

Benefits in Licensing and Litigation

The presence of independent embodiment claims in the issued patent provides benefits beyond their ability to define the invention more broadly than the dependent claims might.

In litigation, for example, judges and juries assessing the validity of a claim may not give separate consideration to the dependent claim limitations, even though they should. Once an independent claim has been found invalid based on prior art, its dependent claims are sometimes declared invalid as a matter of course, improper though that may be. Another possibility is that the limitations in the dependent claims *will* be looked at, but only in isolation, and will be deemed to add nothing nonobvious without the law of nonobviousness being properly brought to bear on the claim as a whole. All in all, then, a litigator's ability to make the case for infringement of an intermediate- or narrow-scope claim may be enhanced by being able to hand to the jury a claim that is self-contained.

Moreover, the dependent claim construct can be confusing to those who do not work with it day in and day out. As a result, jurors may mistakenly import limitations from one dependent claim into another. For example, the fact that claim 9.8 appears ahead of claim 9.9 in the claim family presented above might cause jurors to understand claim 9.9 to include claim 9.8's infrared energy limitation, even though claim 9.9 depends from claim 9.7. Here again, a different result may obtain if claim 9.9 were in independent form.

Additionally, the more independent claims (of all kinds) appearing in a patent, the more time and money a potential licensee or infringer will have to pay her attorney to (a) study the patent's claims and (b) render an infringement and/or validity opinion. The prospective high legal costs may perhaps drive up the minimum license fee that a potential infringer will find palatable.

Balancing Patentability and "Infringeability"

By design, an independent embodiment claim backs off from our broadest view of the invention. The goal, per the philosophy of the Planned Retreat, is to give up a certain amount of claim coverage in exchange for establishing a more secure position of patentability should the broadest claims prove to have been too ambitious.

This is no time to get sloppy, however. The limitations that we include in our less-than-fully-broad claims should still be chosen with care. If the patent's broadest claims prove to be invalid, the patent will be substantially valueless if the remaining claims have no chance of capturing at least some of the commercial marketplace. Yes, we are backing off from our broadest view of the invention. But we should not throw all caution to the wind and just write down whatever comes to mind. An effective independent embodiment claim is one that optimally balances the competing concerns of patentability and "infringeability."

Useful starting points for such claims are intermediate copies of claims and problem-solution statements that arose as the broad ones were being developed. While not achieving the ultimate in breadth, drafts of claims and problem-solution statements will have benefited from an analysis process that eliminated limitations that were deemed particularly unnecessary to the invention. A number of such less-than-fully-broad problem-solution statements appear in Appendix B's account of the author's "real-time" thought processes when analyzing the invention of the backspace key.

Having taken a first cut at an independent embodiment claim, it is desirable to vet the claim to tweak the patentability/infringeability balance. To this end, some of the prescriptions presented in Chapter Eight for keeping undue limitations out of inventive-departure-based claims can be thought about here as well. Most pertinent in this regard are

- Define, Don't Explain[9]
- Use Functional Recitations to Minimize the Number of Claim Elements[10]
- Scrutinize Every Modifier[11]

We would not necessarily apply all of these criteria to all of the claim's limitations; that might result in a claim that defines the invention very broadly, which is not our goal. The point is to make a recitation-by-recitation judgment about where it makes sense to back off to arrive at a claim that has (a) an enhanced probability of distinguishing over the prior art as compared to our broadest claims, while (b) not being *so* specific as to be easily designed around. For example, we would probably still want to call for a "joiner" rather than "a layer of slow-setting epoxy" in all but the intentionally narrowest of claims.

Every claim should be written with a goal in mind. It may be to capture the invention at its full breadth. Or, as here, the goal may be to draft a claim that includes important features of the embodiment(s) while not limiting the defined boundaries *too* much. A claim not expressly derived from the problem-solution statement will inevitably include one or more steps, elements, functions, or interrelationships that the problem-solution statement did not have. Being brought face-to-face with those differences enables the claim drafter to assess whether the claim achieves the intended goal.

Thus, per the philosophy of the Planned Retreat, we can consider each point of difference between our independent embodiment claim and the problem-solution statement and then ask ourselves whether the claim gives up more intellectual property than we had really intended.

Marketed Product Claims

The author uses the term "marketed product claim" to refer to a particular type of independent embodiment claim that can achieve an advantageous balance between patentability and infringeability. A marketed product claim is a claim that includes those embodiment details that are most likely to appear in commercial products embodying the inventive concept. Input from the inventor and/or patent owner is, of course, invaluable in assessing which details those are. If the assessment is correct, it may be difficult for a competitor to design around the claim and still have a saleable product.

---

9. *See* p. 109.
10. *See* p. 112.
11. *See* p. 113.

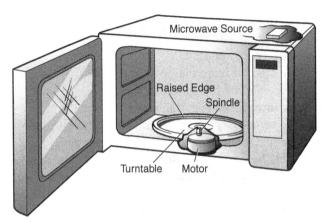

FIGURE 9–2 Microwave oven turntable embodiment serving as the basis for a marketed product claim.

The patent owner's own product, if any, can be a useful guide in this respect. The embodiment details implemented in the patent owner's product represent at least the patent owner's view of those features that are the most desirable to be included in a successful marketplace offering. Such features, then, are more likely than others to also appear in competitors' versions of the product. Certainly a claim that lines up with the patent owner's product will be of value if it is believed that competitors will make an exact knockoff or something very similar to the patent owner's marketed product.

Recall the broad claim 7.4 directed to the preferred embodiment of a way of solving the nonuniform food-heating problem in a microwave oven—namely moving the food around within the oven, or "microwave cavity." That claim is reproduced here as claim 9.12.

> 9.12 Apparatus for heating food comprising
> a microwave cavity, and
> a food support configured to move the food within the cavity while the food is being heated.

A marketed product claim for this invention is claim 9.13, which specifically calls for a turntable as the "food support" and recites two features of the turntable. One feature is that the turntable has a raised edge, which keeps liquids from spilling onto the floor of the enclosure. Another feature is that the turntable is removably supported on a spindle, which allows the turntable to be readily removed from the microwave oven for, say, cleaning. See Figure 9–2.

9.13 A microwave oven comprising
an oven enclosure,
a microwave energy source,
a spindle projecting from the floor of the enclosure,
a motor for rotating the spindle when microwave energy from the
source is being introduced into the enclosure, and
a turntable removably supported on the spindle in such a way that
rotation of the spindle causes rotation of the turntable,
the turntable having an edge that is sufficiently raised to keep liquids
on the turntable from spilling onto the floor of the enclosure.

It is possible to market a microwave oven without those details. But the patent owner might well have been of the opinion that it would be difficult for a competitor to do without them and still sell many microwave ovens.

There are often differences between the patent owner's product and the competitor's version. Thus we do not want to go overboard in packing details into the product claim—particularly since many of those details may not enhance patentability in any event. Rather, we should pursue the goals of the Planned Retreat, undertaking to identify those aspects of the marketed product that are most likely to (a) show up in any commercially practical embodiment of the invention, and (b) enhance the claim's patentability. Some set of the invention's fallback features will typically meet these dual requirements. If more than one set of fallback features seems advantageous in this regard, any number of marketed product claims can be drafted.

Picture Claims

Another type of independent embodiment claim that may prove useful is the *picture claim*. This is a very narrow claim—heavy on structure, light on function, and, most significantly, heavy on the details of a particular disclosed embodiment. The basis for the designation "picture claim" may be that the claim presents a picture of the embodiment—albeit a picture "drawn" in words. Another explanation is that a picture claim is a detailed description of the "picture"—that is, the depiction of the embodiment(s) presented in the patent drawing.

A picture claim is more likely to be allowed than a claim of broader scope; the more limitations a claim has, the less likely it is for there to be prior art that meets them all. On the other hand, a picture claim is usually very easy for a competitor to design around by simply leaving out one of the claim's elements—usually not a difficult task when there are so many elements to choose from. So a picture claim is not likely to be infringed unless the product is a simple one, or unless there is reason to believe that a competitor will slavishly copy the patent owner's product.

On the other hand, by including a picture claim in the patent application, we increase the likelihood that a patent will issue; and just getting a patent, no matter what the breadth of its claims, is sometimes the patent owner's goal.

Maximized Royalty Base Claims

Beyond their role in the Planned Retreat, claims of intermediate and narrow scope can add to the economic value of the patent.

Patent royalties and damages are based on the market value of whatever is encompassed by the claims, this being referred to as the "royalty base." If the claimed invention is a new type of spring usable in ballpoint pens, but all the claims in the patent limit themselves to the spring itself, the royalty base will be the value of the infringing springs.[12] Obviously, the patent owner would rather have a royalty based on the entire value of the pens that include the new spring. The claim drafter would do well, then, to include at least one claim that recites the improved spring in combination with the pen in which it is intended to be used. A claim introduced into a patent application for this express purpose is referred to herein as a "maximized royalty base claim."

There is no guarantee that a court will use the market value of the entire claimed combination when computing damages or lost profits. Common sense says that the owner of an altimeter patent is not going to be awarded royalties or damages based on the combined value of the altimeter and the jet liner in which it is installed, even if the patent includes a claim to that combination. Suffice it to say that whenever it can be plausibly argued that significant cooperation and interdependence exists, it can only help to include claims that define the inventive steps or elements in its likely commercial environment(s), thereby providing the patent owner with the opportunity to argue for the larger royalty base.

Maximized royalty base claims can be either in independent form or dependent form. The latter may prove awkward, however. For example, having started out with a claim directed to a spring, it may prove tricky to add a dependent claim having limitations directed to the pen in which the spring is used. Claiming the pen-spring combination in independent claim form avoids such difficulties.

---

12. Under the right circumstances, pursuant to the so-called entire market value rule, the royalty base may be deemed to extend beyond that which is encompassed by the claims. *See, generally, Uniloc USA, Inc. v. Microsoft Corp.*, 632 F. 3d 1292, 98 USPQ2d 1203 (Fed. Cir. 2011).

Claims of intermediate and narrow scope protect and/or enhance the claim suite's broadest claims in various ways. As we have just seen, these include implementing the Planned Retreat to account for new cited prior art disclosing the inventive concept, maximizing the issued patent's royalty base; and possibly setting the stage for a claim-differentiation argument.

There are at least two other contingencies that claims also need to be protected against. One is that a claim may read on prior art that does *not* disclose the inventive concept. Another contingency is that a claim may be deemed indefinite. Those contingencies are addressed with so-called definition claims—the subject of the next chapter.

CHAPTER REVIEW—Intermediate- and Narrow-Scope Claims

Confirm Your Understanding

1. What is a claim of intermediate scope? Narrow scope? What functions do such claims serve?
2. What is a fallback feature claim?
3. What are three ways that recitations in a fallback feature claim can be used to limit a parent claim?
4. What is the danger in relying on a claim differentiation claim to ensure that a parent claim is interpreted with the intended breadth?
5. Why is it desirable to include independent embodiment claims in the overall claim suite, given that one can always include embodiment details in one or more dependent claims?
6. What does it mean to balance patentability and "infringeability" when drafting an independent embodiment claim?
7. What are "marketed product" claims and how do they contribute to the goals of the Planned Retreat?

Questions for Further Thought

8. The book asserts that every claim should be written with a goal in mind. How many such "goals" can you think of?
9. The drafting of maximized royalty base claims is an example of preparing a patent application with licensing and/or litigation in mind. In what other ways should the composition of the overall claim suite be guided by licensing and/or litigation considerations?

Sharpen Your Skills

10. Draft an independent embodiment claim for the vehicular air bag.
    a. A broad independent claim for this invention is provided below, along with a narrative describing various features of the inventor's embodiment that can be looked to for supplying details for the independent embodiment claim.
    b. Explain why you chose the particular features you included in the independent embodiment claim.

    Broad Independent Claim

    1. An occupant-restraining device for a vehicle, comprising

    an inflatable cushion, and

    an inflation mechanism configured to inflate the cushion in response to a rapid deceleration of the vehicle.

Embodiment Details

The vehicle is an automobile and the air bag, or "cushion," is so positioned, and is of such a size, as to restrain movement of an occupant of the vehicle at the time of impact (or other rapid deceleration) and inflation of the cushion.

The cushion has a mouth that is affixed to a support frame that, in turn, is affixed to the steering wheel of the automobile. The cushion is made of nylon, neoprene, polyester, or rayon and has a volume of about 3 to 3.5 cubic feet when fully inflated. Small holes in the cushion allow it to deflate almost immediately after being inflated so as to minimize the severity of the impact of the occupant against the cushion.

Mounted within a suitable housing within the automobile is a weight whose momentum causes the weight to be displaced forwardly when deceleration of the automobile is sufficiently rapid as to potentially cause injury to the occupant. The displacement of the weight closes an electrical switch. This causes an igniting signal to be generated.

Responsive to the igniting signal, a three-stage pyrotechnic system generates a volume of propellant gas that inflates the cushion within 1/10 second. The pyrotechnic system comprises (a) an igniter charge that is set off by the igniting signal, (b) an enhancer charge that is set off by the igniting charge and that generates sufficient heat to set off, (c) a heat-responsive propellant charge that generates the propellant gas.

The igniting charge, enhancer charge, and propellant charge are, respectively, (a) a mixture of zirconium and potassium perchlorate, (b) a mixture of boron and potassium nitrate, and (c) sodium azide.

The amount of propellant gas that is generated is proportional to the severity of the collision so as to minimize injury to the occupant from the cushion itself. The volume of the cushion when inflated is also proportional to the severity of the collision. The latter feature is implemented by providing a fold in the cushion that is secured with breakaway stitching. The breakaway stitching fails at higher propellant gas pressures.

CHAPTER TEN

Definition Claims

A fallback feature claim stakes out a more limited parcel of intellectual property than its parent. As we saw in the previous chapter, the contingency being guarded against is that prior art teaching of the subject matter intended to be captured by the parent claim may surface after the patent application is filed, rendering the parent claim unpatentable or invalid. A fallback feature claim intentionally retreats from the boundaries defined by its parent claim to a narrower but possibly more patentably secure position, as depicted in Figure 10–1. The author refers to such prior art as "invention-relevant" prior art because not only does the parent claim read on it, but the prior art actually discloses what the inventor thought *she* had invented.

This chapter discusses another important type of claim, referred to as a definition claim. Like fallback feature claims, definition claims are typically in dependent form. Unlike fallback feature claims, however, definition claims are not intended to retreat from what the inventor regarded as her invention. Rather, a definition claim defines more specifically the invention boundaries that were intended all along, as also depicted in

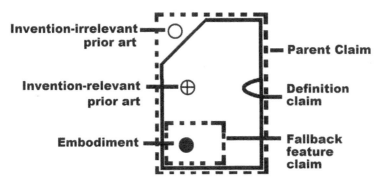

FIGURE 10–1 Fallback feature claims and definition claims address different kinds of prior art.

Figure 10–1. A definition claim thereby addresses two types of potential deficiencies in the parent claim not addressed by fallback feature claims.

One of the potential deficiencies addressed by a definition claim is that the parent claim may read on prior art that does not disclose the inventive concept. The author refers to such prior art as "invention-irrelevant" prior art. The other potential deficiency is that the parent claim may be indefinite under 35 U.S.C. 112(a) because either the parent claim itself or a claim that the parent claim depends from contains indefinite terminology.

Almost anything added to a claim narrows it to a greater or lesser degree. A definition claim thus narrows the subject matter called for in its parent. But in contrast to a fallback feature claim, the subject matter that a definition claim "gives up" is not anything we ever regarded as part of the invention.

Parent Claim Potentially Reads on Invention-Irrelevant Prior Art

We first explain the use of a definition claim to anticipate the possibility that a parent claim may read on invention-irrelevant prior art, that is, prior art that does not disclose the inventive concept. Claim 10.1 is such a claim, reciting the combination of a bimetallic switch with a doodad.

> 10.1 Apparatus comprising
> a bimetallic switch, and
> a doodad connected to the bimetallic switch.

In this claim, the term "bimetallic switch" is intended to refer to a known type of electrical switch made up of two strips of metal having different coefficients of expansion, such as the alloys brass and Invar. Such a switch will bend in response to changes in temperature and is widely used in thermostats. The inventor has discovered that adding a doodad to such a switch improves its sensitivity to temperature changes.

To see how a definition claim functions differently from a fallback feature claim, let us first consider how a fallback feature claim might function for this invention.

Figure 10–2(a) posits the existence of prior art teaching what the inventor thought that *she* was the first to come up with—a two-strip switch that bends with temperature changes, connected with a doodad. There is no hope for a claim as broad as claim 10.1 in this situation. Patentability will have to be predicated on a fallback position defined by a fallback feature claim. Claim 10.2 is such a claim, calling for the (assumedly inventive) addition of a "gizmo" to the subject matter of claim 10.1.

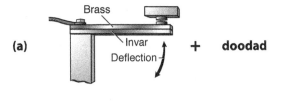

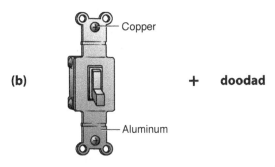

FIGURE 10–2 Two pieces of prior art, each disclosing a "bimetallic switch" in combination with a doodad.

10.2 The apparatus of claim 10.1 further comprising a gizmo connected to the doodad.

By contrast, Figure 10–2(b) posits the existence of certain invention-irrelevant prior art that claim 10.1 also reads on. The dictionary defines "bimetallic" as "consisting of two metals." Therefore, *any* switch made from two kinds of metal is a "bimetallic switch," broadly speaking. Figure 10–2(b) shows such a wall switch—made of copper and aluminum—combined with a doodad. This prior art also anticipates claim 10.1.

Unlike the first case, however, the wall-switch prior art does not anticipate the inventive concept. Indeed, the inventor never intended her claim to encompass the wall-switch arrangement, which doesn't exhibit the problem she set out to solve and certainly does not solve it.

Establishing a position of patentability in *this* situation does *not* require falling back to a more limited parcel of intellectual property, such as the subject matter defined by "gizmo" claim 10.2. The boundaries defined by claim 10.1 are *just fine* if only the term "bimetallic switch" is firmed up to say what was meant by that term all along. There is no need to retreat from the intended claim boundaries—just to clarify them.

Claim 10.3 is a definition claim that addresses this situation, defining the term "bimetallic switch" in the sense that the inventor always intended, thereby excluding the wall-switch prior art.

> 10.3 The invention of claim 10.1 wherein the bimetallic switch comprises at least a pair of substantially overlapping metal strips having different coefficients of expansion.

Claim 10.3 is not a fallback feature claim, because it does not retreat from the intended boundaries of the parent claim 10.1. It simply makes clearer what those boundaries were always intended to be.

Parent Claim Is Potentially Indefinite

Let us now consider the second function of definition claims—anticipating the possibility that the parent claim may be indefinite. This is a violation of § 112(b)'s requirement of claiming the invention "distinctly." A claim is indefinite if the public cannot determine with reasonable certainty what the boundaries of the claimed subject matter are.[1] The so-called notice function of a patent's claims means that potential infringers have to be able to determine whether their actual or contemplated products will be covered by the claim or not.[2] The definiteness requirement is no mere formality. A claim that is indefinite is invalid.[3]

Examples of potentially indefinite terms are the italicized words in the following recitations: *high-resolution* filter; *intelligent* processor; *vigorous* agitation; *quick* and *ready* access; *acceptable* level of pliability. After all, how much resolution is *high* resolution? When is a processor *intelligent*? How vigorous is *vigorous* agitation? What level of pliability is *acceptable*?

Recitations like these often seem perfectly fine to the claim drafter. He knows what he means. Or least he thinks he does. But the examiner (and later, the Opposing Team) may assert that such terms are indefinite.

Claim 10.4 is an example of a potentially indefinite claim making reference to the "complexity" of an algorithm:

1. *See, e.g., Power-One, Inc. v. Artesyn Technologies, Inc.,* 599 F. 3d 1343, 94 USPQ2d 1241 (Fed. Cir. 2010); *In re Borkowski,* 422 F.2d 904, 164 USPQ 642 (CCPA 1970).

2. *See, e.g., Praxair, Inc. v. Atmi, Inc.,* 543 F. 3d 1306, 88 USPQ2d 1705 (Fed. Cir. 2008).

3. *See, e.g., Honeywell Int'l, Inc. v. Int'l Trade Comm'n,* 341 F.3d 1332, 68 USPQ2d 1023 (Fed. Cir. 2003).

10.4 The invention of claim 1 wherein the complexity of the first
algorithm is much less than the complexity of the second algorithm.

How does one assess the complexity of an algorithm? Is it the number of steps or branch points? The level of the sophistication of its underlying mathematics? The time required to execute it? And what level of complexity would satisfy the claim's "much less" recitation? Absent an explicit definition in the specification, e.g.,

as used in this specification and in the claims, the complexity of an
algorithm is measured by the time required for its execution

these are unanswerable questions, which is what probably makes this claim indefinite.

Yet another example of a potentially indefinite term is the word "elongated" in chair claim 6.1, reproduced here as claim 10.5.

10.5 Apparatus comprising
a seat, and
a seat support that supports the seat above an
underlying surface,
the seat support including one or more elongated
support members.

FIGURE 10–3
When is a chair
leg "elongated"?

What minimum length-to-thickness ratio makes a chair leg elongated? As a chair leg gets shorter and shorter, it becomes increasingly unclear as to whether it is "elongated" or not. See Figure 10–3.

Claim 10.6 is a definition claim that addresses the potential indefiniteness of claim 10.5. It defines "elongated" to mean having a length-to-thickness ratio of at least 3 to 1.

10.6 The invention of claim 10.5 wherein each support member has
a length-to-thickness ratio of at least 3 to 1.

That definition of "elongated" should, of course, also appear in the specification as being at least the preferred minimum length-to-thickness ratio.

It is not crucial to distinguish between terminology that may be indefinite ("elongated") and terminology that might cause a claim to read on invention-irrelevant prior art ("bimetallic"). We simply need to focus on each word or phrase in a claim and consider whether either situation may obtain. The two questions to be asked are

1. Might certain terminology encompass more than what we intend?
2. Could it be argued that the terminology is so indefinite that the public cannot discern the boundaries of the claimed subject matter?

If the answer to either question is yes, serious consideration should be given to drafting a definition claim that backstops the terminology in question.

Questions and Answers

Since a definition claim defines what we meant all along, why not put the definition into the parent claim at the outset and not bother with a separate definition claim?

There is always a danger that a definition will be more restrictive than we might have contemplated, thereby giving up claim coverage that we didn't intend to give up. The wall-switch prior art shown in Figure 10–2(b) may not actually exist, in which case independent claim 10.1 would be patentable. Keeping the broad term "bimetallic switch" in independent claim 10.1 and establishing a backup position by defining that term in definition claim 10.3 covers both contingencies.

Virtually any word or phrase has the potential to be interpreted in an unanticipated way. Isn't it impractical to backstop every term with a definition claim?

Yes, it is impractical. The key is to identify terms that intuition and experience say are more likely to need backstopping than others. Terms that are the most crucial for patentability should get particular attention. Patentability of claims 10.1 and 10.5 hinges solely on the terms "bimetallic" and "elongated," respectively. Definition claims that explicitly define those terms are definitely called for.

Rather than including definition claims in the application when first filed, why not wait to see what prior art the examiner has found and then amend the pending claims to define a term during prosecution if this proves necessary?

Amending a claim during prosecution may not be possible if the definition to be relied on is not at least implicit in the specification as filed. Focusing at the outset on the possibility that we may need to rely on a definition claim sometime after the application is filed ensures that appropriate definitions are included in the specification in the first instance.

Moreover, the issue may not come up during prosecution, but only afterward—during a licensing negotiation or a litigation—when it is too late to amend the claims.

———————

This chapter and the previous chapter make clear the crucial role served by claims that are often written in dependent form—notably fallback feature claims and definition claims. But so far, we've talked about these claims mostly in isolation. They must be somehow assembled into claim families, with each dependent claim of the family being dependent from either the family's independent claim or another one of the dependent claims. The number of combinations and permutations is usually too large to include them all. A principled approach to assembling the dependent claims is our next topic.

CHAPTER REVIEW—Definition Claims

Confirm Your Understanding

1. What is the difference between a fallback feature claim and a definition claim?
2. What are the two main functions served by definition claims?
3. What is meant by the terms "invention-relevant" prior art and "invention-irrelevant" prior art?
4. Which provisions of 35 U.S.C. motivate the inclusion of definition claims in the overall claim suite?
5. What are the two main considerations in deciding whether to include a definition claim in the overall claim suite?

Questions for Further Thought

6. Consider the thermostat example in this chapter (p. 138). Does the duty of candor imposed by 37 CFR 1.56 require citation of the wall switch prior art if we knew about it at the time of filing?
7. Claim language is supposed to be interpreted in light of the specification. *Phillips v. AWH Corp.*, 415 F.3d 1303, 75 USPQ2d 1321 (Fed. Cir. 2005) (en banc); *Bancorp Servs., L.L.C. v. Hartford Life Ins. Co.*, 359 F.3d 1367, 69 USPQ2d 1996 (Fed. Cir. 2004). Why, then, are we concerned about (a) claim terms being interpreted in irrelevant ways that bear no relationship to their use in the specification (e.g., "bimetallic" switch (p. 138)), or (b) claim terms being deemed indefinite if one could go to the specification to divine their meaning?

Sharpen Your Skills

8. Explain why the <u>underlined</u> terms in the following claim phrases are prime candidates for being backstopped with a definition claim.

Claim Phrase	Disclosed Embodiment
determining if said parameter is greater than a predetermined <u>industry-standard value</u>	Parameter in question is specified in the MPEG-4 audio/video compression standard
eliminating the <u>most expensive</u> data lines from said list	The data lines in question are particularly prone to malfunctioning, thereby engendering a lot of expense to continually monitor and repair them
processing said data if it is in a <u>predetermined pattern</u>	The predetermined pattern is 001100110011...

Claim Phrase	Disclosed Embodiment
said adhesive being <u>superior to</u> rubber cement	Claimed adhesive does not lose its holding power over time as does rubber cement
a <u>car</u> capable of <u>traversing</u> a railroad track	Automobile outfitted with railroad wheels so that it can travel on railroad tracks
<u>aesthetically pleasing</u> user interface	The user interface uses a color palette that people in focus groups said was pleasing to them
<u>interleaving</u> the bits of said bytes	byte 1: 00000000 byte 2: 11111111 interleaved bits: 0101010101010101
said structure comprising <u>brick or like material</u>	Specification discloses brick and cinder block as possible materials for the structure
<u>translated</u> software	The software in question has been translated from the computer language Java to the computer language C++

CHAPTER ELEVEN

Assembling the Dependent Claims

A claim, be it in independent or dependent form, may recite any number of features, each worthy of a fallback feature claim.[1] It may also include any number of terms, each worthy of being backstopped by a definition claim.[2]

How are all these claims to be arranged? They could all be made to depend as peers from the parent claim. Or they could be strung out in a chain, each claim depending from the next. Mix-and-match combinations of these are also possible. The number of claims required to cover all the possibilities is usually prohibitive, however, and so choices need to be made. This chapter presents guidelines for making those choices and, in so doing, implementing a successful Planned Retreat for the invention.

The Chaining Dilemma

Figure 11–1(A) depicts a claim family comprising claims 1–4. The broad invention is claimed in independent claim 1. A terminology definition X is recited in dependent claim 2. Fallback features A and B are recited in

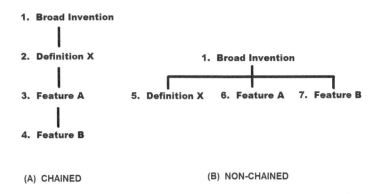

(A) CHAINED

(B) NON-CHAINED

FIGURE 11–1 Dependent claims can be chained or nonchained.

1. *See* Chapter Six.
2. *See* Chapter Ten.

claims 3 and 4, respectively.[3] This is referred to as a claim chain because the claims are linked one to the next. Claim 4 depends from claim 3, which depends from claim 2, which depends from claim 1.

Figure 11–1(B) depicts a claim family in which the same dependent claims are arranged as peers in a nonchained arrangement. Claims 5, 6, and 7 are identical to claims 2, 3, and 4, respectively, except that claims 5, 6, and 7 all depend from claim 1 instead of being dependent from one another.

The nonchained approach of Figure 11–1(B) maximizes the possibility that a competitor's product will infringe at least one valid claim of the claim family. If claim 1 proves to be invalid, infringement occurs as long as the competitor's product includes any *one* of the limitations X, A, and B in conjunction with the limitations of claim 1. For example, claim 6 is infringed as long as the competitor's product includes fallback feature A in conjunction with the limitations of claim 1. If the product also meets limitations X or B, then that many more claims are infringed.

The chained approach of Figure 11–1(A), by contrast, does *not* maximize the possibility that a competitor's product will infringe at least one valid claim of the family. A competitor's product that does not meet terminology definition X will not infringe any of the dependent claims, even if that product includes features A or B, because claims 2, 3, and 4 each incorporate terminology definition X. If claim 1 were to be invalid in *this* situation, this family would contain *no* claim that is both valid and infringed.

The chained approach does have an advantage, however. It provides more robust protection against unforeseen prior art or indefiniteness. Claim 4, for example, encompasses not only its own limitations but those of claims 1 through 3. With the nonchained approach of Figure 11–1(B), by contrast, none of the dependent claims benefit from the potentially enhanced patentability afforded by the others.

If the total number of fallback features and terminology definitions is small, we can cover all bases with a reasonably small number of claims. In that case, the "chain-or-not-chain" (aka the "wide-or-deep") problem goes away. For example, Figure 11–2 shows that only seven dependent claims are required to cover all ways of combining any one or more of limitations X, A, and B with the limitations of claim 1.

The number of possible combinations doubles for each additional claim, however. Accommodating all the combinations of four, five, or six fallback feature claims and/or definition claims within a single claim

---

3. A particular claim may recite more than one fallback feature or terminology definition. For simplicity, this discussion assumes that is not the case.

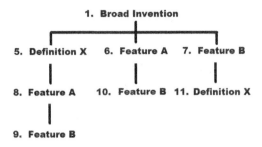

FIGURE 11–2 Seven dependent claims cover all possible combinations of three limitations with an independent claim.

family could require as many as 15, 31, and 63 dependent claims, respectively, although the actual number would probably be smaller since some limitations make sense only when tied in to others. Moreover, it is usually desirable for the overall claim suite to include multiple claim families in order to (a) define the broad invention in more than one way,[4] (b) present the invention in various settings,[5] and (c) employ various statutory claim types.[6] The potential number of claims could thus be quite large. And since the Patent and Trademark Office assesses a fee for each claim beyond a certain number, the filing fees could quickly mount up.

The expense may be justified if the invention is important enough. In the typical case, however, judicious choices need to be made to keep the claim count to a reasonable number. Those choices should be made based primarily on the goals of the Planned Retreat. If retreat to narrower claims becomes necessary, those claims should give up as little valuable intellectual property as possible while establishing a defensible position for what's left. A claim that does not further the Planned Retreat goals or serve some other purpose—such as reciting a terminology definition or serving as a maximized royalty-based claim—is probably superfluous.

Inherent in the Planned Retreat philosophy are two competing considerations: Any word added to a claim has the potential to contract its scope and create an infringement loophole. But that very same contraction in scope may be needed to establish a position of patentability if claims that are broader are found to read on the prior art.

Those competing considerations are effectively balanced by following the guidelines discussed in the sections below.

---

4. *See* p. 243.
5. *See* pp. 211–217.
6. *See* Chapter Fifteen.

- Claims independently imparting patentability to a (dependent or independent) parent claim should be nonchained relative to one another.
- Claims imparting patentability to a parent claim in combination should be chained with one another.
- Claims not imparting patentability to a parent claim in combination should not be chained with one another.
- Claims serving no function should be avoided altogether.
- Claims should be positioned within the claim family hierarchy based on their contribution to the Planned Retreat.

Claims Independently Imparting Patentability Should Be Nonchained

Each significant fallback feature should be recited in a dependent claim that depends directly from the parent claim being backed up.

In the example of Figure 11–3, parent (in this case, independent) claim 1 is directed to a printing-ink formulation believed to be novel and nonobvious. There are two fallback features—an additive that promotes quick drying of the ink and a unique blue colorant (pigment). Both the additive and the colorant are believed to be inventive in combination with the basic printing-ink formulation recited in claim 1. Each of those features thus provides an effective position of retreat should the broad ink formulation turn out to be in the prior art. The nonchained approach is appropriate here because a potential infringer might use the quick-drying additive without the colorant, or vice versa. Thus, as shown in Figure 11–3, claims 2 and 3 directed to these features each depend

FIGURE 11–3 Claims reciting features independently enhancing patentability of the broad invention should each depend directly from the independent claim, as should any claims defining terminology in that claim.

directly from the parent claim 1. Claims 2 and 3 are each defensible positions of retreat. We would therefore not want to only chain these features by, for example, making claim 3 dependent from claim 2. To do so would be to give up potentially valuable intellectual property unnecessarily.

Similar considerations apply to definition claim 4. Claim 1 might recite, for example, that the printing ink is "viscous." The term is potentially indefinite. The printing-ink industry does distinguish between printing inks that are relatively resistant to flow at one extreme and those that are relatively less resistant to flow at the other—the latter presumably being the "viscous" ones. But how could one know whether any particular ink between those two viscosity extremes is or is not "viscous?" Definition claim 4 puts some boundaries on the term "viscous" by defining it as a particular viscosity range, for example, "between 300 and 400 centipoises." By depending directly from claim 1, definition claim 4 protects the broad subject matter of claim 1 from possible invalidity based on indefiniteness.

Of course, a claim defining "viscous" could also be chained with claims 2 and/or 3 in order to also protect *those* claims from the possible indefiniteness of the term "viscous" inherited from their parent claim 1. The desirability of such mixing and matching is discussed below.

Claims Imparting Patentability in Combination Should Be Chained

Claims reciting features that would not be obvious to combine with each other and the parent claim subject matter should be chained. Such claims should also be presented in nonchained form if they appear to be independently novel and nonobvious.

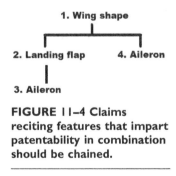

FIGURE 11–4 Claims reciting features that impart patentability in combination should be chained.

This is the situation depicted in Figure 11–4 for a family of claims directed to the airplane wing of Figure 11–5. The inventor of this wing has discovered that the particular aileron and landing flap configurations that she used in her prototype affect the wing's flying characteristics that would be unexpected, even if the aileron and landing flap configurations were to have been individually known, providing an argument for the nonobviousness of the combination of the aileron and the landing flap with the broad wing shape.[7] Claim 3 of this claim family combines all three elements.

The inventor also believes that the aileron and landing flap configurations independently enhance the patentability of the basic wing shape. As a result, those features are set forth in respective fallback feature claims 2 and 4, each depending directly from independent claim 1.

Although claims 3 and 4 are both directed to the aileron feature, each serves a useful function for this invention's Planned Retreat. Aileron claim 4 gives up less intellectual property real estate than aileron claim 3 does. Claim 3, on the other hand, establishes a potentially more secure position of retreat because we have an argument as to the nonobviousness of combining the aileron and the landing flap with the broad wing shape.

Claims Not Imparting Patentability in Combination Should Not Be Chained

When no unexpected results or other indicium of nonobviousness arises from the combination of particular features, chaining them is not going to achieve much from a patentability standpoint. We should *separately* claim each feature in combination with the parent claim and be done with it. If

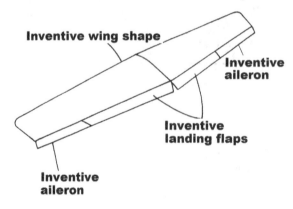

Inventive wing shape

Inventive aileron

Inventive landing flaps

Inventive aileron

FIGURE 11–5 Wing with an inventive shape having two fallback features—an inventive type of aileron and an inventive type of landing flap.

---

7. *Graham v. John Deere Co.*, 383 U.S. 1, 148 USPQ 459 (1966) (unexpected results is a factor to be used in assessing obviousness).

the effect of the aileron on the performance of the wing of Figure 11–5 is the same no matter what landing flap is used (and vice versa), then claim 3 is superfluous from the Planned Retreat point of view.

Specifically, if the wing-shape-plus-aileron combination were not known or obvious, then we could always retreat to aileron claim 4. Claim 3 would be superfluous because claim 4 would be a better position to retreat to, given that claim 3 also requires the wing to have the recited landing flap. Claim 3 is also superfluous if, on the other hand, the wing-shape-plus-aileron combination *were* known or obvious because under the facts assumed above, the patentability of the wing-shape-plus-landing-flap-combination recited in claim 2 would not be enhanced by adding the aileron to the combination.

Claims Serving No Function Should Be Avoided Altogether

A claim that serves no function in a claim family should not be included in the patent application. This statement may seem self-evident, but it needs to be said. In practice, patent applications routinely include claims that serve no useful function whatsoever.

Consider, for example, claims 11.1 and 11.2 directed to a bottle cap.

11.1 A bottle cap comprising

(a) . . .

(b) . . . , and

(c) . . .

wherein the cap includes an array of parallel ribs on the side of the cap and parallel to its central axis.

11.2 The bottle cap of claim 11.1 wherein there are 122 of said ribs.

The recitation in dependent claim 11.2 that the bottle cap has exactly 122 ribs is not a defensible position of retreat. Ribbed bottle caps are in the prior art, and the exact number of ribs is a matter of design choice. Therefore, any number of ribs—including 122—is obvious, assuming no "unexpected results" derive from having exactly 122 ribs. If the parent claim 11.1 proves to be unpatentable or invalid based on prior art, claim 11.2 will fall right along with it. Moreover, such a claim constricts the claimed subject

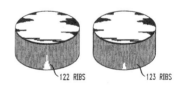

FIGURE 11–6 Absent unexpected results, a dependent claim reciting that a bottle cap has a particular number of ribs serves no useful function and can readily be done away with.

matter to such a small realm as to have virtually no value. It is easy enough for others to manufacture a cap with some other number of ribs. We can see, then, that claim 11.2 achieves neither goal of the Planned Retreat—it gives up a lot and is not a defensible place to fall back to in any event.

**FIGURE 11–7
Claim 3 is limited
to black ink for
no good reason.**

Similarly, the patentability of a ballpoint pen invention is not enhanced by a dependent claim reciting that the ink is black. It is obvious that the ink in any ballpoint pen can be black. Such a claim, then, is not a defensible position of retreat; if the parent claim falls, its black ink dependent claim falls right along with it.

Indeed, the black ink claim can be downright harmful if other claims depending from it *do* serve some function but do not appear elsewhere in the overall claim suite without being burdened by the ink-is-black limitation. Consider the claim family in Figure 11–7. If prior art makes it necessary to retreat from the basic ink formulation recited in claim 1, it will be necessary to retreat down through black-ink dependent claim 2 to inventive quick-drying additive claim 3. Claim 3 stakes out a defensible position of retreat, but that position is limited, for no good reason, to inks that are black.

An old saw has it that "when a dog bites a man, that's not news," which is to say that there is nothing new in what is ordinary or expected. By analogy, it is not "news" when

> . . . said ink is black;
> . . . said computer is a laptop;
> . . . said form of payment is a debit card; or
> . . . said window has a fixed sash.

Claims of this type are almost always superfluous.

Position Claims Within the Claim Family Hierarchy Based on Their Contribution to the Planned Retreat

The preceding guidelines use the philosophy of the Planned Retreat to help us decide whether or not claims should be chained relative to one another. We still need to decide, however, where a given claim or sub-chain ought to appear within the overall claim family hierarchy.

Here again the philosophy of the Planned Retreat is our guide.

A claim should appear relatively high up in the claim family when the claim's subject matter (a) is likely to show up in others' embodiments and (b) seems likely to add patentability based on prior art and/or definiteness concerns. The stronger those likelihoods, the higher in the claim family the claim ought to appear. Conversely, a claim should appear in a relatively low position in the claim family when it meets only one or neither of these criteria.

Here is the guideline in bullet form:

1. Position a claim relatively high in the claim family hierarchy based on the extent to which
   - the subject matter of the claim is believed likely to be incorporated in practical commercial embodiments;
   - the subject matter of the claim is believed likely to support patentability;
   - a term defined by the claim is seen as being vulnerable to attack as being indefinite; and/or
   - a term defined by the claim is seen as potentially excluding invention-irrelevant prior art that may show up downstream.
2. Position a claim relatively low in the claim family hierarchy based on the extent to which the above criteria are not met.

A useful way of implementing this approach is to stop at each point in the process of assembling a claim family and ask, *What is the next most important thing to say?* It might be a particular fallback feature, or it might be a particular terminology definition. Whatever that next most important thing to say happens to be, it is the next claim to be added to the claim family in process.

To the extent that we are dealing with fallback feature claims, the question *What is the next most important thing to say?* is readily answered by a mix-and-match approach guided by the philosophy of the Planned Retreat.[8] What mostly remains is to slot in the definition claims.

As an example, Figure 11–8 is a graphical representation of the claim structure of the Planned Retreat that was developed in Chapter Six for the "elongated support," or "chair" invention[9] (with the claims augmented with definition claims as discussed below). We were concerned in Chapter Six only with the fallback features. But a further concern is that the word "elongated" is potentially indefinite and could cause the broad independent claim 1 to be declared invalid.

---

8. *See* Chapter Six.
9. *See* p. 69.

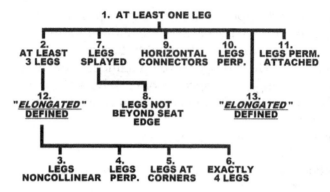

FIGURE 11–8 A mix-and-match approach may be required to cover the important combinations of limitations.

The claim family represented in Figure 11–8 thus includes two definition claims—actually the same definition claim presented in two locations within the claim hierarchy. The definition claim in question, appearing as claims 12 and 13, defines what is meant by the word "elongated," e.g.,

The apparatus of claim 1 wherein each elongated element has a length-to-thickness ratio of at least 3 to 1.

We had decided that we don't want to put a definition of "elongated" directly into claim 1 because a definition always has the potential to limit a claim in unintended ways. Yet we would hate to lose the broad invention to indefiniteness or to invention-irrelevant prior art in which the support members were deemed to be "elongated" even though they were just a tiny bit longer than wide. Thus defining "elongated" is probably every bit as important to say as any particular fallback position, even though there is some potential for a slight loss of coverage due to the 3-to-1 ratio. As shown in Figure 11–8, then, our definition of "elongated" is presented in a claim 13 that depends directly from independent claim 1.

Where else might it be important to define what "elongated" means?

Claim 2, which recites that there are at least three elongated support members, probably covers most of what the chair inventor envisioned as being the important commercial marketplace. And we are somewhat concerned that a rudimentary seating device with an elongated support member as shown in Figure 6–5[10] might actually turn up the prior art, thereby invalidating both claims 1 and 13 and leaving claim 2 as the broadest allowable claim. Since claim 2 inherits claim 1's potential indefiniteness problem vis-à-vis "elongated," it is probably desirable to back-stop claim 2 with a definition claim as well, shown as claim 12.

Beyond this, the question of where else the definition of "elongated" should be slotted is less clear-cut. Claims 7 to 11 also inherit claim 1's potential indefiniteness. Should they also be backstopped with a definition claim? Or perhaps made to depend from claim 13? Claims 3 through 6 are "saved" from any indefiniteness problem since they depend from definition claim 12. But there's always the possibility that the definition in claim 12 will turn out to be limiting in a way that we hadn't anticipated, thereby potentially contracting the scope of claims 3 to 6 unduly. Are further claims that mix and match the fallback feature claims and definition claims thus called for?

Each case is *sui generis*. It is impractical to have each fallback position to appear both with and without an accompanying definition. Rethinking the scheme of Figure 11–8, the inventor may opine that any commercially vended three-or-more-legged seating device is likely to have at least one of the features recited in claims 3 to 6. In that case, we might not be so worried about protecting claim 2 by itself. We might thus eliminate claim 12 and define "elongated" in a definition claim that depends from each of claims 3 to 6. The features of claims 3 to 6 are thus backstopped in the event that "elongated" does turn out to be declared indefinite but, with claim 12 eliminated, those claims would not suffer from the potential of being limited by the definition in an unanticipated way.

In the end, it comes down to a matter of judgment and intuition, based on our assessment of the likelihood of new invention-relevant and/or -irrelevant prior art showing up, the likelihood of a particular term being declared indefinite, and the likelihood that a particular definition may be more limiting than we might have anticipated.

---

10. *See* p. 66.

Manage Claim Counts by Using Dependent Claim Combinations in Different Claim Families

The above guidelines can help us eliminate unnecessary claims and thereby help keep the claim count down. The total number of claims we wind up with can still be undue, however, if all of the worthwhile dependent claim combinations were to be included in every claim family.

If desired, the claim count can be reduced further by putting different combinations of dependent claims into different claim families, albeit with some risk as discussed below.

Consider, for example, the three claim chains appended to broad independent claim 1 in Figure 11–2, based on the nonchained structure of Figure 11–1(B). Replicating these chains for each other independent claim might result in an undesirably large claim total for the application. Figure 11–9 shows how those three chains could be divided among three different claim families, one headed by an independent method claim and two headed by independent apparatus claims.

There is some risk in this approach. If the combination of the broad invention with feature A turns out to be in the prior art, only claims 7, 9, 10, and 11 will remain valid. Our ability to assert a method claim against infringers may then be compromised in that claim 9—the only surviving method claim—incorporates definition X and Feature A. These are limitations that competitors' methods may not meet. Apparatus claim 7 is free of those limitations, but the anticipated enforcement scenario may be such that a method claim is easier to enforce.[11]

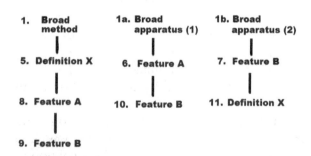

FIGURE 11–9 Claim counts can be managed by dividing different combinations of dependent claims among various claim families.

---

11. *See* pp. 237–238.

These are the kinds of contingencies that caused us to include all possible combinations of limitations for the single independent claim in Figure 11–9. If the invention is important enough, it may be in the patent owner's best interest to incur the excess claims fees rather than risk the loss of claims that may prove vital.

Markush Groups—A Trap for the Unwary

Some practitioners keep the claim total down by using Markush groups. That practice, however, is a trap for the unwary.

A Markush group is a listing within a claim of a group of alternatives. Its original use was in the context of composition of matter inventions in which no generic term was available to encompass a group of alternative constituents within the composition.[12] Markush groups are now used for all types of inventions, as in claim 11.4 below reciting that the processor-based device of claim 11.3 "is a selected one of a (i) computer, (ii) personal digital assistant, or (iii) cellular telephone."

> 11.3 A method for use in a processor-based device, the method comprising . . .
>
> 11.4 The method of claim 11.3 wherein the processor-based device is a selected one of a (i) computer, (ii) personal digital assistant, or (iii) cellular telephone.

By combining the three choices into one claim, the claim drafter has incorporated into one dependent claim what would otherwise require three.

Claim 11.4 is presumably intended to provide a fallback position if the subject matter of parent claim 11.3 is invalid based on prior art. However, if it is known (or obvious) to carry out claim 11.3's method in even one of the three devices—for example, the computer—claim 11.4 is also invalid because it reads on the case where the computer is the "selected one." This is true even if it were not known or obvious to carry out the method in a personal digital assistant or a cellular telephone. We see, then, that the presence of the "computer" in the Markush group ruins claim 11.4 as a fallback vehicle. The longer the list, the worse it is, since it is increasingly likely that the claim will read on some piece of prior art.

---

12. *See, e.g.*, Manual of Patent Examining Procedure, § 2173.05(h) (8th ed., rev. July 2010).

The better practice is to identify those alternatives that could provide an effective fallback position and recite each one in its own dependent claim.

One possible *effective* use of a Markush group in a dependent claim context is in a definition claim, either to protect against indefiniteness or unpatentability based on invention-irrelevant prior art. When a Markush group is included in a dependent claim for *those* reasons, we don't care that the claim does not enhance patentability of its parent, because it is serving a different purpose.

Consider, for example, claims 11.5 and 11.6. The parent claim 11.5 calls for "a network edge device" in a packet network (e.g., the Internet). Such a device is understood in art to mean a router, bridge, or other network switching element at the point where signals enter the packet network. Hence the term "network edge" device. Claim 11.6 includes a Markush group specifically defining the network edge device as being either a router or a bridge.

> 11.5 A packet network comprising
> (a) a network edge device,
> (b) . . . and
> (c) . . .
>
> 11.6 The invention of claim 11.5 wherein the network edge device is one of (a) a router and (b) a bridge.

Claim 11.6 will not save its parent claim from invalidity based on invention-relevant prior art. If the broad inventive concept turns out to be known, it would necessarily use a router, a bridge, or some obvious equivalent at the network edge. Claims 11.5 and 11.6 stand or fall together in the face of such invention-relevant prior art.

However, claim 11.6 *can* save its parent from invalidity based on invention-irrelevant prior art. Claim 11.5 might read on prior art in which the "network edge device" is not a router, a bridge, or anything like them but, rather, a simple screw terminal to which incoming telecommunications lines are connected. Such a terminal is, after all, a "network edge device," broadly speaking. Claim 11.6 firms up the invention boundaries that were always intended, thereby securing coverage for the inventive concept while avoiding such invention-irrelevant prior art.

CHAPTER REVIEW—Assembling the Dependent Claims

Confirm Your Understanding

1. What is meant by "chained" and "nonchained" dependent claims?
2. Complete the following table by inserting the main advantage and disadvantage of dependent claims being chained and not chained.

	ADVANTAGE	DISADVANTAGE
CHAINED		
NON-CHAINED		

3. Explain the rationale behind each of the following rules presented in this chapter:
   a. Dependent claims independently imparting patentability to a (dependent or independent) parent claim should be nonchained relative to one another.
   b. Dependent claims imparting patentability to a parent claim in combination with one another should be chained.
   c. Dependent claims not imparting patentability to a parent claim in combination with one another should not be chained.
   d. Dependent claims should be positioned within the claim family hierarchy based on their contribution to the Planned Retreat.
4. State four factors that militate in favor of a particular dependent claim being positioned relatively high within a claim family.
5. In order to keep to a reasonable number of claims, one might choose to put different combinations of dependent claims into different claim families (claims headed by respective independent claims). What is the potential danger in doing this?
6. What is the potential danger of Markush group claiming?
7. How can a Markush group be effectively used in a definition claim?

Question for Further Thought

    8. In many patents one finds the same set of dependent claims depending from each of a number of independent claims. What advantages and/or disadvantages do you see in this practice?

Sharpen Your Skills

    9. Assume that your client is the inventor of the first vehicular air bag. Using the principles presented in this chapter, create a family of claims for this invention headed up by the independent claim presented on p. 135, per the following guidelines:

        a. Draw your fallback features from the narrative on p. 136.

        b. Include definition claims where appropriate. If you don't know a definition for a particular term X, the definition claim can be in skeleton form, e.g., "The invention of claim 1 wherein said X is . . .".

Explain the rationale for where you positioned each feature or definition within the claim family and why you thought particular terms needed defining.

CHAPTER TWELVE

Claims with Functional Language

Certain kinds of claims are said to be "functional." But what that actually means depends on whom you ask. Judge Giles Rich once observed that "[f]ew words in patent law have acquired more diverse meanings than the word 'functional.'"[1]

The practical importance of this topic is that functional language relied on for patentability may not do so as a matter of law. On the other hand, examiners sometimes reject claims as being "functional" in situations where the claim is perfectly fine.[2]

This chapter has more legal discussion and case citations than other parts of the book. It is important that readers understand and absorb the case law principles that have built up over time in order to deal with the practicalities of drafting, and arguing for the patentability of, claims with functional language. It is vital to know when a claim is, in the lexicon of this chapter, "unduly functional" and thus needs to be revised.

"Functional Language" but Not "Functional Claim"

It proves useful to talk about claims that have "functional language" but, as we will see, it is best to avoid the terms "functional claim" and "functional claiming."

We begin with what it means for a claim to have "functional language" or, equivalently, "functional recitation(s)." We don't need a *strict* definition; in the end, we will be analyzing our claims based on what they actually say, rather than whether any particular recitation meets anyone's idea of what constitutes functional language. Indeed, the goal of this chapter is to enable the reader to readily assess whether a given claim with functional language is patentable or not based on first principles.

---

1. *In re Fuetterer*, 319 F.2d 259, 266 n.9, 138 USPQ 217 (Fed. Cir. 1963).
2. *See, e.g., K-2 Corporation v. Salomon SA*, 191, F.3d 1356, 1366–68, 52 USPQ2d 1001 (Fed. Cir 1999); *Wright Medical Technology, Inc. v. Osteonics Corp.*, 122 F.6d 1440, 1443–44, 43 USPQ2d 1837, 1840 (Fed. Cir. 1997).

A useful working definition of functional claim language is any recitation that is other than a purely physical characterization of a tangible object. Functional language thus encompasses, *inter alia*, statements of function, functionality, or result; actions; relationships in time or space; properties; capabilities; and modes of use. The italicized language in the following claims is functional language at issue in reported cases that we will look at in this chapter:

> 12.1 *The use of . . . electro-magnetism . . . for marking or printing intelligible characters, signs, or letters, at any distances.*[3]
>
> 12.2 A glue comprising cassava carbohydrate rendered semifluid by digestion *and having substantially the properties of animal glue.*[4]
>
> 12.3 In an apparatus for determining the location of an obstruction in a well having therein a string of assembled tubing sections interconnected with each other by coupling collars, . . .
> means . . . for receiving pressure impulses from the well . . . and
> means . . . *for tuning said receiving means to the frequency of echoes from the tubing collars . . .*[5]

In an apparatus context, a functional recitation is often said to be one that defines a structural element by what it *does*, as opposed to what it *is*. A means-plus-function recitation is, by its nature, a functional recitation. Even a single word reciting a structural element can be functional. "Slab" is a structural recitation, while "door" is a functional characterization of a slab having the function of access control. "Filter," "brake," "clamp," "screwdriver," and "lock" are all structural elements expressed in functional terms.[6] A method step is the quintessential functional recitation, being typically a statement of action or mode of use. We do not usually think of method steps as being inherently functional. But it helps to recognize their inherently functional nature because functional characterizations of structural elements are often method-like.

Although we will talk about functional claim *language,* it is best to avoid the terms "functional claim" and "functional claiming" because those terms mean different things to different people. To talk about a *claim* being functional—at least in the pedagogic setting of this book—is to surely sow the seeds of confusion.

---

3. *O'Reilly v. Morse,* 56 U.S. 62 (1854).

4. *Holland Furniture Co. v. Perkins Glue Co.,* 277 U.S. 245 (1928).

5. *Halliburton Oil Well Cementing Company v. Walker et al,* 329 U.S. 1, 71 USPQ 175 (1946).

6. *See, e.g., In re Swinehart,* 439 F.2d 210, 169 USPQ 226 (Fed. Cir. 1971); *Greenberg v. Ethicon Endo-Surgery, Inc.,* 91 F.3d 1580, 39 USPQ2d 1783 (Fed. Cir. 1996).

Here's the difficulty: Many of the guiding cases[7] use the term "functional claim" in a narrow sense, as meaning a claim that (a) purports to distinguish the invention from the prior art based on functional language, but (b) is deemed ineffective to do so as a matter of law. However, many practitioners[8] understand the term "functional claim" much more broadly as meaning any claim containing functional language—including, of course, recitations in means-plus-function form. The Federal Circuit has also used the term "functional claim" in the latter, narrower sense.[9]

Claims 12.4 and 12.5 illustrate the dichotomy between the two kinds of claims that people call "functional." Both are directed to Loud's ballpoint pen discussed in Chapter One and both use the functional language transitional phrase "capable of . . . ":

12.4 A pen having a marking sphere capable of revolving in all directions, substantially as and for the purposes described.

12.5 A pen capable of creating a continuous line on a rough surface.

In the broader sense, both of these are functional claims by virtue of their respective functional recitations—"capable of revolving in all directions" and "capable of creating a continuous line on a rough surface." The word "marking" in claim 12.4 is also a functional recitation since it indicates the function of the recited sphere.

However, in the narrower sense, in which "functional" equates to "unpatentable," claim 12.4 is *not* a functional claim, notwithstanding its functional *language*. Firstly, the recitation of a "marking sphere" in and of itself distinguishes the invention from the prior art pens, none of which had a marking sphere. Like another of Loud's claims,

12.6 A pen having a spheroidal marking-point, substantially as described,

claim 12.4 would have been patentable irrespective of the functional language, "capable of revolving in all directions." That being said, claim 12.4's "capable of revolving . . ." functional language is effective to further distinguish the recited structure from the prior art because it provides an affirmative limitation on the recited sphere when in place in a pen.

---

7. *See, e.g., General Electric Co. v. Wabash Co.*, 304 U.S. 364, 37 USPQ 466 (1938).

8. Informal communications with the author.

9. *See, e.g., Welker Bearing Co. v. PHD, Inc.*, 550 F.3d 1090, 1096, 89 USPQ2d 1289 (Fed. Cir. 2008).

By contrast, claim 12.5—which was not in Loud's patent but was composed by the author for the present discussion—is a functional claim even in the narrower sense—in which "functional" equates to "unpatentable"—because claim 12.5 characterizes Loud's pen solely in terms of a pen that avoids the known problem of prior art pens not being able to create a continuous line on a rough surface. We will see that the case law deems such a claim to be unpatentable.

The terms "functional claim" and "functional claiming" are thus best avoided in order to minimize the potential for confusion. We shall, instead, refer to claims having functional language as just that: "claims having functional language." And we shall use the term "unduly functional" to refer to a claim that, like claim 12.5, has functional language purporting to distinguish the invention from the prior art but that the case law says does not effectively do so.

At bottom, of course, no particular terminology is right or wrong. As long as we understand when a claim containing functional language is or isn't patentable, any particular use of the term "functional claim" is fine and readers can certainly use it in any sense they like as long as the meaning is clear.

Being "unduly functional" is not limited to apparatus claims. As explained below, method claim 12.1 and composition claim 12.2 are both unduly functional.

We haven't yet said why the type of claim that we here call "unduly functional" should, in fact, be unpatentable as a matter of patent jurisprudence. Much about that later. The short answer for now is that to allow an inventor such a claim would be to award her patent coverage of greater scope than her contribution to the art. But before going there, let us discuss how to recognize an unduly functional claim when we see one.

Functional Language at the Point of Novelty

The mere presence of functional recitations in a claim does not, in and of itself, raise the issue of undue functionality.[10] The question comes up only when functional language is relied on as defining how the invention differs from the prior art. Such recitation(s) are said to constitute "functional language at the point of novelty" (with the word "novelty" in this context including nonobviousness as well).

So we need to explore when functional language at the point of novelty does and does not render a claim unduly functional.

---

10. *See, e.g.,* the cases cited at note 2.

When a Claim Is Unduly Functional

The criterion for whether a claim is unduly functional, and thus unpatentable, is consistent with how we *always* assess the patentability of claims—the relationship of the claimed subject matter to what was already known. The focus here, though, is how the functional language in question relates to the problem(s) that the inventor has solved.

The guiding principle can be stated as follows:

> A claim is unduly functional if functional language at the point of novelty recites that a known or obvious problem is overcome without saying anything about how the problem actually *is* overcome.

Or, as the U.S. Supreme Court put it in *General Electric Co. v. Wabash Appliance Corp.*,[11] "[A] characteristic essential to novelty may not be distinguished from the old art solely by its tendency to remedy the problems in the art."[12]

The "known or obvious problem" can take many forms, e.g., a defect or limitation in a known device, process, or material, or the absence of a particular known or obviously desirable quality, capability, or characteristic. Or the problem may be one of those never-fully-solved ones, such as how to make or do things faster, cheaper, or better.

Whatever the nature of the known or obvious problem, a proper claim cannot simply amount to, in effect, a boast that the known or obvious problem has now been solved; the claim has to say something about *how* the problem was solved.

But what about enablement? Innumerable reported cases say that a reference asserted to invalidate a claim must provide an enabling disclosure.[13] A prior-art reference describing a problem in the art does not necessarily enable one to *solve* that problem. So how can such prior art be used to invalidate a claim?

The fact is that cases relying on the above rule involve particular situations—mostly claims directed to compositions of matter and particular kinds of obviousness questions.[14,15] Statements in other cases asserting or implying a wider applicability to the requirement of prior-art-reference enablement are dicta in those cases—usually because the

---

11. *See* note 6.

12. *General Electric Co. v. Wabash Co.*, *supra* note 7 at 372.

13. *See, e.g., In re Donohue*, 766 F.5d 531, 533, 226 USPQ 619, 621 (Fed. Cir. 1985); *In re LeGrice*, 301 F.2d 929, 936, 133 USPQ 365, 371 (1962).

14. 35 U.S.C. §§ 161–164

15. *See, e.g. Impax Laboratories, Inc. v. Aventis Pharmaceuticals Inc.*, 545 F.3d 1312, 88 USPQ2d 1381 (Fed. Cir. 2008).

reference in question was found to *be* enabling.[16] Such statements cannot, in any event, overturn the effect of *O'Reilly v. Morse*[17] discussed below—a seminal U.S. Supreme Court case that relied on unenabled prior art.

In analyzing claims with functional language, we can rely on a different rule: *A reference is prior art for all that it teaches.*[18] Thus the inoperativeness of something asserted in the prior art to solve a problem does not negate the citability of that prior art as teaching that the problem was known.

The above guiding principle can be stated in other, essentially equivalent ways, with varying degrees of colloquiality. Take your pick:

> A claim is unduly functional if it encompasses all ways of solving a known or obvious problem or of achieving a known or obvious result, whether or not the prior art knew how to implement it.

> A concept known to the prior art is *in* the prior art and therefore cannot be claimed at the disclosed conceptual level.

> If the prior art *said* it, or inherently *knew* it, you can't *claim* it, even if nobody knew how to *do* it.

The Cases

The oft-cited U.S. Supreme Court's 1853 decision in *O'Reilly v. Morse*[19] illustrates that prior art is citable for all that it teaches, whether enabled or not. The claim at issue was claim 8 of Morse's reissued telegraph patent of 1848[20]—shown above as claim 12.1. Morse was the first to solve the problem that telegraph signals could not be transmitted very far because the signal weakened with distance to the point of becoming unusable. Claim 12.1 purports to cover all ways of solving the "at any distance" problem. Unfortunately for Morse, the art had already recognized the desirability of this. Prior to Morse, the Court noted,

---

16. *See, e.g., Symbol Technologies, Inc. v. Opticon, Inc,* 935 F.2d 1569, 19 USPQ2d 1241 (Fed. Cir. 1991); *In re Collins,* 462 F.2d 538, 174 USPQ 333 (CCPA 1972); *In re Kehl,* 101 F.2d 193, 40 USPQ 357 (CCPA 1939); *In re Dowty,* 118 F.2d 363 (CCPA 1941).

17. *O'Reilly v. Morse, supra* note 3.

18. *Beckman Instruments, Inc. v. LKB Produkter AB,* 892 F.2d 1547, 1551, 13 USPQ2d 1301 (Fed. Cir. 1989); *In re Hollingsworth,* 210 F.2d 290 (CCPA 1954) ("claims which do not distinguish from a disclosure alleged to be inoperative cannot be allowed"); *In re Crecelius,* 86 F.2d 399 (CCPA 1936) ("It is elementary that the claims must distinguish from the references even if they are inoperative."); *In re Perrine,* 111 F.2d 177 (CCPA 1940); *In re Crosby,* 157 F.2d 198, 71 USPQ 73 (CCPA 1946); *In re Guild,* 204 F.2d 700, 98 USPQ 68 (CCPA 1953).

19. *O'Reilly v. Morse, supra* note 3.

20. U.S. Patent 1,647 (Reissue #118), June 13, 1848.

the conviction was general among men of science everywhere that the object could, and sooner or later would, be accomplished.[21]

Claim 12.1 was thus held invalid, while claims to Morse's repeater technology, which was how Morse actually solved the problem, were upheld.

The Supreme Court ruled similarly in *Holland Furniture Company v. Perkins Glue Company*.[22] The claim at issue there was our claim 12.2. Glues made from "cassava carbohydrate rendered semifluid by digestion" were known, but no one knew how to produce such a glue that had the superior properties exhibited by animal glue, such as greater holding power. The recitation in the claim "having substantially the properties of animal glue" was thus functional language at the point of novelty—functional language purporting to distinguish the claimed subject matter from the prior art. Claim 12.2 was found unpatentable— even though the inventor Perkins was apparently the first to come up with such a glue—because it was known or obvious that such a glue would be desirable. To similar effect is the ruling of the Court of Customs and Patent Appeals (CCPA) in *In re Fullam*.[23]

Finally, we have *General Electric Co. v. Wabash Appliance Corp.*,[24] which involved the claim shown below as claim 12.7. The recitation shown in italics is the functional language relied on for novelty:

> 12.7 A filament for electric incandescent lamps or other devices, composed substantially of tungsten and made up mainly of a number of comparatively large grains *of such size and contour as to prevent substantial sagging and offsetting* . . .

The *Wabash* court relied on the precedent—established by *O'Reilly v. Morse* and *Perkins Glue*—that at a point in a claim where the applicant should state how his invention differs from the prior art, it is not enough to state only that the inventor solved a problem that the prior art did not. Indeed, *Wabash* is frequently quoted for its assertion to that effect:

> [T]he vice of a functional claim exists . . . when the inventor is painstaking when he recites what has already been seen, and then uses conveniently *functional language at the exact point of novelty* [emphasis added].[25]

---

21. *O'Reilly v. Morse*, 56 U.S. at 107.

22. *Holland Furniture Co. v. Perkins Glue Co., supra* note 4.

23. *In re Fullam* 161 F.2d 247, 73 USPQ 399 (CCPA 1947).

24. *General Electric Co. v. Wabash Co., supra* note 7.

25. *General Electric Co. v. Wabash Co., supra* note 7, 304 U.S. at 371, 37 USPQ at 469 (1938).

The Court's reference to language that is "conveniently functional" would seem to have been a sardonic or sarcastic jab at what the Court saw as the greediness of an inventor seeking to capture all ways of solving a known problem by "conveniently" not limiting himself to any details about how he actually solved it.

The legal principles relied on in *Wabash* were sound, but the author is not convinced that the Court got this one right on the facts. Arguably, the Court did not give full and proper consideration to what the claim's functional language actually said. More on that below.

When a Claim Is *Not* Unduly Functional

In a certain sense, there is no compelling need to explore the attributes of a claim that is *not* unduly functional. It could simply be said that a claim that does not meet the criteria for being unduly functional is, well, "*not* unduly functional."

However, being able to affirmatively state why a particular claim is not unduly functional will serve us well in order to identify such a claim when we see it and to effectively argue its patentability in the Patent and Trademark Office.

Halliburton: Ironically, the Perfect Example

A good example of functional language that distinguishes the invention from the prior art is found in the claim at issue in the Supreme Court's *Halliburton v. Walker* case of 1948, shown above as claim 12.3.

Given that the Court found the functional language at issue *not* effective to distinguish the invention from the prior art, this may seem a strange assertion. But the Court's holding was so at odds with sound patent jurisprudential principles that Congress was stimulated to enact what was originally 35 U.S.C. 112, ¶ 3,[26] later became § 112, ¶ 6, and is now § 112(f)[27]—thereby effectively undoing *Halliburton*'s precedential effect. *Halliburton* thus provides a unique vehicle for understanding the kind of functional-at-the-point-of-novelty language that defines a *patentable* invention in our post-*Halliburton* world.

The invention in *Halliburton* related to the then-known use of sound echoes to measure the depth of oil wells. The presence of certain tubing collars in the well made the prior art equipment's measurement read-

---

26. *See* the discussion of the adoption of ¶ 3 in *In re Donaldson Co., Inc.*, 16 F.3d 1189, 29 USPQ2d 1845 (Fed. Cir. 1994); and *In re Fisher*, 314 F.2d 817, 137 USPQ 150 (CCPA 1963).

27. As of September 16, 2012, § 112 is divided into subsections (a) through (f) corresponding to what were previously referred to as ¶¶ 1 through 6.

ings inaccurate. Inventor Walker solved that problem by adding a tuning functionality to the prior art equipment. Per Walker's discovery, claim 12.3 recites a combination of (a) the prior art equipment, with (b) an element cast in means-plus-function form that provided the tuning, viz.:

> means . . . for tuning said receiving means to the frequency of echoes from the tubing collars of said tubing sections . . .

The Supreme Court found Walker's claim to be (in our terms) unduly functional, invoking the above-noted language from *Wabash* about "conveniently functional language at the exact point of novelty." Indeed, it is easy enough to apply the *Wabash* rationale to the claim in *Halliburton*. Walker's claim did just what the claim in *Wabash* had done—recite something in the prior art combined with functional language at the point of novelty.

Why, then, did the *Halliburton* case cause such a stir? Indeed, why was its decision jurisprudentially unsound?

Halliburton would have been on all fours with *Wabash* and the Court's prior cases *if* it had been known in the art that a "means . . . for tuning" was desirable without knowing how to implement such a means. The "known or obvious" problem in the art would then have been the question of how such a means could be implemented. Walker's contribution to the art would then have been his teaching of how the known-to-be-desired "means . . . for tuning" could actually *be* implemented. And the Supreme Court would then have been justified in holding that the claim was invalid due to its failure to recite anything about that implementation.

Likewise, the Court would certainly have been justified in invalidating a claim calling for, say, a "means for ensuring the accuracy of the well-depth measurement" since the inaccuracy of the prior art equipment was a known problem.

But none of that was the case.

The known problem in the art was *not* that nobody knew how to build the tuning means. Nobody knew that such a means was even desirable. The only thing the prior art did know was that the presence of the oil well's tubing collars made the depth readings inaccurate. That being so, functional language directed to Walker's *particular* solution to that problem—improving the prior art equipment to include a tuning means—did not render Walker's claim unduly functional.

The underlying rationale of the pre-*Halliburton* cases was that it gives too much to an inventor to allow a claim so broad as to encompass all solutions to a known problem. However, Walker's claim was not of that nature. The *Halliburton* court went astray by not taking into account what the nature of the known problem was—and thus what Walker's *contribution* was.

One might argue that Walker's claim *did* encompass all ways of solving a problem—namely the prior art's lack of a tuning means. However, that was not a known or obvious problem. It was a "problem"—if we want to call it that—that inventor Walker was the first to recognize. Claiming all ways of solving a problem that the inventor recognized as *being* the problem is not the same as claiming all ways of solving a problem that everybody already *knows* to be a problem.

The *Halliburton* decision was clearly the wrong result—so much so that, as noted above, section 112(f) was enacted with the specific intent of overruling *Halliburton*'s implicit requirement that you can't have a means-plus-function recitation at the point of novelty without reciting something about how the means is implemented. To that end, the statute provides that an element, i.e., *any* element, in a claim for a combination may be expressed as a means or step for performing a specified function *"without the recital of structure, material, or acts in support thereof."*[28]

Section 112(f) eliminates the possibility that a claim with functional language at the point of novelty can be rejected or invalidated on that basis alone. On the other hand, the intent in enacting section 112(f) was only to restore the law to its pre-*Halliburton* state.[29] Thus if a means-plus-function recitation at the point of novelty amounts to nothing more than a statement that a known or obvious problem in the prior art has been solved, it would seem that such a claim will still be deemed unpatentable based on *O'Reilly v. Morse* and its progeny. For an inventor's claim having a means-plus-function recitation at the point of novelty to be patentable, the idea of providing such a means in the recited combination has to have been a contribution of that inventor.

That was, indeed, the case in the Federal Circuit's 2011 decision in *In re Glatt Air Techniques, Inc.*[30] The invention was an improvement in an apparatus for coating particles. Such apparatus had the known problem of particle agglomeration. The inventor recognized that that problem could be solved by shielding a nozzle that was part of the apparatus. The claim at issue was our claim 12.8:

> 12.8 In a fluidized bed coater having a product container, said product container including a . . . partition . . . defining an inner upbed . . . and an upwardly discharging spray nozzle . . .

28. 35 U.S.C. 112(f).

29. *In re Fuetterer*, 319 F.2d 259, 264 n.ll, 138 USPQ217, 221 n.11 (CCPA 1963).

30. *In re Glatt Air Techniques, Inc.*, 630 F.3d 1026 (Fed. Cir. 2011).

THE IMPROVEMENT COMPRISING

shielding means positioned adjacent said spray nozzle for shielding the initial spray pattern developed by said nozzle against the entrance of particles moving upwardly through the upbed.

This claim is functional at the point of novelty, a fact that couldn't be made more clear than by its Jepson-style ("the improvement comprising") format. But while functional at the point of novelty, claim 12.8 is not unduly functional because the idea of shielding the initial spray pattern was not something that the art knew was desirable. *That* was the *inventor's* contribution. Claim 12.8 *would* have been unduly functional if, instead of reciting the shielding means, it had called for a means whose recited function was solving the known agglomeration problem, e.g.,

means for preventing agglomeration of particles moving upwardly through the upbed.

But that, of course, is not what the claim says.

Claims like claim 12.8—where patentability is predicated on the addition of a single new "means" to a prior art combination—are so commonplace that we hardly give it any thought. We have section 112(f), and its statutory overruling of *Halliburton*, to thank for that.

The following passage from the Federal Circuit well summarizes what we have seen to this point:

It was in the Wabash case that the Supreme Court condemned the use of "conveniently functional language at the exact point of novelty." The "exact point of novelty" in the Wabash case resided in statements in the claims which "distinguished [the large grained tungsten filament there involved] from the old art solely by its tendency to remedy the problems in the art met by the patent." . . . We note, however, that the Supreme Court, in a seldom quoted passage in the Wabash case, stated:

"A limited use of terms of effect or result, which accurately define the essential qualities of a product to one skilled in the art, may in some instances be permissible and even desirable."[31]

---

31. *In re Fuetterer, supra* note 29.

It's About Undue Breadth

The Supreme Court invalidated Morse's claim 8—our claim 12.1—in *O'Reilly v. Morse* on the grounds that the claim was "too broad." This presaged what, in the author's view, is the only sound basis on which to find an unduly functional claim unpatentable—namely that it reads on, or is rendered obvious by, the prior art.

This was not the universal route by which the cases came to their conclusions. Any number of opinions subsequent to *O'Reilly v. Morse* advanced other rationales in invalidating unduly functional claims. Since the reader may encounter those other legal theories in reading the cases, it will be helpful to see why they are not in alignment with current jurisprudence, even though the ultimate conclusions were sound.

One rationale used to invalidate a claim with unduly functional language was that the claim extended the patent monopoly "beyond the invention"[32] or that it claimed "more than the applicant invented."[33] Those are not inaccurate characterizations of a claim that is unduly functional. But judges are no longer empowered to invalidate claims as not comporting with what *they* regard as the invention. Per § 112(b), the invention is whatever the *applicant* regards it to be, as defined in her claims. The invention thus defined may or may not be patentable, but that is a different question.

Other post-*O'Reilly* opinions invalidated claims with functional language as being "indefinite." Modern case law, however, reserves indefiniteness—which is a violation of the requirement of § 112(b) that the invention be claimed "distinctly"—for situations where the boundaries of the claimed subject matter are not clear. Being unduly functional and being unclear are two different things.[34] Breadth is not indefiniteness.[35] Certainly there was no doubt as to the boundaries of what Morse attempted to stake out for himself in his invalidated claim 8 (our claim 12.1).

---

32. *Holland Furniture Co. v. Perkins Glue Co., supra* note 4.

33. *In re Ferguson*, 83 F.2d 693 (CCPA 1936).

34. This point is well illustrated by the related cases *In re Fisher*, 307 F.2d 948, 135 USPQ 22 (CCPA 1962) and *In re Fisher*, 427 F.2d 833, 166 USPQ 18, 24 (CCPA 1970). The earlier case based the nonallowability of a functional claim on section 112, asserting that the claim failed to point out that which the applicant regarded as the invention. By the time that the later case was decided, the Federal Circuit had come to the current view that, absent explicit statements to the contrary as to what the applicant regards as the invention, the invention at issue is whatever the claims say it is and should be evaluated on that basis.

35. *In re Gardner*, 427 F.2d 786, 166 USPQ 138 (CCPA 1970).

Cases sometimes use § 112(a) as the basis for invalidating claims as being too broad. But such undue breadth is not founded on prior art considerations. These are, in the main, chemical cases in which the inventor's disclosure of a limited number of species or embodiments is found insufficient to establish that the inventor was in possession of the invention defined by a broad generic claim encompassing innumerable species.[36] The justification for this approach is the unpredictability of chemical reactions, and it is rarely, if ever, applied to mechanical and electrical cases, in which even a single embodiment is regarded as providing broad enablement.[37]

This leaves only sections 102 and 103 as the statutory basis for affirming the invalidity of claims that we here call unduly functional. Indeed, that is a jurisprudentially sound view. A reference disclosing, or rendering obvious, the existence of a known problem is citable for that fact since "a reference is prior art for all that it teaches."[38] Thus claims that are unduly functional are unpatentable, quite simply, because they read on, or are obvious in view of, the prior art.

The foregoing has significant implications in prosecution. The presence of functional language in a claim—even at the point of novelty—is not in and of itself a valid ground for rejection. An examiner may properly reject a claim as "functional" only when (a) functional language at the point of novelty encompasses all ways of solving a known or obvious problem or of achieving a known or obvious desired result, as discussed above, or (b) functional language that *could* serve to render the claim patentable is not properly tied into the recited structure or method steps, as discussed below in the section *Words Matter*.

Why Does It Make Sense?

The above lays out the rules. But why does it all make sense jurisprudentially? Why wasn't Morse—who was the first to come up with a way of using electromagnetism to communicate intelligence over any desired distance—allowed to have a claim to that concept?

Isn't it a bedrock principle that the patent goes to whoever was the first to come up with something?

Yes, that *is* a bedrock principle. But the "something" that Morse was first to come up with was not the naked notion of using electromagnetism to communicate intelligence over any desired distance. People

---

36. *See, e.g., University of Rochester v. GD Searle & Co., Inc.*, 358 F.3d 916, 69 USPQ2d 1886 (Fed. Cir. 2004).

37. *In re Fisher, supra* note 34.

38. *Supra* note 17.

already knew the desirability of that. If others wanted to solve the problem the way Morse did, that would be one thing. Morse was entitled to claims directed to his particular way of solving the problem of signals weakening with distance. Indeed, the Supreme Court upheld the validity of claims directed to the repeater technology that Morse had devised to deal with that problem.

But it is unfair to the public for an inventor who is the first to solve a known problem to be awarded a claim so broad as to dominate others who later solve the known problem in a different way. If others solve the problem that everyone has been working on—or at least knew was waiting to be solved—in a way that takes no advantage of what the first inventor taught, it is not sound jurisprudence to allow that first inventor to extract tribute from others or keep them out of the market. This is what the Court in *O'Reilly v. Morse* was getting at when, in invalidating Morse's claim, it stated that,

> [f]or aught that we now know some future inventor, in the onward march of science, may discover a mode of writing or printing at a distance by means of the electric or galvanic current, *without using any part of the process or combination set forth in the plaintiff's specification* [emphasis added].[39]

Consider, then, time travel. The literature abounds with descriptions of time travel going back to H.G. Wells's *The Time Machine* of 1895. And, indeed, well before that.

At some point in the future, someone might figure out how to actually do time travel and might try to define her contribution in a patent claim such as claim 12.9:

> 12.9 A method comprising
> receiving from a user an indication of a time and place in the past
> or future to which one wishes to travel, and
> transporting the user to that time and place.

The reader should now be able to explain why that inventor will not be entitled to claim 12.9 even though she was the first to build a working time machine and even though the prior art is nonenabling.

---

39. 56 U.S. at 113.

"Words Matter"

Functional language intended to have limiting effect must clearly constitute an affirmative limitation on a recited element, step, or the claimed subject matter as a whole. That may not happen if the language is not carefully worded. Claim drafters sometimes insert functional recitations in a claim without much thought to how they tie into the claim grammatically. Grammar and sentence construction should not be thought of as irrelevant niceties; claims are routinely parsed and then interpreted in accordance with the precepts of English grammar.[40]

Indeed, as was noted by the Federal Circuit,

> a claim may be grammatically constructed in such a manner that a statement therein appears to set forth a mere result, yet closer inspection will reveal that what appears to be a functional statement is not functional at all, but on the contrary, is a positive limitation. . . . [41]

Transitional Phrases

Transitional phrases such as "so that," "such that," and "wherein" can be quite useful in stitching functional claim recitations into the fabric of a claim, but they should be used carefully to ensure that they produce the desired result.

"so that"

For example, what is the role of the "so that" clause in claim 12.10?

> 12.10 Apparatus comprising . . .
> .
> .
> .
> . . . the blower inlet being located at a level below the cavity **so that** when the blower and magnetron are turned off and the thermal element is turned on air is thermally convected from the blower inlet through the air passages into the waveguide and into the cavity.

One possibility is that the "so that" clause is an affirmative limitation on the exact location of the blower inlet. Per that reading, the blower inlet is not just at *any* level below the cavity, but at a *particular* level that

---

40. *In re Hyatt*, 708 F.2d 712 at 714, 218 USPQ 195 at 197 (Fed. Cir. 1983).
41. *In re Krodel*, 223 F. 2d 285, 106 USPQ 195 (CCPA 1955).

results in air being thermally convected in the manner recited in the claim.[42] A different possibility, however, is that the "so that" clause is equivalent to a "whereby" clause—describing an inevitable consequence of the operation of the previously recited structure.[43] In that case the "so that" clause will not be given any independent limiting effect.

In litigation, the Opposing Team may argue that this ambiguity renders the claim indefinite. Or the Opposing Team might urge the court to adopt the second claim reading in order to cause the claim to be invalid as reading on prior art in which the blower inlet is located at *some* level below the cavity, albeit not a level that causes air to be thermally convected in the manner stated in the claim.

If the "so that" clause of claim 12.10 is intended to have a limiting effect, the claim should be phrased to make the words following "so that" more affirmatively limit the word "located." Here are two possible alternatives:

> . . . the blower inlet being located at a level below the cavity ~~so that,~~ the level being such that when the blower and magnetron are turned off . . .

> . . . the blower inlet being <u>so</u> located at a level below the cavity ~~so~~ that when the blower and magnetron are turned off . . .

If no limiting effect is intended, "whereby" might be a better choice than "so that."

"such that"

Here's another example,[44] involving "such that":

> 12.11 A stent having first and second ends with an intermediate section there between, and a longitudinal axis, comprising:
> a plurality of longitudinally disposed bands, wherein each band defines a generally continuous wave having a spatial frequency along a line segment parallel to the longitudinal axis; and
> a plurality of links for maintaining the bands in a tubular structure, wherein the links are so disposed that any single circumferential path

---

42. *See, e.g., Application of Chandler*, 254 F.2d 396, 117 USPQ 361 (CCPA 1958) (recitations preceded by "so that" found to have limiting effect).

43. *Texas Instruments v. US Intern. Trade Com'n*, 988 F.2d 1165, 26 USPQ2d 1018 (Fed. Cir. 1993). However, a "whereby" recitation may be used "against" the patentee to narrow the claimed subject matter when asserted against an infringer. *See, e.g., Hoffer v. Microsoft Corp.*, 405 F.3d 1326, 74 USPQ2d 1481 (Fed. Cir. 2005).

44. *Raytheon Co. v. Roper Corp.*, 724 F.2d 951, 220 USPQ 592 (Fed. Cir. 1983).

formed by the links is discontinuous; ***such that*** *the links and bands define an expandable structure having axial flexibility in an unexpanded configuration.*

Assume that the italicized functional language "such that the links and bands . . ." is necessary to distinguish the invention from the prior art. If "such that" is interpreted to mean "in such a way that," then the clause is an affirmative limitation on how the links are disposed. However, if "such that" is interpreted to mean "with the overall result that" then it is arguably in the nature of a "whereby" clause and thus nonlimiting.

The Federal Circuit found the "such that" language of claim 12.11 to have a limiting effect, thereby saving the claim from reading on prior art. But the patentee was lucky. The manner in which semicolons are used in claim 12.11 suggests that the semicolon preceding "such that" refers to the recited stent as a whole—rendering the "such that" clause equivalent to a "whereby" clause and thus nonlimiting. It could also be argued that if the "such that" clause was intended to have a limiting effect, it would have necessarily referred back to how both the links *and the bands* are disposed—not just the links.

Among the several ways that the last paragraph could have been written more clearly is this:

> a plurality of links for maintaining the bands in a tubular structure, wherein the links are so disposed that any single circumferential path formed by the links is discontinuous; ~~such that~~ the links and bands <u>being so configured as to</u> define an expandable structure having axial flexibility in an unexpanded configuration.

"wherein"

Claim recitations following "wherein" are often structural, e.g., "wherein said computer includes a display screen." But they are just as often functional. Thus in claim 12.12, "retractable" is a functional characterization of the recited landing gear.

> 12.12 An aircraft including
> .
> .
> .
> a forward landing gear mounted to said aircraft by a hinge, wherein said landing gear is retractable.

But there's something wrong with claim 12.12.

The word "wherein" means "in which." As such, it needs an anteced-ent—some "which" for "in which" to relate back to. Substitute "in which" for "wherein" in claim 12.12 and then ask what the claim means. What is being referred back to by "wherein"? It's certainly not the hinge. And it is a grammatical stretch to suggest that "wherein" refers to the landing gear. We might readily talk about a landing gear that *is* retractable, but what does it mean to have a landing gear *in which* that landing gear is retract-able? The claim drafter no doubt intended the claim to mean that the use of a hinge as a mounting device is what causes the landing gear to be retractable, but that's not really—or at least clearly—what the claim says.

Sloppy use of "wherein" occurs a lot, with significant consequenc-es.[45] Any number of cases have turned on the question of what limiting effect a "wherein" clause is to be given,[46] sometimes to the patent own-er's detriment.

Think about what a judge might say about claim 12.12 or what the Opposing Team might argue about it during adversarial licensing nego-tiations or in litigation: The claim is ambiguous and thus indefinite? The "wherein" clause does not limit the claimed subject matter and, as a result, the claim reads on some invention-irrelevant prior art?

One *could* argue that "wherein" refers all the way back to "aircraft" as recited in the preamble. However, the placement of the "wherein" clause in the "forward landing gear" paragraph, rather than its own separate paragraph, makes this something of a syntactical stretch that a judge may decline to entertain.

There's no reason to open the door to this kind of attack. When inserting a "wherein" clause with functional language into a claim, do the following:

a) Substitute "in which" for the word "wherein" in your mind and then look to see if there is a clear antecedent—some "which" being referred back to—either an individual element or step or the claimed subject matter as a whole.

b) If there is any colorable way for it to be argued that the "wherein" clause does not affirmatively limit a claim element or step or the claim as a whole, introduce the functional language in a way that expressly invokes the intended antecedent, as in claim 12.13:

---

45. *See also* the discussion at p. 115.
46. *See, e.g. Griffin v. Bertina,* 285 F.3d 1029, 62 USPQ2d 1431 (Fed. Cir. 2002).

12.13 An aircraft including

.

.

.

a forward landing gear mounted to said aircraft by a hinge, ~~wherein~~ <u>in such a way that</u> said landing gear is retractable.

c) Take care not to use a "wherein" clause to inadvertently introduce a method step into an apparatus claim. The Federal Circuit
declared claim 12.14 invalid on this basis,[47] the Court noting that
the words following "wherein" did not define a functional capability but an out-and-out method step in what was otherwise an
apparatus claim:

12.14 An interface control system . . . comprising:
. . . interface means for providing automated voice messages relating to said specific format to certain of said individual callers,
wherein said certain of said individual callers digitally enter data . . .
through said digital input means [emphasis added] . . .

The "wherein" clause in claims 12.14 could have so easily been written properly, as in the following amended version:

12.14 (Amended) An interface control system . . . comprising:
. . . interface means for providing automated voice messages relating to said specific format to certain of said individual callers, <u>the
interface means being adapted to receive data entered digitally by</u>
~~wherein said~~ certain of said individual callers ~~digitally enter data~~ . . .
through said digital input means.

When functional language is inserted into a claim with the express
intent of it being only explanatory and not of limiting effect, it is much
preferable to use "whereby" instead of "wherein." The word "whereby"
is a conjunction and, as such, does not serve to modify something grammatically, unlike "wherein," which is an adverb.

Statements of Intended Use

A statement of intended use for a recited apparatus is a kind of functional language that is also ineffective to define a patentable invention if

---

47. *In re Katz Interactive Call Processing Patent*, 639 F.3d 1303, 97 USPQ2d 1737 (Fed.
Cir. 2011). *See, similarly, IPXL Holdings, L.L.C. v. Amazon.com, Inc.*, 430 F.3d 1377, 77
USPQ2d 1140 (Fed. Cir. 2005).

the claim otherwise reads on the prior art. Consider the following claim to a dispensing top for a popcorn container:

> 12.15 A dispensing top for passing only several kernels of popped popcorn at a time from an open-ended container filled with popped popcorn, having a generally conical shape and an opening at each end, . . . [other structural limitations omitted]

The fact that the claim characterizes the recited dispensing top as being for use to dispense popcorn does not render this claim patentable over other known dispensing tops meeting all the structural limitations but just not disclosed as being useful to dispense popcorn.[48]

Or consider claim 12.16 directed to a rubber-band-shooting device intended to be used to swat insects:

> 12.16 An *insect swatter* comprising:
> an elongated rod having a distal end *for being aimed at an insect,* and
> an elastic lash connected to the rod in such a way that the lash can be elastically stretched and then released so as to swat *said insect.*

Prior art teaching a rubber-band-shooting device meeting the structural language of the claim will render claim 12.16 unpatentable even if not disclosing the use of the device to swat insects.[49]

What Did the Wabash Functional Language Actually Say?

The above examples illustrate the importance of carefully considering both the meaning and placement of functional language. One more example follows, in which the author takes exception as to how functional-language-at-the-point-of-novelty jurisprudence was applied by the Supreme Court in *General Electric Co. v. Appliance Corp.* discussed above.

The invention related to light bulb filaments. It was known that a problem called "sagging" could be solved by using relatively large-grained tungsten, but that, in turn, was known to induce another problem, called "offsetting." The patentee had discovered that *both* problems could be overcome if the large grains of tungsten had an irregular contour. Among the claims in the subject patent were the following, both having functional language at the point of novelty as indicated in italics and both held invalid by the Supreme Court:

---

48. *In re Schreiber,* 128 F.3d 1473, 44 USPQ2d 1429 (Fed. Cir. 1997).
49. *In re Conte,* No. 2011-1331 (Federal Circuit, November 15, 2011).

12.17 A coiled filament composed substantially of tungsten and capable of use in an electric incandescent lamp *without either substantial sagging or offsetting during a normal or commercially useful life.*

12.18 A filament for electric incandescent lamps or other devices, composed substantially of tungsten and made up mainly of a number of comparatively large grains *of such size and contour as to prevent substantial sagging and offsetting . . .*

Claim 12.17 is unduly functional in anyone's book. It characterizes the invention by saying nothing more than that it solves the known prior art problems.

But claim 12.18 is different.

Claim 12.18 recites not simply that the problems of sagging or offsetting are overcome, but broadly recites *how* they are overcome—namely by a combination of grain size and grain contour. Nothing in the Court's opinion suggests that this was something known, or that would have been obvious, to those skilled in the art (although the prior art did know that large grain size by itself could overcome sagging). The Supreme Court nonetheless invalidated claim 12.18, reversing the Court of Appeals[50] which had found claim 12.18 to be valid, the Court of Appeals having characterized claim 12.18 as being not "wholly functional." The author thinks that the Court of Appeals had the better view.

Beyond the question of defining over the prior art, the Supreme Court expressed doubt as to whether claim 12.18 "conveyed definite meaning to those skilled in the art" because the claim did not teach what size and contour would actually be "of *such* size and contour as to prevent substantial sagging and offsetting."

However, modern patent jurisprudence does not require a claim to teach *anything,* and, specifically, a claim doesn't have to enable the public to determine operable proportions.[51] These are matters for the specification. All that definiteness requires is for a claim to clearly define the boundaries of that which the applicant regards as his invention.[52]

So the question of the definiteness of claim 12.18 comes down to this: Given a nonsagging, nonoffsetting filament, could an experiment be done to determine whether those desirable properties were due to the size and contour of the filament grains? For example, it might be possible to vary the size and/or contour of the grains of such a filament to see whether one or both of the undesirable properties returns. If such an experiment

---

50. *General Electric Co. v. Wabash Appliance Corporation, supra* note 7.

51. *In re Fuetterer, supra* note 1.

52. 35 U.S.C. 112(b).

were possible, it could well be argued that the boundaries of claim 12.18 are not indefinite because one can determine whether the grains in any given nonsagging, nonoffsetting filament are "of such size and contour as to prevent substantial sagging and offsetting," as claim 12.18 recites.

CHAPTER REVIEW—Claims with Functional Language

Confirm Your Understanding

1. What is the difference between structural and functional claim language?
2. What are the two main ways in which practitioners use the term "functional claim" (or "functional claiming")?
3. What does it mean for a claim or claim language to be "functional at the point of novelty"?
4. According to the terminological convention of this chapter, when is a claim unduly functional?
5. What is the statutory basis for disallowing claims that are unduly functional?
6. Under what circumstances is it proper for a claim to have functional language at the point of novelty?
7. If particular functional claim language is desired to have a limiting effect (i.e., to provide a point of distinction from the prior art), how must that language tie in to the rest of the claim?
8. What is the literal meaning of "wherein"? What are the claim-drafting implications of that literal meaning?
9. Using principles of present-patent patent jurisprudence, what is an appropriate response to the assertion that claim 12.7 is indefinite for failing to teach anything about what the size or contour of the grains should be? Why, in the author's view, is claim 12.7 (at least potentially) not indefinite?

Questions for Further Thought

10. Why was the patent bar upset with the decision in *Halliburton v. Walker*?
11. The chapter gives "slab," "filter," "brake," "clamp," "screwdriver," and "lock" as examples of structural elements expressed in functional terms. What are some others?
12. Do you agree with the Court's determination in *O'Reilly v. Morse* that claim 8 (our claim 12.1), if upheld, would have given Morse more than he deserved? In that same vein, do you agree with the author that time travel claim 12.9 is not a claim that the first person to actually implement a time machine ought to get?
13. Many practitioners avoid the use of "so that" when introducing functional recitations in their claims, preferring to use, for example, "such that" or "in such a way that." Can you think of why this might be?
14. Why should statements of intended use in an apparatus claim be ignored when assessing a claim's patentability? Is there any downside to including them?

Sharpen Your Skills

15. Write two claims (or claim fragments) that respectively illustrate proper and improper uses of "wherein."

16. Write two claims (or claim fragments) using the phrase "so that" where one of the uses effectively serves to define the boundaries of the claimed subject matter and the other does not.

17. Write a claim to an everyday item that includes a "whereby" clause.

18. What is the difference in scope between claim 12.7 and the following claim in which the claim's functional language has been re-cast?

> A filament . . . made up mainly of a number of comparatively large grains (a) of such size as to prevent substantial sagging and (b) of such contour as to prevent offsetting . . .

CHAPTER THIRTEEN

Means-Plus-Function

Section 112(f) of the patent statute (formerly designated as its "paragraph 6")[1] says that an element in a claimed combination may be expressed as a means or step for performing a specified function without the claim having to be more specific about, for example, the structure that makes up a recited means or the acts (sub-steps) that make up a recited step. The exact language is as follows:

> An element in a claim for a combination may be expressed as a means or step for performing a specified function without the recital of structure, material, or acts in support thereof, *and such claim shall be construed to cover the corresponding structure, material, or acts described in the specification and equivalents thereof* [emphasis added].

As noted in Chapter Twelve, section 112(f) was enacted to statutorily overrule the holding in *Halliburton v. Walker* and thereby return the law to its pre-*Halliburton* state.[2] *Halliburton*, recall, had held that a claim that is functional at the point of novelty is, *ipso facto*, invalid. The prior law had held such a claim to be invalid, however, only if the functional language was such as to render the claim *unduly* functional as defined in Chapter Twelve.

The Federal Circuit, by contrast, has made the law of means-plus-function more restrictive than it was prior to *Halliburton*. It might well be said that, in doing so, the court has thwarted congressional intent, even while professing to be implementing it.[3]

---

1. As of September 16, 2012, § 112 is divided into subsections (a) through (f) corresponding to what were previously referred to as ¶¶ 1 through 6.

2. *See, e.g., In re Donaldson, Co.,* 16 F.3d 1189, 1194 (Fed. Cir. 1994) (stating that Congress enacted the last paragraph to statutorily overrule the holding in *Halliburton*); *In re Fuetterer,* 819 F.2d 259, 264 n.11, 138 USPQ 217, 222 n.11 (CCPA 1963) (noting that it was Congress's intent to restore the law regarding broad functional language in combination claims to its state prior to *Halliburton*).

3. The reader is referred to the excellent review of the history of the enactment of § 112(f) (originally § 112, ¶ 3 and later ¶ 6), Rudolph P. Hofmann Jr. & Edward P. Heller III,

At the heart of the problem is the Court's application of section 112(f)'s last clause (in italics above) and, in particular, the words "and equivalents thereof." It is not clear from the record what Congress intended by this language.[4] But what *is* clear is that the *Federal Circuit's* interpretation cannot be what Congress intended, since the Court's rulings have not returned the law to its pre-*Halliburton* state but to something much more limiting.[5]

Means-Plus-Function Claim Breadth

One issue is the breadth to be accorded to a means-plus-function element. Prior to *Halliburton*, a means-plus-function element was understood to encompass anything that performed the recited function, subject only to (a) the possible limiting effect of language modifying the word "means,"

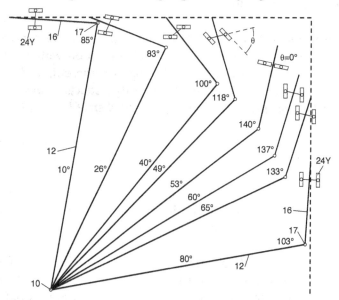

FIGURE 13–1 The invention in Valmont Industries.

The Rosetta Stone for the Doctrines of Means-Plus-Function Patent Claims, 23 RUTGERS COMPUTER & TECH. L.J. 227 (1997).

4. *See generally Graver Tank & Mfg. Co. v. Linde Air Prods. Co.*, 339 U.S. 605, 608–09 (1950); *Roche Palo Alto LLC v. Apotex, Inc.*, 531 F.3d 1372, 1377, 87 USPQ2d 1308 (Fed. Cir. 2008).

5. One reading the opinions rendered by the Federal Circuit over the past 20 years or so could not be faulted for coming away with the impression that the permissibility of means-plus-function claiming originated with the 1952 Congress. That is certainly not the case. Means-plus-function recitations appear in patents issued at least as early as 1898.

e.g., "integrated circuit means," and (b) the possible applicability of the reverse doctrine of equivalents. This understanding arose out of the recognition that an inventive contribution may reside in combining certain functionalities irrespective of how those functionalities might be carried out.

The Federal Circuit, however, has interpreted section 112(f) to require a different result, a perfect illustration of which is its 1993 decision *Valmont Industries, Inc. v. Reinke Manufacturing Co., Inc.*[6]

The invention in *Valmont*, illustrated in Figure 13–1, related to a known type of irrigation system in which an arm 12 with attached sprayers rotates around a center pivot 10. Such an arrangement leaves the corners of a square field unirrigated. The inventor solved this problem by providing an extension arm 16 to extend into each corner of the field as the main arm 12 comes around. The claim element at issue was a "control means" to control the movement of the extension arm—

> control means for operating said moving means to move said extension arm assembly relative to said main arm assembly to irrigate said portions outside of said first portion as said main arm rotates.

The patent owner, Valmont Industries, sued Reinke Manufacturing for patent infringement. Reinke's accused device did, in fact, meet the "control means" language of the claim. Reinke's particular control means sensed electromagnetic signals from a buried cable to control the steering of the extension arm. By contrast, the control means disclosed in Valmont's patent used angle measurement circuitry to determine when the extension arm should be deployed as the main arm traveled its 360° circuit.

The Federal Circuit found that the claim was not infringed. Citing the section 112(f) equivalents language, the Court held that angle measurement circuitry and a buried cable detector were "strikingly different" and thus not equivalent.

There is nothing in the pre-*Halliburton* jurisprudence that would have led to this result—showing that either (a) section 112(f)'s equivalents language was intended only to codify the *reverse* doctrine of equivalents for means-plus-function recitations, as has been suggested in some quarters,[7]and thus not applicable to the *Valmont* situation, or that (b) the Federal Circuit had a way-too-narrow view of what should be regarded as an equivalent. For example, the two electronic ways of implementing the control means (Valmont's angle-measurement-based circuitry and Reinke's buried cable circuitry) don't seem to be so "strikingly different"

---

6. *Valmont Industries Inc. v. Reinke Manufacturing Co., Inc.*, 983 F.2d 1039, 1043, 1044, 25 USPQ2d 1451, 1455 (Fed. Cir. 1993).

7. *Supra* note 3.

when one considers that another possible "control means" might be a horse trained to walk at the periphery of the field and to pull the extension arm into and out of the corners.

The Court's jurisprudence in the aftermath of *Valmont* has been confusing, at best, and inconsistent, at worst. On the one hand, the Court has asserted that "when in a claimed 'means' limitation the disclosed physical structure is of little or no importance to the claimed invention, there may be a broader range of equivalent structures than if the physical characteristics of the structure are critical in performing the claimed function in the context of the claimed invention."[8] Thus a frictional fit of one piece into another can be the equivalent of screw threads or a ball-and-socket joint serving the same function, particularly when these are known to be interchangeable attaching means.[9]

That makes sense.

So go explain, then, why the Court decided in *General Protecht Group v. ITC*,[10] that a magnetic latching means is not equivalent to a mechanical one, even though performing the same function within a claimed combination. Judge Newman raises that very question in her dissent in that case.

Indeed, the physical characteristics of the structure of a means-plus-function element are not only most of the time not *critical* "in performing the claimed function in the context of the claimed invention,"—they are *irrelevant* to it. That is whole reason that the profession, at least as early as 1898, began to use it.[11] So there would have been nothing jurisprudentially amiss for the Court to have been saying all along that to the extent that the physical characteristics of the structure are *irrelevant* in performing the claimed function in the context of the claimed invention, the appropriate range of equivalents encompasses anything that will perform that function.

Unfortunately, the Federal Circuit long ago foreclosed itself from such an approach, as discussed below.[12]

In any event, it is not reasonable to think that Congress enacted section 112(f) with the idea of fostering the kind of departure from accepted means-plus-function practice that the *Valmont* case represents. To the contrary, sound pre-*Halliburton* jurisprudential principles provide every good reason to reward the *Valmont* inventors with a claim broad enough

---

8. *IMS Technology, Inc. v. Haas Automation, Inc.*, 206 F.3d 1422, 54 USPQ2d 1129, 1138 (Fed. Cir. 2000).

9. *Hearing Components, Inc. v. Shure Inc.*, 600 F.3d 1357, 94 USPQ2d 1385 (Fed. Cir. 2010).

10. *General Protecht Group v. ITC*, 619 F.3d 1303, 96 USPQ2d 1292 (Fed. Cir. 2010).

11. *See, e.g.*, U.S. Patent 648,560 filed December 9, 1898, issued May 1, 1900.

12. *See* p. 192.

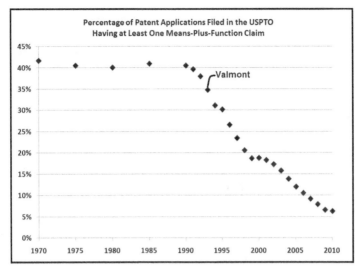

FIGURE 13–2 The decline in means-plus-function claiming in U.S. patent practice.

to cover all ways of controlling the extension arm given that no prior art taught or rendered obvious the idea of having the extension arm at all. Such a claim would be commensurate with, without being any broader than, the *Valmont* inventors' contribution to the art. As it was, the *Valmont* inventors got short-changed.

Given cases like *Valmont*, it is no wonder that there has been a mass exodus from means-plus-function claiming. See Figure 13–2[13] and note how 1992's slight decline in the number of U.S. patents filed with means-plus-function claims turned into an avalanche in 1993—the year in which *Valmont* was decided.

Means-Plus-Function Claim Indefiniteness

The other main piece of fallout from the Court's interpretation of section 112(f) has been in the realm of the disclosure. Prior to *Halliburton*, it was enough for the drawing to depict a particular "means" of the claims as an unadorned "black box" as long as the specification gave enough detail that one skilled in the art would know how to implement what was in the box.

However, the Federal Circuit has said that without any "structure" being shown or described, one cannot tell what the means's equivalents

---

13. Data for Figure 13–2 is based on the filing dates of issued patents having at least one means-plus-function claim.

are; that, therefore, one cannot determine the extent of the means-plus-function element's boundaries; and that, therefore, a claim whose means-plus-function elements are depicted only at the functional level is indefinite and thus invalid.[14] The fact that a person skilled in the art would be readily able to implement the disclosed "means" is not the issue.[15]

Here, again, the Court has gone off track. Recall that the intent of section 112(f) was simply to overrule the effect of *Halliburton* and bring the law back to its pre-*Halliburton* state. There were no such means-plus-function indefiniteness concerns in the pre-*Halliburton* era. Nor is there any evidence that Congress intended section 112(f) to impose any requirements on the disclosure other than the enablement requirements set forth in section 112(a).

The Federal Circuit could have taken a different approach. It could just as easily have said that when a means-plus-function element is shown as a black box, the applicant regards as an equivalent anything that can perform the function. The claim could then be invalidated if the prior art showed, or rendered obvious, any combination meeting the language of the claim, with the inventor having no ability to press for a more narrow interpretation based on a nonequivalence theory. And then the chips would fall where they belong. In the absence of such prior art, the inventor would have coverage for all combinations meeting the language of the claim. There's nothing terrible about that. The absence of such prior art simply means that the inventor was the first to teach the idea of combining the recited various structural (if any) and functional elements in the manner claimed, in which case she *should* be awarded the claim. In the presence of such prior art, on the other hand, the claim would be dead in the water. This is the trade-off that claim drafters had always assumed was in play and, indeed, had relied on.

Unfortunately, the Federal Circuit has now foreclosed itself from such an approach. It has said that allowing a means-plus-function element to encompass all ways of performing the function would amount to impermissible "pure functional claiming."[16]

The court is off base here as well, having confused two different scenarios.

To the extent that one might find an *entire claim* as being impermissible due to its being "purely functional"—like Morse's claim 8 (our claim 12.1)[17]—then fine. But there is no sound jurisprudential basis—other than

14. *See, e.g., Biomedino, LLC, v. Waters Technologies*, 490 F.3d 946, 83 USPQ2d 1118.

15. *Id.*

16. *See, e.g., Blackboard, Inc. v. Desire2Learn Inc.*, 574 F.3d 1371, 91 USPQ2d 1481 (Fed. Cir. 2009); *Net MoneyIN, Inc. v. Verisign, Inc.*, 545 F.3d 1359, 88 USPQ2d 1751 (Fed. Cir. 2008); *Aristocrat Technologies v. International Game Technology*, 521 F.3d 1328, 86 USPQ2d 1235 (Fed. Cir 2008).

17. *See* pp. 164, 168.

the Federal Circuit's own precedent—for objecting to the recital of an *individual element* in purely functional terms. The inventor's broad contribution to the art represented by a combination that includes a means-plus-function element at the point of novelty does not lie in any particular structure that performs the function. If it did, the claim would have to recite that structure in order to be patentable. But otherwise an inventor is entitled to claim a new and obvious combination of elements defined by their structure and/or by the function they perform, *irrespective of their structure*.

The U.S. patent system is much the worse for all of this. With the advent first of electronics, then the digital computer, technological innovations have been increasingly in the realm of new capabilities that clever inventors recognized were made possible by those technologies. This has made ever more problematic the limitations that the Federal Circuit has imposed on inventors' ability to fully define components of inventive combinations in terms not of what they *are* but of what they *do*.

In enacting section 112(f), Congress evinced no intention of departing from the time-honored principle that an inventor is entitled to a claim commensurate with her contribution to the art. The Federal Circuit's failure to take account of that most basic of principles was perhaps the single most significant factor in the Court's derailing of fully effective means-plus-function claiming.

Unfortunately, the Court seems to have come much too far to be able to retrench from what has become decades of precedent. Getting back will undoubtedly require a full reset—either by way of a Supreme Court ruling or an act of Congress.[18]

What's a Poor Claim Drafter to Do?

The tools that the Court has left us with to protect our clients' inventions are confusing and contradictory.

"Don't use the word 'means,'" says the Court, and there will be a presumption against the application of section 112(f), even if the element is defined in functional terms.[19] But that holds only if the functional characterization is accompanied by language that (a) "connotes" a specific structure,[20] with generic terms like "element," "mechanism," and

---

18. Indeed, the Patent Law Committee of the American Intellectual Property Law Association has gone on record as favoring such an amendment. *AIPLA Bulletin*, October-November-December 1994, 137–138.

19. *Inventio AG v. Thyssenkrupp Elevator*, 649 F.3d 1350, 99 USPQ2d 1112 (Fed. Cir. 2011).

20. The "connotes structure" notion seems to have been introduced by the Court in *Personalized Media Communications v. International Trade Com'n*, 161 F.3d 696, at 48 USPQ2d 1880 (1998).

"device" being regarded as equivalent to "means,"[21] or (b) has a generally understood meaning, as demonstrated, for example, by a dictionary
definition. Moreover, since "connotes" means "implies" or "suggests,"
it is not clear, at least to the author, when any particular language will
meet the Court's criterion. Presumably "connote" is a more liberal standard than, for example, "denote," a term that the court has also used.[22]

Apart from the difficulty in applying the connotes-specific-structure
criterion prospectively, it is virtually impossible to predict what the Court
will say as to any particular recitation, as evidenced by the following:

Invokes Section 112(f)	Does NOT Invoke Section 112(f)?
colorant selection mechanism,[23] lever moving element[24]	cooperating detent mechanism,[25] modernizing device,[26] dust collection structure,[27] computing unit,[28] connector assembly,[29] circuit[30]
movable link member[31]	reciprocating member,[32] eyeglass hanger member[33]
detent means,[34] control means,[35] means for metering oil...in predetermined amounts[36]	pumping means,[37] perforation means[38]

---

21. *MIT v. Abacus Software*, 462 F.3d 1344, 80 USPQ2d 1225 (Fed. Cir. 2006).

22. *Lighting World, Inc. v. Birchwood Lighting, Inc.*, 382 F.3d 1354 at 1361; 72 USPQ2d 1344 (Fed. Cir. 2004).

23. *MIT v. Abacus Software, supra* note 21.

24. *Mas-Hamilton Group v. LaGard, Inc.*, 156 F.3d 1206, 48 USPQ2d 1010 (Fed. Cir. 1998).

25. *Greenberg v. Ethicon Endo-Surgery, Inc.*, 91 F.3d 1580, 39 USPQ2d 1783 (Fed. Cir. 1996).

26. *Inventio AG v. Thyssenkrupp Elevator, supra* note 19.

27. *Powell v. Home Depot U.S.A., Inc.*, 100 USPQ2d 1742 (Fed. Cir. 2011).

28. *Inventio AG v. Thyssenkrupp Elevator, supra* note 19.

29. *Lighting World, Inc. v. Birchwood Lighting, Inc., supra* note 22.

30. *Linear Tech. Corp. v. Impala Linear Corp.*, 371 F.3d 1364, 72 USPQ2d 1311 (Fed. Cir. 2004).

31. *Mas-Hamilton Group v. LaGard, Inc., supra* note 24.

32. *CCS Fitness, Inc. v. Brunswick Corp.*, 288 F.3d 1359, 62 USPQ2d 1658 (Fed. Cir. 2002).

33. *Al-Site Corp. v. VSI Int'l, Inc.*, 174 F.3d 1308, 50 USPQ2d 1161 (Fed. Cir. 1999).

34. *Interspiro USA Inc. v. Figgie Int'l Inc.*, 18 F.3d 927, 30 USPQ2d 1070 (Fed. Cir. 1994).

35. *Aristocrat Technologies v. International Game Technology, supra* note 16.

36. *Restaurant Technologies, Inc., v. Jersey Shore Chicken*, 360 Fed. Appx. 120 (Fed. Cir. 2010) (nonprecedential).

37. *TI Group Automotive Systems v. VDO North America*, 375 F.3d 1126, 71 USPQ2d 1328 (Fed. Cir. 2004).

38. *Cole v. Kimberly-Clark Corp.*, 102 F.3d 524, 41 USPQ2d 1001 (Fed. Cir. 1996).

In some of these cases, one can at least understand how the Court might see a particular recitation as connoting a specific structure. "Pumping means," for example, connotes a pump. But what specific structure is connoted by "modernizing device"? We are told that "dust collection structure for collecting dust" is somehow not a means-plus-function element. But by the Court's precedents, "structure for collecting dust" would have to be given means-plus-function treatment inasmuch as (a) the word "structure" is every bit as generic as words like "device," "mechanism," and "element," which the Court says are equivalent to "means," and (b) "collecting dust" is a purely functional recitation. The author does not understand the jurisprudential logic in holding that "dust collecting structure for collecting dust" does not invoke section 112(f) but "means for metering oil . . . in predetermined amounts" does.

In some cases the Court relies on what it finds in the specification to support its finding that a particular recitation connotes structure.[39] This seems inappropriate, if not contradictory, to the Court's precedents. The question is whether the *claim language connotes* a specific structure, not whether the *specification discloses* one. The specifications for most mechanical inventions and many electrical inventions show a specific structure corresponding to each recited claim element. Thus if it were appropriate to prove that particular claim language connotes structure by finding corresponding structure in the specification, then, anomalously, such claims could never be found to invoke section 112(f). And if this is an appropriate analytical approach, why were "lever moving element" and "movable link member"—which corresponded to disclosed structural components—determined to be means-plus-function elements?

The same question is appropriate for "detent means," even though it does use the word "means." The Court has said that even when the word "means" is used, an element that connotes a specific structure will not get means-plus-function treatment.[40] So how did "cooperating detent mechanism [= 'means']" get a pass but "detent means" did not? Perhaps the reader will be more satisfied with the Court's rationale than the author is.[41]

Moreover, we may be hard-pressed to find a structure-connoting word that does not run the risk of being unduly limiting.

Take our microwave oven example.[42] Remember that the reason we want to move the food around within the microwave oven cavity is that

---

39. *Powell v. Home Depot U.S.A., Inc., supra* note 27.

40. *Rembrandt Data Techs., LP v. AOL, LLC,* 641 F.3d 1331, 98 USPQ2d 1393 (Fed. Cir. 2011).

41. *Greenberg v. Ethicon Endo-Surgery, Inc., supra* note 25.

42. *See* p. 55.

standing waves within the cavity create regions where the energy is more intense than average and others where it is less intense than average, which gives rise to uneven heating. We have taken as our hook for patentability the idea of moving the food within the oven cavity as a way of ensuring that more parts of the food will receive their "share" of that more intense energy. But we or the inventor may have realized that there might be some way in which the microwave energy source could be moved, thereby either reducing or eliminating the standing waves or at least causing the standing wave pattern itself to move.

Now then, what structure-specific term will we use to cover the two possibilities of the food being moved and the energy source being moved? "Motion engenderer"? What specific structure does *that* connote? None, really. But then again, neither does "modernizing device," so maybe we would be okay with motion engenderer. Or not.

A way around this problem may be to create a "phantom element" as described in Chapter Eight.[43]

The indefiniteness issue has another dimension. When a claim element that invokes section 112(f) is implemented by a programmed processor (e.g., a computer), the corresponding structure in the specification is the processor programmed to perform the function.[44] Thus unless the algorithm that the processor implements is disclosed, one cannot tell what the functional element's equivalents are. Therefore, one cannot determine the extent of the claimed element's boundaries, and so the claim is indefinite.

So suppose the claimed subject matter includes a word processor as one of its elements. A black box labeled "word processor" will certainly satisfy the enablement requirements of section 112(a); those skilled in the art know how to implement such a black box by loading Microsoft® Word, for example, onto a computer. But a word processor is a computer programmed with word-processing software. Without disclosing the algorithm that the software follows, the claim is indefinite. How is a patent drafter supposed to obtain a description of the algorithm used by Microsoft® Word? More to the point, why should such a thing be required?

In the meantime, we still have claims to draft and inventions to protect. And so the author offers the following (hardly foolproof) suggestions based on what appears to be the state of Federal Circuit precedent as of this writing (early 2012). It is a moving target, though. Each new means-plus-function opinion brings more surprises and, with them, the

---

43. *See* p. 104.
44. *Aristocrat Technologies v. International Game Technology, supra* note 16.

need to adjust one's practice. This is one area of patent practice where keeping up with the latest cases is crucial.

Cast Functional Elements in at Least Some Claims in Non-Means-Plus-Function Form

Given the pervasiveness of computer-implemented technology in virtually every corner of "science and the useful arts," the need to characterize elements of apparatus claims in functional terms continues to increase, even while the percentage of issued patents having claims with "means for" language has dropped from over 40 percent in 1990 to less than 10 percent today (Figure 13–2). This doesn't mean that practitioners have abandoned the use of functional language in claims. It means only that they have abandoned "means for" in favor of other formulae, e.g., "a circuit adapted to."

There is good reason that practitioners have sought to continue to characterize elements functionally while attempting to dodge "means-plus-function treatment" for those elements. To do otherwise—i.e., to characterize an element in purely structural terms—carries with it the risk that the Opposing Team will find a way to design around the claim by doing what the recited physical element does in some other way. Reliance on the doctrine of equivalents to bridge the gap is an unsatisfactory solution. The alleged infringer's way of carrying out the recited function may, indeed, not *be* an equivalent in the doctrine-of-equivalents sense. Even if a good case of equivalence can be made out, convincing the Opposing Team and/or a court to accede to it is no easy matter. As a result, patent owners often forego asserting a patent against an infringer unless they can make out a case of literal infringement. The doctrine of equivalents may not even be available, per the Federal Circuit's and Supreme Court's *Festo* rulings.[45,46]

On the other hand, going back to a means-plus-function formulation carries with it all of the downsides discussed earlier. Not that many patents ever make it to court, where some judge will be called upon to rule on the scope of a means-plus-function recitation. But even in licensing negotiations, the Opposing Team may latch on to a claim's use of means-plus-function language to argue that *their* means is (in the words

---

45. *Festo Corp. v. Shoketsu Kinzoku Kogyo Kabushiki Co.*, 535 U.S. 722, 62 USPQ2d 1705 (2002).

46. *Festo Corp. v. Shoketsu Kinzoku Kogyo Kabushiki, Co.*, 344 F.3d 1359, 68 USPQ2d 1321 (Fed. Cir. 2003) (en banc).

of the *Valmont* court) "strikingly different" from the means disclosed in the patent.

Thus, at least for some claims, we want to be able to define physical elements in functional terms without triggering "means-plus-function treatment."

Here are some guidelines:

- Don't use the word "means," no matter how much other "structure" you think you are claiming. Use of the word "means" gives rise to a presumption that the claim drafter intended to invoke section 112(f);[47] absence of the word "means" gives rise to the opposite presumption.[48]
- Use language that connotes (whatever that may mean) specific structure, with emphasis on the word "specific." Use of modifiers that relate strictly to function, as in "ink delivery means"[49] has been held to not avoid "means-plus-function treatment" for the element.
- Substitutes for the word "means" that do not connote a specific structure will be regarded as synonyms for "means" and thus do not serve to avoid "means-plus-function treatment." It is a little hard to fathom why "circuit for" connotes a specific structure but "element for," "device for," and "mechanism for" do not. But that's what the Court says.[50]
- If you are wedded to using "means" (or other generic terms like "element"), but don't want "means-plus-function treatment," characterize your means with modifiers that evoke a specific or known type of structure. Strangely enough, such means-plus-function recitations are not means-plus-function elements for purposes of section 112(f). Examples are "pumping means,"[51] "connector assembly,"[52] and "trellis encoding means."[53]

Write Beauregard Claims Whenever It Makes Sense

As discussed in Chapter Fifteen,[54] a so-called computer-readable-medium, or "Beauregard," claim is a form of apparatus claim—a "manufacture" in

47. *Net MoneyIN, Inc. v. Verisign, Inc.*, *supra* note 16.

48. *Inventio AG v. Thyssenkrupp Elevator*, *supra* note 19.

49. *Signtech USA, Ltd. v. Vutek, Inc.*, 174 F.3d 1352, 50 USPQ2d 1372 (Fed. Cir. 1999).

50. *Apex Inc. v. Raritan Computer, Inc.*, *supra*; *MIT v. Abacus*, *supra* note 21.

51. *TI Group Automotive Systems v. VDO North America*, 375 F.3d 1126, 71 USPQ2d 1328 (Fed. Cir. 2004).

52. *Lighting World, Inc. v. Birchwood Lighting, Inc.*, *supra* note 22.

53. *Rembrandt Data Techs., LP v. AOL, LLC*, *supra* note 40.

54. *See* p. 235.

the lexicon of 35 U.S.C. 101—directed to a computer-readable medium, such as an optical disc, with programming on it.

Here is a typical example of a Beauregard claim that might have been written to cover the notion of screen editing:

> 13.18 A nontransitory computer-readable medium on which are stored program instructions that, when executed by a processor, cause the processor to perform the operations of
>
> presenting an image on a screen, and
>
> modifying a selected portion of the image in response to user commands.

Except for its preamble, a Beauregard claim reads like a method claim. Thus while providing apparatus claim benefits for the anticipated enforcement scenario,[55] a Beauregard claim allows us to define a software-implemented invention in functional terms without calling for any "means" and thus without invoking section 112(f).

Be sure, however, that defining the invention in terms of a physical readable medium makes sense from the standpoint of the anticipated enforcement scenario. Not that the examiner will disallow a claim on that basis. But the nature of many software-implemented inventions is that no such computer-readable medium will ever come into being, e.g., the invention is a combination of functionalities carried out by diverse elements within a computer network. In that case, it may not be reasonable to think that you will be able to ever find anyone in possession of a computer-readable medium having programming that carries out all the called-for steps. A Beauregard claim would be of questionable value in such a case.

Don't Abandon Means-Plus-Function Claims Altogether

In addition to presenting functional limitations in non-means-plus-function form, consider including some means-plus-function claims as well:

- The Supreme Court or Congress may return means-plus-function claiming to its former status some time during the life of the issued patent, in which case a means-plus-function recitation might be deemed broader than any of the other claims in the patent.
- When an accused apparatus meets a means-plus-function recitation because the apparatus implements an equivalent to the means described in the specification, the means-plus-function recitation

---

55. *See* p. 235.

is met *literally*, per the operation of section 112(f)—*not* as a consequence of the doctrine of equivalents.[56] Thus even if the claim element were amended during prosecution, the *Festo*[57] rule—which severely restricts the use of the doctrine of equivalents for amended recitations—does not apply.

- If you have both means-plus-function and non-means-plus-function claims, the doctrine of claim differentiation[58] may be able to be invoked as a way of demonstrating that the patent's non-means-plus-function claims must be interpreted to be of different, arguably broader, scope than the patent's means-plus-function claims. Or maybe vice versa.[59]

Craft the Specification with Section 112(f) in Mind

To the extent that a claim element does not get "means-plus-function treatment," its presence in the claim does not trigger any special requirements for the specification. That is not the case, however, when section 112(f) is deemed to apply. That may occur either because the claim element explicitly uses the means-plus-function construct or a court gives it "means-plus-function treatment."

Thus whenever functional language is used in a claim, we need to (a) do what we can in the first instance to avoid an element being given "means-plus-function treatment" per the guidelines above (p. 200 unless "means-plus-function treatment" is actually desired, and (b) take account of the requirements that the Federal Circuit has imposed on means-plus-function recitations in the event that an element is given "means-plus-function treatment" despite our best efforts to the contrary.

Here are some guidelines:

- Since reported cases presume an intent on the part of the patentee, based on the claim language, to invoke section 112(f), one might expressly disclaim such intent for all elements not explicitly in "means for . . . " form.[60]
- Secure as broad a range of section 112(f) equivalents as possible.
  - For any disclosed element that might get "means-plus-function treatment," you should explicitly state that any element that

---

56. *See, e.g., Seal-Flex, Inc. v. Athletic Track and Court Const.*, 172 F.3d 836, 50 USPQ2d 1225 (Fed. Cir. 1999).

57. *Supra* notes 42 and 43.

58. *See* p. 124.

59. *AllVoice Computing PLC v. Nuance Communications*, 504 F.3d 1236, 84 USPQ2d 1886 (Fed. Cir. 2007).

60. *See, e.g., Biomedino, LLC v. Waters Technologies Corp., supra* note 14.

can perform the recited function can be used (assuming that that is true)—at least when only one example of the element in question is disclosed. That is the message of *Mettler-Toledo, Inc. v. B-Tek Scales, LLC*[61] which was decided just as this text was being finalized. The Federal Circuit held in that case that a "delta-sigma" analog-to-digital (A/D) converter was not within the scope of the equivalents of the patent's disclosed "multiple slope integrating" A/D converter—claimed as a means-plus-function element—even though any "generic" A/D converter would have functioned equivalently in the context of the claimed combination. The "mistake" that the application drafter apparently made was to not explicitly state that other kinds of A/D converters could perform the recited function. The fact that one skilled in the art would know that a "generic" A/D converter would work in the claimed combination was not enough. By the logic of this case, a) if a claim recites a "means for fastening," b) the specification discloses only a Phillips head screw as doing the fastening, and c) the specification does not explicitly state that other kinds of fasteners could be used to do the fastening, then the "means for fastening" will be limited not only to *screws*, but to *Phillips head* screws.

— Moreover, it is not enough to merely state that other alternatives can be used. One must be *specific* about what the equivalents maybe be. At least that is a take-away of the *Valmont* case. The *Valmont* specification had indicated that the particular form of the recited "control means" was not crucial, stating that "[t]here are a number of ways in which movement of the extension arm 16 may be controlled." But the Court saw no relevance in this statement.

— If you are bold, you might explicitly assert that the applicant regards anything that carries out a function recited in the claim as being an equivalent to that which is shown in the specification. This may backfire, however. The Court might decide that such an assertion serves only to further condemn the means-plus-function element to "purely functional" status and kill the claim as being indefinite.

• Guard against indefiniteness.
— For any functionally defined element whose breadth corresponds to the boundaries of a box shown in the drawing,— e.g., a claimed "means for parsing" is represented in the drawing by a box labeled "parser"— show at least a high-level

61. *Mettler-Toledo Inc. v. B-Tek Scales LLC*, (No. 11-1173, Fed. Cir., February 8, 2012).

implementation of what's inside the box. Otherwise a court may hold that it cannot tell what the equivalents of the recited element are, and thus find the claim indefinite.

— For any functionally defined element that corresponds in the specification to a programmed processor (or computer), you must show something of the algorithm that the processor performs in carrying out the function.[62] The Court says it is not picky about the form of that disclosure.[63] Among the acceptable ways of describing an algorithm, according to the Court, are mathematical formula, prose, or a flowchart. A flowchart, however, should not merely state the ultimate functions performed by the software. Although it is not clear what the Court has in mind, the author believes that the Court is looking for something that would be at a sufficiently detailed level as to represent some degree of program flow.[64]

— Use the word "algorithm" when characterizing the steps of the flowchart or other programming representation.

Step-Plus-Function

Section 112(f) does not distinguish between how a *means* for performing a specific function is to be construed and how a *step* for performing a specific function is to be construed. Indeed, the Federal Circuit has occasionally addressed itself to the issue of what it refers to as "step-plus-function" recitations.[65]

We have already seen that when a means-plus-function element is shown as a box, the specification should give some indication of what "structure" is *inside* the box. Why, then, is there no similar requirement for claims comprising one or more steps—that is, method claims?

According to the Federal Circuit, it's a matter of "for" vs. "of." Since the statute talks in terms of "a means or step *for* performing a specified function" the Court has said that a method claim will get section 112(f) treatment only when the claim drafter signals his intent to invoke section 112(f) by, for example, reciting a step or steps *for* performing a particular

---

62. *Aristocrat Technologies v. International Game Technology, supra* note 16.

63. *Finisar Corp. v. DirecTV Group, Inc.*, 523 F.3d 1323, 86 USPQ2d 1609 (Fed. Cir. 2008).

64. *In re Aoyama*, No. 2010-1552 (Fed. Cir. August 29, 2011).

65. *See, e.g.*, IMS Technology, Inc. v. Haas Automation, Inc., *supra* note 8.

function.[66] Conversely, calling for a step or steps *of* doing something does *not* invoke section 112(f).[67]

The reader should be guided accordingly.

* * * *

In declining to apply section 112(f) to method claims reciting "steps of" and not "steps for," the Federal Circuit reversed the holding of the lower court, saying that

> [c]ourts must be cautious before adopting changes that disrupt the settled expectations of the inventing community.[68]

In view of the profession's wholesale abandonment of means-plus-function claiming, as shown in Figure 13–2, this admonition is ironic indeed.

———

This brings us to the end of Part II. We have identified the invention and its fallback features. And we have seen how to draft claims directed to these. But it is not enough to draft claims in isolation. The patent application's overall claim suite needs to be developed in a way that maximizes the value of the issued patent to the patent owner. That is the subject of Part III, which follows.

66. *See, e.g., Seal-Flex, Inc. v. Athletic Track and Court Const., supra* note 56.

67. *Generation II Orthotics, Inc. v. Med. Tech. Inc.*, 263 F.3d 1356, 59 USPQ2d 1919 (Fed. Cir. 2001); *OI Corp. v. Tekmar Co. Inc.*, 42 USPQ2d 1777 (Fed. Cir. 1997).

68. *Masco v. United States*, 303 F.3d 1316 at 1327, 64 USPQ2d 1182 (Fed. Cir. 2002), quoting the U.S. Supreme Court in *Festo Corp. v. Shoketsu Kinzoku Kogyo Kabushiki Co., supra* note 46.

CHAPTER REVIEW—Means-Plus-Function

Confirm Your Understanding

1. In what two basic ways does the Federal Circuit's interpretation of section 112(f) put limitations on means-plus-function elements as compared to their use prior to *Halliburton v. Walker*?
2. What criteria does the Federal Circuit put forth as determining whether a claim element will be treated as a means-plus-function element for purposes of section 112(f)?
3. What is the train of logic that the Federal Circuit follows in concluding that a means-plus-function claim element supported only by a black box in the disclosure is indefinite?
4. Notwithstanding their potential problems, why might it be good to include some means-plus-function claims in the overall claim suite?
5. In what way(s) does a Beauregard (computer-readable-medium) claim achieve some of the advantages of means-plus-function claiming while avoiding some of its drawbacks?
6. Why does the Federal Circuit insist that when the "means" of a claim is supported in the specification by a programmed processor or computer, that the algorithm that the processor implements needs to be shown?

Questions for Further Thought

7. The author's views notwithstanding, does the Court's holding in *Valmont* sit well with you?
8. The author finds the Federal Circuit's assessments of when functional recitations should or should not get "means-plus-function treatment" to be "confusing and contradictory." (p. 197). If you agree, what do you think might be the root causes?
9. If you had the opportunity to rewrite 35 U.S.C. 112(f), would you leave it as is or change it? If the latter, how would you have the statute read?
10. What might be the consequence(s) of eliminating 35 U.S.C. 112(f) altogether?
11. The Federal Circuit has found that glue is the equivalent of a rivet or a button as a "fastening means." *Al-Site Corp. v. VSI Int'l, Inc.*, 174 F.3d 1308, 50 USPQ2d 1161 (Fed. Cir. 1999). How does this square with the Court's holdings that something must be a "structural equivalent" to be an equivalent under section 112(f)? See, e.g., *Tip Systems, LLC v. Phillips & Brooks/Gladwin*, 529 F.3d 1364, 87 USPQ2d 1254 (Fed. Cir. 2008).

12. The Federal Circuit says that a method claim calling for a step or steps *for* doing something invokes treatment of the claim under section 112(f) whereas a step or steps *of* doing something does not invoke such treatment. What is the basis for the Court's distinction between "for" and "of"? Given that large sums of money often hang in the balance in a patent infringement suit, do you feel that the assessment of whether a claim is infringed should hinge on such a tiny lexical difference?

13. Do you find anything strange about the term "step-plus-function"?

14. Does it bother you that a means-plus-function recitation might not be regarded as invoking section 112(f)?

Sharpen Your Skills

15. Commit section 112(f) to memory. (It will come in handy when you are having means-plus-function discussions with your colleagues.)

16. Create a set of rules, decision tree, or other analytical tool that could be used to show whether a given claim recitation with functional language would or would not be deemed by the Federal Circuit to invoke section 112(f).

17. Prepare an outline of an opinion, or perhaps a full-blown opinion, that the U.S. Supreme Court might issue in affirming or reversing (your option) one of the Federal Circuit's means-plus-function rulings.

PART III

The Claim Suite and the Anticipated Enforcement Scenario

Introduction to Part III: The Claim Suite
and the Anticipated Enforcement Scenario

Drafting claims that will be allowed by the patent examiner is only a part of the patent attorney's job. Another is anticipating what will happen when the patent owner goes to enforce the claims—referred to here as the "anticipated enforcement scenario."

PART III—*The Claim Suite and the Anticipated Enforcement Scenario*—describes how to assemble a suite of claims that maximizes the value of the patent to the patent owner and that minimizes the possibility of something going wrong at enforcement time.

CHAPTER FOURTEEN introduces the idea of invention settings. An invention setting is a particular environment or context in which the invention is manifest. For example, two settings for a lock invention could be the lock itself and a key appropriate to operate the lock. It is desirable to claim an invention in all of its commercially significant settings in order to maximize a patent's value when it comes time to enforce it. Chapter Fourteen also introduces the idea of the "single reachable party." Enforcement of a claim can be difficult or impossible unless all of its limitations are carried out by (a) a single party who is (b) subject to the jurisdiction of the U.S. legal system (assuming a U.S. patent).

CHAPTER FIFTEEN emphasizes the importance of claiming an invention using all appropriate statutory claim types. Consider a patent claiming machinery that implements a novel manufacturing step. Machines on a factory floor, especially their innards, are not easily inspected by outsiders. It may be difficult to prove, therefore, that the competitor's machine meets each recited element of an apparatus claim. However, it may be clear from the vended product that the novel step was used, making it desirable to have method claims and claims directed to the product. A statutory class is not the same thing as an invention setting. For example, a given invention can be claimed in multiple settings using the same statutory claim type, such as the lock and key mentioned above. An invention can also be claimed within a single setting using more than one statutory claim type. In addition, having claims in the right statutory class may be crucial to the patent's realizing its full economic potential.

For example, a percentage royalty based on a claim directed to manufacturing machinery may be only a tiny fraction of the royalty that would be generated by a method or apparatus claim covering the machinery's throughput.

CHAPTER SIXTEEN focuses on claim diversity. This means defining the invention—even within a given statutory class—by using different claim formats, applying different terminology, or presenting claim elements in a different order. This is often referred to as claiming the invention from different "angles." Diversity in the overall claim suite addresses the possibility that any one claim may contain an unappreciated infringement loophole. Drafting both problem-solution-based and inventive-departure-based claims as described in Chapters Six and Seven, for example, provides a measure of diversity to the claim suite.

CHAPTER SEVENTEEN summarizes all the considerations that should be brought to a review of the claim suite with the anticipated enforcement scenario in mind.

CHAPTER FOURTEEN

Invention Settings and Direct Infringers

A patent owner may not realize the full value of her patent unless the invention is claimed in all of its commercially significant settings.

An invention setting—also called a "claim perspective" or "claim point-of-view"—is an environment or context in which the inventive concept is manifest. We will see how a cylinder lock invention, for example, can be manifest in at least three different settings—the lock itself, the key, and the key-cutting machine. An invention setting is "commercially significant" when it is expected that competitors will implement the invention in that particular setting.

Realizing the full value of a patent also requires that the claims will capture the activities of (a) an individual—as opposed to co-acting— parties who (b) would be direct infringers if unlicensed. That goal is largely achieved, as it turns out, when the claims define the invention strictly within the boundaries of its various settings. Drafting and reviewing claims with individual direct infringers specifically in mind helps ensure that the claims will capture the activities of those parties.

This chapter discusses patent value principally in terms of license royalties or monetary damages. The ideas in this chapter, however, apply with equal force when a patent is to be cross-licensed or when the patent owner intends to exercise her right of exclusivity. In any of these cases, the patent owner's goals may be less than fully realized if the claims define the invention in less than all of its commercially significant settings and/or do not capture the activities of individual direct infringers.

Two exercises presented at the end of the chapter—one involving a clothing manufacturing process and the other a web server network— give the reader an opportunity to analyze claims with the ideas of the chapter in mind.

Invention Settings

In this section we explore the notion of an invention's commercially important settings and see why a patent's value depends on claiming the invention in all of them.

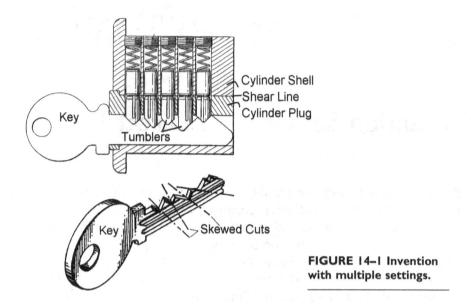

FIGURE 14–1 Invention with multiple settings.

Invention Settings Explained

The cylinder lock invention presented in Figure 14–1 illustrates an invention with multiple settings.

As in cylinder locks generally, the cylinder plug of this lock can rotate within the cylinder shell only if the key raises the top of each tumbler to the shear line. Doing that in this particular lock requires that the key not only raise the tumbler by a particular amount, as in the prior art, but that the key also must *rotate* the tumbler by some amount. The rotation is caused by key cuts that are skewed rather than perpendicular to the plane of the key. Not only are the lock and key unique, but the key must be cut on a unique key-cutting machine.

The novelty in each of these components stems from a single inventive concept—the fact that the tumblers are rotated. Yet the lock, the key, and the key-making machine represent three different settings in which the inventive concept is manifest. The key blank might be a fourth setting if it has some feature that distinguishes it from prior art key blanks.

As another example, two settings for a paper-making invention could be (a) the composition of the paper and (b) the manufacturing of the paper.

An invention setting is not the same as a statutory class. The latter is an invention category—a process, machine, manufacture, or composition of matter.[1] An invention setting, by contrast, is an environment or con-

---

1. 35 U.S.C. 101.

text in which the inventive concept is manifest. In our lock example, the contexts are the lock itself, the key, and the key-cutting machine.

Indeed, an invention can often be defined in a given setting using more than one statutory claim type. For example, the lock invention could be defined within the key-cutting machine setting by apparatus claims defining the structure of the machine as well as by method claims defining how the machine operates to cut the key. In the paper-manufacturing setting, the invention could be claimed both as a method for making the paper and as an apparatus (paper-making machine) that carries out that method.

Nor is an invention setting the same as an invention embodiment. The embodiments of an invention differ in the details of how the invention is implemented. Our paper composition could include synthetic fibers in one embodiment and natural fibers in another. But either embodiment might be claimed in either of the two settings noted above.

Many, if not most, inventions have multiple settings, as in the following further examples:

- (a) Chemical compound useful as a pharmaceutical; (b) making the compound; (c) treating a medical condition using the compound
- (a) Encoding a video signal (to reduce the amount of data required to represent it); (b) decoding the encoded signal
- (a) Plastic container; (b) preform useful in producing the container; (c) producing the container from the preform
- (a) Roadway base intermediate; (b) roadway base containing the intermediate; (c) roadway made of the roadway base that contains the intermediate
- (a) Peptide; (b) cell capable of producing the peptide; (c) manufacturing the peptide

The Importance of Invention Settings

As noted at the outset, the patent owner may not realize the full value of his patent unless the invention is claimed in all of its commercially significant settings. We might think to claim the lock and be done with it; however, others might only cut keys or might only make the key-cutting machine, thus not infringing the lock claim and not being liable to the patent owner.

Claiming an invention in all of its commercially significant settings is particularly important when the royalty base in one setting is significantly larger than in another. One would certainly think to claim a television signal format invention in the setting in which the signal is generated—the broadcast transmitter. However, there are only about 20,000 television stations worldwide, and their owners do not buy new transmitters very often. By contrast, more than 150 million television *sets* and more than 45 million set-top boxes are sold worldwide every year. That's more than 3 billion television sets and set-top boxes over the 15 to 18 years of a patent's enforceable lifetime. The patent owner would certainly not be content to collect royalties on only 20,000 transmitters when, with a properly drafted claim, he could collect royalties on 3 billion television sets and set-top boxes.

It is, in fact, possible to claim such an invention in a receiving-end (e.g., television set, set-top box, decoding chip) setting even though the circuitry required to decode the signal might be obvious given a knowledge of the signal format.

Claim 14.1 is such a claim, in which the inventive concept is the notion of frequency-interleaving the chrominance (color) and luminance (black-and-white) information of a color video signal.[2]

> 14.1 Apparatus comprising
>
> (a) an input for receiving color video signals having interleaved chrominance and luminance information contained within the video signals, and
>
> (b) a signal processor configured to recover the luminance and chrominance information from the received video signals.

A helpful technique for identifying an invention's settings is to make a sketch—perhaps a block diagram, flowchart, functional representation, or pictorial drawing—that can bring to our attention the various contexts in which the invention may be manifest.

Figure 14–2 is a sketch for a video compression invention, which involves both encoding the video signal and, at some point thereafter, decoding the encoded signal. Sketching out the figure helps us to realize that the settings for this invention include

- Encoding and decoding settings—that is, the encoding and decoding algorithms per se may be carried out by integrated circuits vended by an integrated circuit manufacturer or by software on the hard drive of a computer;
- Equipment encoding and equipment decoding settings—that is, video equipment including studio cameras, web cams, broadcast

---

2. Such a scheme is implemented in the NTSB standard broadcast television signal. *See* U.S. Patent 2,635,140 (issued April 14, 1953).

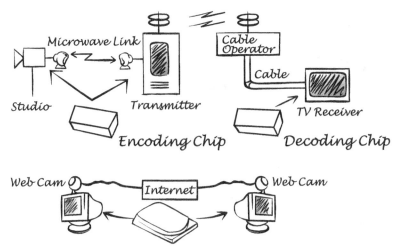

FIGURE 14–2 Making a sketch is a useful way of identifying an invention's settings.

transmitters/receivers, and personal computers, all of which may include the above-mentioned encoding and/or decoding integrated circuit(s) or the software; and

* Transmission setting—that is, transmission media over which the encoded signals might travel, including studio-to-transmitter microwave links, coaxial cables, and the facilities of Internet service providers. (This setting is of mostly academic interest, however, since a claim to the invention in this setting would most likely be directed to the video signal itself. Such a claim has been declared to be directed to nonstatutory subject matter.[3])

Claiming the invention in all of its commercially significant settings ensures that we will have claims that capture the activities of all classes of parties against whom the patent owner may want to assert the issued patent. A claim that defines the invention in the encoding setting, as in Figure 14–3(a), will capture the activities of integrated circuit manufacturers and importers. A claim that, as in Figure 14–3(b), defines the invention in the equipment encoding setting—this by virtue of its including steps or components that are outside of the encoding algorithm per se—will capture the activities of video equipment manufacturers and importers.

Competitors' equipment is also affected by an encoding setting claim since the algorithm is performed within the equipment. An advantage of

---

3. *In re Nuijten*, 500 F.3d 1346, 84 USPQ2d 1495 (Fed. Cir. 2007).

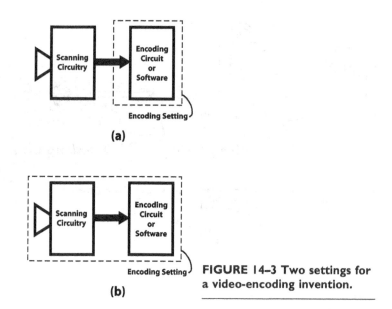

FIGURE 14–3 Two settings for a video-encoding invention.

the equipment claim, however, is its larger royalty base.[4] So the patent owner's licensing strategy might be to license the equipment manufacturers instead of the integrated circuit manufacturers.[5]

A possible disadvantage of a licensing strategy that focuses on the equipment manufacturers is the need to license each equipment manufacturer individually. There may be too many of them to make this practical. The patent holder's strategy might therefore be to negotiate for royalties from, or attempt to secure injunctions against, the relatively few integrated circuit manufacturers rather than attempting to enforce the patent against innumerable equipment manufacturers further down the supply chain.

On the other hand, equipment may implement the algorithms in software, such as software bundled with a personal computer's operating system. The value of that fraction of the operating system software that carries out the video encoding and decoding may be quite small indeed, making it difficult to argue for significant royalties.

The patent owner may therefore want to adopt a dual-pronged strategy, charging royalties from integrated circuit manufacturers for integrated circuits that implement the invention, and charging royalties from

---

4. *See* p. 133.

5. The doctrine of patent exhaustion would typically preclude the patent owner getting royalties from both the integrated circuit manufacturer and the equipment manufacturer. *See, e.g., United States v. Univis Lens Co.,* 316 U.S. 241, 53 USPQ 44 (1942).

equipment manufacturers for equipment that implements the invention in software.

There is no need for any of this to be decided at the time of filing. Indeed, the patent owner's enforcement strategy could change over time. Having claims directed to the invention in all of its commercially significant settings keeps all the options open.

One of the author's colleagues makes it a practice to identify all of the commercially important invention settings before beginning any claim drafting. He then proceeds methodically through the identified settings, drafting claims for each one.

> *"I spend a lot of time thinking through the invention settings before I even get into the guts of a first draft of a claim. Understanding the larger picture of protecting the invention from these different settings allows me to automatically exclude a range of meaningless limitations that might be improperly suggested by a poorly analyzed picture claim. For example, trying to get a claim to the structure of a key will inevitably get me thinking about what parts of the key-cutting machine are just not relevant and meaningful to the exclusionary grant I am crafting when I am drafting key-cutting-machine claims.*
>
> *Only after I have a map in my mind of the settings of all of the independent claims do I move on to fleshing out the guts of each claim."*
>
> *—BSL*

Maintaining the Integrity of the Invention-Setting Boundary

Having decided to claim the invention in a particular setting, we must take care to restrict the claim to that setting. If something outside the boundary of the setting makes its way into the claim, parties whose activities would otherwise infringe the claim may no longer do so.

Consider, for example, claim 14.2, which is intended to define a video compression invention in its encoding (e.g., integrated circuit) setting, as depicted in Figure 14–3(a).

> 14.2 A method comprising
> generating a video signal to be encoded, and
> encoding the video signal by. . .
> (a) . . .
> (b) . . .
> (c) . . .

Unfortunately, the step of "generating a video signal to be encoded" is outside of the intended setting; encoding circuitry or software does not generate the video signal, but receives it from somewhere else. This is a point that integrated circuit manufacturers will lose no time in pointing out when the patent owner approaches them to take a license. And while it would be fairly easy to make a case for contributory infringement or inducement in this situation, those are suboptimal enforcement strategies, as discussed below.

Including the step of "generating a video signal" in a claim intended to define the invention in the encoding setting is an easy trap to fall into. After all, the "work stuff" of the algorithm is the video signal, and it does have to be generated by *something*. True, but that doesn't mean that the video signal has to be generated *in the claim*. Rather, input signals can usually be simply assumed to exist, as though handed to us by a genie; there is no need to explicitly generate an input signal in a claim. In this particular case we can simply eliminate claim 14.2's offending "generating" step and change the encoding step to that of "encoding *a* video signal," per claim 14.3:

> 14.3 A method comprising
> encoding a video signal by. . .
> (a) . . .
> (b) . . .
> (c) . . .

As another example, consider claim 14.4, whose intended setting is a piece of apparatus intended for use in a packet transmission network, such as the Internet. The problematic recitation is a control unit "connected to" a packet transmission network.

> 14.4 Apparatus comprising
> (a) a control unit *connected to* a packet transmission network and configured to monitor traffic on the network,
> (b) . . .
> (c) . . .

This claim goes outside the boundary of the apparatus setting. It requires that the apparatus actually be connected to the network. The claim does not read on the apparatus as sold by the manufacturer, but only after the network owner connects the apparatus to its network. This problem is remedied in claim 14.5.

> 14.5 Apparatus comprising
> (a) a control unit configured to monitor traffic on a packet transmission network,

(b) . . .

(c) . . .

Our goal should be to draft claims that will read on a competitor's product as it sits on the competitor's shipping dock. This might even be thought of as the "shipping dock setting."

Thinking about the advertising disclaimer "batteries not included" is another helpful way of analyzing whether a claim violates a given invention setting boundary. What "batteries" might the Opposing Team not include with their product as shipped?

The Individual Direct Infringer

The invention should be claimed in a way that will capture the activities of individual direct infringers.

Direct infringement of a patent occurs when someone, without authority, makes, uses, offers to sell, sells, or imports something that meets all the limitations of at least one of the patent's claims.[6]

There are other ways in which someone can be liable under a patent, such as by inducing someone else to infringe[7] or by being a contributory infringer,[8] these being forms of so-called indirect infringement. However, contributory infringement and inducement require proof that some party is a direct infringer.[9] Without a direct infringer, there can be no contributory infringer. Nor can there be an inducer of infringement. So a case of direct infringement will have to be proved in any event. Moreover, indirect infringement involves additional proof elements. For example, contributory infringement requires proof that the part of the invention supplied by the accused party constitutes a "material part" of the invention and also requires that the accused party knew of the patent and knew that the part was especially made or especially adapted for use in an infringement of the patent.[10] Going further, the invention should be claimed in a way that will capture the activities of *individual* direct infringers. Multiple parties can be liable as joint direct infringers, such as where Party A carries out the initial steps of a claimed manufacturing method to produce an intermediate product that is completed by Party B

---

6. 35 U.S.C. 271(a).

7. 8. 35 U.S.C. 271(b).

8. 35 U.S.C. 271(c).

9. *See, e.g., Fujitsu Ltd. v. Netgear Inc.*, 620 F.3d 1321, 96 USPQ2d 1742 (Fed. Cir. 2010).

10. 35 U.S.C. 271(c).

carrying out the remaining claimed steps.[11] However, the mere fact that parties can be found whose combined activities meet all the claim limitations does not necessarily establish them as joint infringers. There needs to be either an agency relationship between the parties who perform the method steps or one party needs to be contractually obligated to the other to perform at least one of the steps.[12] Those kinds of connections between the parties are often not there.

Even if those connections *are* there, joint infringement may not exist if a claim encompasses the activities of parties in different countries. For example, the apparatus claims of a U.S. patent are directly infringed only if all of the claimed assembled or unassembled apparatus is made, used, offered for sale, sold, or imported within the United States.[13]

And even if joint infringement *could* be made out in a given case, this is not something we want to have to do. More facts will have to be proved; more parties will have to be deposed; more attorneys will be involved; and so forth.

Moreover, since we have full control over the claims when the patent application is being drafted, there is no excuse for not claiming the invention in a way that will capture the activities of individual direct infringers if there is any way to do it. The idea that "we can always get them for contributory or inducement" or that "we can always just sue them jointly" is not a valid reason to pass up the opportunity to draft claims that will be directly infringed by individual parties when we can do so.

Claiming the invention in all of its commercially significant settings usually takes us most, if not all, of the way there. For example, claiming our video-encoding invention in its coding/decoding setting, per claim 14.3 and Figure 14–2a, ought to make for a pretty airtight case against individual integrated circuit manufacturers or vendors of encoding/decoding software. However, we may have missed a setting altogether.

11. *See, e.g., Shields v. Halliburton Co.*, 493 F. Supp. 1376, 1389, 207 USPQ 304 (W.D. La. 1980), *aff'd*, 667 F.2d 1232, 216 USPQ 1066 (5th Cir. 1982), 182 USPQ 644; *On Demand Mach. Corp. v. Ingram Indus.*, 442 F.3d 1331, 1335, 78 USPQ2d 1428 (Fed. Cir. 2006) (decided on other grounds).

12. *BMC Resources, Inc. v. Paymentech, Lp*, 498 F.3d 1373, 84 USPQ2d 1545 (Fed. Cir. 2007); *Akamai Technologies, Inc. v. Limelight Networks, Inc.*, 629 F.3d 1311, 97 USPQ2d 1321 (Fed. Cir. 2010), vacated, Nos. 2009-1372, -1380, -1416, -1417 (Fed. Cir. April 20, 2011); *McKesson Techs. Inc. v. Epic Sys. Corp.*, 2011 U.S. App. LEXIS 10674, 98 USPQ2d 1281 (Fed. Cir. 2011), vacated, No. 2010-1291 (Fed. Cir. May 26, 2011).

13. 35 U.S.C. 271. By contrast, a party within the United States who interacts with a system, for example, over communication lines, "uses" that system and is therefore an infringer, even if a portion of the system lies outside the United States. *NTP, Inc. v. Research in Motion, Ltd.*, 418 F.3d 1282, 75 USPQ2d 1763 (Fed. Cir. 2005).

Drafting and reviewing claims with the individual direct infringer in mind helps assure that all bases are covered.

Two Frequent "Offenders"

Try as we might to draft claims that individuals will directly infringe, the Opposing Team may outsmart us—figuring out some way we did not anticipate to divide the claim steps or apparatus elements among multiple parties. We will see an example of that below.

At the very least, however, we can avoid claiming the invention in ways where multiple-party action is likely, if not guaranteed.

One typical frequent offender is the so-called system claim. Claim 14.6 is such a claim, directed to a telecommunications network comprising two telephone central offices and interoffice circuits interconnecting them.

> 14.6 A telecommunications network comprising
> (a) an originating central office,
> (b) a terminating central office,
> (c) one or more interoffice circuits interconnecting the originating and terminating central offices, and
> (d) . . .

The difficulty is that the two central offices may belong to two different local telephone companies and the interoffice circuits may include the facilities of yet a third party, such as a long-distance carrier. Under those facts no single party would infringe this claim. And if the parties do not work in sufficiently close concert that they might be deemed joint infringers, that avenue of enforcement would be foreclosed as well.

By comparison, claim 14.7 defines the same invention in the central office setting rather than the system setting. As such, it limits infringement to a single party—the manufacturer of the central office—and reads on the product as it sits on the manufacturer's shipping dock without the apparatus having to be "up and running" or connected into a network as claim 14.6 requires.

> 14.7 A central office adapted for use in a telecommunications network, the central office comprising
> (a) a network adapter configured to transmit signals to another central office in the network via one or more interoffice circuits, and
> (b) . . .

Claim 14.7 offers another advantage over claim 14.6. Even if a single party owned and operated all of the elements called for in claim 14.6, that single party would most likely be a telephone company. The patent owner is likely a manufacturer of telecommunications equipment. In theory, the patent owner could assert the patent against telephone companies that buy infringing equipment from competing manufacturers. Asserting a patent against your own customers is not a good way to engender good will and future sales, however. Claim 14.7 enables the patent owner to avoid that situation since it can be asserted against competing manufacturers directly. Indeed, forcing competitors to pay a royalty increases the competitors' costs and may enable the patent owner to offer her own equipment at a lower price.

Another frequent offender is the consumer action claim. This is a claim that invokes action on the part of a consumer or other private party in what is, in essence, a commercial activity. The claimed subject matter in claim 14.8, for example, is a method in which a computer user selects a displayed icon, causing a signal indicating the selected icon to be transmitted to a web server. The web server, in turn, processes that signal in some novel way. The claim comprises two steps (a and b) performed by the computer user and two steps (c and d) performed by the web server.

> 14.8 A method comprising
> (a) selecting an icon displayed on a screen,
> (b) transmitting to a web server a signal indicative of the selected icon,
> (c) receiving the signal at the web server,
> (d) processing the received signal in such a way that. . . .

A computer user and a web server operator are certainly not likely to be found to be in an agency relationship, nor is one of them likely to be contractually obligated to the other to perform any of the steps.[14] As such, they are unlikely to be adjudged joint direct infringers.

As in the system claim case, there is a ready fix: draft a claim strictly limited to the web server setting. Claim 14.9 is such a claim. It calls for the web server to receive and then process the signal generated by the computer user without affirmatively reciting any user-performed steps.

> 14.9 A method comprising
> (a) receiving a signal indicative of a user-selected screen-displayed icon
> (b) processing the received signal in such a way that. . . .

---

14. *See* p. 220.

Even if a patent were to contain only multiparty claims, the patent owner would not be without some recourse. The Opposing Team's assertion that "we don't do everything called for in the claim" can be responded to by suggesting that the Opposing Team's customers might be liable as joint or contributory direct infringers. Those options may have little legal merit, but the specter of customers being joined in a patent suit may nonetheless bring the target infringer to heel. No businesspeople want their business relationships strained in that way. But the ploy may not work. The accused party may call the patent owner's bluff, forcing her to then bring an action that stands a good chance of failing in the final analysis.

There is no way around it. No opportunity should be missed to claim the invention in a way that captures the activities of individual direct infringers.

Take On an Opposing Team Mind-set

The Opposing Team readily finds infringement loopholes because they are *motivated* to find those loopholes and, indeed, to exploit them. By taking on an Opposing Team mind-set, we can find those loopholes just as easily and close them while the claims are still being drafted. Putting ourselves into an Opposing Team mind-set, then, is a good way to verify that (a) the invention has been claimed in all of its commercially significant settings, and (b) the claims will capture the activities of individual direct infringers to the maximum extent possible.

A colleague of the author puts himself into an Opposing Team mind-set by imagining that the claim is under attack. He thinks in terms of both what he calls easy attacks and subtle attacks.

An "easy" attack occurs when the Opposing Team finds a way to implement the inventor's teachings while avoiding one or more limitations in the claim. A subtle attack occurs when the Opposing Team creates a business model in which even if all the limitations of a claim are met, there is no individual direct infringer.

"Security experts often speak of analyzing 'attacks' in a cryptographic sense and their practical viability in a real-world setting. I think of claims similarly. There are the easy 'attacks,' such as a competitor relying on limitations that clearly do not need to be reflected in the broadest abstraction that is the independent claim. For example, a product claim that includes a 'magnetizable sleeve' as an element could possibly be avoided by introducing a sleeve that is not 'magnetizable.' That would be an 'easy' attack on a claim. Thwarting such an attack is simply a matter of reading closely.

> *Then there are the more subtle 'attacks' that are often overlooked—such as a competitor creating a business model that does not require the practice of certain steps or the construction/use/sale of certain components that are required by a claim.*
>
> *An example of a more 'subtle' attack would be considering alternative business models that avoid the territorial effects of a U.S. patent or that separate the components/activities of a product/service claim in a way that can avoid contributory infringement issues. If a service claim requires steps A, B, and C, consider whether steps B and C can be performed in Cameroon (especially problematic for a lot of Internet-related patents). If a product requires components A, B, and C, consider a business arrangement where you sell only parts A and B and require customers to obtain a licensed version of C."*
>
> —BSL

As an example of such a subtle-attack business model, consider the discovery that the insulation on scrap wire can be removed from the metal by chopping the wire into very fine pieces and agitating the pieces in an ultrasound bath. The insulation will float and the bare metal will sink to the bottom of the bath, from which it can be readily recovered and recycled.

Claim 14.10 recites the process in two steps: chopping the wire and agitating the chopped pieces in an ultrasound bath to separate the insulation from the metal.

> 14.10   A method comprising,
> chopping insulation-covered metal wire into pieces that are no longer than the width of the insulation, and
>   agitating the chopped pieces in an ultrasound bath,
>   whereby the insulation and the metal separate in the bath.

Figure 14-4 shows how this can easily be made a multiparty activity in which Party I does the chopping and Party II does the agitating and recovery of the bare wire. Even if the parties have a close connection, there is no infringement in this country if the Opposing Team sets up its business in such a way that the scrap wire is chopped in Canada and then shipped into New York State for agitation/separation. Or Party II may choose to buy already-chopped wire from an unrelated Party I, who sells chopped wire on the open market for some other use, such as a filler of some kind or for recycling in a process not based on ultrasound removal of the insulation.

Rather than relying on the law or the facts to fall our way, we would do better to turn this into a process that one individual will infringe. Claim 14.11 encompasses the actions of Party II exclusively.

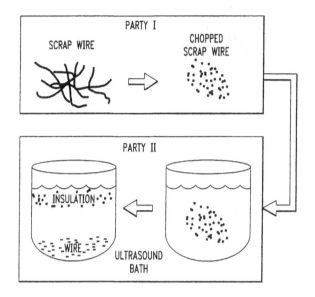

FIGURE 14–4 An invention that the Opposing Team might divide into a multiparty process in the hopes of avoiding infringement.

14.11 A method comprising,
   agitating, in an ultrasound bath, pieces of insulation-covered metal wire that are no longer than the width of the insulation, whereby the insulation and the metal separate in the bath.

Other analytical approaches might also have brought us to claim 14.11. It may have occurred to us when analyzing the invention's settings that the ultrasound bath is a setting in and of itself. Or we might have recognized the chopped wire as being an input to a process that simply involves agitation and, as such, is not required to be generated within the claim, just as a video signal can be treated as an input to an encoding process and, as such, not required to be generated within a claim to the encoding process per se. Or we could have recognized that because the chopped wire is an intermediate product in claim 14.10, further distillation of the claim is possible.

None of the pitfalls discussed in this section are difficult for the alert claim drafter to avoid. The key is simply to recognize that we get a patent not because the patent owner wants to do something, but because someone else may want to do it. Taking on an Opposing Team mind-set will enable us to quickly appreciate all the things someone else might do that take advantage of the invention and to assure ourselves that our claim suite will encompass all the ways that an individual party might carry them out.

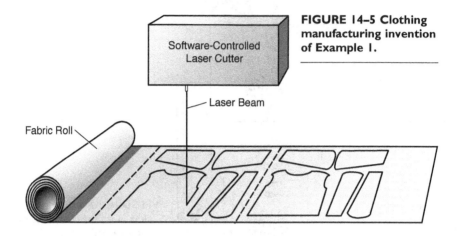

FIGURE 14–5 Clothing manufacturing invention of Example 1.

Exercises for the Reader

The claims in the following two examples violate various precepts set forth in this chapter. They also contain unnecessary elements and other unduly narrowing limitations not necessary to distinguish the invention from the prior art.

The reader is invited to take on the role of the Opposing Team's patent attorney and figure out all the ways in which noninfringement can be argued and/or how the Opposing Team's business model could be arranged so as to ensure noninfringement.

Each example is followed by the author's analysis and a suggested improved claim.

Example 1: Clothing Manufacture

Invention

The typical prior art clothing manufacturing process for making a shirt, for example, cuts through a stack of fabric to produce a large number of shirt fronts, then shirt backs, then sleeves, collars, and so on. One of each component of the shirt is then taken from a respective stack so that the garment can be sewn together. The inventive departure is a process for small-scale manufacturing of garments. As depicted in Figure 14–5, all the pieces of the article of clothing are cut from a particular section of a single ply of textile. As a result, all the pieces for an individual garment are together when they come off the cutting machine and thus are in a "kit" ready to be sewn.

Claim

A method for mass-producing clothing, the method comprising

(a) creating a set of software instructions for a computerized cutting machine, the instructions defining the shapes of a set of pieces of fabric to be cut for an article of clothing to be produced,

(b) loading the instructions into the machine,

(c) providing a roll of fabric,

(d) dividing the fabric into sections,

(e) operating the machine to cut the pieces of the set from a respective one of the sections, and

(f) sewing the set of pieces together to form an article of clothing.

Analysis

Step (a) This step may invoke the activities of a party other than the clothing manufacturer, creating a multiparty activity. In particular, creating the software instructions may be a service provided to the clothing manufacturer by the cutting-machine vendor or yet some third party. Another problem is that the software instructions may be created overseas, creating a multiple-jurisdiction problem. Moreover, the machine may be "programmed" by some mechanical means or by hard-wired circuitry rather than software. Note, too, the potential narrowing effect of the word "fabric," which is not usually thought to encompass such apparel material as leather.

Step (b) This step also potentially invokes the activities of a party other than the clothing manufacturer. The cutting-machine vendor, or some third party, might be the one who loads the instructions into the machine as a service to the clothing manufacturer. This step also raises a potential royalty base issue. Since the instructions are loaded into the machine only once for each different pattern, the Opposing Team will argue that the claim is infringed only a single time for each different pattern, no matter how many articles of clothing are made from that pattern. This argument is bolstered by the fact that the claim recites the creation of only a single article of clothing.

Step (c) This is a worthless step that serves no purpose other than to create mischief. The Opposing Team may argue that it doesn't "provide" the fabric roll, but rather that the fabric roll is provided *to* it by the fabric vendor, thereby invoking the activities of yet another outside party. The argument may not carry the day. It can be argued that "providing" reads on the clothing manufacturer's action of mounting the roll on the machine. But no matter how unmerited the accused infringer's arguments may be, they will have to be *argued* to be unmerited, adding to the complexity and expense of the suit. The "providing" step just gives the Opposing Team something else to argue about. A "providing" step is *always* superfluous because other limitations can be drafted so as to assume the existence of the thing "provided." Ditto for "obtaining." Indeed, "obtaining" may be even more problematic to the extent that the thing obtained might be obtained outside the country. Another potential problem is the word "roll." The fabric might be folded flat rather than being provided in a roll.

Step (d) This step can well be argued never to be infringed, because the cutting machine may not carry out any function that can be characterized as "dividing" the roll into sections, particularly if the fabric advances through the machine in a continuous motion. Even if the machine starts and stops for each set of pieces, one may be hard-pressed to identify what operations of the machine constitute the affirmatively recited step of "dividing" the roll into sections.

Step (e) This step seems all right.

Step (f) This step presents a further potential single-infringer or multiple-jurisdiction issue. The set of pieces may be cut in the United States but shipped to an unrelated party for assembly overseas. It may be possible, however, to argue the applicability of 35 U.S.C. 271(f)(1).

Suggested Claim
A claim that avoids these problems is the following:

> A method comprising
> operating an automatic cutting machine to cut pieces of garments from a length of textile,
> wherein, for each of the garments, all of its pieces are cut from a respective nonoverlapping section of the textile.

Example II: Internet Infrastructure

Invention
The disclosed embodiment involves two web servers. As shown in Figure 14–6, each web server has a backup magnetic storage medium (e.g., hard disc, magnetic tape, etc.) partitioned into two sections, one for storing a backup version of its own data and one for storing a backup version of the other web server's data. In case a particular server's backup data

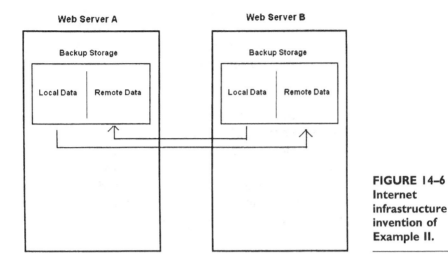

FIGURE 14–6
Internet infrastructure invention of Example II.

gets corrupted, another version is available from the other web server. The patent owner plans to assert the patent against web server manufacturers.

Claim

Apparatus comprising

(a) a communications medium,

(b) first and second web servers interconnected by the medium,

(c) each web server including a backup magnetic storage medium on which data is stored,

(d) each web server including a backup module configured to format the backup storage medium into local and remote partitions and to store, in the remote partition, data received from the other server.

Analysis

Element (a) The web server manufacturer can point out that it does not make or sell the communications medium.

Element (b) The web server manufacturer can point out that the web servers are not interconnected when the manufacturer ships them.

Element (c) The web server manufacturer will point out that, contrary to the claim language, no data is stored on the web server when it leaves the factory. Moreover, the web server manufacturer may arrange its business model such that a server is shipped without the backup storage

medium. The customers are advised that if they want the server to operate with the backup feature, they should order the backup medium separately from a third party. The web server manufacturer can also avoid
this claim by designing the web server to use optical, rather than magnetic, storage media.

Element (d) The web server manufacturer will point out that its servers
do not format the media but come preformatted from the media vendor.
It may design its web servers to back up one another's data in groups of
three or more in round-robin fashion—A backs up B, B backs up C, and C
backs up A—rather than in reciprocal fashion required by the claim. The
web server manufacturer will also argue that the servers aren't "operating" when they leave the manufacturer's shipping dock.[15]

Suggested Claim

A web server adapted to be interconnected with a second web
server, the web server comprising

an interface configured to receive a copy of data that is local to
the second web server, and

a memory storage module operative to store, in a first partition
of a backup storage medium, data that is local to the web server, and
to store, in a second partition of the storage medium, a copy of the
received data that is local to the other web server.

We go a long way toward maximizing the value of the patent by
ensuring that the invention is claimed in all of its commercially significant settings and that the claims capture the activities of individual direct
infringers.

The value of the patent can also depend, however, on the invention
being claimed using various statutory claim types. That is the subject of
the chapter that follows.

------

15. The manufacturer's assertion that it does not meet any "operating" type of limitation can often be countered by pointing out that the manufacturer undoubtedly does
operate the apparatus when testing it in the factory and/or when installing the apparatus
on the user's premises.

CHAPTER REVIEW—Invention Settings and Direct Infringers

Confirm Your Understanding

1. What is an invention setting?
2. What is meant by a "commercially significant" invention setting, and why is it important for an invention to be claimed in all of its commercially significant settings?
3. What does it mean to "maintain the integrity of the invention setting boundary?"
4. Contributory infringers and those who induce others to infringe are liable as indirect infringers (35 U.S.C. 271(b)(c)). Why, then, is it desirable to draft claims that will capture the activities of direct infringers?
5. Parties can be sued as joint infringers. Why, then, is it desirable to draft claims that will capture the activities of individual infringers?
6. Why may a "system claim" be difficult to enforce?
7. What are the legal and practical problems in enforcing claims requiring action by the consumer, i.e., a method step like "clicking on said displayed icon?"
8. How does taking on an Opposing Team mind-set help the claim drafter recognize potential infringement loopholes brought about by a particular setting in which an invention may be claimed?

Questions for Further Thought

9. Assume that the key blank for the lock invention discussed in this chapter (p. 216) would be indistinguishable from prior art key blanks. Why can't the invention nonetheless be claimed in the key blank setting with a claim such as

   A key blank adapted to be cut for use as a key in a tumbler lock of a type in which at least one tumbler is rotated upon insertion of the key.

10. Do you agree with the author's assertion that "receiver" claim 14.1 would be patentable even though the structure of the recited two elements would be obvious given a knowledge of the (assumedly novel/nonobvious) format of the video signal generated at the transmitter?
11. What is the harm in calling for "an energy source" in a claim directed to an electrical or electronic device, given that, as a practical matter, every such device requires a source of energy in order to operate?

Sharpen Your Skills

12. Invention settings
   a) Think of at least two settings for each of the inventions below. Remember that an invention is not claimed in different settings just because the claims are in different statutory classes, e.g., method and apparatus (p. 214).
      i)   Web application for takeout restaurants that uses instant messaging to allow customers to obtain menu information and/ or to place orders.
      ii) Structure for a shoe
      iii) Spreadsheet program
      iv) Method of drying fruit
      v)   Coding format that prevents making unauthorized copies of downloaded music
      vi) Method that forwards e-mails received at a user's personal computer to the user's PDA by way of a relaying server
      vii) Blade for use in a multiblade razor
      viii) Software compiler program (converts software written in a source code language, like Java, into object code (0s and 1s) that a computer can read and execute
   b) Who are the likely infringers of the invention in each setting?
   c) Which settings(s) are likely to be the most important from the standpoint of patent enforcement?

CHAPTER FIFTEEN

Statutory Claim Types

We saw in Chapter Fourteen that maximizing a patent's value requires claiming the invention in all its commercially significant settings. In this chapter we will see that a patent's value also depends on claiming the invention using a particular one or more of the three main statutory claim types—method claims, apparatus claims, and composition claims. These derive from the four statutory subject matter classes defined in 35 U.S.C. 101: method claims for "processes"; apparatus claims for "machines" and "manufactures [manufactured items]"; and composition claims for chemical compounds and other "compositions of matter."

Many inventions lend themselves to being claimed using a particular statutory claim type. A paper clip would certainly be claimed as a manufacture using an apparatus claim; an oil-refining procedure would be claimed as a process using a method claim, and so forth. However, many inventions can be claimed using more than one statutory claim type. In fact, maximizing the patent's value may depend on it.

The central consideration is the anticipated enforcement scenario. A patent infringer is one who, without authority, makes *or* uses *or* offers for sale *or* sells *or* imports a patented invention.[1] As a practical matter, the patent owner will typically want to assert her patent against only some of these, such as manufacturers or importers. This allows the patent owner to collect royalties (or obtain an injunction against infringement) at the wellhead; it is usually impractical to chase after innumerable wholesalers, retailers, or consumers. However, the ability to effectively assert a patent against a particular class of infringers may depend upon the statutory claim type(s) that were used to define the invention.

Apparatus (Machine/Manufacture) Claims

Apparatus Claims Generally

Many inventions are implemented in machines or as manufactures and, as such, are defined by apparatus claims. Indeed, for many inventions this may be the only claim type that makes sense. The chair and

---

1. 35 U.S.C. 271(a).

paper-clip claims appearing throughout the book are examples of apparatus claims. Many biotech inventions, such as transgenic plants, are
"manufactures" and are also defined by what are essentially apparatus
claims, such as claim 15.1.

> 15.1 A transgenic plant comprising a transgenic eukaryotic cell
> encoding a plastid membrane transport polypeptide with at least 17
> consecutive amino acid residues between residues 43 and 323 of SEQ
> ID NO:2.

Many patents have only method claims, even though apparatus
claims could also have been obtained. This happens particularly for
inventions implemented in software-based systems, such as telecommunications gear or medical diagnostic equipment. Signal-processing inventions, such as speech-recognition algorithms, are another example.

Limiting such inventions to method claims is usually not a good idea.
Apparatus claims are readily asserted against manufacturers; they are
infringed the moment the infringing apparatus comes into being at the
end of the assembly line. By contrast, method claims defining the *operation* of an apparatus are infringed only when the operation itself is carried out. The direct infringers are not the manufacturers, but consumers
or other users.[2]

A manufacturer could be accused of inducing infringement of a
method claim or being a contributory infringer.[3] However, as discussed
in Chapter Fourteen, it is preferable to be able to establish a case of direct
infringement.[4] Moreover, damages for activities occurring prior to suit
are available only if the accused contributory or inducing infringer had
actual notice of the patent.[5]

Another problem with method-claim-only patents is that some methods are performed only a few times, severely limiting the royalty base.
An example is a method for arriving at a design parameter for a product.
Consider claim 15.2, which defines a method for determining the optimum area for a semiconductor chip *and* gate to provide it with a very
fast "rise time."

---

2. Manufacturers may be direct infringers of a method in the course of equipment
testing or installation, for example. However, the royalty base for such infringement is
typically significant.

3. 35 U.S.C. 271(b)–(c).

4. 35 U.S.C. 271(a).

5. *Manville Sales Corp. v. Paramount Systems, Inc.*, 917 F.2d 544, 554, 16 USPQ2d 1587
(Fed. Cir. 1990); *DSU Medical Corporation v. JMS Co., LTD* (Fed. Cir. 2006) (en banc).

15.2 A method for use in designing a logic gate of a semiconductor chip, the method comprising
designing the gate to have an area A, given by $A = \langle beta\rangle I_c^{2/3}$, where I_c is an impurity concentration of the semiconductor material, and $\langle beta\rangle$ is the length of the longest intra-gate signal path.

This claim will be infringed only a handful of times—during the semiconductor chip design process. Obtaining any kind of significant royalty or damage award will be an uphill battle. By contrast, apparatus claim 15.3 is directed to the overall semiconductor chip that includes a gate resulting from the design algorithm.

15.3 A semiconductor chip having at least one logic gate whose area A, is given by $A = \langle beta\rangle I_c^{2/3}$, where I_c is an impurity concentration of the semiconductor material, and $\langle beta\rangle$ is the length of the longest intra-gate signal path.

This apparatus claim will entitle the patent owner to a royalty or damages for each chip made.

One final advantage of apparatus claims is that they are not subject to the patent statute's so-called first inventor defense, which applies only to methods.[6]

Computer-Readable Medium ("Beauregard") Claims

The anticipated enforcement scenario for software-implemented inventions gives rise to unique claiming issues.

A software-implemented invention can certainly be defined as a sequence of method steps. And it can be defined as an apparatus that carries out those steps. The latter may be a particularly useful enforcement vehicle when the software comes preloaded in a computer, since the computer manufacturer, and those in the chain of sale, are direct infringers.

However, a great deal of software is sold in stand-alone form on a compact disc (CD) or other computer-readable medium. The anticipated enforcement scenario may then involve asserting the patent against the software house directly. A method claim may be less than ideal in this scenario because the method steps are not performed by the software house but by the end user's computer. Similarly, an apparatus that carries out the method steps does not come into being until the software is loaded from the CD into the consumer's computer. The software house

6. 35 U.S.C. 273(b)(3)(A).

could be accused of inducing infringement or of being a contributory infringer. Again, however, it is desirable to be able to establish a case of direct infringement whenever possible.

These concerns are addressed by the computer-readable medium claim, also referred to as a Beauregard claim.[7] In its typical form, this specialized type of apparatus claim calls for a computer-readable or machine-accessible medium (e.g., a CD) storing program instructions that cause a computer to perform steps that implement the invention. The infringing apparatus is the CD itself, claimed as a manufacture, as in claim 15.4:

> **15.4** An article of manufacture, comprising a machine-accessible medium having instructions encoded thereon for enabling a processor to perform the operations of
> receiving a request from a client comprising an identifier of the client;
> transmitting the identifier to a central registry containing characteristic profiles for plural clients;
> receiving a characteristic profile from the central registry that includes a processing potential for the client; and
> transmitting content to the client over a network, such content scaled according to the characteristic profile.

The usefulness of Beauregard claims extends beyond consumer-oriented software. Manufacturers of software-based industrial and telecommunications equipment distribute programs and program updates to their customers on computer-readable media.

Propagated Signal Claims—No Longer Permitted

A propagated signal claim is a specialized type of apparatus claim that was used for a number of years until the Federal Circuit declared such a claim to be directed to nonstatutory subject matter in 2007 in *In re Nuijten*.[8] Practitioners may encounter this type of claim in patents issued prior to *Nuijten*, so it is of some interest to know what they are.

The subject matter of a propagated signal claim is a signal per se, disembodied from any apparatus or method that generated the signal. Claim 15.5 is a propagated signal claim defining a data encryption invention.

---

7. *In re Beauregard*, 53 F.3d 1583, 35 USPQ2d 1383 (Fed. Cir. 1995).
8. *In re Nuijten*, 500 F.3d 1346, 84 USPQ2d 1495 (Fed. Cir. 2007).

15.5 A propagated signal comprising

a first component representing a public key, said public key signed by a private key, said private key created in a first time interval, said public key created in a second time interval, said first time interval distinct from said second time interval;

a second component representing a digital signature, said signature created during said second time interval if it is determined the certification request was received within the second time interval; and

wherein said signature is created using a second private key, said second private key created during said second time interval.

Practitioners pursued propagated signal claims while they were still permitted because such claims were seen to provide at least two advantages in the anticipated enforcement scenario. Propagated signals can readily be captured electronically and analyzed. This could have made it easier to prove infringement than when the invention is defined as a machine/manufacture or as a process. Moreover, propagated signal claims would have been infringed by parties that would typically not infringe any other claim type. These include telecommunications carriers, cable companies, and Internet service providers over whose facilities the signal would propagate.

The Federal Circuit ruled in *Nuijten* that a transient electric or electromagnetic transmission such as was sought to be claimed by *Nuijten* does not fit within the definition of an article of manufacture as recited in 35 U.S.C. 101 nor in of any of the other classes of patentable subject matter provided for in that statute.

Method (Process) Claims

Many inventions are fundamentally processes or methods—chemical syntheses, computer algorithms, surgical techniques, business methods, and so forth. However, an invention definable in apparatus terms can often be defined as a method that the apparatus performs. See, for example, microwave oven claims 7.1 and 7.3.[9] Indeed, method claims may provide a significant advantage over apparatus claims in the anticipated enforcement scenario.

For one thing, it may be difficult to demonstrate a one-to-one relationship between the structural elements of an apparatus claim and the parts of an allegedly infringing apparatus. For example, the functions of two claim elements may be performed by a single, dual-purpose

---

9. *See* p. 85.

element in the allegedly infringing apparatus. Yet that same apparatus may infringe all the steps of a method claim.

For another thing, it may be impossible to inspect suspected infringing apparatus, such as machinery on a competitor's factory floor. Yet, it may be apparent from the product the machinery produces that the method is being performed. Having a method claim to assert can thus short-circuit a lot of pushback from the Opposing Team and help bring a licensing negotiation or settlement discussion to a successful conclusion.

Even when infringement of an apparatus claim can readily be demonstrated, a method claim may be far more valuable. An apparatus claim covering an improved shoe-making machine may yield a royalty for each machine sold to shoemakers. However, the aggregate value of infringing shoe-making machines that may be constructed during the life of the patent will pale in comparison to the aggregate value of the shoes made by those machines. Thus a method claim reciting novel shoe-fabrication steps performed by the machine can yield a much higher economic return to the patent owner.

A method claim can also prove to be more valuable than a composition claim. For example, a whole year's worth of a chemical composition used to fabricate integrated circuits may have a market value of no more than a few thousand dollars. Thus, unless the patent owner's goal is to enforce her right of exclusivity, a claim directed to the composition per se may be of little benefit. By contrast, a method claim directed to an integrated circuit manufacturing method using the new composition would command a royalty for every integrated circuit made. For example, claim 15.6 recites a standard integrated circuit fabrication process in which the only novelty is in the formula for the new composition.

> 15.6 A process for fabricating a device comprising the steps of
> forming a radiation-sensitive region on a substrate,
> patterning at least a portion of the region, and
> further processing the substrate
> characterized in that the region comprises a composition formed
> by a polymerization process employing a material represented by [formula for the new composition omitted].

Another benefit of method claims relates to recovery of damages for infringement occurring prior to bringing suit. It is possible to recover such damages in general. However, if the patent owner sells a product covered by apparatus claims, damages based on infringement of the apparatus claims are awarded only for the period beginning when the infringer had actual notice of the patent *unless* the product was marked with the patent number.[10] This marking requirement does not apply, however, if the patent contains only method claims.[11]

Yet another benefit is that even if a claimed process was used to make a product in a foreign country, the subsequent importation of the product into the United States constitutes an infringement of the method claim.[12]

Composition Claims

Inventive compositions of matter—organic compounds, ceramics, peptides, biological material, and so on—should be claimed as such. Claim 15.7 is a composition claim.

> 15.7 A composition comprising an underfill material and an anhydride adduct of a rosin compound that comprises an ester of an organic rosin acid moiety.

A composition claim encompasses the composition itself, even if made by a process not contemplated by the inventor of the composition. It may also be advantageous to pursue method claims defining process(es) for producing the composition—either in the same patent application or a separate one.

Product-by-Process Claims

A product-by-process claim is not a statutory claim type per se. It is a specialized type of apparatus or composition claim that defines a product in terms of the process by which it is made. Claims 15.8 to 15.10 are product-by-process claims for a chemical composition, a frozen fruit gel, and a molded shoe innersole:

> 15.8 A polycarbonate produced by the process of
> (a) forming a reaction mixture that comprises a dihydroxy compound, a carbonic acid derivative, a solvent, and sufficient base to bring about the formation of polycarbonate; and
> (b) employing in said reaction mixture a chain terminator containing a hydroxy group, such that monocarbonate does not form.

---

10. 35 U.S.C. 287(a).

11. *American Medical Systems, Inc. v. Medical Engineering Corp.*, 6 F.3d 1523, 1537, 28 USPQ2d 1321, 1331 (Fed. Cir. 1993).

12. 35 U.S.C. 271(g).

15.9 A firm fruit gel having fibrous tissues that resemble those of a peach, which is produced by the steps of:

(a) adding a fruit juice component to a component consisting essentially of konjak flour, alkaline agent, and water and stirring these components to form a mixture;

(b) freezing the mixture; and

(c) thawing the frozen mixture.

15.10 A molded innersole produced by the steps of

(a) introducing an expandable, polyurethane material into a mold;

(b) placing an elastomeric insert material into the mold, the insert material having greater shock-absorbing properties and being less resilient than the molded, open-celled polyurethane foam material;

(c) etc.

Even though it recites method steps, a product-by-process claim is a claim to the product itself. The process steps are only the vehicle by which the product is defined. That being said, a product defined by a product-by-process claim infringes that claim only if the competitor uses the same method to produce it.[13] On the other hand, a product-by-process claim is unpatentable if the product is in the prior art, even if the process steps recited in the product-by-process claim are new.[14]

If the product in question can be defined by a composition or manufacture (apparatus) claim, it can be claimed that way as well.

Even under the constraints of a chosen claim scope, setting, and statutory claim type, there are virtually an unlimited number of ways to draft a claim to a given invention. Indeed, there is a good reason to draft several different versions of the broadest claims. The chapter that follows explains why and shows how.

---

13. *Abbott Labs. v. Sandoz, Inc.*, 544 F.3d 1341, 89 USPQ2d 1161 (Fed. Cir. 2009) (en banc).

14. *Id.*

CHAPTER REVIEW—Statutory Claim Types

Confirm Your Understanding

1. What is dangerous about drafting only method claims for an invention that could also be claimed as an apparatus?
2. What is dangerous about drafting only apparatus claims for an invention that could also be claimed as a method?
3. What is dangerous about drafting only composition claims for an invention that could also be claimed as a method that uses the composition?

Question for Further Thought

4. Some practitioners include computer-readable medium (Beauregard) claims as a matter of routine for every invention that can be implemented by computer. Can you think of situations where such a claim, while possible to draft, would be of little or no value?

CHAPTER SIXTEEN

Claim Diversity

A patent's enforcement is fraught with uncertainty. Claims may contain unappreciated loopholes—unnecessary elements, unduly narrow terminology, or limitations whose meaning seemed perfectly clear but could be argued to be indefinite. Another uncertainty is the discovery of prior art not cited during prosecution.

These problems may not surface until the patent owner attempts to license or sue on the patent, at which point it is usually too late to do much about them. Fallback feature claims[1] and definition claims[2] can go a long way toward addressing these uncertainties, but it is difficult to anticipate every possible invalidity scenario.

Yet another source of uncertainty is what the law will be at the time a patent is asserted.

Claim diversity—the subject of this chapter—is an approach to constructing the overall claim suite that addresses these and other uncertainties. A diverse claim suite presents the invention in different ways, for example, by organizing the limitations differently, using different terminology, or employing different combinations of functional and structural recitations. A particular defect in a claim that renders it too broad or too narrow or indefinite may not show up in another claim if the invention is expressed differently, albeit at the same level of breadth, in the same setting, and using the same statutory claim type. Like the Planned Retreat, then, claim diversity improves the odds that the issued patent will have at least one claim that is both valid and infringed.

We never actually know whether any potential problems have been fixed. Any *known* claim defects are fixed before the application goes out the door. We simply take it as an article of faith that the more one claim differs from another, the more likely it is that any hidden defects in the first will not appear in the second.

---

1. *See* Chapter Six.
2. *See* Chapter Ten.

Achieving a significant level of diversity in the claim suite may be easier said than done. Most types of inventions can be defined in a wide variety of ways. But once having slaved over a claim to get it just right, it is sometimes difficult to force one's brain to think about how the invention might be defined differently. It can be hard to put aside a particular ingrained view of the invention—or a particular approach to claiming it—and head off in new directions.

This chapter presents some ideas for jump-starting the claim-drafting process into those new directions. These ideas apply to drafting not only broad claims, but claims at any desired level of breadth.

Recast the Problem-Solution Statement

Drafting a new version of the problem-solution statement will readily yield a new claim, particularly when the problem-solution-based claim-drafting technique introduced in Chapter Seven is used. A different problem-solution statement may also provide us with a new "take" on the inventive departure, thereby yielding a different claim when using the inventive-departure-based approach of Chapter Eight. Two such claims are those drafted by William Dowss for John Loud's ballpoint pen invention, discussed in Chapter One and presented again here:

> 16.1 A pen having a spheroidal marking-point, substantially as described.
>
> 16.2 A pen having a marking sphere capable of revolving in all directions, substantially as and for the purposes described.

Drafting a new version of the problem-solution statement may prove difficult, however. Just as with a claim we have lived with for a while, the original problem-solution statement may dominate our thinking to such a degree that nothing useful comes from an attempt to draft a new one. If that happens, simply move on to the other techniques described below.

In other cases, however, new ways of seeing the problem or the solution may arise as we become more familiar with the invention—particularly after the specification has been written. Such insights can be brought to bear in developing a different formulation of the problem and/or the solution.

Use Both Functional and Structural Recitations

The book emphasizes the importance of functional claim limitations when reaching for claim breadth. Here, for example, is the typewriter backspace key expressed in purely functional terms:

16.3 A typewriter adapted to move its carriage to a previously typed-at position through an intra-typewriter operation initiated in response to a predetermined user action.

This claim calls for no particular structure or, indeed, *any* structure by which the carriage movement is effectuated. Defining an invention functionally, rather than structurally, makes it harder for others to avoid the claim by implementing the functions and relationships inherent in the claim but using them with different structural elements.

Having drafted a very functional claim, however, we can endeavor to write one that has more structure to it and, in so doing, enhance the diversity of the overall claim suite.

Structural limitations in a claim can be specific physical elements or means-plus-function elements. The former are primarily defined by what they *are*, the latter by what they *do*. For example, claim 16.4 defines the invention of the backspace key in terms of physical elements, and claim 16.5 defines the same invention using means-plus-function elements.

Physical Elements Claim

16.4 A typewriter comprising

a plurality of alphabet keys,

a carriage that moves in a first direction when one of the alphabet keys is depressed,

a control key, and

a mechanical linkage interconnecting the control key and the carriage and that moves the carriage in a second direction when the control key is depressed.

Means-Plus-Function Claim

16.5 A typewriter comprising

printing means for creating printed characters on a carriage-carried platen in response to the operation of alphabet keys,

advancement means for moving the carriage forward after each character is printed, and

backspace means responsive to user operation of a backspace key for moving the carriage backward when the control means is operated.

As noted above, a wider range of equivalents may be accorded to a structural recitation than to a means-plus-function recitation. In the backspace key example, claim 16.4's combination of the control key and mechanical linkage may be interpreted more broadly than claim 16.5's backspace means. Then again, a means-plus-function element may be given the wider range of equivalents, depending on the invention in

question and the state of the law at the time the claim is being interpreted. The Federal Circuit has developed a large body of case law that
has severely limited the desirability of using the means-plus-function
construct. Means-plus-function claiming is the topic of Chapter Thirteen.

Claim diversity is enhanced by using all three types of recitations—
purely functional, structural, and means-plus-function—either in a con-
sistent-throughout-the-claim form, per claims 16.3 through 16.5, or in
mix-and-match combinations.

Vary the Terminology

Varying the claim terminology is another facet of claim diversity. Certain
words or phrases may be interpreted more narrowly or more broadly
than others, even while seeming to convey the same idea. Advantageously, then, varying the terminology may narrow a claim that would
otherwise be so broad as to read on prior art or may broaden a claim that
would otherwise be narrower and miss certain competitors' implementations of the inventive concept.

Just thinking about different ways of expressing things may open the
door to invention-broadening insights that can be used more extensively
throughout the claims. For example, we may have started out using the
term "cooking" in all of the claims directed to a microwave oven invention. But upon searching for other ways to express the invention, we may
realize that the word "heating" might be a better choice for most of the
claims, "heating" undoubtedly being a broader term.

Here are some other examples of claim terminology alternatives:

- peptide/protein
- fastener/attachment mechanism
- telecommunications network/telephone system
- refreshing the web page/fetching a new version of the web page

These alternatives might be deemed to mean exactly the same thing
as one another. In some contexts, however, one might prove to be broader
or narrower than the other. Or one term might be deemed indefinite but
the other not.

Enforced-Format Claiming

Enforced-format claiming is yet another way to get our thinking onto
a different track. Per this technique, we arbitrarily impose one or more
claim format options on the claim to be drafted. For example, if an
already-drafted claim has a minimal preamble, the imposed claim format

option may be to pack the preamble with as many of the claim limitations as possible. A number of other claim format alternatives are suggested below, followed by three illustrations of the technique.

Enforced-format claiming forces us to head off in a new direction in defining the invention. The selected format options may be ones that we do not employ regularly or that may seem unnatural. This is all to the good, as it can shake us out of the very comfort zone that may stand in the way of achieving a more diverse claim suite.

Enforced-format claiming is analogous to painting a landscape. Before an artist begins to paint the scene, she must first make some format choices. What will the orientation of the canvas be? What direction does the light come from? Where is the vanishing point? Only after deciding on these aspects does the artist begin to inform the chosen framework with the subject matter itself.

Enforcing certain format choices will typically have a ripple effect on the more substantive aspects of the claim. Certain format options may force the claim elements into a different order of presentation. This, in turn, may require different recitations to stitch the claim elements together. Limitations that seemed unavoidable when the claim was put together in one way may need to be stated differently—or may prove to be unnecessary altogether—when the claim is assembled in some other way. The resulting claim may well be quite different from any of those already drafted.

It may become apparent as a claim evolves that certain format choices will not work well with others, or that they may not be suitable for the invention at hand or for the chosen setting. Other format choices can be tried out in real time as the claim is being drafted. Any chosen format options should be abandoned if the claim seems to work better without them. They were, after all, chosen arbitrarily in the first instance.

Many format alternatives work well for claims in almost any technology. Others are more technology-specific. Some common format choices of both kinds are presented below.

Readers who have been drafting claims for a while will recognize particular format choices that they normally gravitate to. The point of the enforced-format technique is to force ourselves to try out some others.

The discussion of the format choices is followed by some exemplary claims illustrating the enforced-format technique.

Functional vs. Structural Limitations

An invention can be expressed in functional or structural terms. Structural components, in turn, can be recited as physical or means-plus-function elements. Use of this option is illustrated above in connection with the backspace key invention.

Number of Elements or Steps

An apparatus claim can have 0, 1, 2, or more individual claim elements. Similarly, a method claim can have 0, 1, 2, or more individual method steps.

Preamble Length

The claim preamble can be very minimal, for example, "Apparatus comprising. . . ." Another option is to pack into the preamble as many of the claim recitations as possible, leaving for the body of the claim as few as one method step or structural element or something in between.

Preamble Content

The preamble can contain functional statements, method steps, apparatus elements, or mix-and-match combinations of these. It is common, for example, for a method claim preamble to establish an apparatus context for the recited method steps. It is also possible for the preamble to have no content other than a standard phrase such as "A method comprising."

Problem to Be Solved

It can be dangerous for a claim to recite the problem to be solved, as discussed earlier (p. 88 in Chapter 7). In the interest of claim diversity, however, some claims may explicitly recite the problem.

Treatment of the Inventive Departure

The inventive departure appears at the end of many claims—the natural result of defining an invention in terms of a structure or process in the prior art to which something new is added. However, a different set of words defining the invention can evolve by forcing the novel part of the claim to appear elsewhere.

Another format choice is the relationship of the inventive departure to the other limitations. There are at least three choices here. The inventive departure can be recited as

- one or more stand-alone elements or steps,
- a sub-element or substep of another element or step, or
- a functional characterization of one of the other elements.

Underlying Scientific or Engineering Theory

Many inventions are based on some underlying engineering or scientific discovery or theory. For inventions of this type, the claim drafter can choose either to

- ignore the discovery or theory and simply recite the structure or steps that take advantage of it, or
- make the discovery manifest in the claim.

We definitely want claims of the first type; the inventor's theory as to how or why the invention works as it does may prove to be incorrect, providing the Opposing Team with an opening to argue against the claim's validity. But, again, in the interest of claim diversity, claims that explicitly recite the invention's underlying theory can be drafted as well.

Mathematical Limitations

Certain kinds of method steps, interrelationships among physical elements, and other aspects of many inventions can be described using mathematical expressions. Mathematics provides a precision that words often cannot. On the other hand, math in a claim has the potential to limit the boundaries of the claimed subject matter in unintended ways. The aims of claim diversity are served by using both mathematics and words.

Granularity

Certain inventions appear in modules or basic building blocks that are interconnected with like units. An example is a novel integrated circuit memory element that is interconnected in a matrix with millions of other identical elements. The invention can be claimed as a stand-alone memory element. It can also be claimed as an interconnected matrix of such elements.

Time Perspective

Some inventions involve an algorithm or other set of method steps that are performed repetitively. For example, an MPEG encoder operates on successive video frames, applying the same set of encoding steps to each frame. The format choice here is the time-domain equivalent of the granularity choice just described. The algorithm can be defined in terms of the operations applied to a single video frame or, alternatively, to a sequence of frames. In a similar vein, some processing inventions can be claimed statically, as though frozen in time, or in terms of an ongoing operation.

Signal Domain

Many signal processing inventions—perhaps most, these days—are carried out in the digital domain and operate on digital signal samples. A claim can certainly define an invention in those terms. However, we may be able to define the invention without putting it in any specific signal domain by reciting the processing of generic "signals" rather than digital "signal samples."

Enforced-Format Examples

The enforced-format claiming technique is illustrated below using three inventions. The claims shown in the examples are of varying scope, in the interest of illustrating a wide range of format choices.

The table following these examples indicates which of the above-listed options are implemented in which claims. As noted earlier, those options are but a sampling of the various ways in which claims and their recitations can be formatted.

Example I—Web Search

Statement of Invention
There are thousands of Internet search engines that specialize in particular topics, or "search domains," such as medical, sports, jobs and careers, and so forth. By knowing the name of the search engine for a particular topic, it is of course possible to visit the search engine's site and input a search string there. In general, however, users know few, if any, specialized search engines, relying on the general-purpose search engines instead. A problem is that the general-purpose search engines often return many irrelevant hits.

The inventive concept is for software to perform an automatic analysis of the content (text) of an input search string to identify a relevant search domain and to submit the search string to a search engine that specializes in that search domain.

Claims

    1. A computer-readable storage medium that is not a transient signal, the computer-readable medium having stored thereon instructions that, when executed by a processor, causes words of an input search string to be submitted to a specialized search engine identified by an automatic computer analysis of the search string.

    2. A computing system of a type that receives an input search string and submits it to a search engine, the computing system comprising
      a processor,

a subsystem including the processor arranged to identify the search engine based on an automatic computer analysis of the contents of the search string, and

a subsytem including the processor arranged to submit the input search string to a specialized search engine.

3. A method in which the number of extraneous search engine hits in web searches is minimized by submitting search strings to respective search engines, each specializing in a search domain relevant to the respective search string, the method comprising

automatically identifying the relevant search domain for each search string based on the contents of that search string.

4. A method for submitting an input search string to a search engine, the method comprising

minimizing the number of extraneous returned hits by submitting the search string to a search engine that specializes in a search domain relevant to the search string, said minimizing comprising

(a) automatically identifying at least one search domain based on the search string, and

(b) identifying as said search engine a search engine that specializes in the identified search domain.

5. A method performed by a computer system, the computer system including a screen, browser software that displays a search window on the screen, a keyboard for inputting search strings into the window, and a memory that stores a list of specialized search engines, the method comprising

analyzing each search string to identify a particular search engine on the list based on the contents of the search string, and

submitting each said search string to the identified search engine.

Example II—Run-Length Coding

Statement of Invention

It is always desired to be able to transmit or store as much information content as possible using as few bits as possible.

The inventive concept is to exploit the fact that certain kinds of signals have long runs of identical or substantially identical data. For example, a scanned black-and-white image will typically have long runs of 0s (representing, say, "white") and/or long runs of 1s ("black"). This fact is exploited by generating a coded signal that contains digital words whose values represent the length of the runs, rather than the runs themselves. Thus the bit string 00000001111000111111 would be represented as 111 100 011 110, these being the binary values of the run lengths 7, 4, 3, and 6.

Claims

    6. A method that compresses a signal by encoding the lengths of successive runs of portions of the signal that are identical.

    7. A method for processing a binary input signal to reduce the number of bits needed to represent it, the method comprising

    (a) incrementing a count if the value of an individual bit of the input signal is the same as the value of the previously input bit,

    (b) outputting the count and then resetting the count to the value "1" if the value of the bit is different from the value of the previously input bit, and

    (c) repeating (a) and (b) for each successive bit of the input signal.

    8. A method of generating a sequence of output words $W(i)$, $i = 1, 2, 3, \ldots$ in response to an input signal comprised of interleaved runs of 0s and 1s, the output words being given by

    $W(i) = \text{count } (i)$

wherein count (i) is the number of bits in the ith run.

    9. Apparatus for encoding an input signal made up of 0s and 1s, the apparatus comprising

    a counter configured to generate counts of the number of 0s in each run of 0s in the signal and the number of 1s in each run of 1s in the signal, and

    an encoder configured to generate an encoded signal comprising digital words each representing a respective one of the generated counts,

    the input signal having a sufficiently large average run length that the number of bits required to represent the run lengths is less than the number of bits in the signal being encoded.

    10. Apparatus of a type that performs the steps of receiving a binary signal, converting the signal into a succession of code words that represent the values of the bits of the signal and applying the code words to an output,

    characterized in that in the converting step, the apparatus generates, as the code words, digital words representing the lengths of runs of 0s and 1s in the binary signal.

Example III—Modular Flooring

Statement of Invention

Computer rooms and other facilities are built with a raised floor made up of floor panels supported by an underlying framework, so that wiring, plumbing, and other utilities can be run along the "real" floor below. The panels can be lifted up individually at any time for utility access.

Normally the panels are supported solely by the underlying framework. The inventive concept here is for each panel to have a projection that extends under at least one adjacent panel, thereby providing additional support for that panel. The benefit is reduced flexure of the flooring.

Claims

11. A rectilinear modular floor panel having a projection extending from its underside projecting beyond an edge of the floor panel and having a ledge on the opposite edge adapted to engage a similar projection extending beyond an edge of another floor panel when the panels are installed on a grid.

12. A modular floor panel adapted to be installed in a modular floor along with at least two adjacent floor panels, the modular floor panel comprising
a panel body,
a support configured to support one of the adjacent panels, and
an interface configured to be engaged, and supported, by the other of the adjacent panels.

13. A modular floor comprising
a support grid, and
a plurality of panels arranged in spaced relation and supported by the grid, each of the panels comprising
a panel body,
means for supporting an adjacent panel, and
means resting on a supporting means extending from another supporting panel.

14. A modular floor of the type in which floor panels are supported above a floor of a building by a supporting understructure, the floor panels providing further support for one another in such a way that the floor has less flexure at the interface between adjacent panels than if said further support were not provided.

The table on the following page indicates which enforced-format claim options were used in drafting the claims of the above three examples.

⎯⎯⎯⎯⎯⎯⎯⎯⎯⎯⎯

This brings us to the end of what the book has to say about drafting claims. The chapter that follows completes Part III by presenting a collection of checklists setting forth the main claim-drafting points and prescriptions offered in Parts II and III, with references to the relevant material in the text.

	Web Search					Run-Length Coding					Modular Flooring			
Invention Example														
Claim Number	1	2	3	4	5	6	7	8	9	10	11	12	13	14
Functional v. Structural Limitations (Apparatus Claims)														
Pure Function	■									■				■
Means + Function													■	
Physical Elements											■	■	■	
Number of Apparatus/Method Elements														
0	■					■		■		■				■
1			■								■			
2+		■		■	■		■					■	■	
Preamble Length														
Minimal	■					■		■			■		■	■
In-between		■		■			■		■			■		
Extensive			■		■					■				
Preamble Content														
None	■					■		■			■		■	■
Functional			■	■			■		■			■		
Apparatus (in method claims)					■									
Method (in apparatus claims)		■								■				
Problem to Be Solved														
Recited			■	■			■							
Inventive Departure Position														
End of claim		■	■	■				■		■		■	■	
Elsewhere	■				■		■		■		■			■
Inventive Departure Relationship to Other Recitations														
Stand-alone			■		■		■		■		■	■	■	■
Sub-element/step		■		■						■				
Functional	■					■		■						

	Web Search					Run-Length Coding					Modular Flooring			
Time Perspective														
Ongoing process or multiple			■		■		■	■	■	■				
"One-time"	■	■		■		■								
Mathematics														
Used								■						
Granularity														
Individual element											■	■		
One of many													■	■
Underlying Theory														
Recited									■					■
Signal Domain														
Signals generically						■								
Binary/Digital							■	■	■	■				

CHAPTER REVIEW—Claim Diversity

Confirm Your Understanding

1. What are the characteristics of a diverse claim suite?
2. Why is a diverse claim suite desirable?
3. Name at least three approaches to arriving at diverse ways of defining the broad invention. What are the advantages of the various approaches?

Questions for Further Thought

4. Functional claims like claim 16.3 (p. 245) are frequently rejected by examiners as being improper. Which section(s) of 35 U.S.C., if any, could properly be brought to bear in support of such a rejection?
5. The book advises using different terminology in different claims as a way of achieving claim diversity. Do you see any potential problems in doing this? If so, how would you deal with them?
6. Try to think of some format choices other than those presented in the book that could be used to further the goal of claim diversity.

Sharpen Your Skills

7. Try out some of the enforced-format options presented in this chapter (or others) to draft at least three claims for the inventions described below. (Further explanation of these inventions can be found, for example, at wikipedia.com.) For each claim, indicate the format choices that you "enforced" on yourself.

   a. Web Cache

   A web page, once downloaded ("served") to a user's computer ("client"), it is stored in one or more temporary memories ("caches") in the client itself, at the user's Internet service provider (ISP), and/or in one or more intermediate "proxy" servers between the client and the original source of the page ("origin server"). When the client re-requests the page (e.g., via the browser's "back" button), or when the page is requested by another client served by the same proxy server or ISP, the page is served from one of these caches if it is found there—looking first in the cache in the client itself—rather than the request being sent all the way back to the origin server. This use of caches reduces the load on the origin server, speeds up delivery of the page to the requester, and reduces the overall level of Internet traffic.

   b. Bubble Sort

   An array of numbers is sorted into numerical order by making multiple passes through the array and comparing adjacent numbers. If the two adjacent numbers are already in the right order (e.g., lowest number first for a sort into ascending order), move on. If they are in the wrong order, swap their positions and then move on. Repeat this process until a pass through the array results in no swaps being made.

c. Video Compression—Interframe Coding
   Instead of transmitting every pixel of a video image, compare the pixel values within blocks of pixels that are at corresponding spatial locations of successive video frames.
   i. If the pixel values for a block at a particular spatial location in a current frame are the *same as* the pixel values at the corresponding spatial locations in the previous frame, do not transmit pixel information, but only a message indicating that the pixel values for the block have not changed;
   ii. If the pixel values for the block are *different from* those in the previous frame, transmit information indicating how the pixel values differ.
   This methodology exploits the great deal of redundancy in a video signal from one frame to the next to reduce the amount of information needed to store or transmit the video signal while preserving all of its picture information.

8. Evaluate the claims of some issued patents in terms of their claim diversity.
9. Take a patent for which you found that there is little or no claim diversity and draft two additional independent claims that would make the claim suite more diverse.

CHAPTER SEVENTEEN

Claim Review with Enforcement in Mind

Having drafted all our claims, we need to review them with the anticipated enforcement scenario in mind. The claim review should be carried
out at two levels: the overall claim suite level and the individual claim
level.

At the overall claim suite level, we need to assure ourselves that the
patent application contains all the claims that it should. And at the individual claim level, we should assure ourselves that each individual claim
fulfills the function that was intended for it.

This chapter presents of a set of checklists for carrying out both levels
of review. Page references for each checklist item point the reader to the
relevant material.

Reviewing the Overall Claim Suite

Unpatentability/Invalidity

The overall claim suite should have claims that address the possible
unpatentability/invalidity of the application's broadest claims. To this
end, the claim suite should include

- Fallback feature claims (pp. 123–124)
- Independent embodiment claims (pp. 126–133)
- Claims that are optimally chained within families (pp. 147–150)
- Claims that define the invention in diverse ways (pp. 243–255)

Maximizing the Patent's Value to Its Owner

The overall claim suite should be reviewed to ensure that the claims will
maximize the patent's value to the patent owner. To this end, the claim
suite should include

- Claims that define the invention in all of its commercially signifi-cant settings and capture individual direct infringers (pp. 211–230)
- Claims that define the invention using all appropriate statutory claim types (pp. 233–240)
- Claims that capture the maximum royalty base (pp. 133–134)

Reviewing Individual Claims

The claims need to be reviewed individually to be sure each carries out the function intended for it.

It is virtually impossible to review a claim in all of the ways that are appropriate in one editing pass. There is too much to think about. It is better to focus on each aspect in turn and pass through the claims with that one aspect in mind.

Unduly Narrowing Limitations

A claim should not include limitations that define the invention more narrowly than intended. The "usual suspects" include limitations that

- explain rather than define (pp. 109–112)
- are needed only to support some dependent claim recitation (pp. 117–118)
- are "structural" when they could be functional (pp. 112–113)
- are modifiers (adjectives and adverbs) not necessary to define the invention over the prior art (pp. 113–114)
- are data values, parameters, or measurements that a genie could provide and that, therefore, do not have to be generated from within the claim (pp. 115–117)

Claim Overbreadth and Indefiniteness

Claims should also be evaluated to make sure that they are not so broad as to read on the prior art. In doing so, we should

- read the claim as broadly as possible, as an examiner will (pp. 51–53)
- fix an overbroad claim by narrowing/adding claim elements *or* by narrowing the environment or context in which the invention is claimed (pp. 53–58)
- backstop terminology with definition claims to anticipate possible overbreadth based on invention-irrelevant prior art (pp. 138–140)
- backstop terminology with definition claims to anticipate possible indefiniteness (pp. 140–142)

- evaluate claims with functional language to ensure that (a) they are not "unduly functional" (pp.163–168), (b) the functional recitations are appropriately tied into the rest of the claim language (pp. 177–182), and (c) the functional language does not inadvertently invoke "means-plus-function treatment" when it is not desired (p. 198)

Violations of the Invention-Setting Boundary

Make sure that the claim does not spill over its setting to involve the activities of more than one party. Discovering violations of the invention-setting boundary is a matter of asking the following:

- Do all the affirmative claim limitations read on that which a single infringer will do (pp. 219–223)? The "usual suspects" here include
  - Inputs and other signals that could come from elsewhere (pp. 115–117)
  - Limitations that affirmatively recite the environment and/or recite that the inventive apparatus is connected to that environment (pp. 221–222)
  - Method steps that might be performed by multiple parties, especially if one of them is outside the United States (pp. 223–225)
- Does the claim read on the product as it will be vended, sitting on the competitor's shipping dock (p. 219)?
- What "batteries" might the Opposing Team not include with its product as shipped (p. 219)?
- What limitations in this claim could a competitor latch on to in order to avoid infringement, especially if the competitor is willing to change its manufacturing regime or business model (pp. 223–225)?

Formalities

Finally, we need to attend to various housekeeping matters and formal requirements. These include the following:

- Consistent internal logic. The recited claim elements should "hang together" in a logical way. Each element or step should have some physical or functional relationship with each other element or step—either directly or through some other step.
- Conformity with the requirement that the drawing must show every feature of the invention specified in the claims.[1] This is a

---

1. 37 CFR 1.83(a).

good way of verifying that a claim does not call for more elements (particularly "means for" doing this or that) than are actually present in the embodiment(s).[2]

- Antecedent basis for all "the" and "said" recitations.
- Grammar and punctuation.

---

2. *Default Proof Credit Card Sys. v. Home Depot U.S.A., Inc.*, 412 F.3d 1291, 75 USPQ2d 1116 (Fed. Cir. 2005) (nothing in the specification found to correspond to a recited "means for dispensing").

CHAPTER REVIEW—Claim Review with Enforcement in Mind

Confirm Your Understanding

1. What are the issues to be considered when reviewing the claim suite as a whole?
2. What are the issues to be considered when reviewing each individual claim?
3. Why does the author recommend reviewing the claims with only one issue (e.g., proper antecedents) in mind at a time?

Sharpen Your Skills

4. Evaluate the claims of one or more issued patents based on the criteria presented in this chapter.

PART IV

Preparing and Prosecuting the Patent Application

Introduction to Part IV: Preparing and Prosecuting the Patent Application

PART IV—*Preparing and Prosecuting the Patent Application*—addresses three topics: preparing the specification, responding to claim rejections during prosecution, and working with the inventor. These activities may seem unrelated, but each should be informed by the same notions that inform the analysis and claiming of the invention—the inventive concept, the problem, the solution, and the fallback features.

CHAPTER EIGHTEEN begins the overall topic of preparing the specification by considering who its audience is and what their needs are. It then focuses on the first two sections of the specification—the Background of the Invention and the Summary of the Invention—and explains how the problem-solution statement can serve as the basis for an effective, story-telling Background and Summary that can engage that audience and, in the process, advance the interests of the patent owner.

CHAPTER NINETEEN shows how the Background and Summary provide a framework on which the Detailed Description can be built to advance the problem-solution story. The chapter also offers suggestions for streamlining the process of writing the Detailed Description more efficiently. The prescription *Be Detailed Where the Invention Lives* is introduced as a guide for determining which details of the embodiment(s) the Detailed Description should actually include.

CHAPTERS TWENTY and TWENTY-ONE then turn to claim rejections and amendments. The heart of Chapter Twenty is a flow diagram laying out the six options one can take when a claim is rejected under 35 U.S.C. 102 or 103, based on the answers to four questions about the cited prior art. Chapter Twenty-One then homes in on the use of the invention analysis principles described in earlier chapters as the basis for amending claims in the most appropriate way, should amendment prove to be the desirable option.

CHAPTER TWENTY-TWO describes a methodology for the inventor interview. Over time, each practitioner develops an approach that seems to work best for him. This chapter was written mostly with the novice in mind. It introduces the notion of "self-directed learning" as an efficient way of using the inventor as an information resource to get at the problem, the solution, and the fallback features. The chapter then goes on to describe a collaborative process through which the patent lawyer and inventor can write the patent application together.

CHAPTER EIGHTEEN

Writing the Background and Summary

The writing of a patent specification should be guided by the same principles that guide invention analysis and claiming: problem, solution, and inventive concept. Another important consideration is the specification's intended readership.

This chapter begins with a discussion of "the audience" and then focuses in on the specification's Background and Summary. The chapter that follows discusses the Detailed Description.

The Audience

A patent specification must be detailed enough to enable a person skilled in the art to practice the invention. This is the so-called enablement requirement of 35 U.S.C. 112(a):

> The specification shall contain a written description of the invention . . . [sufficient] to enable any person skilled in the art . . . to make and use the same . . .

Enablement is only a minimum legal requirement, however. An effective specification speaks to an audience extending far beyond the person skilled in the art. In fact, although we often say that the audience for the specification is the person skilled in the art, there is no such real-life reader. The person skilled in the art is only a legal construct defining a standard for the specification's required level of detail.

The specification's real-life audience is multifaceted, comprising the patent examiner, the Opposing Team, and possibly a judge and jury. When written with this wider audience in mind, the specification can further the interests of the patent owner in ways that a specification that is minimally enabling may not. Such a specification can facilitate allowance in the Patent Office, make the patent easier to license, and provide an effective platform from which a litigator can argue the merits of the invention to the judge and jury.

In one sense, everything ultimately does come down to the claims. The examiner, for example, is principally focused on ensuring that the claims do not read on the prior art. However, allowance of the claims is helped along when the examiner understands what the invention is and is convinced that there is inventive subject matter to *be* claimed. The specification is the place to convince him of that.

The Opposing Team is also focused on the claims. They want to know whether or not the claims read on their product. But even if the claims do read on the Opposing Team's product, they will resist taking a license unless convinced that their product takes advantage of something novel taught by the patentee. The patent owner's goal is for the Opposing Team to lay down their arms and take a license with as little fuss as possible. They certainly will not do so if they feel they are being asked to pay something for nothing. The specification is a place to convince the Opposing Team that they are *not* being asked to pay something for nothing.

Judges and juries must decide whether the claims are valid and infringed. But before they hand over millions of dollars to the patent owner, judges and juries want to believe that justice is being done—that the essence of the invention has actually been appropriated by the accused infringer. They are therefore likely to look to the specification to be assured that justice *is* being done. Patent claims are a mystery to most non-patent professionals—a seemingly impenetrable morass of "saids" and "means for." The specification should be expressed in "regular" English to encourage judges and juries to try to read and understand it. Indeed, a patent application that is easy to read and understand is more likely to get the attention of a busy judge. A jury convinced that the inventive essence has been appropriated may return a finding of infringement even if the claims somewhat miss the mark.

A specification that achieves all of this is more than just a compendium of technical facts. It tells a story. It is a story of a problem, and of a solution made possible by the patentee's recognition of something that others did *not* recognize. Ideally, that story is told twice—once in the Background and Summary, as discussed in this chapter, and again in the Detailed Description, as discussed in the chapter that follows. Each of the two tellings is built upon and amplifies the problem-solution statement.

The Background

The Background tells the story of a problem that others could not solve, or could solve only partially or only in a complex or expensive way.

An effective Background brings the reader to a point of dramatic tension. By the end of the Background, the reader should be thinking two things: "Yes, I see that there is a problem," and "I wonder how they solved it. Let me read on."

It is not difficult to construct such a Background, but there are ways to enhance its story-telling effectiveness. These are illustrated both by examples in the discussion below and by a fictional patent for the invention of the chair presented in Appendix C.

Begin with the End in Mind

Chapter Eight alluded to Stephen Covey's exhortation, "Begin with the End in Mind." There we were talking about drafting a claim by working backward from the inventive departure. The same idea applies to the Background. Its presentation of the prior art is driven by where the story is headed—the inventive solution. As discussed below, the style of Summary recommended by the author starts out with a one-sentence statement of the inventive solution. This is possible only if the necessary groundwork has been laid in the Background. Indeed, anything that is in the Background should be there because, one way or the other, the Summary relies on its being there.

Keep It Short and Conclusory

The problem is best described at a high level, without a lot of detail. This does not mean skimping on the story line. The Background should provide a full accounting of the problem and how the prior art falls short of solving it. But the technical details of the prior art should be kept to a minimum. The story moves along just fine if the prior art is described only in general terms. The Background best holds the reader's attention when it says as little as needed to make its point.

The following Background, for example, goes into too much detail about the prior art. The writer seems to have felt compelled to *prove* the stated prior art disadvantage—namely that it "requires a considerable amount of control equipment." Readers are rarely interested in all of that. They are usually happy to accept the writer's word for it, and so a version that eliminates the crossed-out material serves perfectly well.

Background of the Invention

A known metal extraction technique described in U.S. Patent 6,—,— involves use of an extraction cylinder equipped with timing controls for sequentially pulsing a slurry and controlling the operation of various valves. The operation is controlled based on the proportions in percent of metal extracted from the cylinder as the process proceeds. The extracted metal is thereby maintained at a substantially constant purity.

Disadvantageously, this approach requires a considerable amount of control equipment. ~~For instance, it requires interface control~~

~~means positioned at one or several interfaces in the cylinder to detect a change in position of the liquid-metal interface during operation of the cylinder as well as another timing device in communication with the interface control means and with the first timing means to adjust the first mentioned timing means, which control the introduction and withdrawal of the material so as to maintain the interface in substantially the same position throughout the extracting operation.~~

We might even consider limiting the first paragraph to just its opening sentence, resulting in the following perfectly serviceable Background that tells readers everything they need, or want, to know about the problem.

Background of the Invention

A known metal extraction technique described in U.S. Patent 6,—,— involves use of an extraction cylinder equipped with timing controls for sequentially pulsing a slurry and controlling the operation of various valves. Disadvantageously, this approach requires a considerable amount of control equipment.

There are always exceptions. Describing particular prior art in intricate detail may be the only way to convey an understanding of the problem to the reader. Or we may feel that the argument for the nonobviousness of the invention is bolstered by presenting a long litany of others' failed attempts. The key is for the Background to include only that prior art—and only at the level of detail—that is necessary to bring home to the reader (a) that there really is a problem, (b) what that problem is, and (c) that the prior art hasn't solved it in the most effective way, if at all.

The Background is the first and best opportunity to engage the reader. Typically the reader will start reading the specification at its beginning— the Background—and will continue reading as long as he can follow what's being said. The Background should therefore be as engaging to a broad readership as possible. This is sometimes a tall order. An esoteric technology can make for difficult reading. All the more reason to write a streamlined Background that makes its points and moves on.

Don't Refer to the Drawings in the Background

It is usually better not to refer to the Drawings in the Background. A difficulty in articulating the problem without reference to the Drawings may well signal that we haven't fully come to grips with what the problem is. This can result in an unduly narrow understanding of the invention and, therefore, unduly narrow claims. In addition, diverting attention to the Drawings and away from the text can disrupt the Background's story-telling.

If a more full-blown exposition of the problem—including reference to the Drawings—is desired, it is better to present it at the start of the Detailed Description.

Don't Give Away Inventor Discoveries to the Prior Art

The typical problem-solution scenario involves a problem already known in the art. Sometimes, however, the inventor's contribution to the art is discovery of the source of a *known* problem or even simply the *existence* of a problem. In either case, that discovery should be introduced in the Summary, not the Background. Otherwise, the Opposing Team can argue that the inventor has admitted that the prior art already knew about the problem and/or its source. There may be no invention left to patent if that were to be the case, because often the solution is quite obvious once the source, or existence, of a problem is known.

Consider, for example, the discovery that a source of rear-end automobile collisions is that the traditional height of brake lights causes them to be less noticed by the driver behind than if they were higher. The inventor's solution is to have at least one brake light at about 45 inches above the ground, the typical driver line-of-sight height. This, then, is the desired claim:

> A motor vehicle having at least one brake light at a height of about 45 inches off the ground.

Patentability of this claim is best supported by putting the inventor's recognition in the Summary, not in the Background. Otherwise, the whole invention is given over to the prior art; the solution is a no-brainer once the source of the problem is identified. One is reminded of the old doctor/patient joke:

> Patient: Doctor, it hurts when I do this. (Low brake lights).
>
> Doctor: Then don't *do* that. (Don't put them so low.)

The idea that the brake lights are too low should not, therefore, be discussed in the Background. The Background should focus on the problem of rear-end collisions and other *known* sources of the problem, such as tailgating. The discovery that the traditional standard brake light height is not optimal for collision avoidance should be saved for the Summary.

The following are two versions of a Background and Summary for this invention. The "Wrong Approach" puts the inventive realization in the Background. The "Right Approach" puts it in the Summary.

Wrong Approach	**Right Approach**
Part of Inventor's Contribution Appears in the Background	**All of Inventor's Contribution Appears in the Summary**

Background

Rear-end automobile collisions continue to be a problem. The principal sources of such collisions have been believed to be driver inattention and tailgating. Defensive driving courses and public service announcements have helped somewhat, but these measures have not been fully effective.

Another source of rear-end collisions is that brake lights positioned at the traditional height of about 25 inches above the roadway are not in the direct line of sight of the driver in the vehicle behind and, as a result, can escape that driver's notice, especially when the driver is daydreaming or focused on something to the side of the road.

Summary

In accordance with the invention, an automobile is provided with at least one brake light that is located approximately 45 inches above the roadway, a height that is more in line with the typical driver line of sight.

Background

Rear-end automobile collisions continue to be a problem. The principal sources of such collisions have been believed to be driver inattention and tailgating. Defensive driving courses and public service announcements have helped somewhat, but these measures have not been fully effective.

Summary

At the heart of the present invention is my discovery that another source of rear-end collisions is that brake lights positioned at the traditional height of about 25 inches above the roadway—and thus not in the direct line of sight of the driver in the vehicle behind—can escape that driver's notice, especially when the driver is daydreaming or focused on something to the side of the road.

In accordance with the invention, then, an automobile is provided with at least one brake light that is located approximately 45 inches above the roadway, a height that is more in line with the typical driver line of sight.

Note how the "Wrong Approach" gives over the heart of the inventor's discovery to the prior art. It focuses the question of patentability on whether it would be obvious to raise the brake light height if one knows that the traditional height contributes to rear-end collisions. It could be argued that this version of the story admits that the prior art already knew that, taking all the wind out of the sails of the invention and, indeed, possibly scuttling it altogether.

The "Right Approach," by contrast, gives no clue as to the inventor's discovery. Unlike the first version, this one does not imply that anyone knew that the 25-inch height was a contributing factor to rear-end collisions. Desirably, the inventor's contribution to the art comes as a surprise when it emerges in the Summary. The stage on which patentability will be played out will be whether it was known or obvious that the traditional brake light location contributed to rear-end collisions—not whether it was obvious to raise the height once that fact is known.

An examiner is not likely to reject an invention based on what might be seen as a technicality of formatting. But the Opposing Team will make as much of it as possible in licensing discussions or litigation. "If your inventor supposedly discovered the source of the problem," the Opposing Team will argue to the patent owner, "how come she talks about it in the Background?"

As noted above, the inventor's contribution is sometimes her recognition that there even *is* a problem. An example is the repeating typewriter (and later, computer) key, where a character or space is repeated for as long as its key is depressed. Typists typed for almost a century without this convenience (no doubt made possible by the advent of the electric typewriter). The problem of having to repetitively strike the "dash" key in order to create a dashed line across the page was not experienced by typists as a problem to be fixed. It remained for the inventor of the repeating key function to show typists (and later users of word processors) that they had this "problem."

As with the brake light invention, the inventor's contribution should be saved for the Summary, as in the "Right Approach" version below.

<u>**Wrong Approach**</u>	<u>**Right Approach**</u>
Part of Inventor's Contribution Appears in the Background	**All of Inventor's Contribution Appears in the Summary**
Background	**Background**
Typewriting has contributed greatly to the speed and legibility with which words can be put to paper. However, improvements are always desired in any art. For example, when the same character or space is to be typed multiple times, it is inefficient for a typist to have to depress the corresponding key that same number of times.	Typewriting has contributed greatly to the speed and legibility with which words can be put to paper. However, improvements are always desired in any art.
Summary	**Summary**
Typewriters embodying the principles of the invention type a character or space continuously for as long as the corresponding key is depressed.	I have observed that when the same character or space is to be typed multiple times, it is inefficient for a typist to have to depress the corresponding key that same number of times. Based on this observation, typewriters embodying the principles of the invention type a character or space continuously for as long as the corresponding key is depressed.

The invention is sometimes even given away to the prior art at the very outset of the Background, in its Field of the Invention. In the following example, the italicized words go beyond the field of the invention to disclose the invention itself:

Field of Invention

The present invention relates to typewriting and, in particular, to a function of a typewriter *wherein a character or space is repeated for as long as the corresponding key is depressed.*

This is to be avoided for all of the reasons discussed above.

The Summary

The Summary presents the solution to the problem laid out in the Background.

There are two schools of thought about the Summary.

Many attorneys, including the author, subscribe to the view that the Summary should present the invention in narrative form, thereby continuing the story-telling that was begun in the Background. This is referred to here as the story-telling type of Summary.

The other school of thought holds that the Summary should be a substantially verbatim reprise of the broadest claim, and perhaps other claims, with only minor reformatting or wording changes, such as changing "said" to "the." This is referred to here as the claim-restatement type of Summary.

Proponents of the claim-restatement type of Summary have litigation in mind. It is felt that a court may rule that one or more embodiment details are essential to the invention because they are mentioned in the Summary. The claimed subject matter is then interpreted as being limited by those details, even when the claims don't recite them, creating a loophole for the accused infringer. This is avoided if the Summary exactly mimics the claims. Indeed, in at least one reported case, recitations in a "whereby clause," which are not normally given limiting effect, were deemed to be an integral part of the claimed process at least in part because of language in the Summary.[1]

Unfortunately, the claim-restatement type of Summary usually leaves the reader in the dark as to what the invention is, as in the following example:

---

1. *Hoffer v. Microsoft Corp.*, 405 F.3d 1326, 1329, 74 USPQ2d 1481, 1483 (Fed. Cir. 2005).

Summary of the Invention

The above problems are solved in one aspect by a vacuum pump having a drivable worm gear comprising a screw thread made of plastic and being formed as one piece, the worm gear having a first longitudinal section configured for being coupled to a pinion via which a torque can be transmitted from the pinion to the worm gear and the first longitudinal section being formed as one piece with the worm gear and wherein the worm gear comprises first and second support sections, a second longitudinal section and a third longitudinal section and the second and the third longitudinal sections being formed as one piece with the worm gear and the worm gear having a slot for the receipt of an anti-seize-up arm.

This type of Summary invariably leaves the reader with only one reaction—"Huh?"—and squanders a golden opportunity to bring the reading audience on board with the invention. Like the claims that underlie it, a claim-restatement type of Summary *defines* the invention but does not *explain* what it is. Such a Summary does not speak to the patent's intended audience. In fact, it does not speak to anyone. Readers invariably stop reading a claim-restatement type of Summary after the first few lines because it conveys little readily digestible information and is tedious to wade through. One might just as well read the claims themselves. The reader is particularly frustrated with this type of Summary when the Background has done a good job of describing the problem. Having been brought to a point of dramatic tension, the reader wonders "How *are* they going to solve this problem?" only to encounter a lexical brick wall that does not provide an understandable answer.

The advantage of the claim-restatement type of Summary is, moreover, speculative and theoretical. Only a tiny percentage of patents are ever involved in litigation. An even smaller number are subjected to a claim-narrowing interpretation based on language in the Summary. Furthermore, although claims are usually amended during prosecution, practitioners rarely amend the Summary, and so the Summary in the issued patent does not jibe with the issued claims anyway.

By contrast, many more patents are the subject of licensing negotiations. A Summary that effectively explains what the invention is goes a long way toward showing the would-be licensee that he is not being asked to pay something for nothing. It helps smooth the way toward a successful deal-closing, particularly if a business executive or other non-patent-professional is involved in the negotiations. A story-telling Summary is something he can understand. "Are we doing this?" he may ask his people, "And, if so, why are we fighting this?"

A patent whose Summary makes the invention clear is less likely to get into litigation because the Opposing Team is more likely to agree (at least among themselves) that their product implements the inventor's teachings. They are also more likely to conclude that the jury will see it that way as well.

A story-telling Summary can even play a positive role in litigation by helping the judge and jury understand what was invented. It is compelling when the Summary is read aloud in court and the patent owner's expert testifies that it describes just what the defendant's product does.

A Summary cannot help but "come out broader" when it is written unconstrained by claim-drafting mechanics and formalisms. Indeed, this is one of the important reasons that the author advocates characterizing the invention in problem-solution form in the first instance, rather than through an invention-analysis-by-claim-drafting approach.

This is not to negate the concern that informs some practitioners' preference for a claim-restatement type of Summary. We certainly do not want claimed subject matter to be limited by embodiment details contained in the Summary but not present in the claim itself. But the claim-restatement type of Summary throws out the baby with the bathwater. One gives up a lot by foregoing the advantages that flow from a well-thought-out Summary in anticipation of a speculative and infrequent litigation contingency.

It is possible, in any event, to address that contingency and still employ the story-telling type of Summary by following the guidelines presented below. As with the discussion of the Background, use of these guidelines is illustrated both by specific examples and by a fictional patent for the invention of the chair as presented in Appendix C.

State the Inventive Solution in One Sentence

Whenever possible, the Summary should contain a one-sentence statement of the invention. It should usually be the Summary's first sentence and is typically lifted right out of the problem-solution statement. Any contextual or terminological antecedents for the solution will have been provided in the Background. This is what allows the solution to be stated in the Summary so directly.

Here are three examples of such Summaries, in which the second sentence closes the problem-solution loop—a desirable feature of the Summary discussed below.

Summary of the Invention

A. In a traffic signal embodying the principles of the invention, the indicia displayed for the first direction of travel are changed automatically in predetermined coordination with changes in the indicia displayed for the second direction of travel. Such automatic changing of the indicia avoids the inconsistencies that can result when the indicia are changed manually.

B. In accordance with the invention, light pen locations determined during previous scans are used to predict the location of the pen during the upcoming scan and thus to determine where the scanning patch is to be centered on the screen. This technique allows the patch to be made smaller than in the prior art, substantially decreasing the average time required to identify the new pen location.

C. In accordance with the invention, each display point is energized to have an intensity proportional to the average intensity of a cluster of cells of the dithered image rather than the intensity of a single dithered image cell, as in the prior art. This has the effect of averaging the brightness of each two-line pair, which, in turn, eliminates the flicker.

As noted above—and as in these examples—it is usually appropriate for the one-sentence solution to be the Summary's opening sentence. But this is not always the case. For example, when the inventor's contribution to the art includes discovery of something about the problem, or when the inventor has discovered the very existence of the problem or its source, the Summary should begin by explaining that discovery. The one-sentence solution follows that. Examples are the above Summaries for the automobile brake light and repeating key inventions.

Other Summaries that lead off with something other than the one-sentence solution are presented below under the heading *Be Creative.*

Present the Solution Functionally

The inventive solution should be stated as functionally as possible with a minimum of "hardware" limitations. See the examples above. Just as in the problem-solution statement, the Summary should specify *what* is done to solve the problem rather than *how* the embodiment happens to carry it off. Indeed, if a problem-solution statement has been developed following the methodology presented in this book, the "solution" portion of the problem-solution statement will already meet this criterion. Even for something as apparatus-focused as the chair invention, it is still possible to state the solution with a fair amount of functionality, as seen in Appendix C. A Summary that defines the invention principally in apparatus terms is often narrower than it has to be.

Close the Problem-Solution Loop

The Background has laid out a problem, and the Summary presents the solution to that problem. How the solution actually solves the problem is sometimes immediately apparent, but not always so. In the latter case, the story-telling function of the Background and Summary is enhanced when the Summary closes out the problem-solution loop by explicitly stating how the inventive steps or structure solve the problem. See the last sentence of each of the Summaries above.

Designate Optional Features as Such

The Summary can safely refer to the solution portion of the problem-solution statement as "the invention." At the same time, however, the Summary must make clear that fallback features or other embodiment details that it mentions are only illustrative or optional. There should never be a question about what is absolutely required by the broad invention and what is not.

This is accomplished by appropriate use of appropriate qualifying terms, as in the following examples:

- "If desired, particular embodiments may optionally include step S."
- "Element E may be, for example, the particular type of E known as an E_1."
- "The invention may be used to particular advantage in context C."

Use the "Inverted Pyramid" Style

The Summary should follow the "inverted pyramid" format used in newspaper stories. The first sentence presents the essential kernel of the story. Important details appear in the next few paragraphs. Quotes, fill-in information, and less important details come after that. Very little that is unimportant appears ahead of anything more important. Here is an example of such a newspaper story:

> FREEDONIA, April 2—An earthquake of monumental proportions struck this island nation today, killing hundreds of people and injuring thousands more. Property damage was estimated at $900 million.
>
> The quake, which began at 5 A.M. AST, measured 8.5 on the Richter scale. It was the second major earthquake to strike this island nation in five years.

The previous quake measured 7.6. Since the Richter scale is logarithmic, today's event was considerably more powerful.

"We have barely recovered from the last one," Prime Minister Alexander Wagstaff said at a press conference shortly after, "and now this."

Note how the story could be pruned paragraph by paragraph from the end and would still make sense. This is because the paragraphs are self-contained, convey the most important information first, and leave less important details for later.

The Summary in a patent specification should be similarly constructed. Only what is essential to defining the invention appears in the one-sentence solution. This should be followed by the most important details—the important fallback features, advantageous contexts in which the invention may be implemented, and so forth. Further details, such as less important fallback features, come after that. See the example in Appendix C.

Any news story always omits some details because they are not significant enough to report. So too when constructing a Summary. There is always a point where further embodiment details, even if included in one or more of the narrower claims, are not sufficiently important to be highlighted in the Summary. The dividing line is arbitrary. There is no particular harm in going "too far" as long as it is made clear that such details are merely illustrative or optional. A useful test is to ask whether a particular detail would be helpful to the first-time reader in understanding the invention or how it can be advantageously implemented.

The author refers to this process for constructing the Summary as pushing the details "down and out." After having presented the one-sentence statement of the invention solution, the next most important detail—for example, the most important fallback feature—is presented next. The next most important detail comes after that. Each other detail continues to be pushed down further into the pool of as yet unmentioned details until it emerges as the most important of those that remain. At some point, any other embodiment details that *could* be presented are not important enough to *be* presented.

The effectiveness of the inverted pyramid technique in presenting the most important details first can be further appreciated by comparing the earthquake story above with the following alternative version, in which the format is violated in the extreme:

FREEDONIA, April 2—Freedonia Prime Minister Alexander Wagstaff called a press conference at 8 A.M. AST this morning. Mr. Wagstaff
reminded the assembled journalists that some five years ago Freedonia was hit by an earthquake measuring 7.6 on the Richter scale. It
was only within the last several months, he pointed out, that all damage from that quake had been repaired and all services restored.

It was against that backdrop that Mr. Wagstaff announced a new
incident that brought thousands of people to the hospital, and caused
at least $900 million in damage. Hundreds more were killed when, at
5 A.M. AST, Freedonia was hit with another earthquake, measuring 8.5.

Be Creative

The Summary provides a lot of opportunity for story-telling creativity.
In each of the following examples, the Summary does not begin with the
one-sentence solution. Rather, it features a lead-in that paves the way
for it. We saw earlier how such a lead-in is appropriate when at least a
part of the inventor's contribution to the art was the inventor's discovery
of the problem or of the source of a known problem. A preinventive-
concept lead-in can actually serve any number of different functions, as
illustrated by the following examples.

Lead-in A

This lead-in presents a key recognition on the part of the inventor as to
the desirability of providing a new functionality to an old device.

We have recognized that what is needed in order to solve this
problem is to provide each codec in a connection with the ability to
recognize the presence of another codec on its high-bit-rate side of
the connection. In accordance with the invention, a codec, upon recognizing the presence of another codec on its high-bit-rate side of a
connection, switches from its conventional encoding/decoding operating mode to a mode in which it embeds the coded speech bits in its
output signal directly. As a result, only one encoding/decoding cycle is
performed across the connection.

Lead-in B

This lead-in describes how the inventive circuit is similar to the prior art
as a way of highlighting the difference between them.

A differential amplifier solving the above problem is similar to
prior art differential amplifiers that generate an intermediate differ-

ential signal, from which an output signal is normally generated. In accordance with the invention, however, the output differential signal is generated by output circuitry that combines each component of the intermediate differential signal with an auxiliary signal component in phase therewith.

Lead-in C

This lead-in uses the Summary as the vehicle to mention certain known properties of the material comprising the device, thereby steering clear of presaging the invention in the Background.

At the heart of our micro-positioner is a monolithic body of a crystalline material of a type in which (a) domains of differing crystal axis orientations can coexist stably, (b) domain walls can be moved via applied electrical signals, and (c) domain wall movement results in relative motion between the non-interfacing domain ends. We have recognized that these properties can be exploited to provide a micro-positioner in which an object to be moved is secured to a free end of the crystalline body while the other end is held fixed. Movement of a domain wall via application of an appropriate electrical signal gives rise to the desired micro-movement of the object.

Lead-in D

This lead-in describes a phenomenon observed in the laboratory that the inventors went on to exploit.

We have discovered that storage of wall voltage can be minimized by using a scan write pulse shaped in such a way that the wall voltage just stored by the pulse can give rise to a so-called "second breakdown," which actually reduces the wall voltage. This advantageously allows the selection of scan write pulse parameters that are sufficiently large to overcome the above-noted problem of ensuring that the OFF cell flashes without threatening to switch other OFF cells to the ON state. A plasma panel embodying the principles of the invention utilizes just such a scan write pulse.

Having told a concise version of the problem-solution story in the Background and Summary, we are primed to tell it again—but in expanded form—in the Detailed Description. Writing *that* part of the specification is the subject of the next chapter.

CHAPTER REVIEW—Writing the Background and Summary

Confirm Your Understanding

1. According to the author, what are the hallmarks of an effective Background of the Invention ("Background")?
2. Why might it be desirable for a Background to be long and detailed?
3. When is it preferable to introduce the problem solved by the invention in the Summary of the Invention ("Summary") rather than the Background?
4. What are the two main Summary styles? What are the arguments for and against using each style?
5. According to the author, what are the hallmarks of an effective Summary?
6. What is meant by "closing the problem-solution loop" in the Summary?

Questions for Further Thought

7. Since the boundaries of the patented invention are defined by the claims, not the specification, why does the book insist that the Summary (indeed, the entire specification) must make clear that fallback features or other embodiment details that it mentions are only illustrative or optional?
8. Why does constructing the Summary in the "inverted pyramid" style (pp. 280–281) help the patent drafter to tease out the inventive concept from the inventor's embodiment(s)?

Sharpen Your Skills

9. Evaluate the Background and Summary of one or more issued patents based on the following criteria presented in this chapter:

Background
- Does the Background make clear what problem(s) the invention solves?
- Is the Background of suitable length?
- Does the Background avoid giving away inventor discoveries to the prior art?

Summary
- Is it clear from the Summary what it is that solves the problem(s), broadly speaking?
- Is the inventive concept stated as functionally as possible?
- Does the Summary make clear what features of the disclosed embodiment(s) are merely optional or preferred, as opposed to being inherent in the broad invention?
- Does the Summary close the problem-solution loop?
- Use the precepts discussed in this chapter to edit or rewrite the Background and/or Summary of a patent for which some number of the above criteria are not met.

CHAPTER NINETEEN

Writing the Detailed Description

The Detailed Description, along with its accompanying Drawings, is a second telling of the problem-solution story. Actually, the Detailed Description *illustrates* the story rather than simply telling it.

The Background and Summary of many patents do a good job of telling the invention story. However, the invention often disappears from view once the Detailed Description starts up. The reader is set loose to negotiate an expanse of details without being shown how they relate to the invention story.

A Detailed Description that does not continue to focus on the invention story misses an opportunity to help the reading audience better understand the invention. The fact that "it's all in there somewhere" only satisfies the minimum legal requirement of enablement.[1] It does not guarantee that the reader will be able to align the broad statements in the Background and Summary with the specifics in the Detailed Description. Most of the details in the Detailed Description (and Drawings) do not illustrate the invention per se. Their purpose is to provide an enabling disclosure—showing particular implementations of functional blocks, explaining the overall context in which the invention is implemented, and so forth. Even in a moderately simple Detailed Description it may not be at all clear which aspects of the disclosed embodiment(s) corresponds to the elements of the invention unless the correspondence is explicitly pointed out.

The Detailed Description, then, should not be a flat, featureless field of undifferentiated details. It should be an attention-grabbing landscape with a central focus and clearly delineated features that stand out from the overall setting.

The Detailed Description as Expansion of the Background/Summary

Many attorneys write the Detailed Description before the Background and Summary. There is much to be said, however, for writing the

---

1. 35 U.S.C. 112(a).

Background and Summary first. Indeed, that is the author's preferred approach.

A Background and Summary based on the guidelines of the previous chapter serve as a perfect outline for the Detailed Description. The Background and Summary guide the writer as to what should be introduced when in telling the expanded version of the invention story. In fact, the author's Detailed Descriptions typically contain each sentence of the Summary, or sometimes whole paragraphs, augmented or expanded with the embodiment details. Key sentences from the Background are sometimes also included. A Detailed Description written in this way provides its reader with a clear picture of which aspects of the Detailed Description illustrate the broad, general statements made in the Background and Summary. It imbues the overall specification with a pedagogic unity and cohesiveness that is hard to achieve when the Detailed Description is written first.

This approach is used in the sample patent shown in Appendix C.

Illustrating the Problem

The Detailed Description's telling of the problem can be at various levels of detail, depending on what seems useful. The problem story can be as short as a sentence or two that refer the reader to the Background. Often, however, it is useful to illustrate the problem with reference to a block diagram of an illustrative system, or a flowchart of an illustrative prior art process in which the problem arises. If the invention is a simple article of manufacture, such as a hand tool, a piece of sports equipment, or a gadget of some kind, it may be useful to show a prior art version.

The stage is thus set for the problem to be shown in context and to be explained in greater depth than is typically desirable for the Background. As mentioned above, whole sentences appearing in the Background describing the problem may be presented again at this point, and then amplified with reference to the system block diagram or process flowchart. The reader may have understood the problem in a general sense from having read the Background, but may not have understood specifically how the problem arises or why solving it is so important. The Detailed Description is a vehicle through which these things can be made clear.

Illustrating the Solution

The stage is now set for the Detailed Description to illustrate the solution to the problem. The following are some specific ideas for illustrating the solution in a pedagogic way that moves the invention story forward.

Point Out the Inventive Departure

There will be points in the Detailed Description where the reader will encounter the structural element(s) or method step(s) that constitutes the inventive departure. These should be explicitly pointed out by making specific reference to "the invention." Such lead-in phrases as "In accordance with the invention" serve well here. Indeed, the first embodiment in the Detailed Description is a place where the Summary's one-sentence statement of the inventive concept can be inserted and then amplified with specific reference to the embodiment.

Use the Word "Invention" Carefully

The word "invention" should be used with great care. This is a point that cannot be emphasized often enough or strongly enough. The word "invention" should be used without qualification only when referring to the broad inventive concept. We should not call something "the invention" unless we are willing to have the patent coverage limited to that.

If the specification says that something is "the invention," the Opposing Team will argue to the court that it *is* the invention, regardless of what the claims say, and various reported decisions will back up that argument. Broad terms in claims have been interpreted narrowly because the specification characterized something as being a part of "the invention." Indeed, entire claim elements nowhere to be found in a claim have been imported into it based on such a characterization of "the invention" in the specification.

An issue in a reported Federal Circuit case[2] was whether a certain functionality called for in the claims should be regarded as (a) encompassing an alleged infringer's one-step process for performing that function, or (b) limited to a two-step process as was used in the patentee's illustrative embodiment. The claim itself said nothing about the number of steps. The Court deemed construction (b) to be the correct one based in part on use of the word "invention," rather than "implementation of the invention," in the Detailed Description. The Court pointed to the following Detailed Description lead-in to the details of the two-step process:

> The decoding algorithm employed in accordance with the present invention operates to …

and then asserted that "[t]he specification characterizes the two-step process as 'the invention,' not merely an implementation of the invention."

---

2. *Harris Corp. v. Ericsson, Inc.*, 417 F.3d 1241; 75 USPQ2d 1705 (Fed. Cir. 2005) (construing claim terms in U.S. Patent 4,365,338).

Or consider the seemingly innocuous statement

> FIG. I is a circuit diagram of the invention.

This sentence implies that every component shown in the diagram is required to implement the inventive concept. It is not likely that that is what the patent drafter meant. Unless one is willing to have the patent's coverage limited to the circuit exactly as shown, it would be better to write

> FIG. I is a diagram of a circuit in which the invention is implemented.

Or consider the statement

> The invention employs a nickel oxide shell-type catalyst to speed up the reaction between X and Y.

This statement implies that the invention necessarily involves use of a nickel oxide shell-type catalyst. This is fine if reacting X and Y using a catalyst is known in the prior art and the inventive departure is that the catalyst is of the nickel oxide shell-type. But if the invention resides simply in reacting X with Y, it would be better to write

> Particular embodiments of the invention may use a nickel oxide shell-type catalyst to speed up the reaction between X and Y.

These considerations apply, of course, to the Summary as well. Indeed, it is even more important to observe the specialness of the word "invention" in the Summary since the Summary is supposed to be a summary of the invention per se.[3] However, the point is brought up here—in connection with the Detailed Description—because we are already quite focused on stating what the invention is when writing the Summary, and so we are not as likely to make a mistake. The Detailed Description is less formalized and more wide-ranging. There is a lot more to think about than just the invention per se when drafting the Detailed Description. It may thus be easier to slip up when writing the Detailed Description and refer to something as "the invention" when it is not.

When the claims in a litigated patent get interpreted more narrowly than they "should," the specification is often the culprit.

---

3. Manual of Patent Examining Procedure, § 608.01(d) (8th ed., rev. July 2010).

Use the Inverted Pyramid Style to Get to the Invention Early

A way to keep up reader interest is to structure the Detailed Description using the inverted pyramid style described above in connection with the Summary.[4] For example, the inventive concept may reside in a new functional relationship between the elements of a known type of system. In such a case the Detailed Description can lead off with a description of a high-level block diagram or simplified mechanical drawing illustrating that functional relationship. The details of the various components of the disclosed system can be introduced later on.

Indeed, it is the author's practice to push down to the end of the disclosure descriptions of components or steps that are not involved in the invention but are simply included to fulfill the enablement requirement.[5] Few readers will actually be interested in that material, and it can get in the way of the story-telling. An inverted-pyramid-style Detailed Description will, in fact, evolve naturally if the Summary is used as a template.

If the subject matter is not amenable to an early introduction of the inventive concept, we can at least clue the reader in on where a discussion of the invention may be found, as in the following:

> "In order to explain the invention, this description first presents some tutorial material relating to sonar-based prospecting. The present invention, relating to our technique for processing the sonar data, is described below under the heading 'sonar signal processing.'"

Have the Invention Well in Hand Before Starting the Detailed Description

The key to writing an effective Detailed Description is to have the invention well in hand *before* the writing begins. This is automatically accomplished if the Summary has already been written, as suggested above. But even if the Detailed Description is written first, we still should know what the invention is before we start.

A contrary view holds that familiarity with the embodiment gained by writing the Detailed Description helps the attorney determine what the invention actually is. We have seen, however, that analyzing the embodiment to identify the invention rather than carrying out a problem-solution analysis can easily result in the broad invention being missed.

Even if the invention does get properly identified at some point during or after the writing of the Detailed Description, the Detailed

---

4. *See* p. 280.
5. 35 U.S.C. 112(a).

Description probably will not point out the invention in desirably broad, functional terms. Aspects of the embodiment that were thought to be central to the invention, and described as such, may prove to be only optional fallback features. Conversely, features that were thought to be optional might prove to be crucial to patentability once the invention has been fully analyzed and vetted against the prior art. Terminology used in the Detailed Description may prove to be too narrow in light of what was later realized to be the invention. The overall structure of the Detailed Description may prove to be less than optimally suited for telling and illustrating the invention story.

Revision is always an option, of course, but involves time and effort that would not have to have been expended if the invention had been identified at the outset.

Preparing the drawings is also more efficient if we know what the invention is. Since the drawings must show every feature recited in the claims,[6] we can be sure that the drawings are complete only once we know what the claims will say. This, in turn, requires knowing what the invention is and what its fallback features are. Revising the drawings can be tedious and may entail further revision of the specification to make it consistent with the revised drawings.

There are other issues. Major revision of the Detailed Description is error-prone. The editing process may miss an unduly limiting statement about what "the invention" entails. Not all changes in terminology may be caught. The narrative is likely to read like the patch job that it was. As with any composition, writing the Detailed Description without a clear goal can result in a tangle that is very hard to unravel.

Be Detailed Where the Invention Lives

How detailed should the Detailed Description actually be?

An effective rule of thumb is *Be Detailed Where the Invention Lives*. This means that aspects of the embodiment that relate most closely to the invention should be described in the greatest detail. Conversely, aspects of the embodiment that are further removed from the invention can be described in less detail.

In the book's chair example, for instance, the approximate height of the seat above the supporting surface—about 18 inches, say—is close to where the invention lives because the invention relates to how the seat is supported, and the height of the seat is determined by the length of the chair's "elongated support members," the latter constituting the inven-

---

6. 37 CFR 1.83.

tive departure. On the other hand, methods for felling trees in order to obtain wood to build a chair are far from where the invention lives, and one could feel safe in leaving a discussion of tree-felling methods out of the specification (assuming the prior art knew some way to fell a tree).

Details that are closest to where the invention lives are most likely to be details that can be effectively relied on to distinguish the invention from invention-irrelevant prior art, as will now be explained.

Recall from an earlier discussion[7] that "invention-irrelevant" prior art is prior art that anticipates a claim, rendering it overbroad, but does not disclose the inventive concept and/or does not solve the problem. The words of the claim just happen to read on that prior art.

There is no need to fall back to a narrower view of the invention in such a case by, for example, incorporating one of its fallback features into the broadest claims. Rather, what needs to be done when faced with invention-irrelevant prior art is to add language to the claim that firms up the invention boundaries that were always intended. This is further discussed in Chapter Twenty-One.

It becomes clear soon enough what additional language is needed to firm up the intended invention boundaries. Sometimes that language will define a context to which the invention applies or in which the problem arises. Sometimes it is an operational parameter or a relationship between parameters. Sometimes it is an explicit definition for a term that an examiner might interpret more broadly than the claim drafter intended or envisioned. In all these cases, amending the claim to include the additional language does narrow the claim, but only to the extent of reining it in to the subject matter intended to be encompassed in the first place.

Here's the catch: Whatever the additional language is to be, it needs to find support in the specification. Therein lies a dilemma. On the one hand, it is difficult to predict just what additional language might be needed. The nature of the invention-irrelevant prior art that may come up during prosecution is unpredictable. On the other hand, it is not cost-effective or practical to disclose every minute detail of every element or method step in the embodiment on the off chance that any particular one of them might hold the key to firming up the invention boundaries in the face of invention-irrelevant prior art. Choices have to be made in order to meet realities of time and budget.

Being detailed where the invention lives is an effective way of making those choices.

Returning to our chair example, the height of the seat above the supporting surface may seem like an irrelevant detail not worthy of mention. If

---

7. *See* p. 138.

the invention is that the support members are "elongated," who cares how high they position the seat? This detail could save the day, however, if prior art comes to light after the patent application is filed disclosing a standard-height table. The claim could then be amended to recite the seat height.

The author was once called upon to study an issued patent whose claims referred to a "stripe." The file history showed that the examiner was able to read the claims on invention-irrelevant prior art by interpreting the term "stripe" very broadly. The prior art's "stripe" was quite different from what the patent applicant had in mind. It would not have given up any significant invention coverage to amend the claim to include a geometrical definition of the kind of "stripe" that would be appropriate to solve the problem the invention was directed to. Unfortunately, the specification nowhere defined what the inventor meant by "stripe," so there was no support for such an amendment. Indeed, the file history showed that the attorney had a great deal of trouble getting the patent application allowed.

Adherence to the prescription *Be Detailed Where the Invention Lives* would certainly have helped in that case. A term used in a claim, such as the "stripe" of this example, is not just *close* to where the invention lives, It is at the very *heart* of where the invention lives. Following this prescription would therefore have led the attorney to indicate in the specification the meaning of "stripe" in the context of the invention at hand.

Collect Variations and Alternatives as You Go; Save Them for the End

It is desirable for the Detailed Description to point out ways that the disclosed embodiment can be changed while still carrying out the invention. This includes different environments in which the invention may be used, equivalents for various elements and functional blocks, alternative materials, and so forth, referred to here as "embodiment alternatives."

Pointing out embodiment alternatives serves at least two functions. One is to help ensure that a broad range of equivalents is accorded to the various claim limitations—including means-plus-function elements.[8]

The other function served by disclosing embodiment alternatives is to put them into the prior art. This forecloses others from later arguing that those alternatives are nonobvious and thereby possibly obtaining patents that cover them.

---

8. "An element . . . expressed as a means or step for performing a specified function . . . shall be construed to cover the corresponding structure, material, or acts described in the specification *and equivalents thereof.*" 35 U.S.C. 112(f) (emphasis added).

Many embodiment alternatives may occur to the attorney on his own. Others may be offered up by the inventor. If the attorney is writing the application collaboratively with the inventor, as suggested later in the book,[9] he can urge the inventor to mention embodiment alternatives during the writing process.

The author likes to set up a space at the end of the draft specification where alternatives that come to mind can be quickly noted. That way they won't be forgotten, but attention can stay focused on composing the main story line. Those alternatives can later be integrated into the body of the Detailed Description. Or, they can be cleaned up and retained at the end of the specification along with the other usual "savings language" typically included at the end of the Detailed Description. Too many embodiment alternatives introduced into the main text can get in the way of the story-telling.

When Should the Detailed Description Be Written?

Having identified the invention—and perhaps drafted at least some claims—many attorneys write the Detailed Description next, then the Background, and finally the Summary.

As described above, the author always writes the Background and Summary before writing the Detailed Description. In fact, the author usually writes the sections of the application in their order of presentation: Background, Summary, Detailed Description, and then Claims. This is a methodology that can work only if one has the invention fully in hand and the fallback features have been identified. A nailed-down answer to the question *What is the Invention?* is absolutely required for this approach to work.

Some of the advantages of writing the Background and Summary before the Detailed Description have already been discussed, but there are others.

The process of writing the Background and Summary provides an opportunity to "tweak up" the description of the invention within a compact lexical space. This includes refining our view of the broad invention, establishing a terminology to describe the invention and the environment in which it is going to be disclosed, and establishing a logical flow of ideas, from the problem to the solution to the fallback features. It is more time-consuming to go back through an extensive Detailed Description and make changes if our view of the invention has changed or if new terminology was introduced in midstream.

---

9. *See* pp. 329–332.

Writing the Background and Summary in this way can be painstakingly slow. But it pays for itself many times over. A thoroughly vetted Background and Summary serves as an invaluable guide for writing the Detailed Description, assisting with terminology as well as the logical flow of ideas.

The author writes the claims last. Insights may evolve during the writing of the specification—particularly the Background and Summary. Claims written last benefit from all of that.

Final Review

Once the Detailed Description and then the claims (if not written previously) have been completed, the specification is in condition for a final attorney review before being sent to the inventor. The following review points apply not only to the Detailed Description, but to the Background and Summary as well.

Important things to check are the following:

- Consider every mention of the word "invention." If properly used, it should never imply or allow for an inference that the inventor regarded some optional feature as being required for the broad invention.
- Proceed down through the claims and confirm that every term, functional recitation, and concept in the claims has a clear antecedent basis in the specification and that every claim term is well-defined. (This would have saved one attorney a lot of grief in the case of the claim term "stripe" recounted above.)
- Confirm that the Summary's definition of the invention aligns with the broadest claim(s). Any limitations in the Summary that are not in the broadest claims should be qualified as being "illustrative" or "optional" and/or should be pushed down into a later part of the Summary. The Summary in its final form should conform to the claims in *their* final form.
- Tend to editorial and administrative matters. Is the terminology used in the specification consistent throughout? Does the specification mention every element in the drawing that was given a reference numeral? Are spelling, grammar, and punctuation correct?

The application can then go to the inventor for her review.

The activities involved in securing patent protection for an invention—preparing the patent application and then prosecuting it in the Patent and Trademark Office—are colloquially referred to as "prep and pros." To this point in the book, we've addressed "prep." We will return to it in Chapter Twenty-Two when we discuss working with the inventor.

The upcoming two chapters focus on "pros." They address the topic of claim rejections and how the problem-solution paradigm is brought to bear when amending claims.

CHAPTER REVIEW—Writing the Detailed Description

Confirm Your Understanding

1. According to the author, what are the hallmarks of an effective Detailed Description in a patent application?
2. What difference does it make how the Detailed Description is constructed as long as it satisfies the "enablement" and "best mode" requirements of 35 U.S.C. 112, ¶ 1?
3. What advantages can flow from writing the Background and Summary first, i.e., before writing the Detailed Description? What disadvantages can flow from writing the Detailed Description first?
4. Why does the book admonish the patent drafter to use the word "invention" carefully?
5. Why is it desirable to have the invention well in hand before beginning to write the Detailed Description?
6. What is the rationale for the prescription *Be Detailed Where the Invention Lives*?

Question for Further Thought

7. The author writes the claims last when preparing a patent application. Since the invention is what the claims say it is, how does this practice jibe with the author's assertion that is it desirable to have the invention well in hand before the Detailed Description is written?

Sharpen Your Skills

8. Evaluate the Detailed Description of one or more issued patents based on the following criteria presented in this chapter. Specifically, does the Detailed Description—
   - Point out the inventive concept?
   - Use the word "invention" carefully and appropriately?
   - Follow the prescription *Be Detailed Where the Invention Lives*?

CHAPTER TWENTY

Claim Rejections—Amend or Argue?

The problem-solution paradigm is central not only to claiming the invention in the first instance, but also to amending the claims during prosecution, should that prove necessary.

This chapter presents an overview of the six main options available when a claim is rejected as unpatentable under § 102 or § 103. The next chapter describes how the problem-solution paradigm is used to identify the best way(s) to amend a claim, should amending prove to be the appropriate option.

In both chapters, the term "cited prior art" includes both (a) subject matter disclosed in a single prior art reference and cited in a § 102 rejection, and (b) subject matter that results from modifying or combining teachings in one or more references as advanced by the examiner in a § 103 rejection.

Four Questions, Six Options

The answers to four questions determine which of six options should be taken when a claim is rejected under § 102 or § 103. The four questions are:

1. Is the examiner's position on obviousness well-founded? (This question applies to § 103 rejections only.)
2. Does the claim read on the cited prior art?
3. Is the cited prior art the same subject matter intended to be captured by the claim (i.e., does it disclose the inventive concept)?
4. Does the invention predate the cited prior art reference(s)? (This question is relevant only until the revised version of 35 U.S.C. 102 comes into effect on March 16, 2013.)

And the six options are:

1. Argue the nonobviousness of combining or modifying prior art teachings used to reject the claim. (This question applies to § 103 rejections only.)
2. Argue that the rejected claim does not read on the cited prior art.

3. Avoid the cited prior art by amending the claim to retreat from the invention boundaries previously intended to be staked out.
4. Avoid the cited prior art by amending the claim to better define the intended invention boundaries.
5. "Swear behind" the cited prior art reference(s). (This option is relevant only until the revised version of 35 U.S.C. 102 comes into effect on March 16, 2013.)
6. Cancel the claim.

The flow diagram of Figure 20–1 shows how the options are chosen based on the answers to the four questions. The flow diagram also shows that the option to cancel a claim (box 10) can be pursued independent of the answers to any of the four questions—that is, irrespective of the merits of the rejection. For example, a claim may be deemed expendable because other, allowed claims afford adequate coverage for the invention. Or the client may not wish to incur the cost of fighting the rejection. Of course, a claim may also be canceled because the cited prior art renders it unpatentable. This is accounted for elsewhere in the flow diagram (boxes 16 and 18).

It is assumed in this discussion that the effective date of a reference is early enough to render it properly citable against the invention.[1] This is something to be checked, although examiners rarely make such a mistake.

Question 1: Is the Examiner's Position on Obviousness Well-Founded? (Boxes 11, 12)

The examiner rejects a claim under § 103 when his opinion is that the claim reads on obvious subject matter, that is, subject matter that would have been obvious to a person of ordinary skill in the art at the time the invention was made. This can be an allegedly obvious modification to the teachings in a single prior art reference or an allegedly obvious combination of the teachings of two or more references.

The threshold consideration when faced with a § 103 rejection is whether the examiner's position on obviousness is well-founded. It may not be. For example, the prior art may "teach away" from making the asserted modification or combination of references. Or it may arguably be the product of hindsight, given the benefits of our inventor's disclosure.

It is beyond the scope of this book to delve into the law of obviousness. The reader may wish to consult a general patent law treatise for an

---

1. *See, e.g.,* 35 U.S.C. 102 (a), (b), (e).

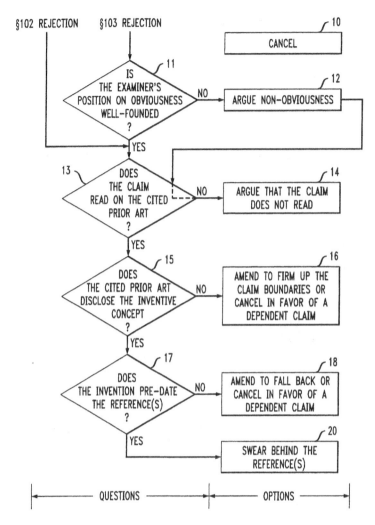

FIGURE 20–1 Decision process for rejected claims. (After March 16, 2013, box 15 "YES" arrow goes directly to box 18. See text.)

in-depth discussion of this area of the law. Suffice it to say that if there is a basis for arguing the nonobviousness of the cited modification/combination, that is the option to take. There is usually no reason to narrow a claim to avoid reading on subject matter that we can argue is nonobvious—not, at least, until after we have attempted to convince the examiner that his position on obviousness is not well-founded.

Question 2: Does the Claim Read on the Cited Prior Art? (Boxes 13, 14)

The examiner's position that the claim reads on the prior art needs to be evaluated. Claims are often rejected even though the cited prior art does not meet every claim limitation.

If the claim does not read on the cited prior art, we should argue against the rejection on that basis. An argument should be made even if we have argued against the obviousness of a modification/combination of references advanced by the examiner in a § 103 rejection. That is, we can argue that even if the cited prior art were obvious, the claim still doesn't read on it.

Try to See It the Examiner's Way

In assessing whether a claim reads on cited prior art, it is important to read the claim and the prior art from the examiner's perspective. The examiner is not required to interpret a claim term narrowly based on what is disclosed in the specification. In fact, he is duty-bound to give claim language its broadest reasonable meaning.[2]

For example, computer scientists use the term "active database" to mean a database that takes an action when a particular event happens. An active database operated by a stock brokerage firm, for example, may be programmed to send an e-mail message to client A when stock B reaches a certain price level. However, the examiner may choose to read "active database" on any database that is "up and running." It is not unreasonable to say that such a database is "active," as opposed to dormant or unresponsive.

There is an exception. If the specification explicitly defines a term, then the examiner is supposed to accord it the narrow meaning provided in the definition, for example:

> The term "active database" as used in this specification and claims means a database that takes an action when a particular event happens.

---

2. *See, e.g., In re Morris, supra,* and *In re Vogel,* 422 F.2d 438, 164 USPQ 619 (CCPA 1970). But *see In re Donaldson,* 16 F.3d 1189, 29 USPQ2d 1845 (Fed. Cir. 1994) (en banc) (specification sets a limit on how broadly the Patent and Trademark Office may construe means-plus-function language under the rubric of reasonable interpretation).

Specifications rarely include such statements, however, and for good reason. The definition may exclude something we will want the claim to cover after the patent issues.

It is usually futile, therefore, to argue for a narrower reading of a claim if the examiner's way of reading it has any merit. More importantly, if an examiner can make all of the words of the claim congruent with something irrelevant to the invention, then something fundamental to the inventive concept is probably missing. As such, the claim is susceptible to being read on a whole raft of other invention-irrelevant prior art that might not turn up until after the patent has issued. This is an opportunity for the attorney to ask himself, "How did I manage to write a claim that covers something not the invention?" and to fix the claim so that it no longer does so.

Of course, we should fight for a claim in its unamended form if a rejection is not well-founded. But it is just as important to recognize when it's time to stop, rethink, and amend rather than argue.

Don't Read Too Much into the Reference(s)

We should be wary of reading too much into a reference by bringing our knowledge of the invention to the reading. A reference may seem to be describing the inventive subject matter, but a careful reading may reveal otherwise.

The author once supervised a prosecution where the invention related to a facsimile machine that would detect that it was almost out of paper and would thereupon generate a paper order form containing the facsimile telephone number of the company's paper supplier. A user could then simply fill out the order form while still at the fax machine and fax it to the supplier, without having to look up the supplier's facsimile number or search for a blank order form.

The cited prior art was the following translated abstract of a Japanese patent:

> A facsimile machine detects an out-of-paper condition and, in response, outputs, either on a screen or on paper, ordering information including the telephone number of the paper vendor.

The attorney handling the prosecution recommended that the application be abandoned based on this abstract. But his knowledge of the invention caused him to read too much into the prior art disclosure. The full translation was ordered, and it revealed that the prior art fax machine did not output an order form but only the paper supplier's telephone number—an arguably nonobvious distinction.

Don't Rely Exclusively on the Inventor's Reading of the Reference(s)

The inventor's opinion as to what the cited prior art reference(s) teach can be invaluable. But we should not rely on the inventor's reading exclusively. Inventors tend to focus on the broad outlines of a prior art disclosure. They sometimes don't find, or appreciate the significance of, out-of-the-way statements buried in a patent specification that may anticipate the claimed subject matter. Sometimes they will assert that "it's not the same thing" because the prior art is directed to a different problem, even though the prior art's solution inherently solves the problem that the inventor sought to solve. It is therefore important that the attorney also review the reference.

Question 3: Does the Cited Prior Art Disclose the Inventive Concept? (Boxes 15, 16, 18)

Even though a rejected claim reads on the cited prior art, it may be invention-irrelevant prior art. Our next topic of inquiry, then, is "Does the cited prior art disclose the inventive concept?"

If the answer is yes, we will have to swear behind the cited prior art (if we can) if we want to pursue the claim in its present form. This option is further discussed in the next section.

Otherwise, we will have to amend the claim or, equivalently, to cancel it in favor of a dependent claim that recites the limitations we would have added by amendment. The discussion here assumes that we will amend.

The *strategy* we use in deciding how to amend a claim, however, depends on whether or not the cited prior art discloses the inventive concept.

For example, suppose the inventive concept is mounting a building or other large structure on springs to dampen earthquake vibrations and thereby protect the structure from damage or collapse. The patent application contains the following broad claim to that concept:

> 20.1 Apparatus comprising a structure, and one or more springs supporting the structure.

If the examiner finds prior art disclosing the inventive concept, claim 20.1 must be amended to retreat from the invention boundaries originally staked out. The inventor and the attorney thought that the naked notion of mounting structures prone to earthquake damage on springs was new, but that turned out not to be so. Patentability will have to be predicated on at least one fallback feature, such as a unique type of spring that the inventor may have devised for this particular use.

But even if the examiner does not find prior art disclosing the inventive concept, he would still reject claim 20.1 because it reads not only on earthquake-protected buildings but also on pogo sticks, bathroom scales, vibration-damped machinery, and all kinds of other spring-mounted "structures" known in the prior art. Here, however, there is no need to retreat to a narrower view of the invention—to fall back—by adding limitations related to embodiment details. Rather, the claim should be amended to more precisely define what was always intended by the term "structure"—buildings and other structures prone to earthquake damage—thereby preserving coverage for the inventive concept at its full breadth while excluding "invention-irrelevant" prior art like pogo sticks and bathroom scales.

There is a process for determining just what limitations should be added to a claim in either situation. It involves the same problem-solution paradigm that we used in drafting the claim in the first instance. We will see in Chapter Twenty-One how our claim describing a spring-mounted building is to be amended in accordance with those principles, depending on what kind of prior art shows up.

Question 4: Does the Invention Predate the Reference(s)? (Boxes 17, 20)

N.B. This question is relevant only until the revised version of 35 U.S.C. 102 comes into effect on March 16, 2013, at which time applicants will no longer be able to "swear behind" a reference.

Pursuant to PTO Rule of Practice 131,[3] a reference is not citable against an invention if the invention predates the reference. "Predates the reference" means that prior to the effective date of the reference, the inventor (a) conceived the claimed subject matter, and (b) either reduced the invention to practice or was diligent toward that end. Procedurally, the inventor's dates of conception and reduction to practice are presented in a so-called Rule 131 affidavit or declaration. The process is referred to as "swearing behind" the reference. This procedure is not available, however, if the rejection is based on a statutory bar under 35 U.S.C. 102(b).

The best practice is to use this option only as a last resort, when no option other than narrowing or canceling the claim is available. As shown in Figure 20–1, then, all of the following should apply before we consider swearing behind a reference:

---

3. *Id.*

(a) We have no argument to make for nonobviousness; *and*

(b) The claim reads on the cited prior art; *and*

(c) The cited prior art is invention-relevant.

Stated in the negative, it is the best practice *not* to swear behind a reference if the cited prior art

(a) Is arguably nonobvious; *or*

(b) Does not anticipate the claim; *or*

(c) Is not invention-relevant.

We should thus swear behind a reference (assuming the relevant dates allow us to do so) only when a reference or an obvious modification or combination of reference(s) discloses the inventive concept.

There are several reasons for this.

Prior art similar or identical to the cited prior art—but too early to swear behind—may show up after the patent issues. By having sworn behind the cited prior art rather than arguing against it, we will have passed up an opportunity to establish on the record that the examiner changed his mind and agreed with us that the cited prior art was not obvious or that the claims did not read on it. This can only help strengthen the presumption of validity[4] vis-à-vis similar but too-early-to-swear-behind prior art that may show up downstream.

One might think to take a belt-and-suspenders approach, both arguing against rejection on the merits and swearing behind the prior art. But then it will not be clear on the record that the examiner accepted our substantive arguments, as opposed to having simply accepted the Rule 131 affidavit. Indeed, the Opposing Team will argue to the court that the latter was the case. If our arguments on the merits are ultimately unsuccessful, we can consider filing a Rule 131 affidavit at *that* time.

Moreover, a claim reading on invention-irrelevant prior art—that is, prior art that does not disclose the inventive concept—has probably missed the essence of the invention. Such a claim is always in danger of reading on other prior art that is also invention-irrelevant but is too early to swear behind. Thus by simply swearing behind the cited invention-irrelevant prior art, we pass up the opportunity to improve the claim and, hopefully, get around invention-irrelevant prior art that may turn

---

4. *See, e.g., Central Soya Co. v. Geo. A. Hormel & Co.,* 723 F.2d 1573, 220 USPQ 490 (Fed. Cir. 1983); *Hewlett-Packard Co. v. Bausch & Lomb, Inc.,* 909 F.2d 1464, 15 USPQ2d 1525 (Fed. Cir. 1990).

up only after the patent has issued, when there is little or nothing that can be done about it.

Assuming that we've decided to amend a claim per boxes 16 and 18 of Figure 20–1, we need to decide *how* to amend it. That second part of the story is addressed in the next chapter.

CHAPTER REVIEW—Claim Rejections—Amend or Argue?

Confirm Your Understanding

1. What are the questions to ask oneself when deciding how to respond to the rejection of a claim under 35 U.S.C. 102-103?

2. What are the options that can be taken based on the answers to the four questions?

3. Why do we need to specifically determine whether a rejected claim reads on the prior art, given that the examiner has already made that determination?

4. Since the patent attorney should be an advocate for the inventor and the invention, what is the point in trying to "see it the examiner's way" in assessing whether a rejected claim reads on the prior art?

5. What is the danger in relying solely on the inventor's reading of the prior art in assessing whether it anticipates a claim?

6. A claim that reads on prior art is too broad, whether or not the prior art is invention-relevant (discloses the inventive concept) or is invention-irrelevant (does not disclose the inventive concept). Why, then, is it important to assess whether or not the cited art discloses the inventive concept?

7. Why is it the best practice to not swear behind a reference under 37 CFR 1.132 ("Rule 132 Declaration") if (a) prior art cited in a § 103 rejection is arguably nonobvious, or (b) the cited prior art is not "invention-relevant"?

Questions for Further Thought

8. Using your answers to questions 1 and 2 above, try to reconstruct from memory the flowchart that ties them together.

9. A patentee is allowed to act as his or her own lexicographer. See, e.g., *Chef Am., Inc. v. Lamb-Weston, Inc.*, 358 F.3d 1371, 69 USPQ2d (Fed. Cir. 2004). How, then, is it that examiners are allowed to ignore the clear intended scope of a claim term when reading a claim on the prior art?

Sharpen Your Skills

10. Using the flowchart of Figure 20–1, plan out a strategy for responding to an Office action on your docket at work or a sample Office action that you might get from a colleague or course instructor.

CHAPTER TWENTY-ONE

Claim Amendments

This chapter is of a piece with the one preceding. It describes the role of the problem-solution paradigm in deciding how to amend a rejected claim, should that prove to be the desirable option, per boxes 16 and 18 of Figure 20–1 (p. 299).

Rethink the Invention; *Then* Rethink the Claim

The final form of a claim should not depend on when the prior art that shaped it comes to light. But the reality is sometimes different.

When drafting a claim initially, we may deem it "done" only to realize that it still reads on some piece of prior art we thought we were avoiding. Or a supervisor or colleague reviewing the claim may point out that it reads on prior art we weren't even aware of.

Returning to the word processor to further rework the claim, we may discover that avoiding that last piece of prior art may be no simple matter. As new limitations are added to deal with the new piece of art, others may be able to be taken out or the context may be redefined—all to make the claim as broad as possible without reading on any prior art, including that last new piece. Everything in the claim is up for grabs until the day the application is sent over to the inventor for signature.

However, once the patent application is filed, a different mind-set seems to take over and the claim and its limitations take on a sacrosanct quality. So when examiner-cited prior art makes amending the claim necessary, our tendency is to "bandage" the claim by simply engrafting some new limitation onto what's already there. This can result in the claim we would have arrived at had we known about the cited prior art ab initio. Often, however, it does not, and the resulting claim defines the invention suboptimally, conceding more than it needs to.

This is not how it should be. It's the same invention. It's the same prior art. And so the way we define the invention in view of that prior art should not depend on when the prior art comes to light.

The antidote to all of this is not simply to rethink the *claim*. We should first rethink the *invention* and only then rethink the claim.

Amending When Prior Art Does *Not* Disclose the Inventive Concept

We first consider the case of invention-irrelevant prior art, that is, prior art that does not disclose the inventive concept (Figure 20–1, box 16). A claim can always be amended to include *some* distinguishing limitation. But unless that limitation is arrived at in a principled way, it may be the *wrong* limitation. A "wrong" limitation, while overcoming the cited prior art, may give up more intellectual property than it has to. Or it may leave the claim vulnerable to other invention-irrelevant prior art that may turn up only after the patent has issued, when there is little, if anything, that can be done about it.

Let us return to the concept of spring-mounted buildings for earthquake protection presented in the previous chapter[1] and depicted in Figure 21–1(a). Assume that the examiner did not find prior art disclosing that concept. He has, however, rejected claim 20.1 (repeated here for convenience as claim 21.1) as reading on certain invention-irrelevant prior art—namely pogo sticks, bathroom scales, and spring-mounted machinery (Figure 21–1(b)).

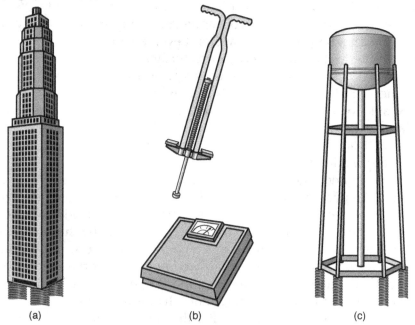

(a)   (b)   (c)

FIGURE 21–1 Spring-mounting for earthquake protection. (a) Illustrative embodiment, (b) invention-irrelevant prior art, (c) embodiment not thought of by the inventor.

---

1. *See* pp. 302–303.

21.1 Apparatus comprising a structure, and one or more springs supporting the structure.

An embodiment-based approach to amending this claim could be to observe that buildings contain floors and windows—something that pogo sticks, bathroom scales, or spring-mounted machinery do not have—and to use that as the hook for patentability:

21.2 Apparatus comprising a structure <u>of a type that has floors and windows</u>, and
      one or more springs supporting the structure.

The approach sounds plausible. But there may be other kinds of structures that the inventor hadn't taken the time to think of that have no floors or windows but yet might benefit from being spring-mounted (Figure 21–1(c)).

Nor would it be appropriate to add a fallback-feature-type limitation, such as details of a particular type of spring the inventor has devised for this use. Since the prior art does not disclose the inventive concept, there is no reason to retreat from it by invoking a fallback feature. Rather, we want to contract the scope of the claim *only* to the point of bringing the claimed invention boundaries into line with the boundaries that were always intended—boundaries that do not encompass invention-irrelevant prior art like pogo sticks and bathroom scales.

A problem-solution analysis readily yields the right claim language. The problem the invention solves is that certain kinds of structures are prone to damage or collapse from earthquake vibrations. Pogo sticks, bathroom scales, and (let us assume) machinery do not have that problem. Amending the claim to put the invention into the context in which the problem arises firms up the invention boundaries to encompass what was always intended, while avoiding the cited invention-irrelevant prior art:

21.3 Apparatus comprising a structure <u>of a type that is subject to collapse due to earthquake vibrations</u>, and one or more springs supporting the structure.

This claim talks about "collapse" rather than "damage" in order to avoid reading on relatively small objects, like the pogo stick, that might somehow get "damaged" in an earthquake but are not subject to full-scale "collapse." A large structure, like a building, may be no more than damaged in a small earthquake. It is nonetheless a structure of a type that is

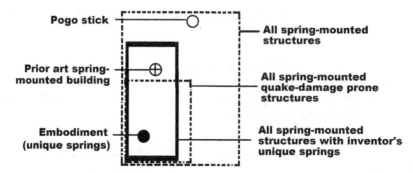

FIGURE 21–2 The strategy for amending a claim depends on whether the prior art discloses the inventive concept.

subject to collapse and so the word "collapse" captures the structures we are interested in without reading on such invention-irrelevant prior art as pogo sticks.

Figure 21–2 shows graphically how claim 21.3 redefines the invention boundaries to avoid the pogo stick (and similar) prior art.

The same claim results from a more formal approach based on this problem-solution statement:

> *The problem of* how to prevent a structure from collapse due to earthquake vibrations *is solved by* supporting the structure on one or more springs.

There may be other ways of amending claim 21.1 to define structures prone to damage or collapse from earthquakes. For example, amending the claim to replace "structure" with "building" might suffice, at least if the specification were to have explicitly defined "building" to include other earthquake-prone structures like freestanding towers.

Definition claims[2] already in the application may well contain the limitations needed to fix a claim rejected on invention-irrelevant prior art. So our earthquake-damage-protection patent application may already have included a definition claim such as the following:

> 21.4   The apparatus of claim 21.1 wherein said structure is of a type subject to collapse due to earthquake vibrations.

---

2. *See* Chapter Ten.

Indeed, one of the main functions of definition claims is to anticipate the possibility that invention-irrelevant prior art may show up during prosecution or after the patent has issued.

Otherwise, as in the example above, we will have to rethink the problem-solution with the newly cited prior art in mind and come up with a fix that firms up the invention boundaries without retreating from what the invention boundaries were always intended to be.

Amending When Cited Prior Art *Does* Disclose the Inventive Concept

If the cited prior art *does* disclose the inventive concept, clarifying the intended invention boundaries isn't an option; the intended boundaries actually encompass the prior art.

We need to fall back, retreating from the boundaries previously envisioned for the invention (Figure 20–1, box 18).

This is the very scenario for which we developed our Planned Retreat for the invention.[3] Thus the current claim suite and the Planned Retreat that it implements can be looked to to supply limitation(s) to overcome the cited prior art. It will be worthwhile, however, to rethink our plan of retreat since in prosecution we still have the opportunity to do so. New insights or changes in the commercial picture may change what we think is the most important fallback feature(s). Indeed, something that may not have been seen as being a meaningful fallback feature when the patent application was first filed may now emerge as being so.

Figure 21–2 depicts the retreat to a fallback position based on the unique building-support springs devised by the inventor.

Dropping Limitations No Longer Needed

Amending claims must be done thoughtfully. A limitation added to a claim to differentiate the invention from the newly cited prior art may distinguish the invention from *all* the prior art, including prior art that shaped the claim originally. As a result, limitations previously thought to be crucial to patentability may now serve only to limit the invention definition unduly. Claiming the invention at its full breadth may thus mean dropping certain limitations at the same time we are adding new ones, as a problem-solution analysis will quickly reveal.

Assume as our example that our client was the inventor of laser-read bar codes (Figure 21–3(a)). The closest prior art we knew about at the time of filing was the use of magnetic ink to print account numbers and

---

3. *See* Chapter Six.

FIGURE 21–3 Identifying an object by machine-reading reflected light (a) Illustrative embodiment, (b) prior art known prior to filing, (c) prior art cited during prosecution.

other information on bank checks (Figure 21–3(b)). This approach is perfectly serviceable for the bank check context because the check layout is uniform, prescribed, and the checks are read in a controlled environment ensuring that the magnetically encoded information is perfectly aligned, and in direct physical contact, with the magnetic read head.

On the other hand, the requirements of coded-object uniformity and controlled physical contact between the object and the code-detection apparatus are major problems in a point-of-sale application. Indeed, any one of these problems is a show-stopper for the use of magnetic ink labels for point-of-sale checkout. Our inventor's solution—using laser or other light reflected from a bar code—overcomes all of those problems. Indeed, the broadest claim in the patent application as filed recited reflected light as the hook for patentability:

21.5 A method comprising identifying an object by machine-reading light reflected from an identifying code on the object.

Assume, however, the examiner finds prior art in which coded patterns are affixed to freight cars and are machine-read by a tracksidemounted photocell that reads light reflected from the coded patterns as the freight cars pass by (Figure 21–3(c)). That prior art renders claim 21.5 too broad, and we need to amend.

Rethinking the solution, we realize that we could limit the claim to laser light. We reject that approach, however, because it is probably obvious to use a laser in the prior art freight car system. Rethinking the *problem*, however, opens the door to a fix that still retains a great deal of commercially valuable subject matter. Redefining the problem as being how to achieve quick and accurate checkout of a retail product leads us to a limitation that retains the solution at its full breadth but puts that solution into the narrower retail context.

> 21.5 (Amended) A method comprising identifying ~~an object~~ a retail product by machine-reading light reflected from an identifying code on the ~~object~~ retail product.
>
> 21.6 A method comprising identifying a retail product by machine-reading light reflected from an identifying code on the retail product.

A freight car is not a retail product. And we will argue that the freight car prior art would not have rendered it obvious to place machine-readable codes on retail products.

Claim 21.6 is not optimal, however. The reflected-light limitation was a good hook for patentability when the only known prior art was magnetic ink encoding. But once the freight car prior art surfaced, the reflected-light limitation does nothing for the claim except to narrow it unduly, and so it needs to be dropped. Indeed, it appears that the day will come when bar codes on groceries and other consumer goods will be replaced by radio-interrogatable printed electronics[4]—an embodiment that would not be captured by claim 21.6. The same retail-product limitation that distinguishes the invention from the freight car prior art also distinguishes the invention from the bank check prior art, rendering the reflected-light limitation no longer needed.

The better way to amend claim 21.5, then, would have been to remove the reflected-light limitation at the same time that the retail-product limitation was added:

> 21.5 (Amended) A method comprising identifying ~~an object~~ a retail product by machine-reading ~~light reflected from~~ an identifying code on the ~~object~~ retail product.

---

4. Lisa Grossman, "New RFID Tag Could Mean the End of Bar Codes," www.wired .com/wiredscience/2010/03/rfid/.

21.7 A method comprising identifying a retail product by machine-reading an identifying code on the retail product.

A problem-solution analysis undertaken with the freight car prior art in mind will, in fact, readily yield the broader claim 21.7. It is true that having decided to use the retail product angle as the hook for patentability, we might have arrived at a problem-solution statement that initially *included* the reflected light limitation:

> The problem of being able to automatically identify a retail product is solved by machine-reading light reflected from an identifying code on the retail product.

However, upon trying this problem-solution statement on for size—questioning the necessity of each limitation—we would have seen that the reflected-light limitation could be eliminated while still not reading on the prior art:

> The problem of being able to automatically identify a retail product is solved by machine-reading ~~light reflected from~~ an identifying code on the retail product.

This problem-solution statement yields claim 21.7 straightaway.

The formalism of drafting a new problem-solution statement may not be needed in a simple case. The key is to evaluate each limitation in the claim to be sure that it is still necessary once a new limitation is added. In a more complicated case, however, redrafting the problem-solution statement in light of all the prior art can help us pinpoint limitations that are no longer needed. The new problem-solution statement may occasionally yield a claim that is so different from the one rejected that it may prove cleaner to completely cancel the pending claim in favor of the new one.

One caveat is in order: There is some risk in removing an existing claim limitation, particularly if another attorney wrote the claim. That attorney may have had some particular prior art in mind that requires the limitation's continuing presence in the claim. Even though such prior art should have been cited to the examiner and should be found within the file, the next attorney picking up the case may not appreciate its applicability to the claim. And if the prior art was invention-irrelevant, it might not have been cited at all if it was far afield.

On the other hand, we *do* want to claim the invention at what appears to be its broadest allowable scope. The conservative approach is to do both: narrow the existing claim without eliminating any existing limitations (as in claim 21.6) but also present a new claim based on the new problem-solution analysis (as in claim 21.7).

A patent attorney can usually prepare a patent application with relatively little inventor involvement. However, there are many benefits to working with the inventor to the greatest extent possible, both in identifying the invention and preparing the patent application.

That aspect of the practice is discussed next.

CHAPTER REVIEW—Claim Amendments

Confirm Your Understanding

1. Assume we have concluded that a claim rejection based on prior art is proper. Why is it important to then rethink the invention before rethinking the claim? Why not simply retreat to one of the narrower claims already in the application?

2. Why does the way in which we amend a claim depend on whether the cited prior art is invention-relevant or invention-irrelevant?

3. When adding limitations to a claim in response to a prior art rejection, why might it be desirable to eliminate one or more other limitations?

Questions for Further Thought

4. An Office action may indicate that a particular dependent claim would be allowable "if rewritten in independent form to incorporate the limitations of the base claim and any intervening dependent claims." Upon rewriting the allowable claim in independent form, why might it be desirable to eliminate certain limitations in the base claim and/or intervening dependent claims? (One would, of course, point out to the examiner that that's what has been done.)

5. The bar-coding example presented in the book narrows claim 21.5 (p. 312) into the patentable realm by stating that the bar-coded item is a "retail product." What potential problem(s) do you see with the resulting claim 21.6? How would you address that problem? How could following the specification-oriented prescription *Be Detailed Where the Invention Lives* (p. 290) prove to be a life-saver in this situation?

6. The book suggests that a proper analysis of the bar-coding invention could result in a claim that would cover radio-interrogatable printed electronics (p. 313). What are some arguments for and against a court allowing such a claim to be enforced against the printed electronics embodiment?

Sharpen Your Skills

7. For each of the following examples, rethink the originally claimed invention in view of prior art cited in the first Office action. How would you amend the claim to avoid reading on the cited art? (For purposes of this exercise, do not consider other prior art that may come to mind, nor any questions of obviousness.)

a. Scale

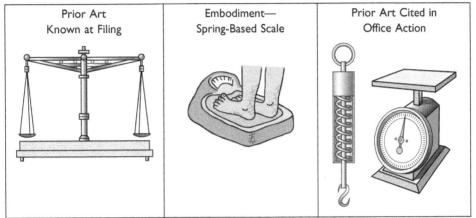

1. (Original) A scale comprising

a spring,

a platform adapted to be displaced against a restoration force of the spring in response to the placing of an object to be weighed on the platform, and

an indicator that indicates the weight of the object as a function of the amount of displacement of the platform

b. Cabinet with "Disappearing" Door

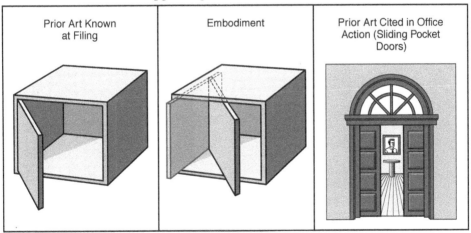

1. (Original) A door for an enclosure having an opening, the door having a first position in which the door extends across at least a portion of the opening and the door being slidable to a second position in which the opening is fully uncovered.

CHAPTER TWENTY-TWO

Working with the Inventor

The inventor is the patent attorney's single most valuable invention-analysis resource. This chapter presents a methodology called "self-directed learning" that helps us make the best possible use of that resource in learning about the invention and formulating the problem-solution statement.

The inventor's participation in the process of preparing the patent application itself can also be invaluable. A four-stage collaborative process for working with the inventor to prepare the application is presented.

The Limitations of Classroom-Style Learning

Unless guided by some other modus operandi, a patent attorney and his inventor will typically gravitate to the classroom-style model of information delivery we all grew up with. The inventor (teacher) determines what information will be presented, in what order, and at what level of detail. Yellow pad and pen at the ready, the attorney (student) dutifully takes down the information the inventor has determined he needs to know, in the order the inventor has decided to present it, and at the level of detail the inventor thinks will be useful.

This may all seem appropriate. The inventor has come up with something new, and the attorney needs to learn about it. How better to do that than to enlist the inventor as technology teacher? The attorney is an empty vessel waiting to be filled and the lecture begins.

The classroom model is not, however, the best learning paradigm for patent work. The attorney has specific tasks to accomplish, the most central of these early on being to identify the problem the inventor set out to solve and how she solved it. The attorney must also gather details about the embodiments. But this is a task for later, and even then only at a level sufficient to satisfy the requirements of "enablement" and "best mode."[1]

Unless the inventor has worked on prior patent applications or comes to the problem-solution paradigm intuitively, she has none of this in mind. For example, the inventor may not offer any information

---

1. 35 U.S.C. 112(a).

about the problem or the broad solution unless prompted to do so. More-over, details may be presented by the inventor at too early a stage for the attorney to appreciate their significance or to see how they fit into the overall picture. Invariably this means the inventor will be asked to repeat those details later. This is not necessarily a concern if the invention is simple and the "detail load" is small. However, many high-tech inventions involve a great deal of complex information. While some inventors are quite patient, others become *im*patient with having to re-explain large chunks of information. Repetition wastes the attorney's time as well.

In short, an attorney making the open-ended request, "Tell me about your invention," and then settling in to a classroom-style learning session runs the risk of receiving the wrong type of information, or receiving too much information, or receiving it in a less than optimum order.

Self-Directed Learning

Many attorneys eventually come around to the more efficient inventor-interview strategy that the author calls "self-directed learning." Here, the patent attorney *teaches himself* what he needs to learn, using the inventor as a resource. The attorney takes charge of the conversation rather than being the passive, classroom-style recipient of whatever the inventor thinks to tell him. The attorney controls the quantity of technological information delivered by the inventor, as well as the order and speed of its delivery. Information is thereby received from the inventor at a level of detail, in an order, and at a pace that most efficiently provides the attorney with what he needs to know.

Self-directed learning is analogous to a well-managed courtroom examination. An effective trial attorney stays in control of the witness, asking pointed questions that elicit answers in small bites. He does not let a confusing answer pass by but, rather, follows up with questions aimed at securing a clearer answer.

Another analogy is that of an expedition in a search for the inventive concept. In this paradigm, the inventor and attorney alternate between being the guide and the guided. The inventor is the guide as to the technological landscape, supplying technological information about what she has invented and the prior art that she knows. The attorney is the guide as to the process by which the inventor/attorney team can bring that information to the attorney's understanding and thereafter analyze it to draw out the inventive concept.

The attorney should take the lead at the outset, giving the broad outline of what needs to be accomplished. He must then cede his role as expedition leader to the inventor, so that the technological facts can begin to unfold. But the attorney should be ready to jump in and redirect the course of the discussion if it begins to veer off course. This back-and-forth interaction actually repeats itself in three main phases coinciding with the general outline of a patent. The first is the Background phase, in which the inventor is encouraged to talk about the problem she set out to solve. Then the overview or Summary of the Invention phase where the inventive concept and the fallback features are discussed. The third, Detailed Description, phase focuses on teaching the public how to practice the invention. At the outset of each of these phases, the attorney is the teacher and the inventor is the student. However, in order to complete the mosaic, the roles are reversed.

Begin from a Known Starting Place

Every patent attorney has had formal technical training or experience. He therefore comes to any invention discussion with at least some technological foundation. The breadth and depth of that foundation will, of course, vary. An attorney experienced in patenting analgesics brings to the analysis of a new analgesic compound a richer fund of knowledge than does an attorney whose pharmaceutical experience has been in vaccines. The latter, in turn, is better prepared to discuss analgesics than is an attorney with no pharmaceutical experience whatever.

No matter what the attorney's level of expertise, however, the process to be used in proceeding from problem to solution, and in gathering the details needed to prepare the written disclosure, is essentially the same. It is a process that enables the attorney to establish and maintain control over the flow of information no matter how much or how little he initially knows about the technology in question.

The process is grounded in the prescription *Begin from a Known Starting Place.* The "known starting place" is the body of knowledge relevant to the invention that the attorney brings to his initial meeting with the inventor. The key is to impart to the inventor at the outset an understanding of what the attorney knows about the subject matter at hand. It may be a lot or a little, but what matters is that a well-defined jumping-off point for the discussion is established.

For example, an initial meeting with an engineer who has made an improvement in elevator counterweighting might start out as follows:

> *"Ben, I can see from your invention disclosure write-up that you have an improved counterweighting system for elevators. Compared to people like you, I am in kindergarten. Let me tell you what I do know and we can proceed from there."*

Picking up his pencil at this point, the attorney continues, while sketching the drawing of Figure 22–1:

> *"I know that the cab rides up and down on rails, and there's a cable that goes over and around a motor-driven pulley system and then down the side of the elevator shaft. There's a counterweight at the end of the cable, and it weighs about the same as the cab, so the motor-and-pulley combination needs to have only enough power and mechanical advantage to deal with the difference in weight between the cab and the counterweight and to counteract inertia, to start it and stop it. There are enough cables to provide a large margin of safety.*
>
> *Let's start from there, beginning with the problem you set out to solve. What else should I know in order to understand the problem?"*

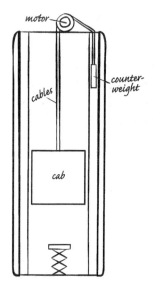

FIGURE 22–1 Patent attorney's view of how elevators work.

This attorney doesn't know much about elevators or their counterweights. But it is better for the inventor to know at the outset just what it is that the attorney does and doesn't know.

On the other hand, the attorney may know the technology intimately, so that his known starting place is at a more advanced level. The initial discussion can then be more narrowly focused on the specifics of the problem and solution.

Beginning from a known starting place is a powerful way of jump-starting the learning process. The attorney's initial exposition of what he knows about the technology establishes his role as discussion leader. It also acclimates the inventor to the attorney's level of familiarity with the technology and establishes common terminology. The inventor can tailor his information to the attorney's level of understanding. And since the inventor will supply information based on what the attorney has already laid out, each increment of information can be placed in the attorney's mind within a well-understood framework.

Proceed Slowly and Carefully

Think about how a tree increases its girth over time by adding successive layers of wood to the existing trunk. Or how an oyster, beginning with a grain of sand, continuously deposits tiny amounts of calcium carbonate around the grain of sand to create a pearl. These natural-world processes build slowly on an initial core, consolidating the new material with the old without leaving significant holes or gaps in the new structure.

The same is true of an attorney expanding his core of knowledge about an invention. He needs to begin from what he knows and then proceed slowly and carefully—eliciting information in small steps and consolidating the new information with the old.

The order in which the information is elicited from the inventor is also important to efficiently gain an understanding of the invention story—first, enough prior art to understand the problem, then the problem itself, then the broad solution, then the implementational features. Early on, we want to hear about the problem and the prior art. The inventor should be gently guided to hold off talking about the solution until everything useful to know about the problem has been set out. The inventor should likewise be guided to hold off talking about implementational features until it seems that the broad inventive concept is well in hand.

Don't Let Any Necessary Detail Get By

Proceeding slowly and carefully involves controlling the pace of information delivery and gently restraining the inventor from moving forward until the attorney is satisfied that either he has understood everything or that any details not understood do not *have* to be understood—at least not just yet.

This aspect of the process is embodied in the prescription *Don't Let Any Necessary Detail Get By*.

The danger in letting a necessary detail get by is that the attorney risks losing control of the information flow, jeopardizing his position as the discussion leader. Certain details are sometimes crucial to understanding what's coming next. The author recalls early in his practice allowing details to get by, with the thought that "I'll figure that out by myself later." But once a few details are allowed to get by, the solid core of understanding being built up can get spongy at the edges. Gaps open up. Confusions build on one another. It gets harder to ask meaningful questions. The attorney's role as discussion leader quickly gives way to that of discussion follower. The self-directed learning process self-destructs, and the interaction lapses into classroom mode.

Recovery is always possible, but we must be proactive. Having realized that a necessary detail has gotten by, the attorney must bring the inventor back to a place where everything was clear so that the discussion can set out again from there.

*"Joanna, I got lost about two minutes ago when you started talk-
ing about the protein folding. I understood what you said about the
protein itself, but tell me again about the folding."*

The sooner we circle back and recover, the better. The small amount
of backtracking needed to return to solid ground and repair whatever
holes in our understanding have developed will not disrupt the discussion. The inventor, rather than being annoyed, will appreciate requests
for clarification because they show that the listener is being attentive and
is genuinely interested in what the inventor is trying to explain.

There is no point in letting the inventor continue on in the hope
that things will become clear later. Invariably, they become increasingly
*un*clear. Sometimes it *can* all be figured out later, but usually only after
expending a great deal more time than if we had simply stopped the
inventor and asked a few pointed questions. And many times we cannot
figure it out at all, requiring a follow-up session or extended phone call
that might not otherwise have been necessary.

Depending on the context, a detail may or may not be "necessary." Is
it important to know that a screw holding two parts together is copper
rather than steel? Probably not, if all that matters is the screw's function
as a fastener. But this detail could be important if proper functioning of
the overall device requires that it be completely nonmagnetic.

A detail may be important to know, but not at present. Certain
details may be required for the specification to meet the requirements of
"enablement" or "best mode" but can get in the way at an early stage of
the discussion, when the focus is on the problem and the broad solution.
Letting such details get by early on is a good thing. They can be revisited
later, when they *are* necessary.

One develops a facility for making on-the-fly judgments as to whether
particular details can be safely allowed to get by. But if it is not immediately apparent whether a detail needs to be understood at a point in
time, we need to interrupt the inventor and find out:

*"I didn't understand what you just said about how the counter-
weight is held together. But maybe I don't need to. We're still talking
about the problem you set out to have the invention solve. Am I going
to have to understand how the counterweight pieces are held together
to understand the problem?"*

Finally, a few other techniques that help ensure that necessary details
do not get by:

- Question the meaning of jargon used by the inventor. The inventor
  will not think you stupid or ill informed. Inventors do not actu-

ally expect people outside their field to know their jargon. It is just that they've been using it so long that to *them* it seems like regular English; just as patent attorneys routinely use terms like "prior art" and "Office action" as though these are common phrases that everyone would know.

- Interrupt the flow of technical facts to comment on or redirect the communication, as needed. The attorney needs to be both the guide and the guided. Don't be afraid to alternate between those two roles.
- Don't be afraid to talk about process. Most of the inventor-attorney dialogue will be about the invention per se. But one can also communicate about the communication process itself. It is always appropriate to say things like:

"I don't understand."

"Let's go back."

"This is going too fast for me to take in."

"Is this relevant to the problem that the invention solves?"

"Let me feed back to you what I think you just said."

"I thought I knew what a hidden Markov model is, but now I'm not sure."

"This is too much detail for me right now."

"I think I just had an insight."

- Be sensitive to twinges of uneasiness that arise upon realizing that necessary details have gotten by. Those little feelings warn that something is wrong. Stop the process and circle back.
- Periodically confirm that your understandings are correct. Suspend the inventor's delivery of new information every so often in order to summarize what you think you've been told, so that the inventor can correct any errors. Restate things in a way that makes sense to *you*. If analogies come to mind, share them. A creative repackaging of the inventor's disclosure rewards her efforts as technological tutor. It can also generate insights that help the attorney-inventor team come to a more complete appreciation of the inventive concept.

Engage Your Technological Curiosity

The active attorney involvement that lies at the heart of the self-directed learning approach should be driven by an engaged curiosity about the invention. If the inventor says something that seems technologically improbable, the attorney needs to ask, "Why *is* that?" Something that seems wrong may actually be something remarkable that lies at the heart of the invention. On the other hand, the inventor may simply have said something incorrect. Or the attorney may have misunderstood what he was told.

An engaged curiosity about the invention not only supports the learning process, but can also lead to insights about the invention and its true breadth. Questions from the attorney may stimulate the inventor to rethink certain assumptions about what she had thought was absolutely required for the invention.

An engaged curiosity about the invention also helps establish rapport with the inventor and often bolsters her interest in the patent application process. This may be crucial to getting the patent work completed if other matters vie for the inventor's time.

On the other hand, the attorney has to know when to stop satisfying his curiosity and move on. At some point he will have heard enough details to recognize that any *further* details are clearly too far "down in the noise" to aid in an understanding of the invention or coming to any insights about it. That is the point at which the discussion needs to be redirected to other topics.

Just when that point has been reached may not be apparent until at least some unnecessary details have already been laid out. With experience, the attorney develops a sense of when he's probably heard enough. This is a matter to be checked out with the inventor:

> *"It sounds like we're now just talking about routine implementational details that don't impact on what's really novel here. Am I right, or is it possible that further discussion on this point will help us to further understand the invention?"*

Figuring out when we've learned enough is analogous to following a vein in a gold mine. The miner keeps digging in a particular direction as long as the rocks being dug out contain meaningful amounts of gold ore. It is difficult to know whether the vein has really run out until the miner has dug at least a little past it. But once it becomes clear that the vein has run out, it is time to begin digging elsewhere.

Rely on the Inventor from the Outset

New practitioners sometimes avoid relying on the inventor for background information about the technology in question. We certainly would like to present ourselves as technologically sophisticated, ready from the outset to absorb the specifics of the inventor's narrative. When there is a helpful write-up or treatise with information that can give the attorney a leg up—a chapter in a textbook, or perhaps a previously written patent or patent application—we can certainly consult it.

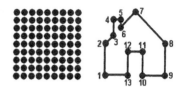

FIGURE 22–2 Trying to learn relevant background without the inventor's guidance is like trying to complete a connect-the-dots picture in which most of the dots are irrelevant and there are no numbers.

Usually, however, securing a suitable technological background from sources other than the inventor is difficult. Professional journal articles are usually too advanced to be of much help. The well-written textbook chapter or patent that can convey to the technological nonspecialist "everything you always wanted to know about . . ." seldom exists.

The attorney must therefore rely on the inventor from the outset.

In the law firm setting, this is rarely even an issue. The pressures of pushing the work through preclude spending hours on preliminary research. In corporate patent departments, however, the emphasis on "numbers" is often not as great, particularly for "new-timers" getting their feet wet. It is usually possible, then, to search the Internet or take oneself down to the company's corporate library and dig in.

It is still not a good idea, however.

Imagine being given a connect-the-dots picture in which most of the dots are not actually part of the picture, and the little numbers aren't there either. Which dots are actually needed for the picture? How are they supposed to be interconnected? Obviously, it's an impossible task.

Similarly, the attorney trying to get up to speed in a particular technology without the inventor's guidance doesn't know which aspects of the prior art—the dots—are actually part of the picture, nor can he know how those that *are* important interrelate in the context of the problem the inventor set out to solve. Every area of technology is replete with countless facts and concepts, most of which will turn out to have nothing to do with the invention at hand. No doubt it is possible to study written sources and ultimately acquire the necessary technological background; but the process will be inefficient because it cannot be sharply focused and will sweep in a substantial amount of extraneous matter along the way.

By contrast, using the inventor as one's resource via the discipline of self-directed learning avoids waste. The inventor points out the relevant dots and explains how they interrelate in the context of the invention. Inventors—particularly first-time patent applicants—are usually pleased to have someone else pay close attention to their work, and they are willing to put in the time to bring the attorney on board with the technology. Certainly, if the inventor is the one who will own the resulting patent, she has the incentive to help. Moreover, an attorney's skillful active engagement with the inventor usually serves as a satisfying substitute for an attorney's lack of specific technological background. It is satisfying because, in return for her time investment, the inventor gets to see her invention framed from a patent attorney's perspective. Inventors are often astounded when presented with the broad inventive concept that the attorney has teased out of the embodiment(s). The more mature an attorney's skills, the more the inventor relishes the opportunity of working with him in all aspects of the patenting process. Indeed, inventors often report having gained valuable insights about their inventions as the result of discussions with their patent attorneys.

However, if the inventor balks at spending the time needed for the attorney to come up to speed in the technology, someone else should be sought. A surrogate for the inventor can sometimes be assigned, such as a coinventor or knowledgeable engineer elsewhere in the inventor's company. Sometimes a different patent attorney with more specific knowledge of the technology in question is available.

The library and the Internet should be the last resort.

It Can Be Hard to Get Started—But You Have To

Beginning practitioners may find it hard to get started with the self-directed learning approach, but it has to be done.

It is not uncommon to have a sense of inadequacy in the face of the inventor's depth of technical knowledge. We are loath to be seen as less than fully competent or as wasting other people's time.

One of the more comfortable places to retreat in the face of such doubts is the technical library—there to postpone making contact with the inventor until we have taught ourselves the basic technology. As we saw earlier, that is not a way to go. The other place of refuge is the familiar and comfortable learning paradigm of our youth—the classroom model and role of the student as empty vessel. Indeed, as long as we sit there taking notes, nodding, and hoping to sort it all out later, we *can* fake it—but only for so long.

Getting it all straight may require any number of follow-up phone calls with the inventor—or another entire face-to-face interview session. Or if we just plow ahead based on whatever we *think* is correct, the draft patent application may have significant mistakes. In either case, our fears of being seen as less than fully competent may ultimately be realized, but magnified many times over.

That's for starters. Inventors encountering significant errors in a patent application often just put it aside, not having the mental energy, the interest, or the time to fix it up. The draft may sit on the inventor's desk for weeks or months, even in the face of attorney follow-ups and reminders. Or what is just as bad—and happens all too often—the inventor may just give up and approve the draft as is, mistakes and all.

The self-directed learning approach can help us avoid all of that. Actively enlisting the inventor's help—not as lecturing teacher, but as a resource that we use to teach *ourselves* about the invention—pays off handsomely for all concerned.

Involve the Inventor in Preparing the Application

For many practitioners, one face-to-face meeting with the inventor is all that the parameters of their practice allow. However, inventor involvement in preparing a patent application can extend over a wide range— from virtually no involvement all the way up to joining the attorney at the keyboard and the two of them writing the entire application together, even the claims. Many factors determine the degree of inventor involvement: the extent to which the attorney is interested in and capable of involving the inventor in the writing process, the inventor's interest and aptitude in doing so, other demands on the inventor's time, and how close their offices are to one another.

All this having been said, the greater the inventor involvement in preparing the application, the better the application. It will certainly be more efficient for the attorney, and often for the inventor as well.

Having blocks of time set aside to work with the inventor allows the attorney to work in a more concentrated fashion than if working alone, subject to interruptions from phone calls and e-mail. The application's logical structure and terminology stay fresh in the attorney's mind. As a result, because the attorney knows where he is in the process and knows the terminology, the writing process requires fewer total hours than when the application is worked on for shorter periods of time that may stretch out over weeks or months.

The inventor's participation in the writing process avoids what would otherwise be stopping points where the attorney would have to pause to figure out things that are unclear or to suspend the process while awaiting a callback from the inventor to answer questions. This way, the inventor is right there to answer any questions and the writing moves forward smoothly. Fewer hours will be spent on the application, and the terminology will be more consistent, because everything stays fresh in the writer's mind.

Inventor involvement also pays dividends when it is time for her to review the final draft. Even if the inventor is prompt in beginning the review of an application that the attorney wrote on his own, she may quickly put the application aside if she becomes confused about what she's being asked to review. If there are significant mistakes that she can't readily fix, especially if she is expected to do the revision, she may just put it aside. Even worse, she may pass over errors without correcting them, thinking that "well, that's just the legalese." All of these concerns substantially go away when the inventor is there with the attorney in the first instance—any errors in the writing will have been pointed out by the inventor and corrected in real time.

A Four-Stage Collaborative Process for Preparing the Application

The following is a four-stage process favored by the author for working with the inventor to learn about the invention and prepare the patent application.

Stage I: Problem-Solution Statement/Fallback Features/Drawings

The attorney and inventor meet to discuss the invention. The attorney may already have some idea about the invention based on a technical memorandum or other written material that the inventor may have supplied in advance. In any event, the goal of this meeting is to develop a refined problem-solution statement based on discussion about the problem, how the inventor solved it, and whatever prior art the inventor is aware of.

The output, or "deliverable," of this first stage is a refined problem-solution statement and identification of the important fallback features. If there is time, this is a good opportunity to sketch out at least the high-level drawings for the patent application. Indeed, sketches made by the inventor as she gives her narrative often serve as the basis of at least some of those drawings. For this reason, the inventor should be encouraged to make her sketches on paper so that a hard copy is available at the end of the session and nothing will have gotten erased in the process. Or a digital camera might be used to capture whiteboard drawings.

If circumstances permit, it is a good idea to put off proceeding to Stage II for at least one day. Stage II is devoted to writing the Background and Summary. That effort benefits from the attorney having a little time "off-line" to let his subconscious solidify his understanding of the invention. Indeed, some of the author's best insights about an invention have arisen on the drive home and at other random moments. This is also an opportunity to develop a general sense of the first few sentences of the Background. The stage is thereby set to hit the ground running when sitting down with the inventor to compose the Background and Summary in Stage II.

Stage I may take about two to three hours, depending on the complexity of the invention and the nature of the prior art to be distinguished from.

Stage II: Background and Summary

Writing the Background and Summary is often a painstaking process, even with the problem-solution statement in hand. Sometimes it is hard to find the right "handle" to get the Background under way. It takes time to work in all the terminology that will be relied on in the Summary's one-sentence invention statement. Additional insights as to the breadth of the invention, or as to how the invention can be articulated in alternative ways, may develop as the text evolves. Revision of the problem-solution statement or developing alternative problem-solution statements may be a lengthy process.

A lot of time will be spent writing relatively few words. Every word added to the writing—particularly in the Summary—will be critically evaluated to ensure that the one-sentence statement of the broad invention is as perfect as it can be. But this is time well spent. This is when the structure of the invention story gets laid out and terminology for the application gets developed. The investment of time will pay dividends in the efficiency with which the Detailed Description will be able to be written, based on the foundation thus laid.

Expect to spend as much as three to four hours when writing the Background and Summary. This could well extend to a full day if the invention is particularly complex.

Stage III: Detailed Description

With the invention story well in hand, the Detailed Description can be written quickly and efficiently, proceeding from one figure of the drawing to the next, using the Background and Summary as a template and highlighting the invention and its fallback features as the narrative evolves.

If a technical memorandum or other detailed write-up authored by the inventor already exists, that document can be used pretty much "as is" to supply all the details required for enablement. A two-part Detailed Description often works. The first part will be a "General Description" or "Overview" mostly comprising newly written material that expands upon the invention story as told in the Background and Summary, using several high-level figures to illustrate the invention and its fallback features. The inventor's write-up can then be dropped into the Detailed Description as the second, more detailed part.

Stage III can sometimes be completed in a single day for a simple invention and a single disclosed embodiment. More complicated applications may require much more time. If the inventor's time is limited, the attorney can work alone to complete the Detailed Description.

Stage IV: Claims

Inventors who have found the time to help write the specification often welcome the opportunity to work on the claims as well. Most attorneys would prefer to work alone at this task. Yet, there are benefits when the attorney and inventor work on the claims together, and the reader is urged to try it. Infringement loopholes are more likely to be identified by the inventor if she is actively engaged in the claim-drafting process than if she reviews the claims after the fact, even with attorney guidance. The inventor is similarly more likely to perceive claim overbreadth based on prior art that she is aware of when she is fully participating in the claim-drafting process.

For a relatively simple invention, two or three claim families can be written over the course of several hours. More time will be required for complex inventions or for more extensive claim treatments.

The classic question of the new patent attorney is, "What should I write first?"

Some mentors suggest that it should be the Detailed Description. It is thought that this is a good way to get the juices flowing and for the attorney to "get a feel for" what has been invented. Others instruct that at least some of the claims be written first to ensure that the Detailed Description—in fact, the entire specification—will be drafted in a way that provides the claims with the necessary conceptual and terminological underpinning.

However, the author's answer to the new attorney's question, "What should I write first?" is this: "You shouldn't write *anything* first. Figure out what the invention is and then you can write whatever you want."

It is hoped that these pages have brought the reader to that point of view. The patent attorney's first task is to answer the question *What Is the Invention?* After that, the order in which things get written down is of little moment. The end product will be fabulous no matter what. A patent application prepared with the inventive concept fully in hand at the outset will be one that best serves the inventor, the patent owner, and, indeed, the invention itself.

CHAPTER REVIEW—Working with the Inventor

Confirm Your Understanding

1. Compare "classroom-style learning" to "self-directed learning" as presented in this chapter.
2. What does the author mean by the prescriptions
   a. Begin From a Known Starting Place
   b. Proceed Slowly and Carefully
   c. Don't Let Any Necessary Detail Get By
3. What are the benefits of following these prescriptions?

Question for Further Thought

3. The attorney-directed interview methodology described in this chapter precludes the inventor from describing the invention in her own way. However, some attorneys advise that it is desirable to do just that—letting the inventor describe her invention in whatever way she wants to and then going back to ask questions. What do you see as the advantages and disadvantages of each approach?

Sharpen Your Skills

4. If you are already working in the field, interview the inventor of the next patent application that you start on using the principles of self-directed learning presented in this chapter. It may be useful to explain those principles to the inventor before you start.
5. Alternatively, have someone play the part of an inventor coming to talk to you about patenting her invention. The "inventor" should study the disclosure of an issued patent so that she will be able to sketch a drawing, come forth with lots of details, and so on. The following U.S. patents have relatively simple disclosures and would be suitable:

4,128,616	4,153,944
4,479,115	4,534,776
5,065,309	5,091,931
5,267,304	5,440,620
6,009,138	6,373,229

Do not review the disclosure yourself ahead of time, the idea being to try to re-create a realistic inventor-attorney interaction.

APPENDIX A

Inventive Concepts and Their Problem-Solution Statements

The following is a sample of inventions for which United States patents have been granted over the past hundred years or so. Each invention is represented by a statement of its inventive concept and a problem-solution statement (both drafted by the author). A claim from the issued patent is also presented.

Ammonia Production

U.S. Patent 971,501—Fritz Haber et al.

Inventive Concept: Use osmium as the catalyst in combining nitrogen and hydrogen to make ammonia.

Problem-Solution: *The problem of* producing ammonia at a low temperature and as quickly as possible *is solved by* passing gases containing nitrogen and hydrogen over a catalyst containing osmium.

Claim: The process of producing ammonia by passing gases containing nitrogen and hydrogen over a catalyst containing osmium.

Fuel-Propelled Rocket

U.S. Patent 1,103,503—Robert H. Goddard

Inventive Concept: Keep the fuel for a rocket in a casing that is separate from the combustion chamber.

Problem-Solution: *The problem of* enabling a rocket to carry a large amount of combustible material while keeping the weight of the rocket as low as possible *is solved by* successively feeding portions of the material to the combustion chamber from a separate casing containing the supply of combustible material.

Claim: A rocket apparatus having, in combination, a combustion chamber, a casing containing a supply of combustible material, and means for successively feeding portions of said material to said combustion chamber.

Packaging Frozen Food

U.S. Patent 1,773,079—Clarence Birdseye

Inventive Concept: Package food in its container and then freeze under pressure.

Problem-Solution: *The problem of* being able to package and preserve food in an economical and commercially practical way *is solved by* first packing the food in the container in which it is to be marketed and freezing the same under pressure applied to substantial surface areas of the packed container.

Claim: A method of packaging and preserving food, which consists in first packing the food in the container in which it is to be marketed and freezing the same under pressure applied to substantial surface areas of the packed container.

Negative Feedback

U.S. Patent 2,102,671—Harold S. Black

Inventive Concept: Reduce the distortion created by an amplifier by using negative feedback.

Problem-Solution: *The problems of* distortion and inconstant gain in a wave translating device having amplifying properties that receives fundamental waves at its input and that carries fundamental components and other wave components at its output *is solved by* controlling the relative magnitudes of the fundamental and other components at the output by feeding waves from the output to the input to decrease the gain of the system.

Claim: In a wave translating device or system having amplifying properties, an input portion and an output portion, means to apply fundamental waves to said input portion, said system carrying fundamental components in said output portion and having means producing other wave components in said output portion, and means controlling the relative magnitudes of said components in said output portion comprising means to feed waves from said output portion to said input portion to decrease the gain of the system.

Magnetic Recording

U.S. Patent 2,351,004—Marvin Camras

Inventive Concept: Record signals by generating a modulated magnetic field and passing the recording medium (e.g., steel wire) through the modulated magnetic field parallel to the lines of force.

Problem-Solution: *The problem of* distortion in magnetically recording fluctuating electrical energy on a paramagnetic body *is solved by* passing the paramagnetic body through a high-frequency magnetic field produced by the joint action of a high-frequency exciting current and the fluctuating electrical energy, the direction of motion of the body through the field being parallel to the direction of the lines of force of the magnetic field.

Claim: The method of magnetically recording fluctuating electrical energy on a paramagnetic body, which includes passing the paramagnetic body through a high-frequency magnetic field produced by the joint action of a high-frequency exciting current and the fluctuating electrical energy, the direction of motion of the body through the field being parallel to the direction of the lines of force of the magnetic field.

Telephony

U.S. Patent 3,500,000—John L. Kelly Jr. et al.

Inventive Concept: Subtract echo replicas from outgoing signals in a communication system and use the resulting signal to adapt a processor that generates the replicas.

Problem-Solution: *The problem of* preventing echoes of speech signals in a first one-way transmission path of a communication system from appearing in a second one-way transmission path of the system *is solved by* algebraically combining the speech signals in the second path with speech signals supplied from an adjustable signal processor connected in the first path, and adjusting the signal processor in response to the combined signals.

Claim: An echo canceller that comprises adjustable signal processing means connected in the first of two one-way transmission paths of a communication system,

means connected in the second of said two one-way paths for algebraically combining speech signals in said second path with speech signals supplied from said processing means, and

means responsive to said algebraically combined speech signals for adjusting said signal processing means.

Superconducting Devices

U.S. Patent 3,600,644—Robert E. Eck

Inventive Concept: Use only one superconductive member rather than two in a Josephson effect circuit.

Problem-Solution: *The problem of* easily and inexpensively fabricating a low-temperature Josephson effect circuit of the type comprising a first, tapered metal member having a small area contact with a flat surface of a second metal member *is solved by* having only one of the members constructed of a material that is superconductive at cryogenic temperatures.

Claim: A low-temperature circuit exhibiting Josephson effects comprising a first metal member and a second metal member, one of said members being constructed of a material that is superconductive at cryogenic temperatures, the second member being constructed of a material that is normal or nonsuperconductive, one of said members having a flat surface and the other of said members having a tapered end positioned in contact with said flat surface to form a small area contact.

Laser Vision Correction

U.S. Patent 4,665,913—Francis A. L'Esperance Jr.

Inventive Concept: Use ultraviolet irradiation and attendant ablative photodecomposition of the cornea to reshape the anterior surface of the cornea and thereby correct sight, e.g., for myopia.

Problem-Solution: *The problem of* correcting sight *is solved by* operating solely upon the anterior surface of the cornea of the eye using selective ultraviolet irradiation and attendant ablative photodecomposition of the anterior surface of the cornea in a volumetric removal of corneal tissue and with depth penetration into the stroma and to a predetermined curvature profile.

Claim: The method of changing optical properties of an eye by operating solely upon the anterior surface of the cornea of the eye, which method comprises selective ultraviolet irradiation and attendant ablative photodecomposition of the anterior surface of the cornea in a volumetric removal of corneal tissue and with depth penetration into the stroma and to a predetermined curvature profile.

Two-Stroke Engines

U.S. Patent 5,375,573—Timothy J. Bowman

Inventive Concept: Atomize lubricating oil in a two-stroke engine using the same compressed air source that atomizes the fuel.

Problem-Solution: *The problems* associated with the use of oil jets and feed valves in a two-stroke engine to atomize lubricating oil that is to be injected into the crankcase directly upon points requiring lubrication *are solved by* atomizing the oil using compressed air taken from the pressurized air rail that produces an atomized fuel spray for injection into the individual combustion chambers.

Claim: A two-stroke engine having a pressurized air rail for producing an atomized fuel spray for injection into individual combustion chambers, in which oil for lubrication is atomized by metering said oil into a stream of compressed air taken from the rail or from a reservoir connected thereto and the resulting oil/air mist is injected into the crankcase directly upon points requiring lubrication.

Mass Spectronomy

U.S. Patent 5,376,791—Lynwood W. Swanson et al.

Inventive Concept: Increase the yield of secondary ions in a secondary ion mass spectrometry system by having iodine vapor in the chamber.

Problem-Solution: *The problem of* increasing the secondary ion yield of sample materials bombarded by an ion beam directed toward a location on a sample material *is solved by* directing iodine vapor at that location while the ion beam is incident thereon, thereby enhancing secondary ion yield.

Claim: A method of increasing the secondary ion yield of sample materials bombarded by an ion beam, said method comprising the steps of:
  directing an ion beam toward a location on a sample material, and
  directing iodine vapor at said location while said ion beam is incident thereon for enhancing secondary ion yield.

Optical Communications

U.S. Patent 5,371,815—Craig D. Poole

Inventive Concept: In a spooled-fiber dispersion compensator, align the mode pattern of the signal relative to the plane of the bend of the spooled fiber.

Problem-Solution: *The problem of* bending losses in a dual-mode fiber dispersion compensator comprising a spooled length of optical fiber *is solved by* energizing the fiber with an optical signal having a single spatial mode including one or more mode null lines that lie in the plane of the bend of the spooled fiber.

Claim: A spooled length of optical fiber; and means for energizing said fiber with an optical signal having a single spacial [*sic*] mode including one or more mode null lines that lie in the plane of the bend of said spooled fiber.

Integrated Circuit Fabrication

U.S. Patent 5,389,554—William U.C. Liu et al.

Inventive Concept: Use an AlGaAs layer as both a ballast resistor and as the active emitter for a heterojunction bipolar transistor.

Problem-Solution: *The problem of* fabricating a heterojunction bipolar transistor having ballasting resistance for its plurality of emitter fingers without encountering hot spotting, space charge conduction, and other disadvantageous phenomena *is solved by* epitaxially depositing an emitter layer of Alx Ga1-x As, where x = 0.4, adjacent a base layer, whereby the emitter layer provides ballasting resistance for each of the fingers.

Claim: A method for fabrication of heterojunction bipolar transistors having a plurality of emitter fingers, comprising the step of:

epitaxially depositing an emitter layer of Alx Ga1-x As, where x = 0.4, said emitter layer is adjacent a base layer, whereby said emitter layer provides a ballasting resistance to distribute a current approximately evenly through each of said emitter fingers.

Internet Technology

U.S. Patent 5,960,411—Peri Hartman et al.

Inventive Concept: Enable a customer to order an item from an online vendor with a single action, e.g., clicking on an icon.

Problem-Solution: *The problems of* customer inconvenience and potential security breaches inherent in the "shopping cart" model of ordering an item in a client/server environment *are solved by* displaying information identifying the item and an indication of a single action that is to be performed to order the item and in response to only the indicated single action being performed, sending to a server system a request to order the identified item.

Claim: A method for ordering an item using a client system, the method comprising:

displaying information identifying the item and displaying an indication of a single action that is to be performed to order the identified item; and

in response to only the indicated single action being performed, sending to a server system a request to order the identified item.

Manufacturing Technology

U.S. Patent 6,016,817—Hans Henig

Inventive Concept: When using a liquid or gaseous fluid to treat a circuit board having small holes, slide the board back and forth and vibrate it at the same time.

Problem-Solution: *The problem of* being able to use liquid or gaseous treatment agents to treat plate-shaped work pieces that have extremely fine holes through which the fluid would normally flow too slowly *is solved by* locating the work piece in a horizontal operational position and imparting a combined movement of (a) a first continuous and/or periodically intermittent sliding movement in a horizontally extending transport path, and (b) a second movement consisting of vigorous vibrational oscillations, both movements being simultaneous with and independent of one another during any such first movement.

Claim: Method of treating plate-shaped work pieces provided with extremely fine holes by means of liquid or gaseous treatment agents, in which to the work piece located in a horizontal operational position is imparted a combined movement, which is made up of

a first continuous and/or periodically intermittent sliding movement in a horizontally extending transport path, and

a second movement consisting of vigorous vibrational oscillations,

both movements being simultaneous with and independent of one another during any said first movement.

Photolithography

U.S. Patent 6,316,152—Hong-Chang Hsieh et al.

Inventive Concept: Generate line jog inexpensively by allowing sharp corners in the line as masked and relying on optical proximity effects to smooth out the corners when the line is actually formed.

Problem-Solution: *The problem of* being able to inexpensively generate a jog in a line within a pattern on a photolithographic reticle *is solved by* a line layout comprising two equal-width line segments laterally displaced from one another by less than their width, each line segment having pointed corners at respective ends that touch.

Claim: A line layout within a pattern on a reticle for use during photolithography, comprising:

a first line segment, having a width and a lower end having pointed corners;

a second line segment having said width and an upper end having pointed corners;

the second segment being laterally displaced, by an amount less than said width, relative to the first segment; and

said upper and lower ends touching, whereby said segments are part of a single continuous line in which there is a jog.

Medical Devices

U.S. Patent 6,444,324—Dachuan Yang et al.

Inventive Concept: Lubricate the inside of a balloon catheter.

Problem-Solution: *The problem of* being able to prevent portions of a dilatation balloon from sticking to one another while also preventing "watermelon seeding" of the balloon *is solved by* disposing a lubricious hydrophilic material on the inner surface of the balloon.

Claim: A dilatation balloon comprising an inner surface and an outer surface, said inner surface having a lubricious hydrophilic material disposed thereon.

Electric Lamps

U.S. Patent 6,525,491—Andreas Huber et al.

Inventive Concept: Switch the polarity of a discharge lamp current before a focal point can form.

Problem-Solution: *The problem of* flickering phenomena in gas discharge lamps *is solved by* operating the lamp in an AC mode such that a gas discharge is established between electrodes serving alternately as an anode and a cathode, and switching over the polarity of the lamp current before a focal point is formed on the cathode.

Claim: A method for operating at least one gas discharge lamp having electrodes, the method comprising

operating the gas discharge lamp in an AC mode wherein a gas discharge is established between the electrodes which alternate as an anode and a cathode during lamp operation, and

switching over polarity of lamp current before a focal point is formed on the cathode,

whereby flickering of the gas discharge lamp is reduced.

Recording Media

U.S. Patent 6,526,005—Johannes J. Mons

Inventive Concept: Encode the diameter of a CD within the CD data.

Problem-Solution: *The problem of* being able to take the inertia of a disclike record carrier (e.g., compact disc) into account in order to control its rotation *is solved by* including the actual physical diameter of the carrier in a machine-readable information track in which record carrier control information is provided.

Claim: A disc-like record carrier having an actual physical diameter, the carrier comprising a machine-readable information track in which record carrier control information including the actual physical diameter is provided.

Integrated Circuit Manufacture

U.S. Patent 6,569,580—Jim G. Campi

Inventive Concept: Use diamond-like carbon in the energy-blocking regions of an integrated circuit mask.

Problem-Solution: *The problem of* improving the strength, resolution, and mask error factor of a binary mask of a type comprising an energy-transparent substrate and having energy-transmitting and energy-blocking regions *is solved by* adhering diamond-like carbon (DLC) to the energy-blocking substance that is adhered to the substrate in the energy-blocking regions.

Claim: A binary mask having energy-transmitting regions and energy-blocking regions, comprising:

an energy-transparent substrate;

an energy-blocking substance adhered to the substrate in the energy-blocking regions; and,

diamond-like carbon (DLC) adhered to the energy-blocking substance.

Semiconductor Memories

U.S. Patent 6,574,148—Christophe Chevallier

Inventive Concept: Drive the bit lines of a voltage programmable memory from both ends.

Problem-Solution: *The problem of* being able to use lower-than-usual voltage levels to program an array of voltage programmable memory cells of a type having bit lines coupled to respective portions of the memory cells *is solved by* coupling driver circuits to both end regions of each of the bit lines.

Claim: A memory device comprising:

an array of voltage programmable memory cells;

a bit line coupled to a portion of the memory cells; and

first and second driver circuits respectively coupled to first and second end regions of the bit line.

Memory Drives

U.S. Patent 6,577,463—Gregory Frees

Inventive Concept: Adjust timing window for reading from a storage device based on a calculation of the tangential misalignment.

Problem-Solution: *The problem of* tangential misalignment in a direct access storage device *is solved by* pre-compensating for the misalignment by adjusting a timing window during which the transducer head reads the information located on the storage surface based on a calculation of tangential misalignment of the transducer head with respect to the information located on the storage surface.

Claim: A method of pre-compensating for tangential misalignment in a direct access storage device having information located on a storage surface and having a transducer head for reading the information, the method comprising:

generating a calculation of tangential misalignment of the transducer head with respect to the information located on the storage surface; and

adjusting, in accordance with the calculation of tangential misalignment, a timing window during which the transducer head reads the information located on the storage surface.

APPENDIX B

An Exercise for the Reader— and the Author

Here is an invention-analysis exercise involving the invention of the backspace key. The reader can use this exercise to try out the invention-analysis techniques presented in the book—begin from the problem, draft a problem-solution statement, and then hone it to a sharp edge by trying it on for size and making changes as needed to make it as broad as possible without reading on the prior art. If it is not clear whether some particular feature of the disclosed embodiment should be regarded as being in the prior art, the reader should make an assumption one way or the other and go from there.

The exercise is followed by a transcript of the author's thought processes when working the exercise himself. It is presented in the first person and the present tense to accentuate the stream-of-consciousness thought process that plays such a big role in invention analysis. Presenting the author's answer in this way will hopefully impart some feel for how the iterative process of hypothesizing a problem-solution statement and trying it on for size can actually play out.

The reader's train of thought and ultimate conclusions will be different from the author's. Seeing the invention in different ways, however, is an important facet of claim diversity.[1] Much will depend on what the reader perceives as the problem(s), if any, solved beyond the problem explicitly indicated in the exercise itself. A lot will also depend on what assumptions were made about the prior art.

Backspace Key Exercise

It is some time in the past. An inventor arrives at her patent attorney's office carrying the typewriter of Figure B–1. Like prior art typewriters, it has alphabetic keys and a space bar. However, a feature of this typewriter that no other typewriter has ever had is a backspace key. The embodiment includes a mechanical linkage between the backspace key

---

1. *See* Chapter Sixteen.

FIGURE B–1 The invention of the backspace key (in circle).

Anthony Casillo, Garden City, NY.
www.typewritercollector.com

and the carriage that causes the carriage to back up by one character position when the backspace key is depressed.

The inventor explains that prior to her invention, typists would have to manually move the carriage back to the location where it was desired to retype a particular letter. This is a tedious and inconvenient process that interrupts the flow of typing. Moreover, having to reposition the carriage by hand is not as easy as it sounds. In moving the carriage backward, it is all too easy for the typist to overshoot the immediately preceding location and then have to "space" over to it.

Prepare a problem-solution statement for this invention.

The Author's Solution

My initial problem-solution hypothesis is based essentially on what the inventor said.

First Hypothesis:

The problems of inaccuracy and inconvenience in having to manually move a typewriter carriage backward to retype a character at the previously typed location *are solved by* providing a key that will back up the carriage by one character location.

Trying this first hypothesis on for size, it seems much too focused on the exact problem and the exact solution. I wonder if there's something else really going on, both from the standpoint of the problem and of the solution. It occurs to me that the problem isn't so much being able to back up, but being able to go to any desired location on the paper without having to type a character in order to get there. Broadly speaking, it seems then that the solution is to provide some mechanism for doing so other than moving the carriage by hand. This leads me to my second hypothesis.

Second Hypothesis:

The problem of having to manually move a typewriter carriage in order to thereupon be able to type at any desired location *is solved by* providing a key that will move the carriage to a desired location without requiring manipulation of the carriage by the typist.

It is immediately clear that this problem-solution statement is too broad. I have managed to write words that read on the very prior art I am trying to avoid—the character keys and the space bar. The hypothesis needs to be narrowed. What problem, I ask myself, is solved by the backspace key that is not solved by the character keys and space bar? What's really going on[2] with the backspace key that isn't going on with the other keys? One characteristic of the backspace key, I realize, is that it does not create any mark on the paper. No good. This distinguishes the backspace key from the character keys, but not from the space bar. I despair of defining this invention without including the notion of backing up. Indeed, it occurs to me all of a sudden that the backspace key is the exact opposite of the space bar. Each one moves the carriage one character location without creating a character—the space bar moves it forward, and the backspace key moves it backward. Given how close the prior art space bar function is, I have convinced myself that the invention necessarily involves the notion of backing up. I do recognize, in a broadening sense, however, that a key that causes the carriage to back up is a new functionality, irrespective of how far it backs up. So I see that I don't have to limit the invention to backing up by only one space. A key that takes the carriage to an "already-passed location" ought to do.

Third Hypothesis:

The problems of inaccuracy and inconvenience in having to manually move a typewriter carriage backward in order to type at an already-passed character location *are solved by* providing a key that, when operated, will place the carriage at that character location.

Certainly not too broad, but my sense is that maybe there is something else. Is there an inventive forest to which the backspace key belongs—but to which the space bar and character keys do not—other than the fact that it moves the carriage backward? It comes to me. The character keys and space bar create written language. Even though the space bar doesn't create a printed character, the thing that it does is integrally a part of the writing process. A space is a character in that sense. The backspace key doesn't do that. It is a control key, I realize. It is the first-ever tree in the typewriter control-key forest. The problem solved was broader than the inventor thought. By a lot. The invention is something that effectuates the operation of the typewriter while not creating a character. I decide to be my own lexicographer and define something I

---

2. *See* p. 36.

will call a "control function," which I will define to mean any operation other than creating printed characters or spaces. I then re-hypothesize the invention for a fourth time.

Fourth Hypothesis:
   The problem of being able to conveniently effectuate at least one control function of a typewriter *is solved by* providing a keyboard key that is operable to effectuate such an operation.

I'm pretty happy with this hypothesis. I feel I'm getting close. Trying this one on for size, though, I find myself wondering if it is functional enough. "What's the underlying functionality?" I ask myself. If the inventive realization was the idea of providing some shortcut way to effectuate a control function, is a "key" necessary? I decide to try out some far-fetched alternatives.[3] The notion of something that will respond to voice commands is a far-fetched embodiment that often bears fruit. Any way to effectuate a control function ought to do, I think to myself, including speaking a command to the typewriter. To worry about the particular way this particular typewriter effectuates the control function is really about *what* rather than *how*. And at the same time as I'm thinking about being unduly fixated on "hardware," I'm worrying that maybe the term "typewriter" is too limiting. Functionally speaking, the invention relates to effectuating a control function of an apparatus that creates lines of printed characters. Here we go again.

Fifth Hypothesis:
   The problem of being able to conveniently effectuate at least one control function of an apparatus that creates lines of printed characters *is solved by* providing a mechanism that is operable to effectuate such an operation.

I like the problem statement now, but the solution is once again too broad. Per my current definition of "control function," this language reads on the knob and related mechanism that allows the typist to roll the paper onto the machine. By my own definition, that is certainly a "control function." Should I limit myself to a control function that relates to the positioning of the carriage in a left/right sense? The roller knob certainly doesn't do that. But such a limitation is not problem-solution based. I worry that to limit the invention to a control function that deals with left/right operations of the carriage is to merely latch on to any con-

---

3. *See* p. 39.

venient limitation, with the result that I might be allowing something to escape. What's really going on with the backspace key that isn't going on with the roller knob? The roller knob is convenient, I tell myself. I realize I have allowed myself to lose focus on the problem—lack of convenience was the problem. So then are we back to the fact that the control function is performed by a key, that being more convenient than the manual moving of the carriage? I hope not. Don't forget the far-fetched embodiment about speaking a backspace command, I tell myself. So whence arises the convenience? There's a sort of remote-control feel to this. Rolling the paper onto the platen with the little knob is a direct, non-remote-control type of operation that directly manipulates the platen.

Aha! An intermediary operation. By allowing for an intermediary operation, we can achieve convenience, albeit at the possible cost of additional complexity. If it's a backspace key, the intermediary operation is the activation of some linkage or other mechanism that moves the carriage by remote control. If it's voice command, the intermediary operation is the electronic recognition of the command and the consequent operation of some physical intermediary that can actually move the carriage.

Sixth Hypothesis:

The problem of being able to conveniently effectuate at least one control function of an apparatus that creates lines of printed characters *is solved by* providing a mechanism responsive to a user action to effectuate an intermediary operation that, in turn, effectuates the control function.

I'm done with the problem-solution statement and can now draft a claim based on it.

Apparatus comprising

a printing mechanism configured to print characters,

a mechanism configured to effectuate at least one control function of the printing mechanism, and

a user interface device configured to respond to a user action to effectuate an intermediary operation that, in turn, effectuates the control function.

Some Afterthoughts

Some of my thinking here was no doubt tainted by my knowledge of what was to come: typing-ball-based typewriters, computer keyboards, and cell

FIGURE B–2 The existence of a carriage return lever (oval) in the assumed prior art would have been a complicating factor in the analysis of the backspace key invention.

Anthony Casillo, Garden City, NY.
www.typewritercollector.com

phones with a backspace key. I tried to put them out of my mind, but I'm not sure how successful I was. In any event, the final problem-solution statement does a pretty good job of capturing the embodiments of the future, it would seem. Backspace functionality in manual typewriters, electric typewriters, computer keyboards—all seem to be covered, including the possibility of voice control. My use of "printed" is a potential sticking point since electronically displayed characters on a screen might arguably not be "printed." I did decide to leave the word "printed" in the problem statement on the theory that a patent attorney in the early twentieth century probably would not have had an inkling of thinking beyond the printed word to computer screens.

Note, too, that the assumed prior art typewriter did not include a carriage-return/paper-advance lever, as shown in Figure B–2. If it did, further thought would have to be put into the problem-solution statement because the sixth hypothesis above would read on such a typewriter.

Finally, I note that I had rejected the first, third, and fifth hypotheses not because they did not define patentable subject matter, but because they did not seem broad enough. But since those problem-solution statements were not found to read on prior art, claims based on them could also be included in any patent application to be filed. The desirability of having such claims is discussed in Chapter Fourteen.

APPENDIX C

Sample Patent

The sample patent on the following pages is directed to the book's chair example. It illustrates the principles of specification construction discussed in Part IV.

The figures of the patent application appear below.

Fig. 1 (Prior Art)

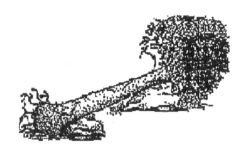

Fig. 2 (Prior Art)

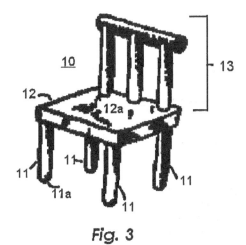

Fig. 3

US 0,000,001

1

SEATING DEVICE

BACKGROUND

The present invention relates to
seating devices.

Several devices are known that
allow people to assume a comfortable
sitting position. Among these are seating
devices comprising a seating platform,
or "seat," held above the ground by some
kind of support structure. One such seating device comprises two or more rocks
piled one on top of the other to a suitable
height. Another is made from a felled
tree laid across two rock supports.

Advantageously, all of these devices,
especially when the seating platform,
or "seat," is set at a comfortable height,
allow people to sit more comfortably,
and for longer periods of time, than the
prior practice of sitting on the ground.

SUMMARY

The known seating devices are not readily portable because of their bulk and
weight. People have not seen this as a
problem but, rather, a fact of life. The
present inventor, however, has recognized that making seating devices more
portable would provide numerous benefits, such as enabling them to be moved
into the shade as the day progresses and
to enable groups of seating devices to
be rearranged to suit different types of
gatherings.

In accordance with the invention,
the portability of seating devices is
enhanced by utilizing one or more elongated members as the support structure
for the seat. Such a support member can
hold up a large load relative to its own
weight when compressed along its longitudinal axis, thereby achieving a significant reduction in weight. Such a seating
device is referred to herein as a "chair"
and the elongated support members as
"legs."

2

The chair can have any desired number of legs. Three or four legs have proven
to be the most advantageous, however.

In particular embodiments of the
invention, the legs may be perpendicular to the seat and may be attached near
the seat edge. Also in particular embodiments, the seat is more or less rectilinear
and has four legs attached at the corners.
Each of these details provides particular advantages and can be implemented
independently of the others.

The legs can be made from any
desired material. Indeed, they can be
integral with a chair carved from stone,
resulting in a seating device that is much
lighter than those having solid-stone
support structures as in the prior art.
Particular embodiments of the invention may, however, advantageously, use
wood for at least the support members.

The legs can be friction-fit into
recesses formed in the underside of the
seat. If desired, however, greater structural integrity for the chair as a whole
can be achieved by securing the legs in
the recesses with an adhesive material.

BRIEF DESCRIPTION
OF THE DRAWING

Fig. 1 depicts a type of seating
device known in the prior art;

Fig. 2 depict another type of seating
device known in the prior art; and

Fig. 3 depicts a seating device, or
"chair," embodying the principles of the
present invention.

DETAILED DESCRIPTION

Among the seating devices known in the
prior art are those shown in Figs. 1 and 2.
The Fig. 1 device comprises two or more
rocks piled one on top of the other. The
Fig. 2 device comprises a felled tree, or
log, laid across a pair of rocks, enabling
more than one person to sit side-by-side.
Other known types of seating devices

5

10

15

20

25

30

35

40

45

US 0,000,001

3

are a flattened-off tree stump, and a single large rock.

The known seating devices are not readily portable because of their bulk and weight. As noted above, it remained for the present inventor to recognize that making seating devices more portable would provide numerous benefits, as detailed hereinabove. Indeed, rocks of the type depicted in Figs. 1 and 2 may weigh hundreds of pounds. A felled tree of sufficient girth to support human sitters may also be extremely heavy.

Fig. 3 depicts a seating device, or "chair," 10, embodying the principles of the present invention that is more portable than those known in the prior art.

The chair comprises a platform, or "seat," 12, having an upper seating surface, 12a, where the buttocks of the sitter are placed. In accordance with the invention, seat 12 is supported above a floor or the ground by support members, 11, that are elongated and that carry the weight of the seat and of a person on the seat substantially along their longitudinal axes. The present inventor has discovered that such an elongated support member can be made quite thin. Such a support member can hold up a large load relative to its own weight when compressed along its longitudinal axis. This achieves a significant reduction in weight for the seating device as a whole and makes it significantly more portable than the seating devices of the prior art.

Elongated support members 11 are hereinafter referred to as "legs." Legs 11 illustratively have rounded bottoms, 11a, and circular cross-sections.

A chair embodying the principles of the invention can have any desired number of legs. For example, if the chair has three legs, it is guaranteed not to wobble. However, tipping over is a concern with three legs unless they are splayed outward. But then structural strength of the legs becomes an issue because splayed legs are not being compressed

4

directly along their axes, leading to the need for thick legs, horizontal reinforcements, and very strong joints at the leg/seat connection points, adding to the cost of fabrication.

In accordance with an advantageous feature of the invention, and as can be seen from Fig. 3, chair 10 illustratively has four legs, 11. The present inventor has discovered that four legs can be made perpendicular to the seat without giving rise to the tipping problem. And since they are compressed directly along their axes, the four vertical legs don't have to be as thick as the three splayed-out legs. Also, since there are four of them, they can be made thinner yet and still support as much weight as three thicker legs. With careful cutting to make the legs as equal in length as possible, wobbling is not a major concern. Five legs adds to the wobbling problem and also increases the weight of the chair. So four legs is regarded by the present inventor as a preferred embodiment.

In accordance with another illustrative feature of the invention, the legs are attached near the edge of the seat. This has been found to further enhance the stability of the chair, no matter how many legs it has. The present inventor has also found that the chair is particularly stable when the seat is more or less rectilinear and has four legs attached at the corners. Indeed, those features are implemented in chair 10.

A seating device having legs pursuant to the principles of the invention can be made from any desired material. Indeed, it can be carved from stone, resulting in a seating device that is much lighter than those having solid-stone support structures as in the one elongated support member prior art. Legs 11 of the illustrative embodiment are made of wood, however. The present inventor has found that wood is sufficiently strong to be used for this application while being significantly less weighty

US 0,000,001

than stone. Indeed, seat 12 is also made of wood in this embodiment.

An aspect of the design of chair 10 is how to hold all the parts together. If the chair is left in one spot, it was found sufficient to have a friction fit of the legs in recesses formed in the underside (not shown) of the seat 12. However, the legs tended to fall out when the chair was moved, thereby compromising its portability. This problem is solved in this embodiment by securing the legs in the recesses with an adhesive material. Tree resin was used in a particular chair that was built.

Chair 10 includes a structure, 13, attached near one edge of seat 12. This structure, which is referred to as a "seat back," is an innovation in sitter comfort that provides support for the back of the sitter. The concept of the seat back is an invention independent of the present invention and is the subject of a separate patent application being filed by the present inventor on the same day as this application.

The foregoing merely illustrates the principles of the invention. For example, although the elongated supports of the illustrative embodiment are below the seat, it may be possible to support the seat by elongated supports from above, such as vines or animal sinew. In addition, although legs 11 of the illustrative embodiment have circular cross-sections and rounded bottoms, other shapes and configurations are possible.

It will thus be appreciated that those skilled in the art will be able to devise numerous alternative arrangements that, while not shown or described herein, embody the principles of the invention and thus are within its spirit and scope.

What is claimed is:

1. Apparatus comprising
a seat, and

a seat support that supports the seat above an underlying surface,

the seat support including one or more elongated support members.

2. The apparatus of claim 1 wherein the seat support includes at least three support members.

3. The apparatus of claim 2 wherein the one or more elongated support members are noncollinear.

4. The apparatus of claim 2 wherein the one or more elongated support members are substantially perpendicular to the seat.

5. The apparatus of claim 2 wherein the seat has a plurality of corners and each of the elongated support members supports the seat substantially at a respective one of the corners.

6. The apparatus of claim 2 wherein the seat support includes exactly four support members.

7. The apparatus of claim 1 wherein the one or more elongated support members are splayed.

8. The apparatus of claim 7 wherein the splayed support members do not extend beyond the perimeter of the seat.

9. The apparatus of claim 1 further comprising at least one horizontal connector connecting at least one pair of the elongated support members.

10. The apparatus of claim 1 wherein the one or more elongated support members are substantially perpendicular to the seat.

11. The apparatus of claim 1 wherein the one or more elongated support members are permanently attached to the seat.

APPENDIX D

Selected Sections of Title 35, United States Code,

Effective as of March 16, 2013

Sec. 101. Inventions patentable

Whoever invents or discovers any new and useful process, machine, manufacture, or composition of matter, or any new and useful improvement thereof, may obtain a patent therefor, subject to the conditions and requirements of this title.

Sec. 102. Conditions for patentability; novelty

(a) NOVELTY; PRIOR ART.—A person shall be entitled to a patent unless—
  (1) the claimed invention was patented, described in a printed publication, or in public use, on sale, or otherwise available to the public before the effective filing date of the claimed invention; or
  (2) the claimed invention was described in a patent issued under section 151, or in an application for patent published or deemed published under section 122(b), in which the patent or application, as the case may be, names another inventor and was effectively filed before the effective filing date of the claimed invention.

(b) EXCEPTIONS.—
  (1) DISCLOSURES MADE 1 YEAR OR LESS BEFORE THE EFFECTIVE FILING DATE OF THE CLAIMED INVENTION.—A disclosure made 1 year or less before the effective filing date of a claimed invention shall not be prior art to the claimed invention under subsection (a)(1) if—
    (A) the disclosure was made by the inventor or joint inventor or by another who obtained the subject matter disclosed directly or indirectly from the inventor or a joint inventor; or
    (B) the subject matter disclosed had, before such disclosure, been publicly disclosed by the inventor or a joint inventor or another who obtained the subject matter disclosed directly or indirectly from the inventor or a joint inventor.
  (2) DISCLOSURES APPEARING IN APPLICATIONS AND PATENTS.—A disclosure shall not be prior art to a claimed invention under subsection (a)(2) if—

(A) the subject matter disclosed was obtained directly or indirectly from the inventor or a joint inventor;

(B) the subject matter disclosed had, before such subject matter was effectively filed under subsection (a)(2), been publicly disclosed by the inventor or a joint inventor or another who obtained the subject matter disclosed directly or indirectly from the inventor or a joint inventor; or

(C) the subject matter disclosed and the claimed invention, not later than the effective filing date of the claimed invention, were owned by the same person or subject to an obligation of assignment to the same person.

(c) COMMON OWNERSHIP UNDER JOINT RESEARCH AGREEMENTS.— Subject matter disclosed and a claimed invention shall be deemed to have been owned by the same person or subject to an obligation of assignment to the same person in applying the provisions of subsection (b)(2)(C) if—

(1) the subject matter disclosed was developed and the claimed invention was made by, or on behalf of, 1 or more parties to a joint research agreement that was in effect on or before the effective filing date of the claimed invention;

(2) the claimed invention was made as a result of activities undertaken within the scope of the joint research agreement; and

(3) the application for patent for the claimed invention discloses or is amended to disclose the names of the parties to the joint research agreement.

(d) PATENTS AND PUBLISHED APPLICATIONS EFFECTIVE AS PRIOR ART.—For purposes of determining whether a patent application for patent is prior art to a claimed invention under subsection (a)(2), such patent or application shall be considered to have been effectively filed, with respect to any subject matter described in the patent or application—

(1) if paragraph (2) does not apply, as of the actual filing date of the patent or the application for patent; or

(2) if the patent or application for patent is entitled to claim a right of priority under section 119, 365(a), or 365(b), or to claim the benefit of an earlier filing date under section 120, 121, or 365(c), based upon 1 or more prior filed applications for patent, as of the filing date of the earliest such application that describes the subject matter.

Sec. 103. Conditions for patentability; non-obvious subject matter

A patent for a claimed invention may not be obtained, notwithstanding that the claimed invention is not identically disclosed as set forth in section 102, if the differences between the claimed invention and the prior art are such that the claimed invention as a whole would have been obvious before the effective filing date of the claimed invention to a person having ordinary skill in the art to which the claimed invention pertains. Patentability shall not be negated by the manner in which the invention was made.

Sec. 112. Specification

(a) IN GENERAL.—The specification shall contain a written description of the invention, and of the manner and process of making and using it, in such full, clear, concise, and exact terms as to enable any person skilled in the art to which it pertains, or with which it is most nearly connected, to make and use the same, and shall set forth the best mode contemplated by the inventor or joint inventor of carrying out the invention.

(b) CONCLUSION.—The specification shall conclude with one or more claims particularly pointing out and distinctly claiming the subject matter which inventor or a joint inventor regards as the invention.

(c) FORM.—A claim may be written in independent or, if the nature of the case admits, in dependent or multiple dependent form.

(d) REFERENCE IN DEPENDENT FORMS.—Subject to subsection (e), a claim in dependent form shall contain a reference to a claim previously set forth and then specify a further limitation of the subject matter claimed. A claim in dependent form shall be construed to incorporate by reference all the limitations of the claim to which it refers.

(e) REFERENCE IN MULTIPLE DEPENDENT FORM.—A claim in multiple dependent form shall contain a reference, in the alternative only, to more than one claim previously set forth and then specify a further limitation of the subject matter claimed. A multiple dependent claim shall not serve as a basis for any other multiple dependent claim. A multiple dependent claim shall be construed to incorporate by reference all the limitations of the particular claim in relation to which it is being considered.

(f) ELEMENT IN CLAIM FOR A COMBINATION.—An element in a claim for a combination may be expressed as a means or step for performing a specified function without the recital of structure, material, or acts in support thereof, and such claim shall be construed to cover the corresponding structure, material, or acts described in the specification and equivalents thereof.

Sec. 271. Infringement of patent

(a) Except as otherwise provided in this title, whoever without authority makes, uses, offers to sell, or sells any patented invention, within the United States or imports into the United States any patented invention during the term of the patent therefor, infringes the patent.

(b) Whoever actively induces infringement of a patent shall be liable as an infringer.

(c) Whoever offers to sell or sells within the United States or imports into the United States a component of a patented machine, manufacture, combination or composition, or a material or apparatus for use in practicing a patented process, constituting a material part of the invention, knowing the same to be especially made or especially adapted for use in an infringement of such patent, and not a staple article or commodity of commerce suitable for substantial noninfringing use, shall be liable as a contributory infringer.

(d) [Provisions preserving patent owner's right to relief under certain circumstances]

(e) [Provisions specifically relating to drugs and veterinary biological products]

(f)

  (1) Whoever without authority supplies or causes to be supplied in or from the United States all or a substantial portion of the components of a patented invention, where such components are uncombined in whole or in part, in such manner as to actively induce the combination of such components outside of the United States in a manner that would infringe the patent if such combination occurred within the United States, shall be liable as an infringer.

  (2) Whoever without authority supplies or causes to be supplied in or from the United States any component of a patented invention that is especially made or especially adapted for use in the invention and not a staple article or commodity of commerce suitable for substantial noninfringing use, where such component is uncombined in whole or in part, knowing that such component is so made or adapted and intending that such component will be combined outside of the United States in a manner that would infringe the patent if such combination occurred within the United States, shall be liable as an infringer.

(g) Whoever without authority imports into the United States or offers to sell, sells, or uses within the United States a product which is made by a process patented in the United States shall be liable as an infringer, if the importation, offer to sell, sale, or use of the product occurs during the term of such process patent. In an action for infringement of a process patent, no remedy may be granted for infringement on account of the noncommercial use or retail sale of a product unless there is no adequate remedy under this title for infringement on account of the importation or other use, offer to sell, or sale of that product. A product which is made by a patented process will, for purposes of this title, not be considered to be so made after—

  (1) it is materially changed by subsequent processes; or

  (2) it becomes a trivial and nonessential component of another product.

(h)–(i) [Definitions]

Glossary

This glossary will be of interest principally to inventors or other non-patent practitioners who may pick up this book. Patent practitioners are already intimately familiar with the terms herein, with the possible exceptions of the terms "claim family" and "claim suite" and the book's somewhat unconventional use of the term "prior art" as encompassing subject matter defined by both 35 U.S.C. 102 and 35 U.S.C. 103.

Terms in *italics* are terms defined in the glossary itself.

Anticipated Said of a *claim* that reads on the *prior art*. A claim that is anticipated will be either *unpatentable* or *invalid*.

Broad Said of a *claim* with relatively few *limitations*, thereby causing the claim to encompass a wider range of implementations of the *inventive concept*. Such a claim is said to be of broad "scope." (Compare with *narrow*.)

Claim A single sentence, arranged in one or more paragraphs, defining what a patent owner has exclusive rights to. (See *infringement*.)

Claim Family Set of *claims* consisting of one *independent claim* and all of its *dependent claims*.

Claim Suite Entire set of *claims* in a *patent*—that is, the collection of all of its claim families.

Dependent Claim A *claim* that refers to another *dependent* or *independent claim* (*parent*) in such a way as to incorporate the parent's limitation into this claim.

Embodiment Method, apparatus, or composition of matter that implements the *inventive concept*.

Indefinite Claim *Claim* having one or more *limitations* that render it not possible to determine with reasonable certainty when the claim would be *infringed*.

Independent Claim A *claim* that does not refer to, and thus does not incorporate the limitations of, any other claim.

Infringed, Infringement A *claim* is infringed when an accused *method, apparatus, or composition of matter* meets every *limitation* in the claim. A *patent* is infringed when at least one of its claims is infringed.

Infringer Any party who *practices* a patented invention without authority from the patent owner to do so.

Intellectual Property (IP) Knowledge and ideas amenable to legal protection. Inventions are a form of intellectual property and are protected by *patents*. Other forms of intellectual property include literary and artistic works, product names, and business information, which are protected by copyrights, trademarks, and trade secret law, respectively.

Invalid Said of an *overbroad* or *indefinite claim* in an *issued patent*. (Compare with *unpatentable*.)

Inventive Concept The essence of what makes a particular invention different from the *prior art*. The inventive concept of the original ballpoint pen, for example, is the fact that it had a spheroidal marking-point.

Limitation A word or phrase in a *claim*.

Narrow Said of a *claim* with a relatively large number of *limitations*, thereby causing the claim to encompass a smaller range of implementations of the *inventive concept*. Such a claim is said to be of narrow "scope." (Compare with *broad*.)

Parent *Claim* to which a *dependent claim* refers, thereby incorporating the *limitations* of the *parent* claim into the dependent claim.

Patent, Issued Patent Government-issued document giving its owner the right to exclude others, for a prescribed period of time, from making, using, offering for sale, selling, or importing an invention.

Patent Application The *specification, claims,* drawings, and formal papers submitted to the Patent and Trademark Office with the goal of obtaining an *issued patent*.

Pending *Patent application* has been submitted to the Patent and Trademark Office, but the Office has not yet issued a patent.

Practice (an invention) One practices a patented invention by making, using, selling, offering for sale, or importing *a method, apparatus, or composition of matter* that *infringes* at least one of the patent's *claims*.

Preamble The introductory words of a *claim*.

Prior Art The body of information published or known by those working in a technical field—normally associated with subject matter defined in various subsections of 35 U.S.C. 102. This book also uses the term "prior art" to include subject matter that would have been obvious to those of ordinary skill in the art per 35 U.S.C. 103.

Read on A claim "reads on" *prior art* when all of the *limitations* in the *claim* can be found in that prior art.

Specification Portion of a *patent application* that describes the *inventive concept* and its *embodiments*.

Unpatentable Said of an *overbroad* or *indefinite claim* in a *pending patent application*. (Compare with *invalid*.)

INDEX